The BOYS™

volume seven: THE INNOCENTS

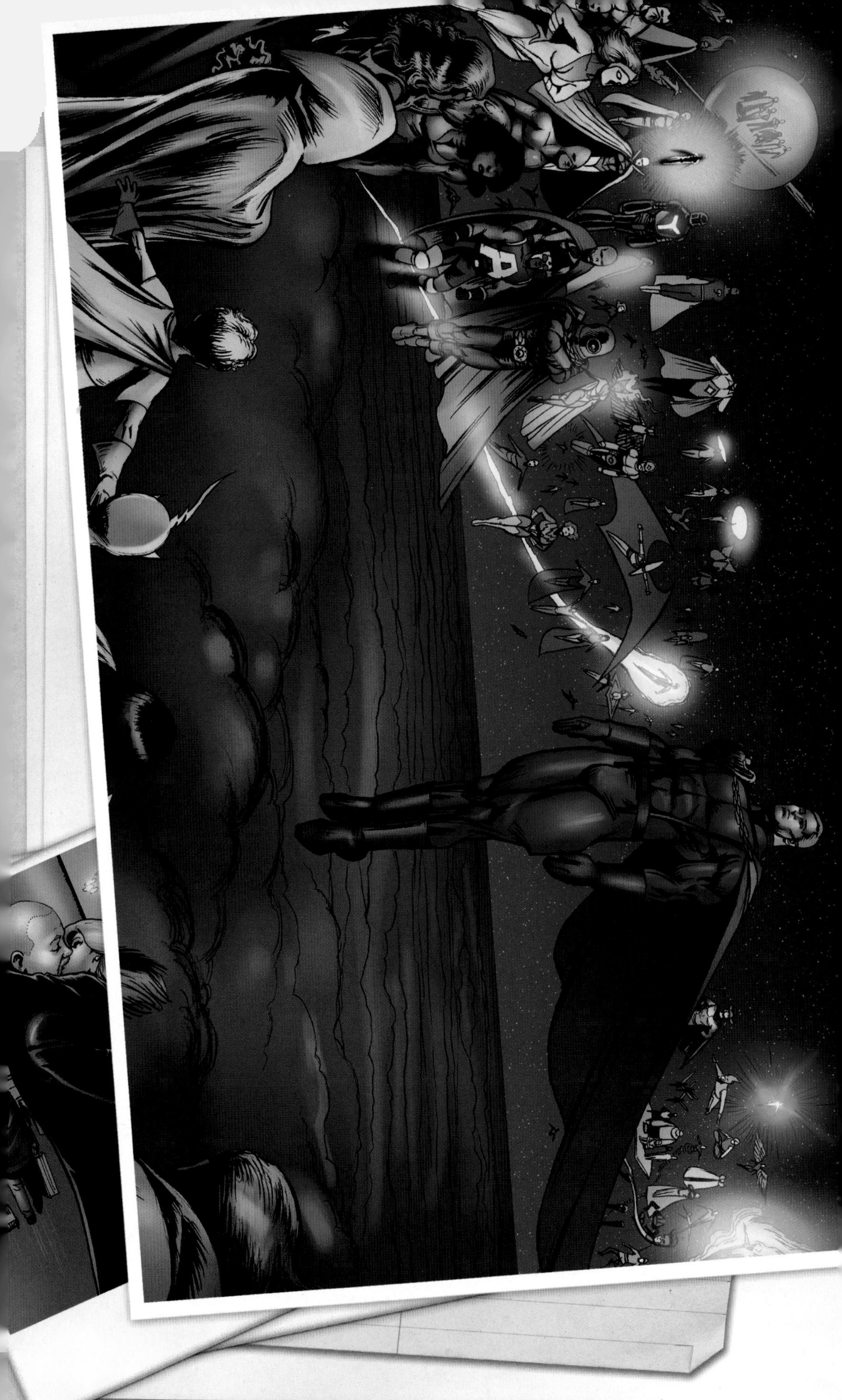

The BOYS ™

volume seven: THE INNOCENTS

Written by:
GARTH ENNIS

Lettered by:
SIMON BOWLAND

Illustrated by:
DARICK ROBERTSON
RUSS BRAUN
& JOHN McCREA w/
KEITH BURNS

Colored by:
TONY AVIÑA

Covers by:
DARICK ROBERTSON
& TONY AVIÑA

Additional inks by:
KEITH BURNS w/
JOHN McCREA

The Boys created by:
GARTH ENNIS &
DARICK ROBERTSON

Collects issues thirty-nine through forty-seven of
The Boys, originally published by Dynamite Entertainment

Trade Design By: JASON ULLMEYER

DYNAMITE ®
Visit us online at **www.DYNAMITE.com**
Follow us on Twitter **@dynamitecomics**
Like us on Facebook **/Dynamitecomics**

Nick Barrucci, CEO / Publisher // **Juan Collado**, President / COO // **Brandon Dante Primavera**, V.P. of IT and Operations // **Joe Rybandt**, Executive Editor // **Matt Idelson**, Senior Editor // **Kevin Ketner**, Editor // **Cathleen Heard**, Art Director // **Rachel Kilbury**, Digital and Multimedia Associate **Alexis Persson**, Graphic Designer // **Katie Hidalgo**, Graphic Designer // **Alan Payne**, V.P. of Sales and Marketing // **Rex Wang**, Director of Consumer Sales // **Pat O'Connell**, Sales Manager // **Vincent Faust**, Marketing Coordinator // **Jay Spence**, Director of Product Development **Mariano Nicieza**, Marketing Manager // **Amy Jackson**, Administrative Coordinator

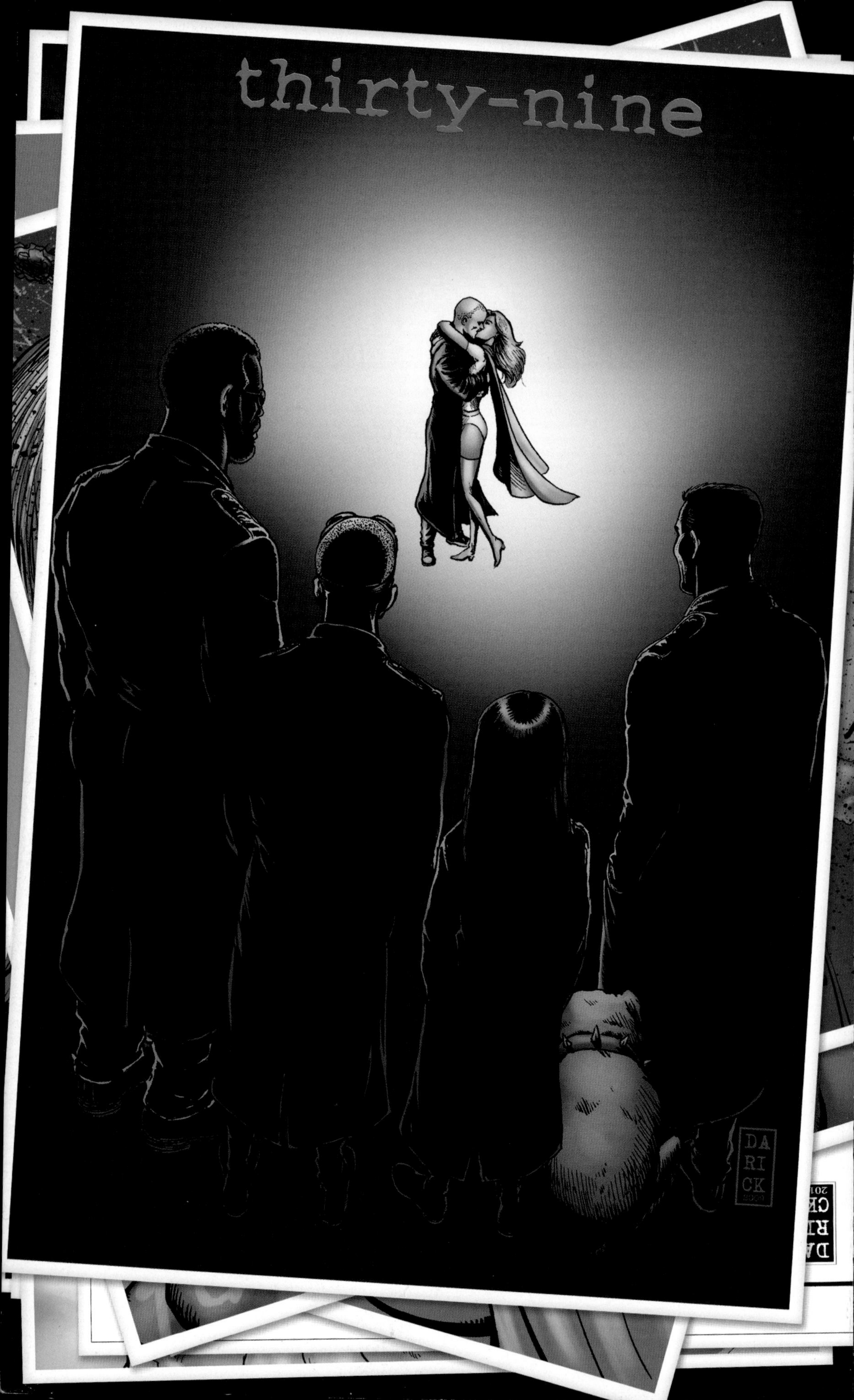
thirty-nine
DA
RI
CK

WHAT I KNOW

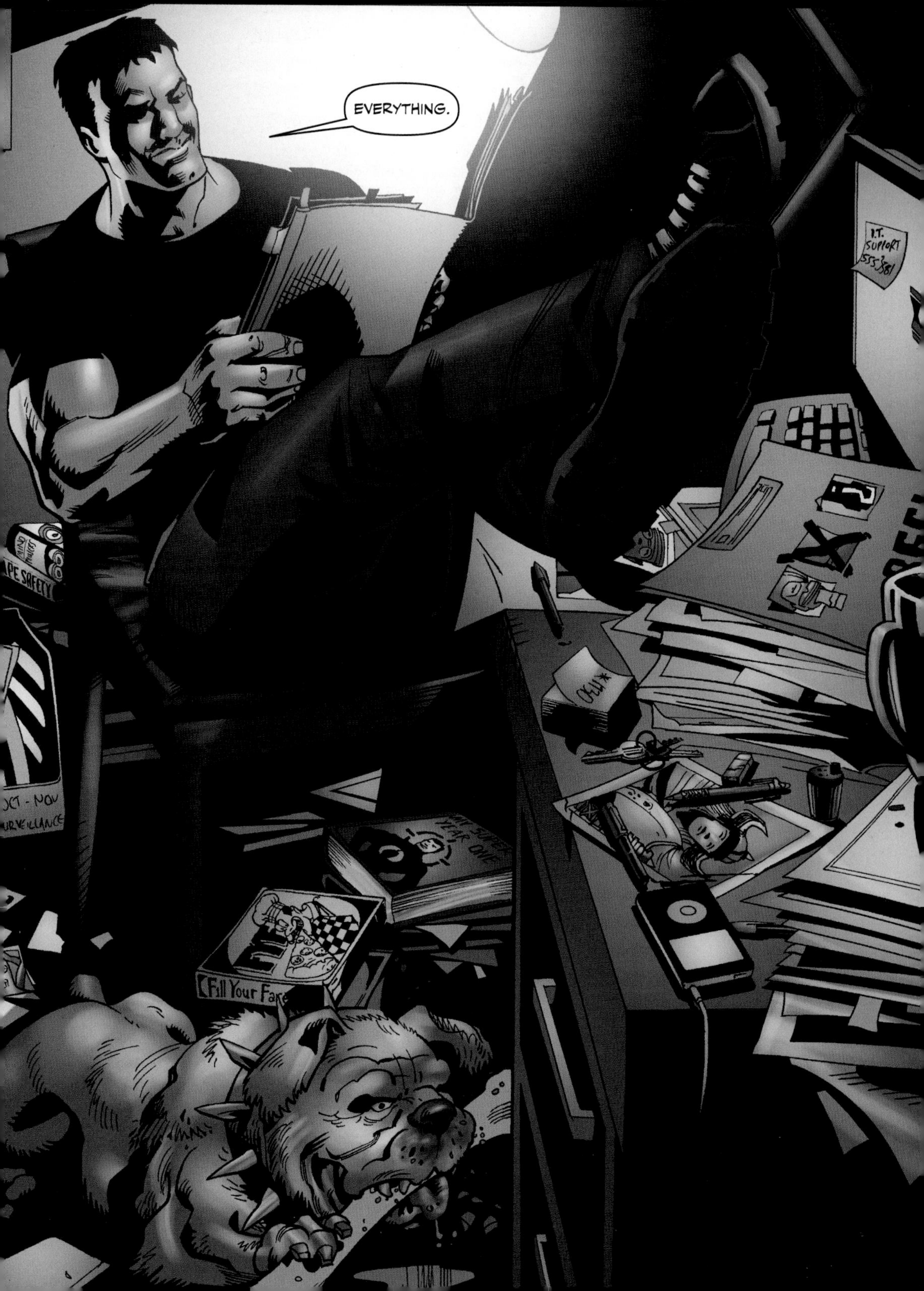
EVERYTHING.

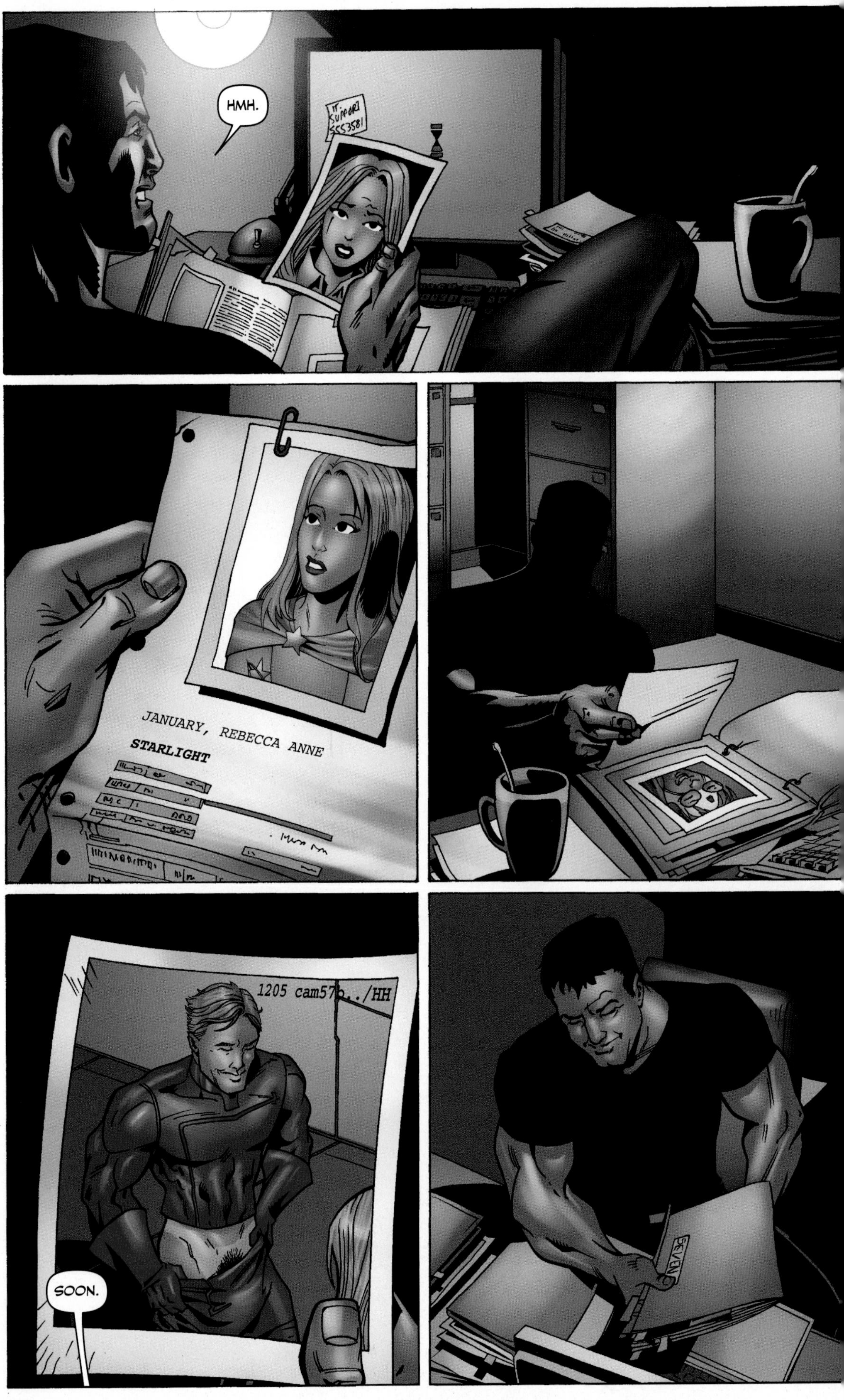

HMH.
IT SUPPORT 5553581
JANUARY, REBECCA ANNE
STARLIGHT
1205 cam57b../HH
SOON.
SEVEN

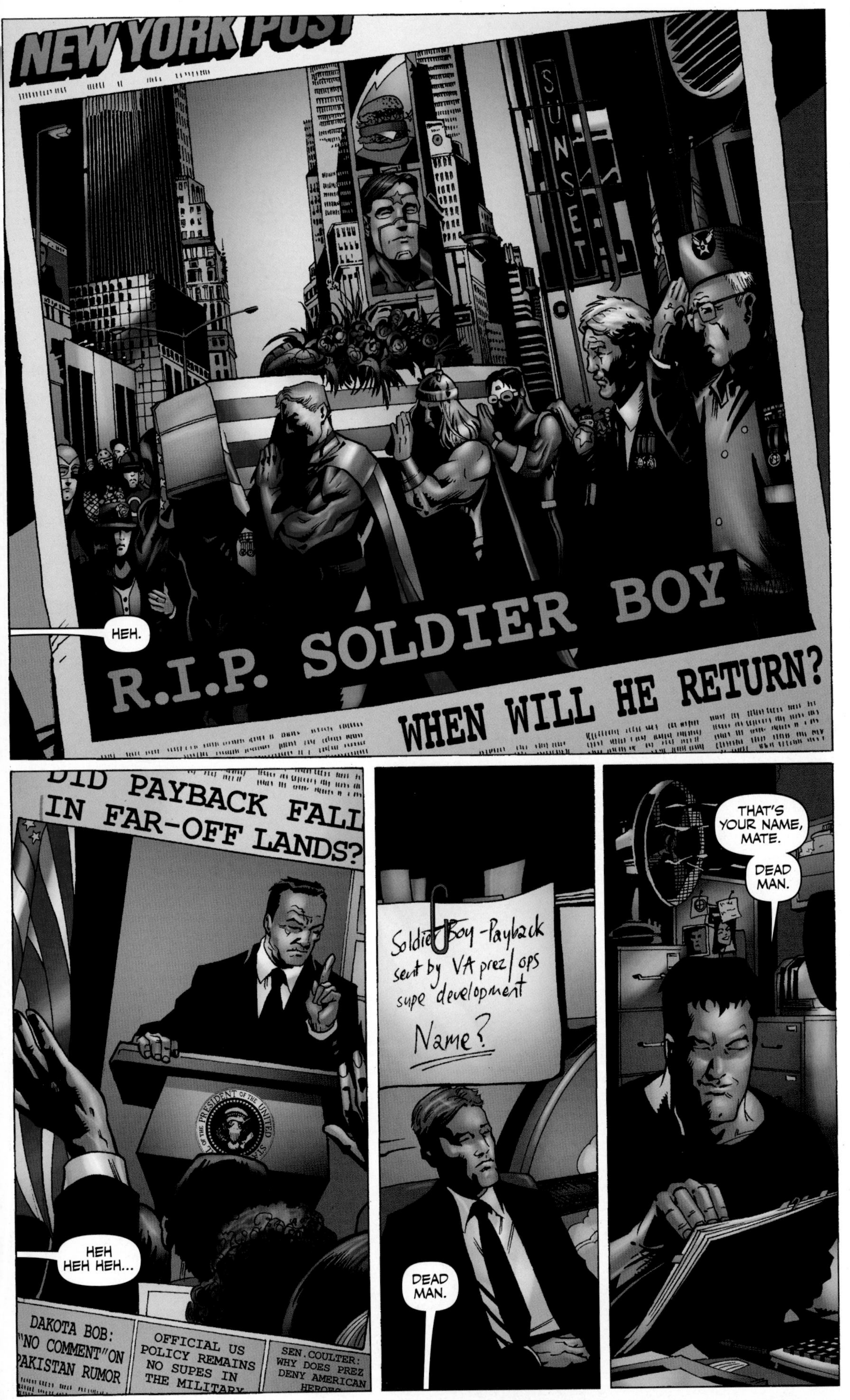
NEW YORK POST
SUNSET
R.I.P. SOLDIER BOY
WHEN WILL HE RETURN?
HEH.
DID PAYBACK FALL IN FAR-OFF LANDS?
HEH HEH HEH...
DAKOTA BOB: "NO COMMENT" ON PAKISTAN RUMOR
OFFICIAL US POLICY REMAINS NO SUPES IN THE MILITARY
SEN. COULTER: WHY DOES PREZ DENY AMERICAN
Soldier Boy - Payback sent by VA prez/ops supe development
Name?
DEAD MAN.
THAT'S YOUR NAME, MATE.
DEAD MAN.

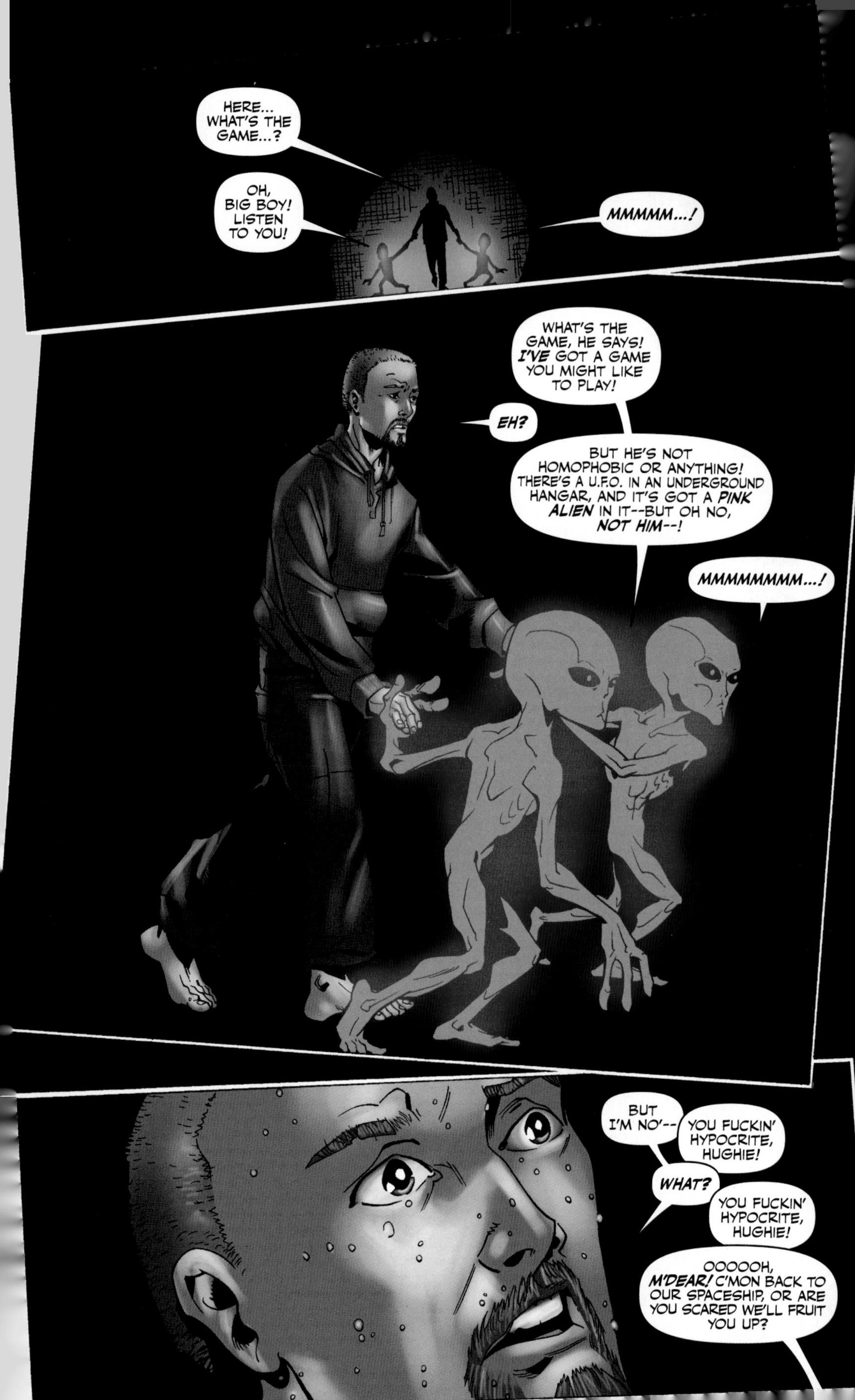
HERE... WHAT'S THE GAME...?
OH, BIG BOY! LISTEN TO YOU!
MMMMM...!
WHAT'S THE GAME, HE SAYS! I'VE GOT A GAME YOU MIGHT LIKE TO PLAY!
EH?
BUT HE'S NOT HOMOPHOBIC OR ANYTHING! THERE'S A U.F.O. IN AN UNDERGROUND HANGAR, AND IT'S GOT A PINK ALIEN IN IT--BUT OH NO, NOT HIM--!
MMMMMMMM...!
BUT I'M NO'--
YOU FUCKIN' HYPOCRITE, HUGHIE!
WHAT?
YOU FUCKIN' HYPOCRITE, HUGHIE!
OOOOOH, M'DEAR! C'MON BACK TO OUR SPACESHIP, OR ARE YOU SCARED WE'LL FRUIT YOU UP?

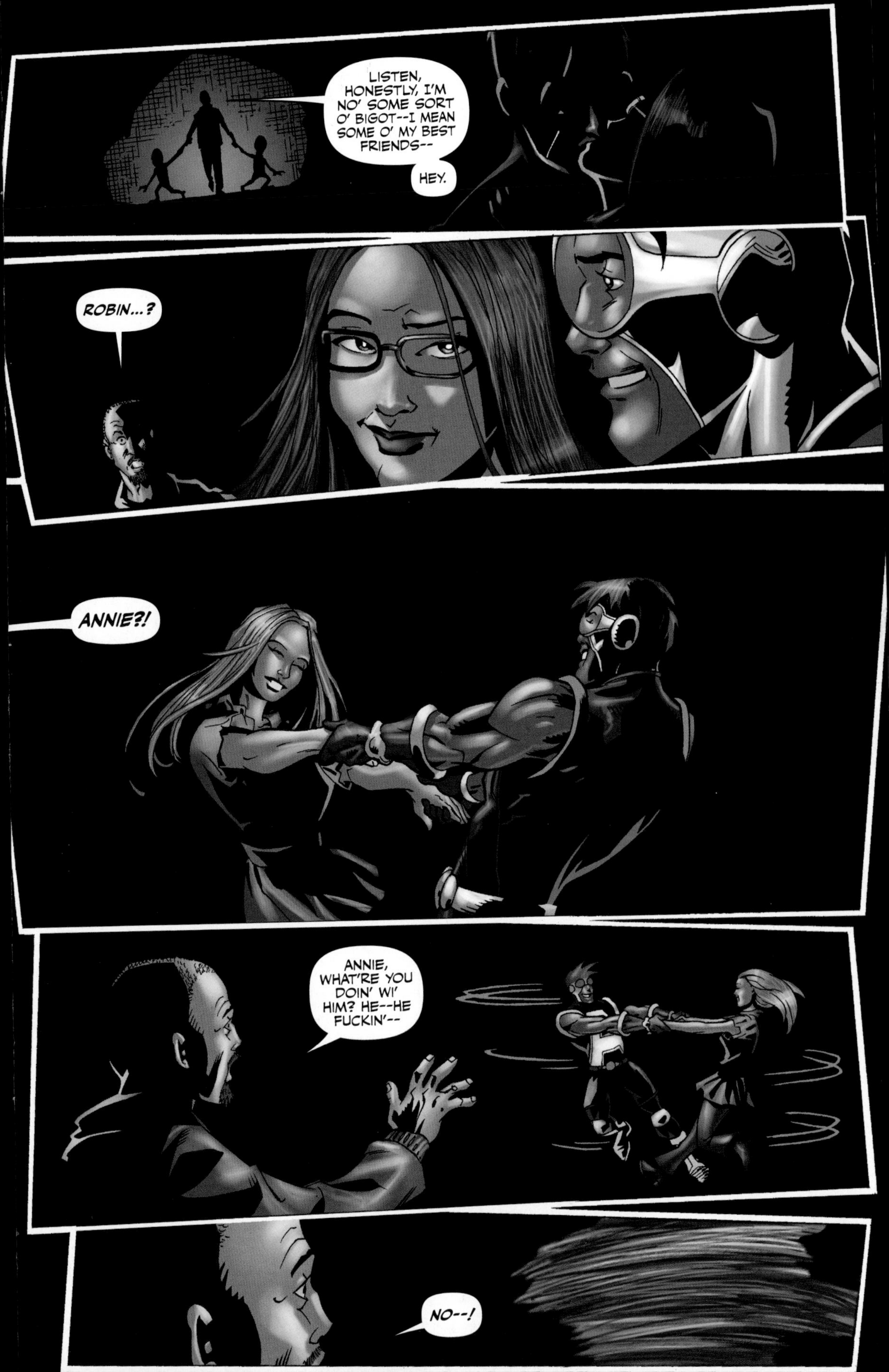
LISTEN, HONESTLY, I'M NO' SOME SORT O' BIGOT--I MEAN SOME O' MY BEST FRIENDS--
HEY.
ROBIN...?
ANNIE?!
ANNIE, WHAT'RE YOU DOIN' WI' HIM? HE--HE FUCKIN'--
NO--!

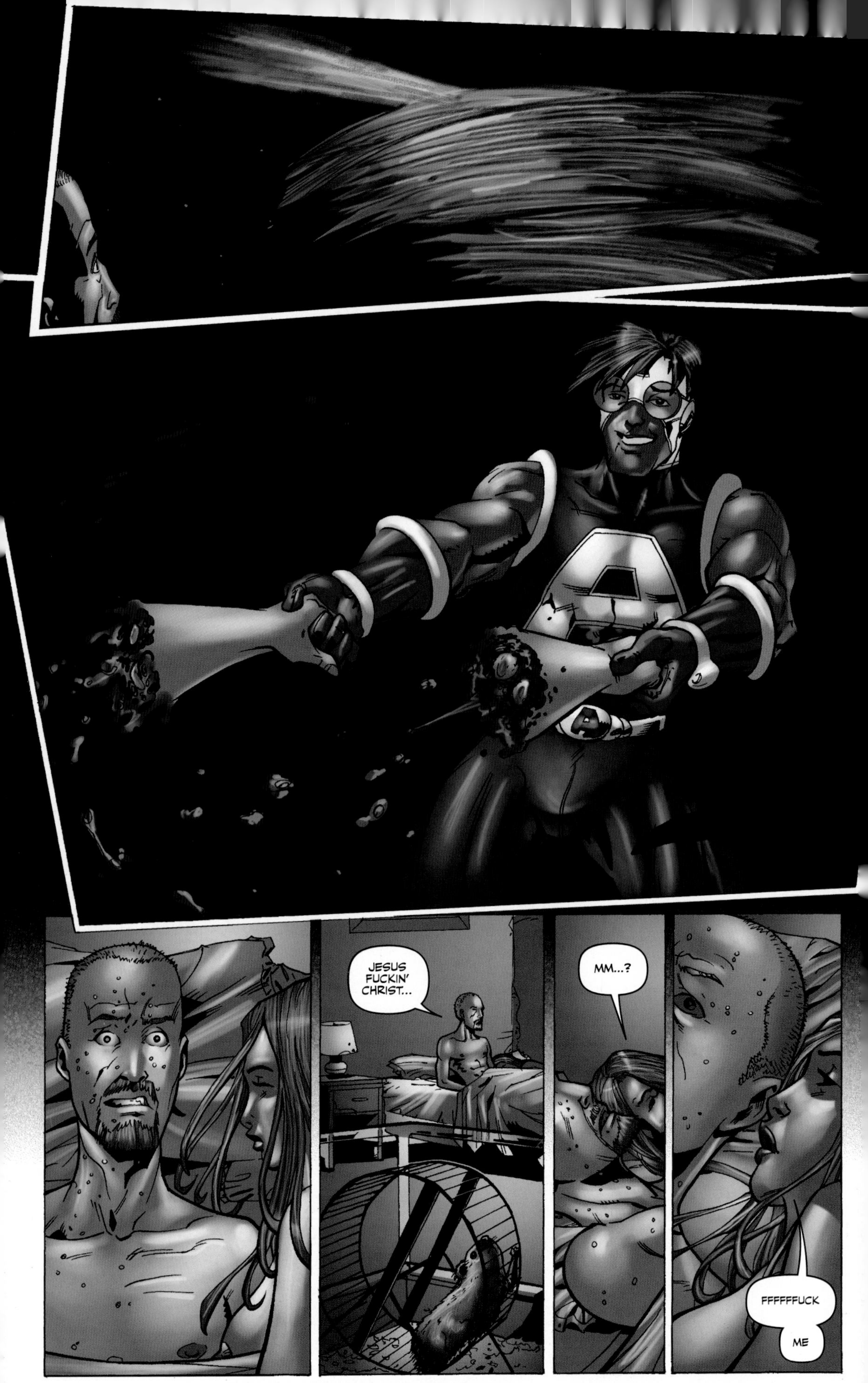
JESUS FUCKIN' CHRIST...
MM...?
FFFFFFUCK
ME

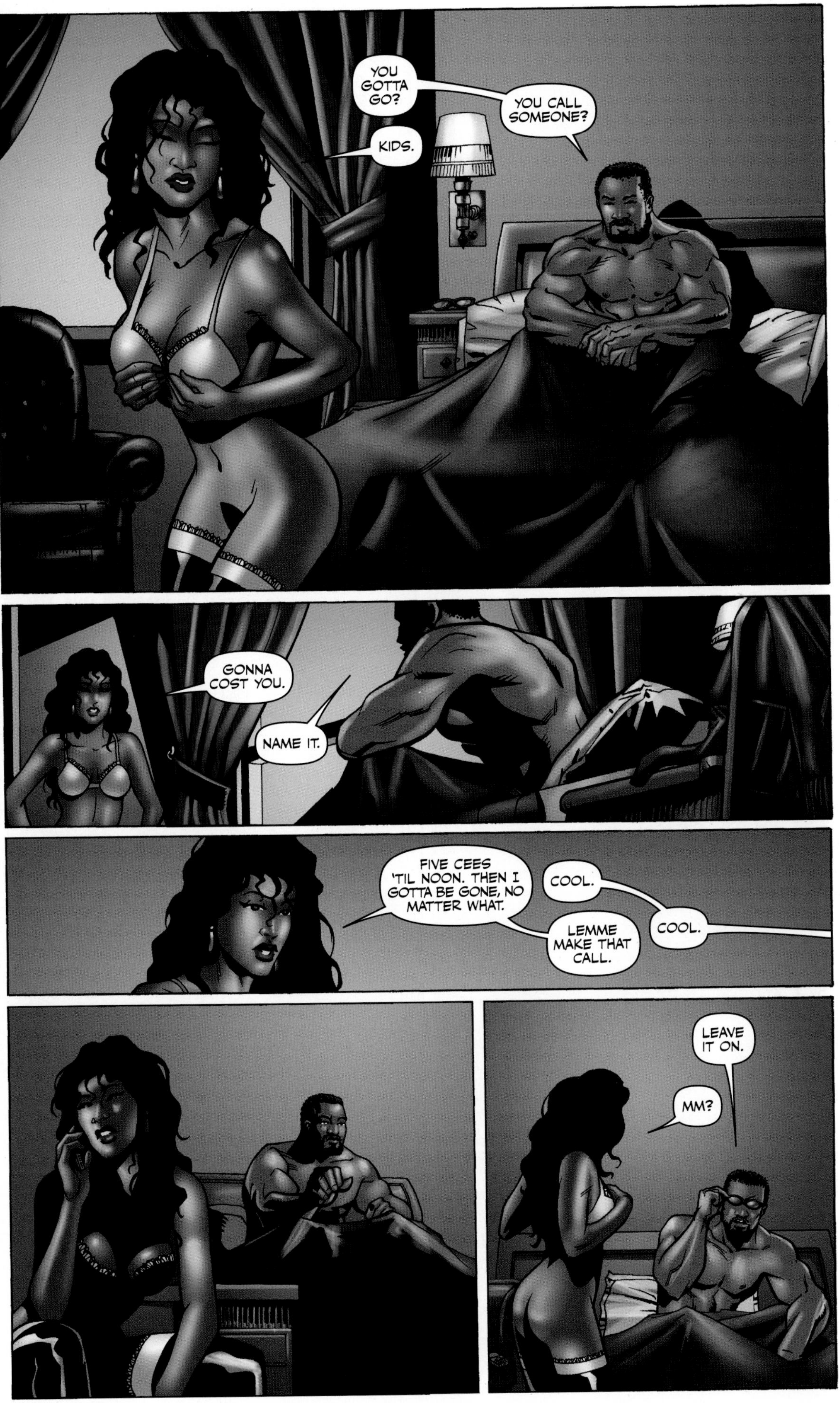
YOU GOTTA GO?
YOU CALL SOMEONE?
KIDS.
GONNA COST YOU.
NAME IT.
FIVE CEES 'TIL NOON. THEN I GOTTA BE GONE, NO MATTER WHAT.
COOL.
COOL.
LEMME MAKE THAT CALL.
LEAVE IT ON.
MM?

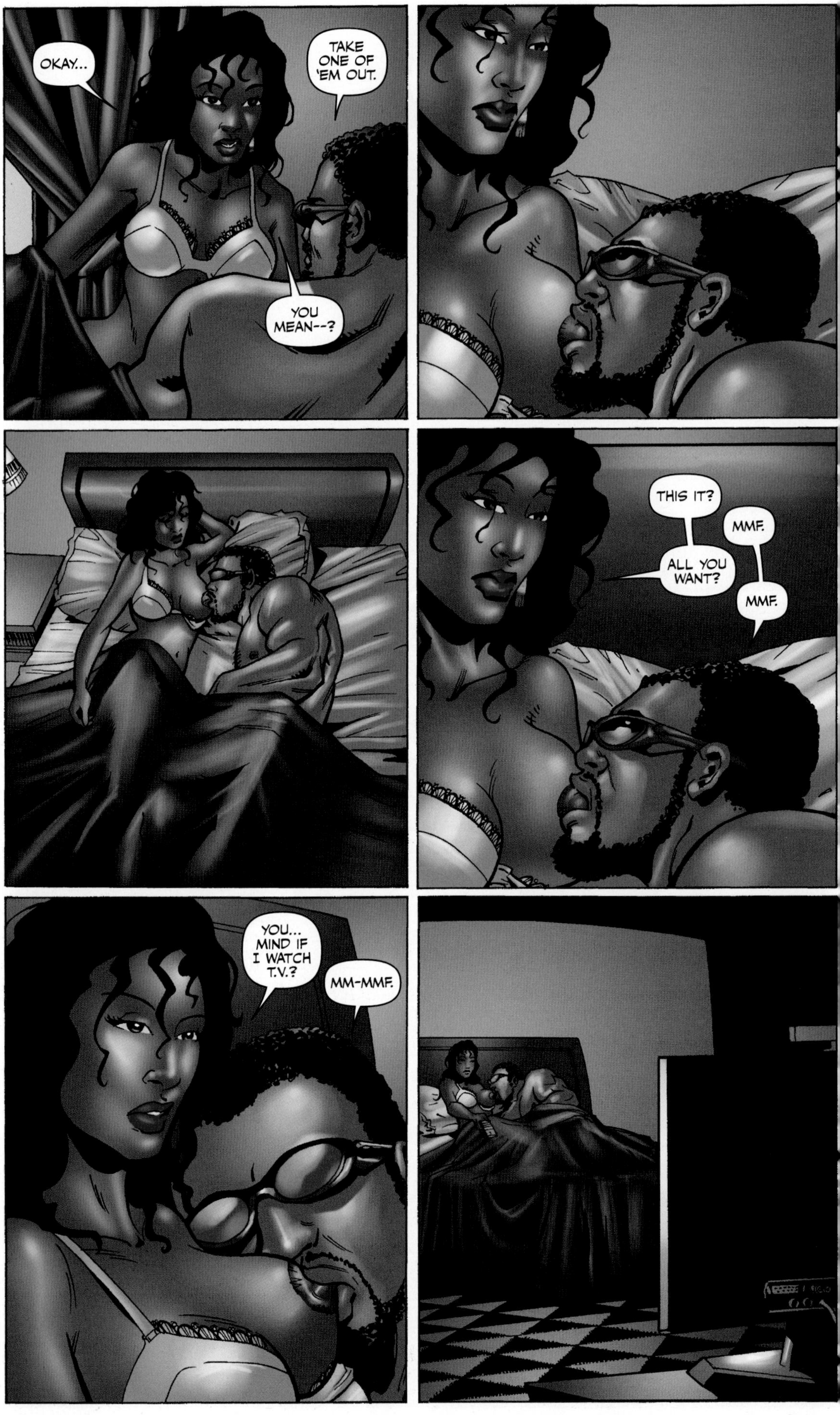
OKAY...
TAKE ONE OF 'EM OUT.
YOU MEAN--?
THIS IT?
MMF.
ALL YOU WANT?
MMF.
YOU... MIND IF I WATCH T.V.?
MM-MMF.

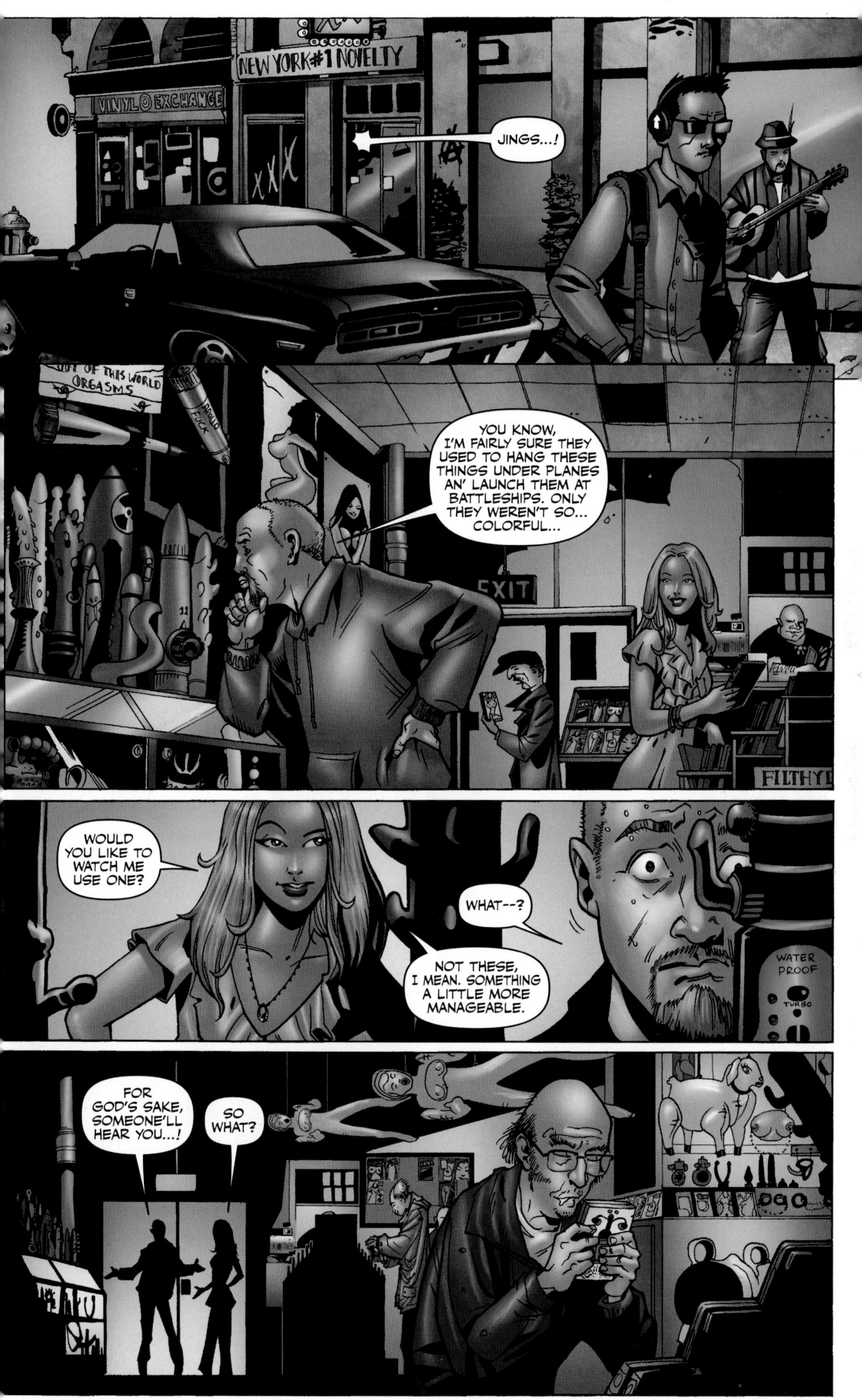

VINYL EXCHANGE
NEW YORK #1 NOVELTY
XXX
JINGS...!
OUT OF THIS WORLD ORGASMS
APOLLO FUCK
YOU KNOW, I'M FAIRLY SURE THEY USED TO HANG THESE THINGS UNDER PLANES AN' LAUNCH THEM AT BATTLESHIPS. ONLY THEY WEREN'T SO... COLORFUL...
EXIT
FILTHY
WOULD YOU LIKE TO WATCH ME USE ONE?
WHAT--?
NOT THESE, I MEAN. SOMETHING A LITTLE MORE MANAGEABLE.
WATER PROOF
TURBO
FOR GOD'S SAKE, SOMEONE'LL HEAR YOU...!
SO WHAT?

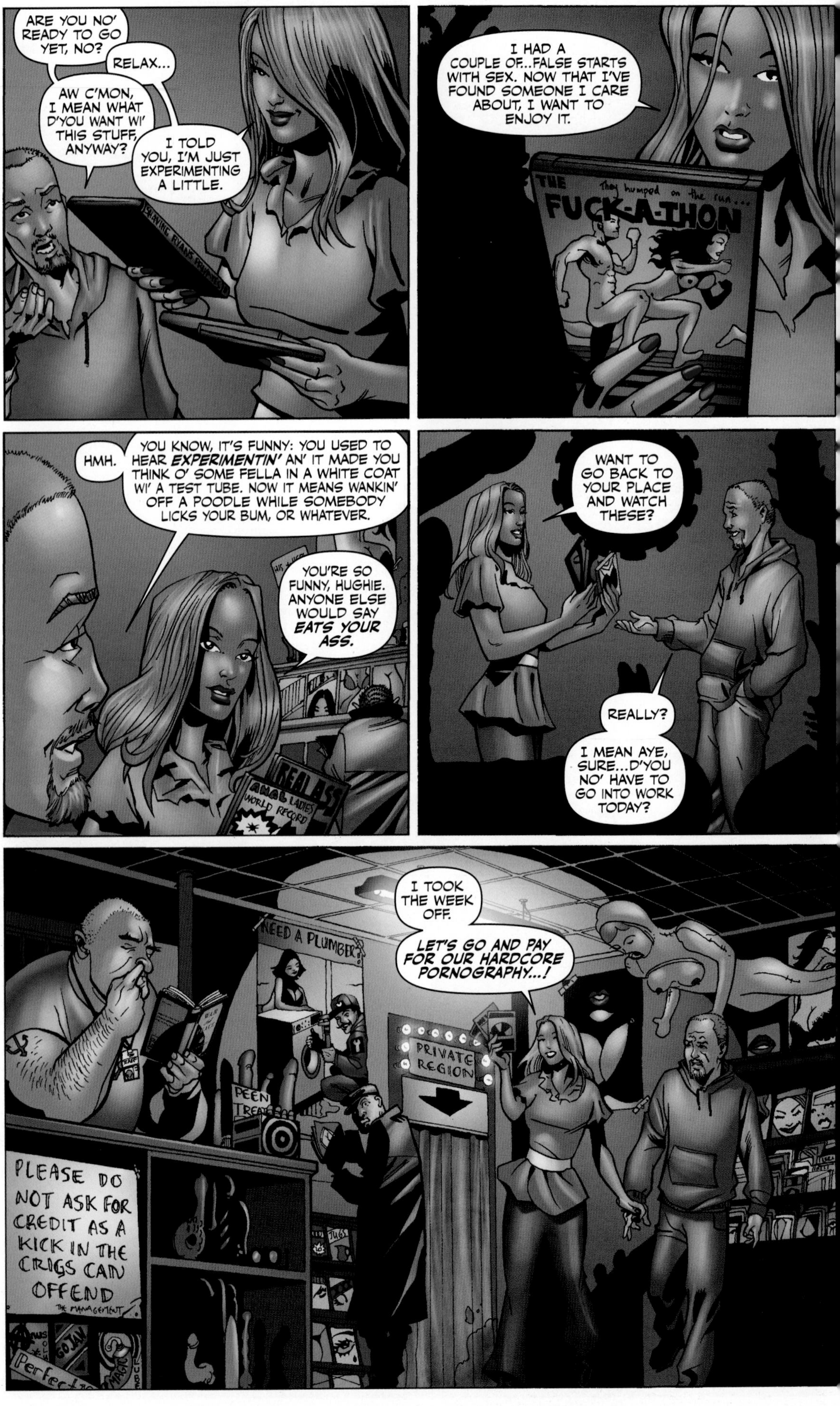
ARE YOU NO' READY TO GO YET, NO?
RELAX...
AW C'MON, I MEAN WHAT D'YOU WANT WI' THIS STUFF, ANYWAY?
I TOLD YOU, I'M JUST EXPERIMENTING A LITTLE.
I HAD A COUPLE OF...FALSE STARTS WITH SEX. NOW THAT I'VE FOUND SOMEONE I CARE ABOUT, I WANT TO ENJOY IT.
THE FUCK-A-THON
They humped on the run...
HMH.
YOU KNOW, IT'S FUNNY: YOU USED TO HEAR *EXPERIMENTIN'* AN' IT MADE YOU THINK O' SOME FELLA IN A WHITE COAT WI' A TEST TUBE. NOW IT MEANS WANKIN' OFF A POODLE WHILE SOMEBODY LICKS YOUR BUM, OR WHATEVER.
YOU'RE SO FUNNY, HUGHIE. ANYONE ELSE WOULD SAY ***EATS YOUR ASS.***
REAL ASS
ANAL LADIES WORLD RECORD
WANT TO GO BACK TO YOUR PLACE AND WATCH THESE?
REALLY?
I MEAN AYE, SURE...D'YOU NO' HAVE TO GO INTO WORK TODAY?
I TOOK THE WEEK OFF.
LET'S GO AND PAY FOR OUR HARDCORE PORNOGRAPHY...!
NEED A PLUMBER
PRIVATE REGION
PLEASE DO NOT ASK FOR CREDIT AS A KICK IN THE CRIGS CAN OFFEND
THE MANAGEMENT

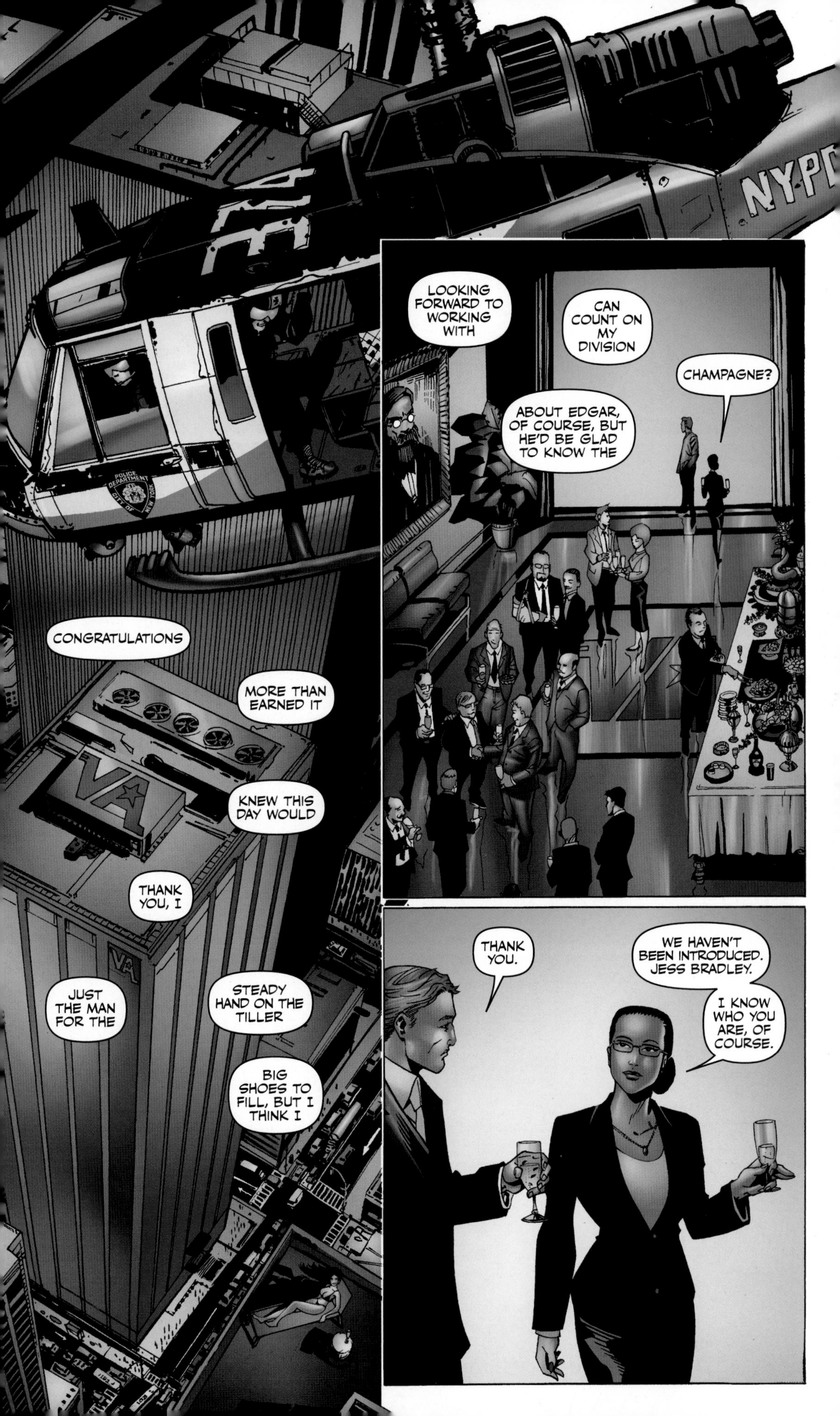
NYPD
POLICE DEPARTMENT CITY OF NEW YORK
CONGRATULATIONS
MORE THAN EARNED IT
KNEW THIS DAY WOULD
THANK YOU, I
JUST THE MAN FOR THE
STEADY HAND ON THE TILLER
BIG SHOES TO FILL, BUT I THINK I
LOOKING FORWARD TO WORKING WITH
CAN COUNT ON MY DIVISION
CHAMPAGNE?
ABOUT EDGAR, OF COURSE, BUT HE'D BE GLAD TO KNOW THE
THANK YOU.
WE HAVEN'T BEEN INTRODUCED. JESS BRADLEY.
I KNOW WHO YOU ARE, OF COURSE.

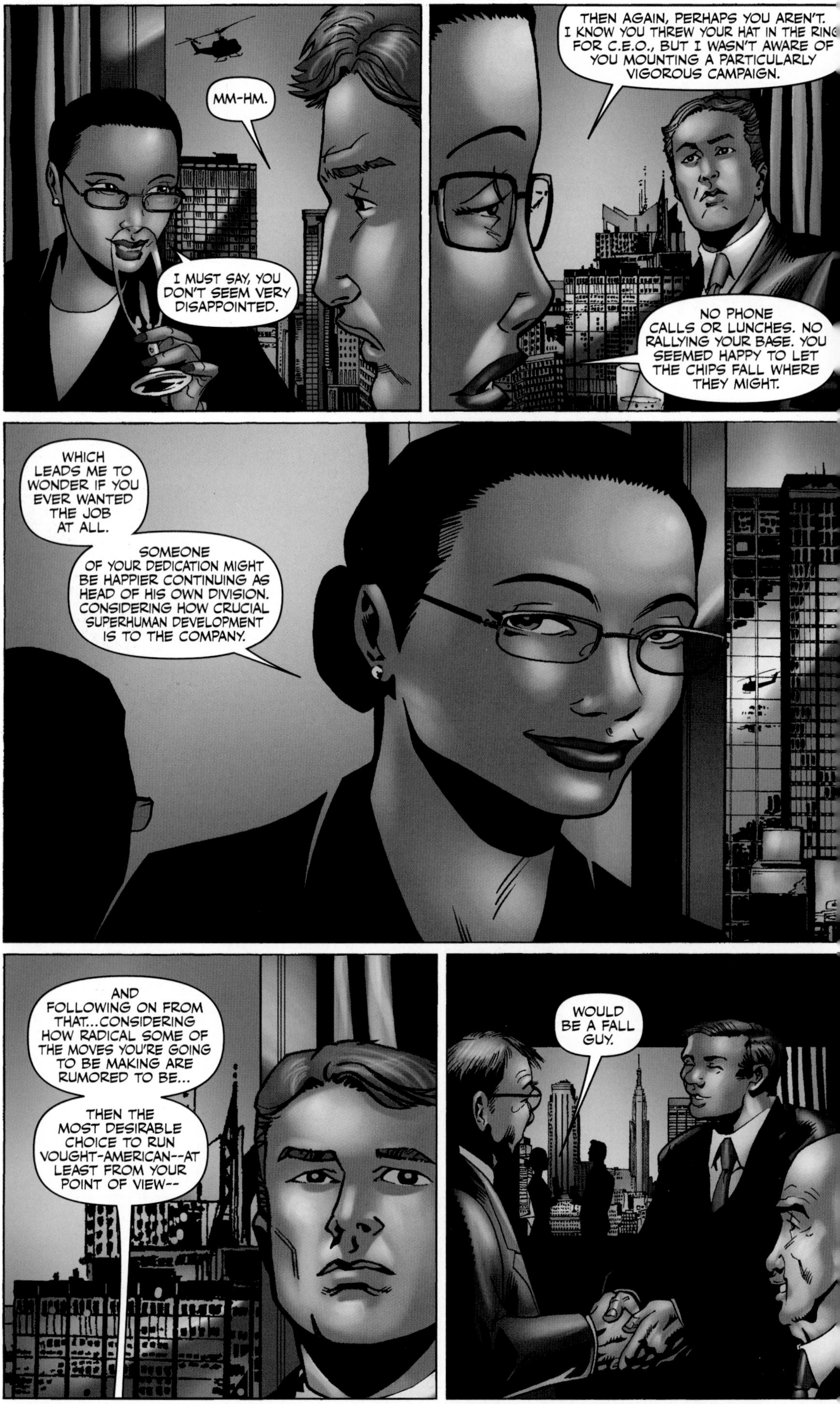
MM-HM.
I MUST SAY, YOU DON'T SEEM VERY DISAPPOINTED.
THEN AGAIN, PERHAPS YOU AREN'T. I KNOW YOU THREW YOUR HAT IN THE RING FOR C.E.O., BUT I WASN'T AWARE OF YOU MOUNTING A PARTICULARLY VIGOROUS CAMPAIGN.
NO PHONE CALLS OR LUNCHES. NO RALLYING YOUR BASE. YOU SEEMED HAPPY TO LET THE CHIPS FALL WHERE THEY MIGHT.
WHICH LEADS ME TO WONDER IF YOU EVER WANTED THE JOB AT ALL.
SOMEONE OF YOUR DEDICATION MIGHT BE HAPPIER CONTINUING AS HEAD OF HIS OWN DIVISION. CONSIDERING HOW CRUCIAL SUPERHUMAN DEVELOPMENT IS TO THE COMPANY.
AND FOLLOWING ON FROM THAT...CONSIDERING HOW RADICAL SOME OF THE MOVES YOU'RE GOING TO BE MAKING ARE RUMORED TO BE...
THEN THE MOST DESIRABLE CHOICE TO RUN VOUGHT-AMERICAN--AT LEAST FROM YOUR POINT OF VIEW--
WOULD BE A FALL GUY.

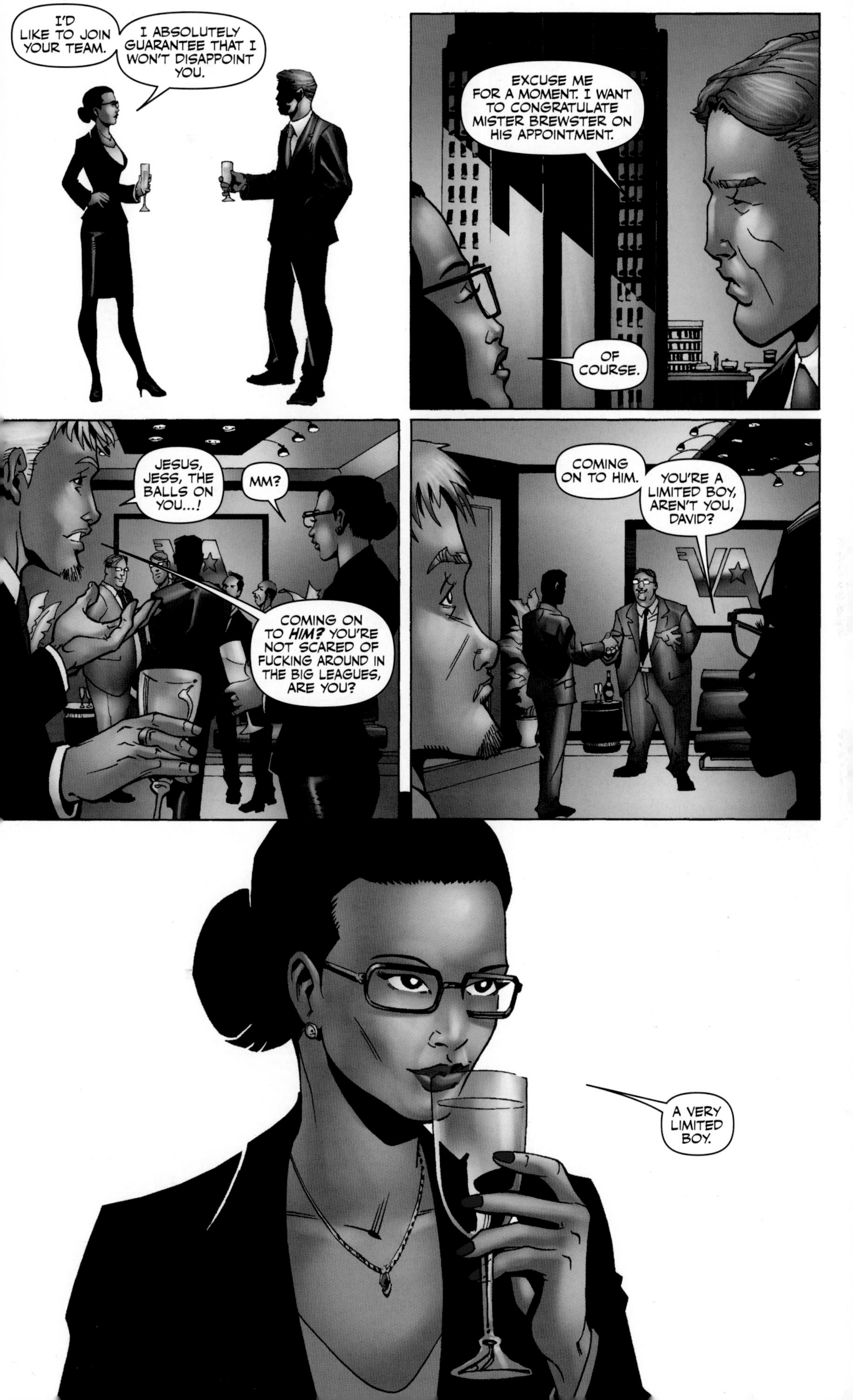
I'D LIKE TO JOIN YOUR TEAM.
I ABSOLUTELY GUARANTEE THAT I WON'T DISAPPOINT YOU.
EXCUSE ME FOR A MOMENT. I WANT TO CONGRATULATE MISTER BREWSTER ON HIS APPOINTMENT.
OF COURSE.
JESUS, JESS, THE BALLS ON YOU...!
MM?
COMING ON TO HIM? YOU'RE NOT SCARED OF FUCKING AROUND IN THE BIG LEAGUES, ARE YOU?
COMING ON TO HIM.
YOU'RE A LIMITED BOY, AREN'T YOU, DAVID?
A VERY LIMITED BOY.

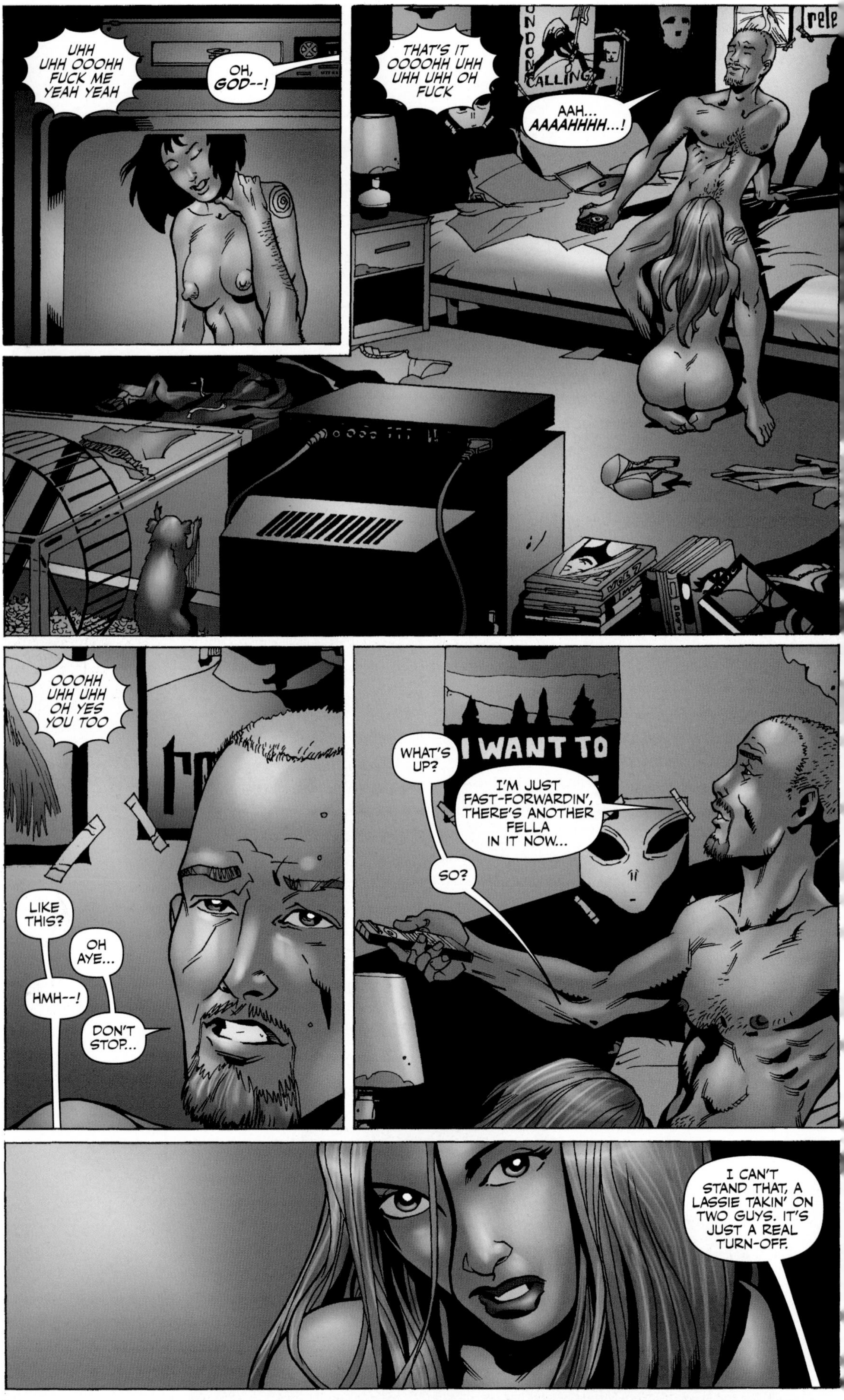
UHH UHH OOOHH FUCK ME YEAH YEAH
OH, GOD--!
THAT'S IT OOOOHH UHH UHH UHH OH FUCK
AAH... AAAAHHHH...!
OOOHH UHH UHH OH YES YOU TOO
LIKE THIS?
OH AYE...
HMH--!
DON'T STOP...
I WANT TO
WHAT'S UP?
I'M JUST FAST-FORWARDIN', THERE'S ANOTHER FELLA IN IT NOW...
SO?
I CAN'T STAND THAT, A LASSIE TAKIN' ON TWO GUYS. IT'S JUST A REAL TURN-OFF.

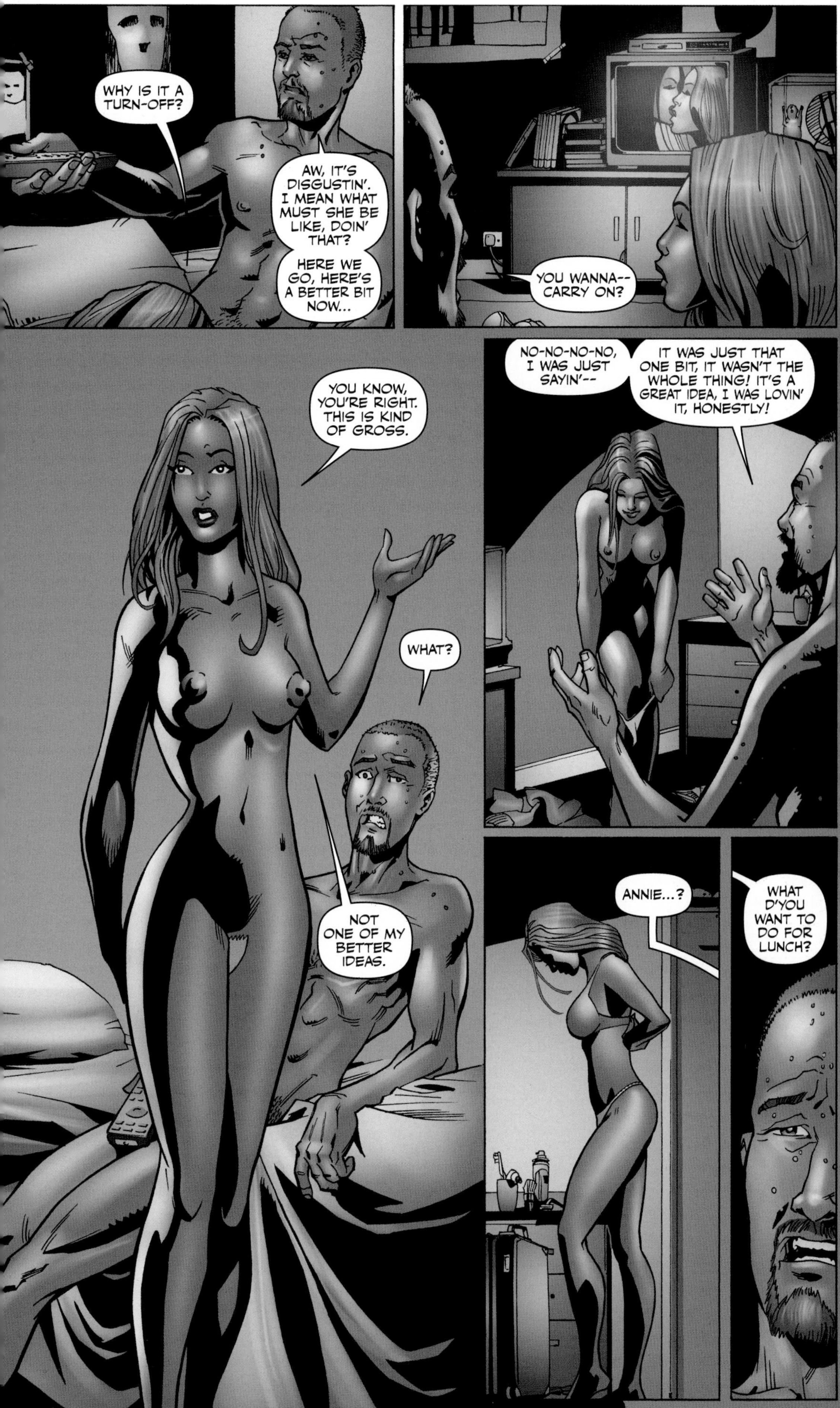
WHY IS IT A TURN-OFF?
AW, IT'S DISGUSTIN'. I MEAN WHAT MUST SHE BE LIKE, DOIN' THAT?
HERE WE GO, HERE'S A BETTER BIT NOW...
YOU WANNA-- CARRY ON?
YOU KNOW, YOU'RE RIGHT. THIS IS KIND OF GROSS.
WHAT?
NOT ONE OF MY BETTER IDEAS.
NO-NO-NO-NO, I WAS JUST SAYIN'--
IT WAS JUST THAT ONE BIT, IT WASN'T THE WHOLE THING! IT'S A GREAT IDEA, I WAS LOVIN' IT, HONESTLY!
ANNIE...?
WHAT D'YOU WANT TO DO FOR LUNCH?

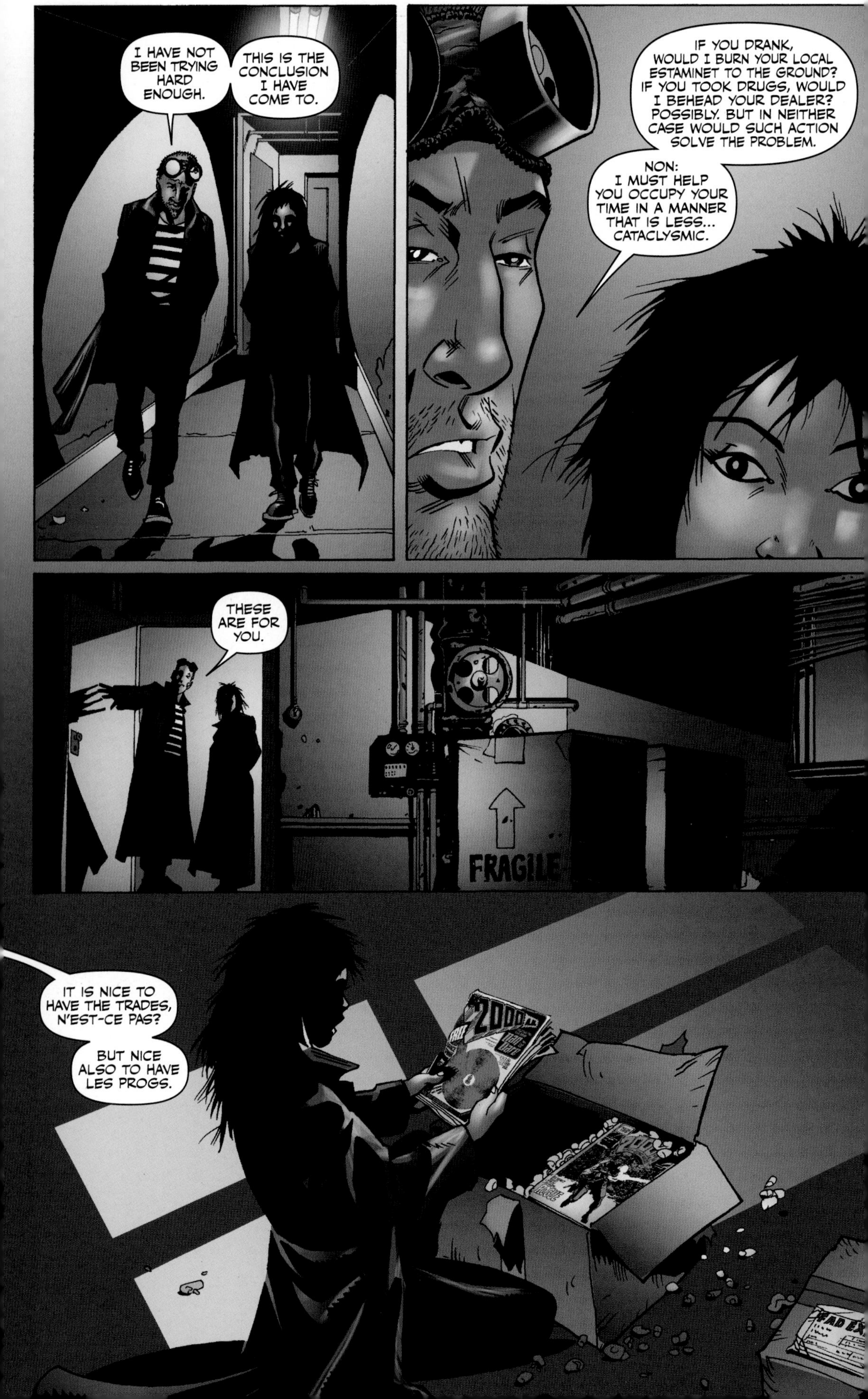
I HAVE NOT BEEN TRYING HARD ENOUGH.
THIS IS THE CONCLUSION I HAVE COME TO.
IF YOU DRANK, WOULD I BURN YOUR LOCAL ESTAMINET TO THE GROUND? IF YOU TOOK DRUGS, WOULD I BEHEAD YOUR DEALER? POSSIBLY. BUT IN NEITHER CASE WOULD SUCH ACTION SOLVE THE PROBLEM.
NON: I MUST HELP YOU OCCUPY YOUR TIME IN A MANNER THAT IS LESS... CATACLYSMIC.
THESE ARE FOR YOU.
FRAGILE
IT IS NICE TO HAVE THE TRADES, N'EST-CE PAS?
BUT NICE ALSO TO HAVE LES PROGS.

AFTER ALL, NO ONE WILL EVER REPRINT DEATH PLANET.

DE L'UN A CINQ-UN-NEUF. NEVER AGAIN SHALL I DOUBT THE POWER OF EBAY.

I WILL NOT GIVE UP ON YOU.

ENJOY.

SO WHAT'S THE SCORE?

SHE IS ENGROSSED.

ALAS, NOT PERMANENTLY.

MEANWHILE, THE WIRETAP ON HER PHONE COPIES ALL INCOMING MESSAGES TO MINE. THE BUG ENABLES ME TO MONITOR HER MOVEMENTS.

ALL YOU GOTTA DO IS BEAT HER TO IT, EH?

SHE WILL SEE NO NEED FOR URGENCY. SHOULD AN EMPLOYER REQUEST A MEETING, I WILL HAVE TIME TO REMONSTRATE WITH HIM.

SHOULD SHE BE REQUIRED TO MOVE DIRECTLY ON A TARGET, I CAN ENFORCE THEIR RAPID EMMIGRATION.

SIMPLE AS THAT...

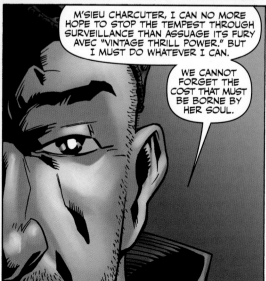

M'SIEU CHARCUTER, I CAN NO MORE HOPE TO STOP THE TEMPEST THROUGH SURVEILLANCE THAN ASSUAGE ITS FURY AVEC "VINTAGE THRILL POWER." BUT I MUST DO WHATEVER I CAN.

WE CANNOT FORGET THE COST THAT MUST BE BORNE BY HER SOUL.

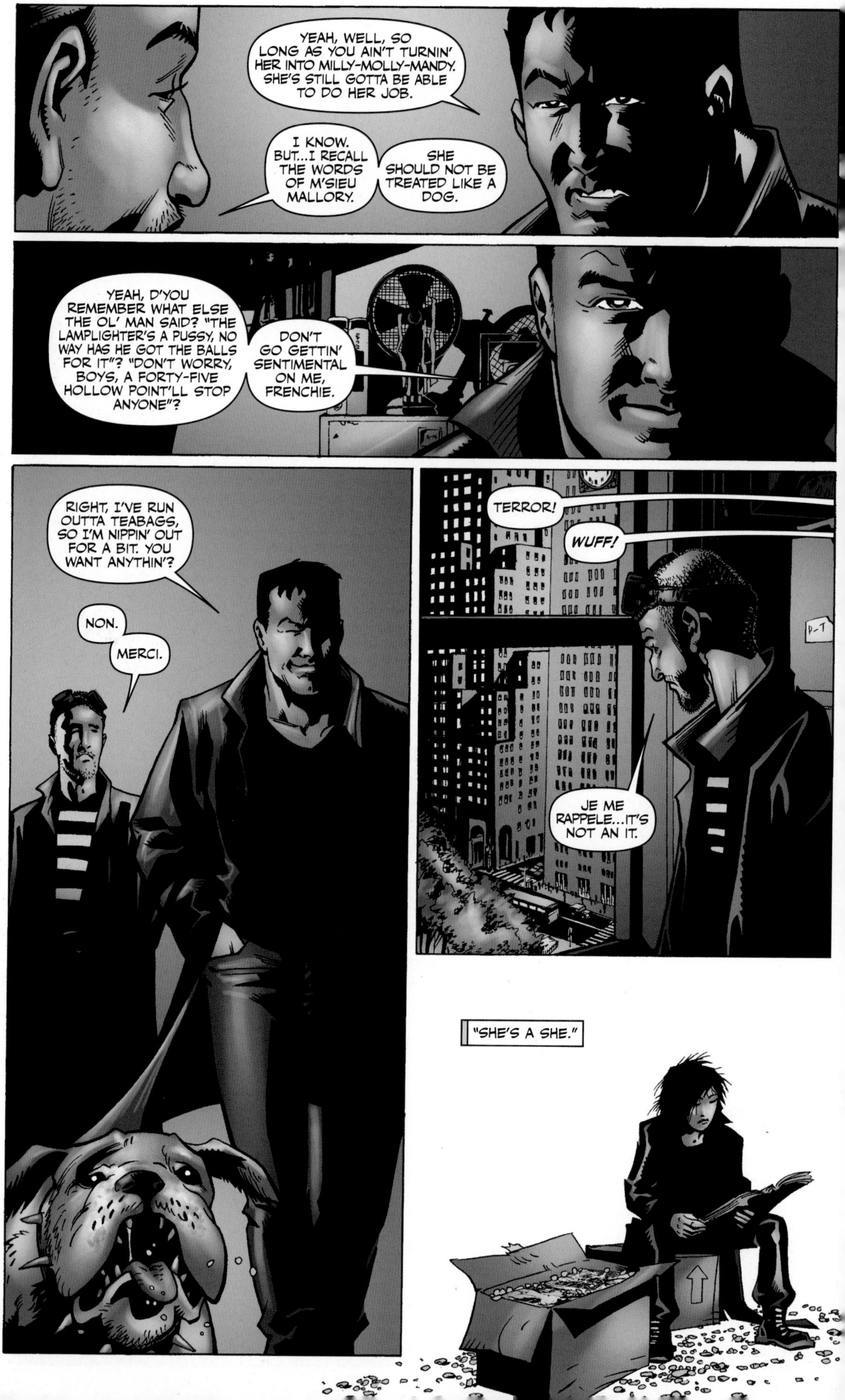
YEAH, WELL, SO LONG AS YOU AIN'T TURNIN' HER INTO MILLY-MOLLY-MANDY. SHE'S STILL GOTTA BE ABLE TO DO HER JOB.
I KNOW. BUT...I RECALL THE WORDS OF M'SIEU MALLORY.
SHE SHOULD NOT BE TREATED LIKE A DOG.
YEAH, D'YOU REMEMBER WHAT ELSE THE OL' MAN SAID? "THE LAMPLIGHTER'S A PUSSY, NO WAY HAS HE GOT THE BALLS FOR IT"? "DON'T WORRY, BOYS, A FORTY-FIVE HOLLOW POINT'LL STOP ANYONE"?
DON'T GO GETTIN' SENTIMENTAL ON ME, FRENCHIE.
RIGHT, I'VE RUN OUTTA TEABAGS, SO I'M NIPPIN' OUT FOR A BIT. YOU WANT ANYTHIN'?
NON.
MERCI.
TERROR!
WUFF!
JE ME RAPPELE...IT'S NOT AN IT.
"SHE'S A SHE."

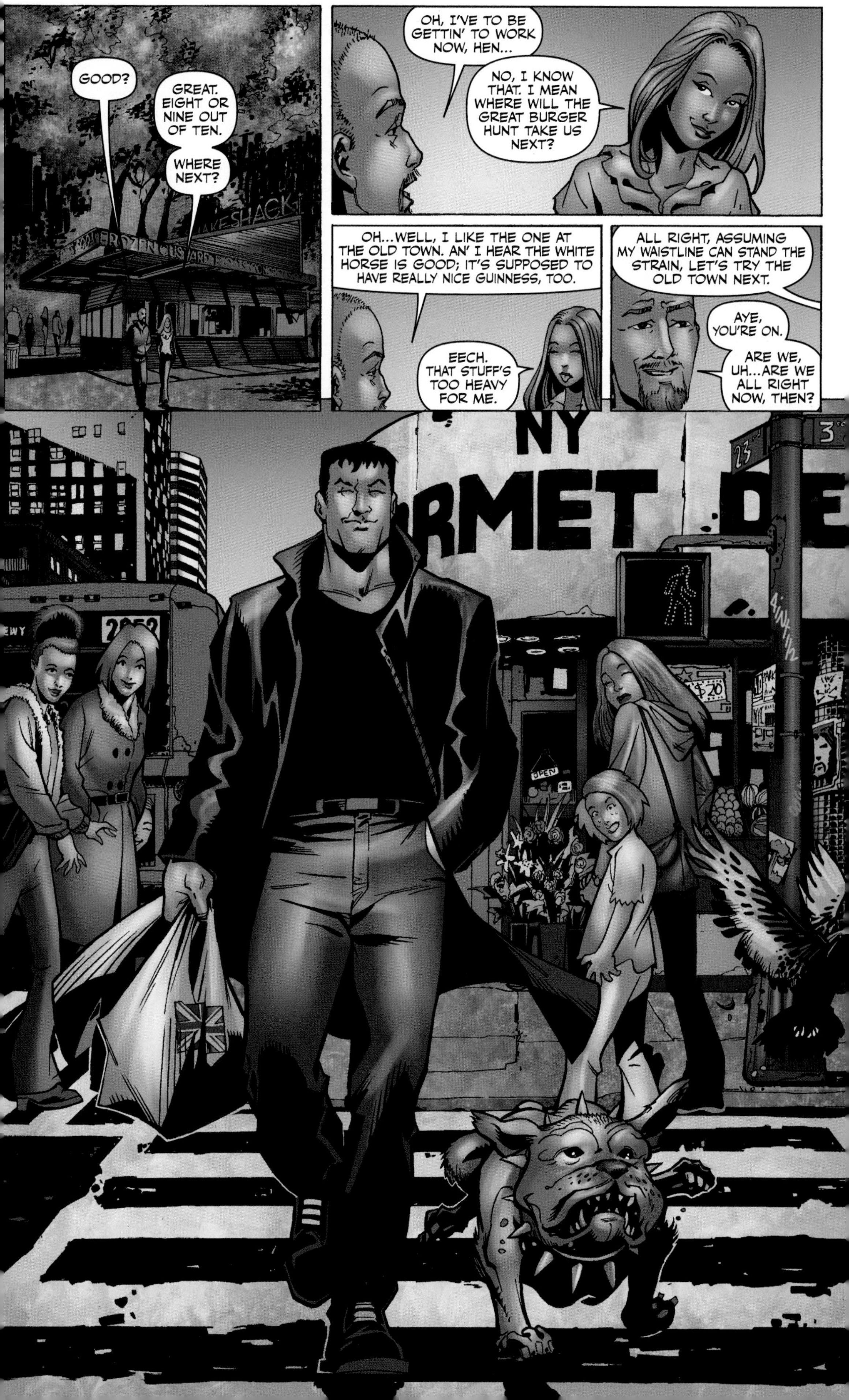
GOOD?
GREAT. EIGHT OR NINE OUT OF TEN.
WHERE NEXT?
FROZEN CUSTARD
OH, I'VE TO BE GETTIN' TO WORK NOW, HEN...
NO, I KNOW THAT. I MEAN WHERE WILL THE GREAT BURGER HUNT TAKE US NEXT?
OH...WELL, I LIKE THE ONE AT THE OLD TOWN. AN' I HEAR THE WHITE HORSE IS GOOD; IT'S SUPPOSED TO HAVE REALLY NICE GUINNESS, TOO.
EECH. THAT STUFF'S TOO HEAVY FOR ME.
ALL RIGHT, ASSUMING MY WAISTLINE CAN STAND THE STRAIN, LET'S TRY THE OLD TOWN NEXT.
AYE, YOU'RE ON.
ARE WE, UH...ARE WE ALL RIGHT NOW, THEN?
NY
RMET
OPEN
$20

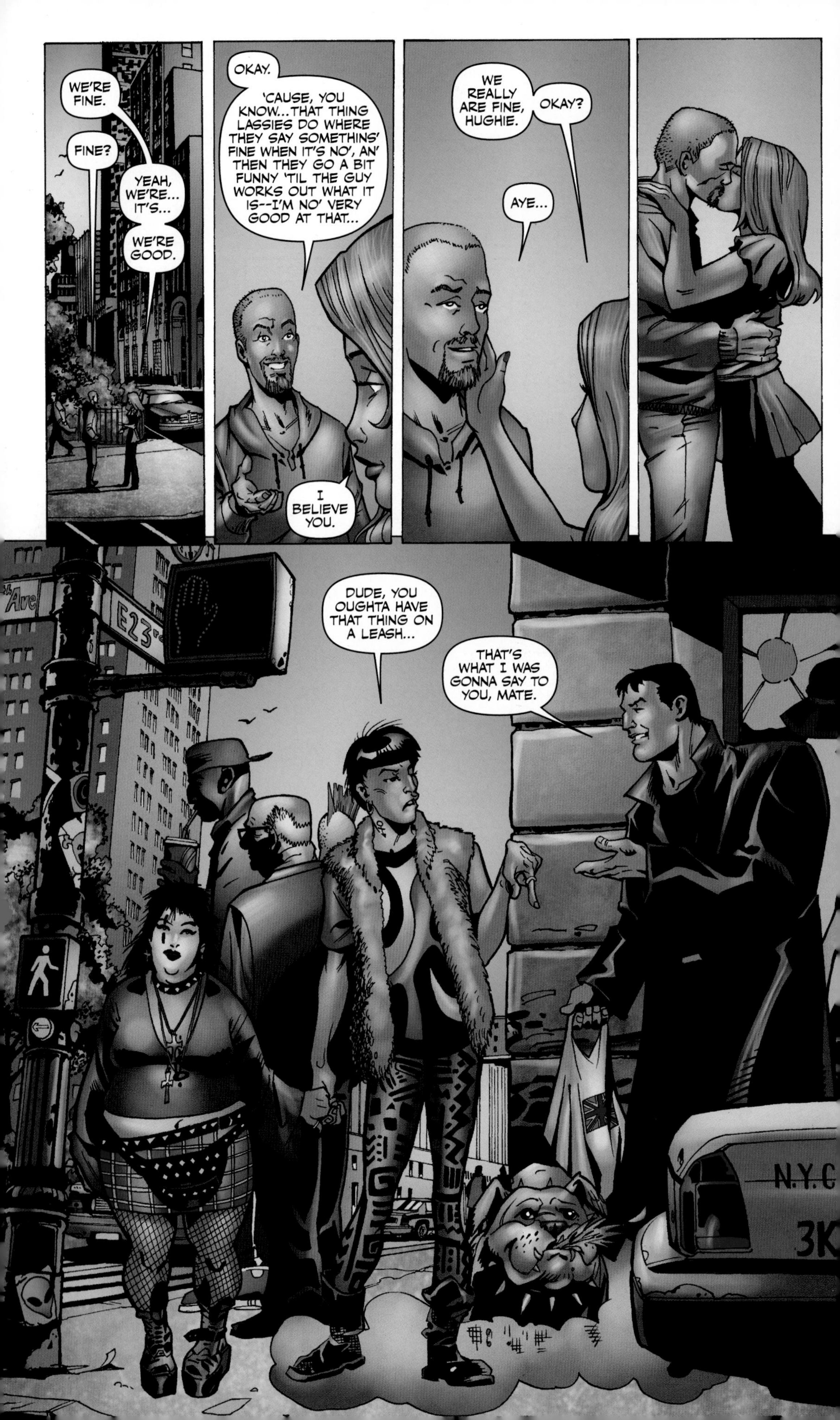
WE'RE FINE.
FINE?
YEAH, WE'RE... IT'S...
WE'RE GOOD.
OKAY.
'CAUSE, YOU KNOW...THAT THING LASSIES DO WHERE THEY SAY SOMETHINS' FINE WHEN IT'S NO', AN' THEN THEY GO A BIT FUNNY 'TIL THE GUY WORKS OUT WHAT IT IS--I'M NO' VERY GOOD AT THAT...
I BELIEVE YOU.
WE REALLY ARE FINE, HUGHIE.
OKAY?
AYE...
Ave
E23rd
DUDE, YOU OUGHTA HAVE THAT THING ON A LEASH...
THAT'S WHAT I WAS GONNA SAY TO YOU, MATE.
N.Y.C
3K

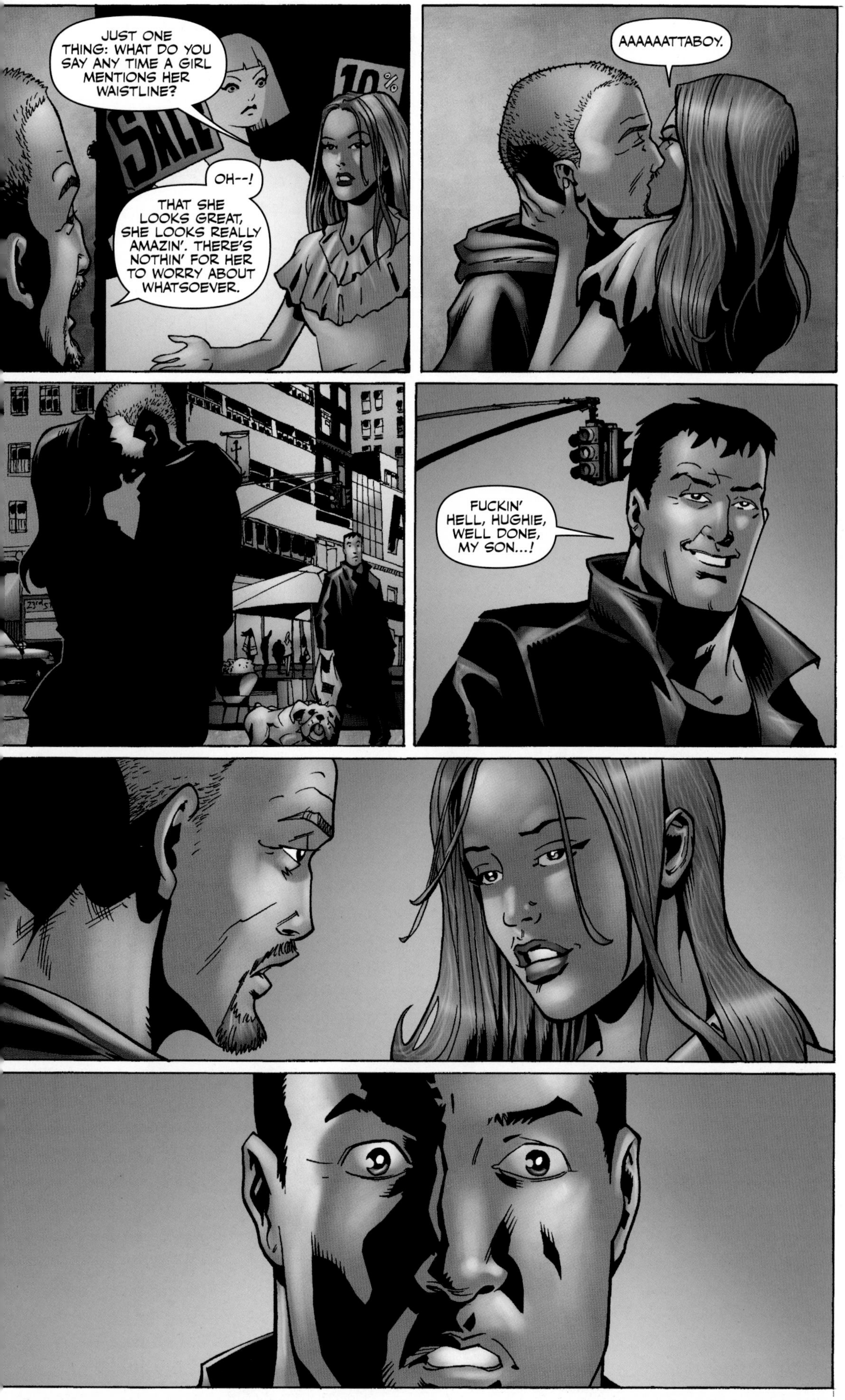

JUST ONE THING: WHAT DO YOU SAY ANY TIME A GIRL MENTIONS HER WAISTLINE?
SALE
10%
OH--!
THAT SHE LOOKS GREAT, SHE LOOKS REALLY AMAZIN'. THERE'S NOTHIN' FOR HER TO WORRY ABOUT WHATSOEVER.
AAAAAATTABOY.
FUCKIN' HELL, HUGHIE, WELL DONE, MY SON...!

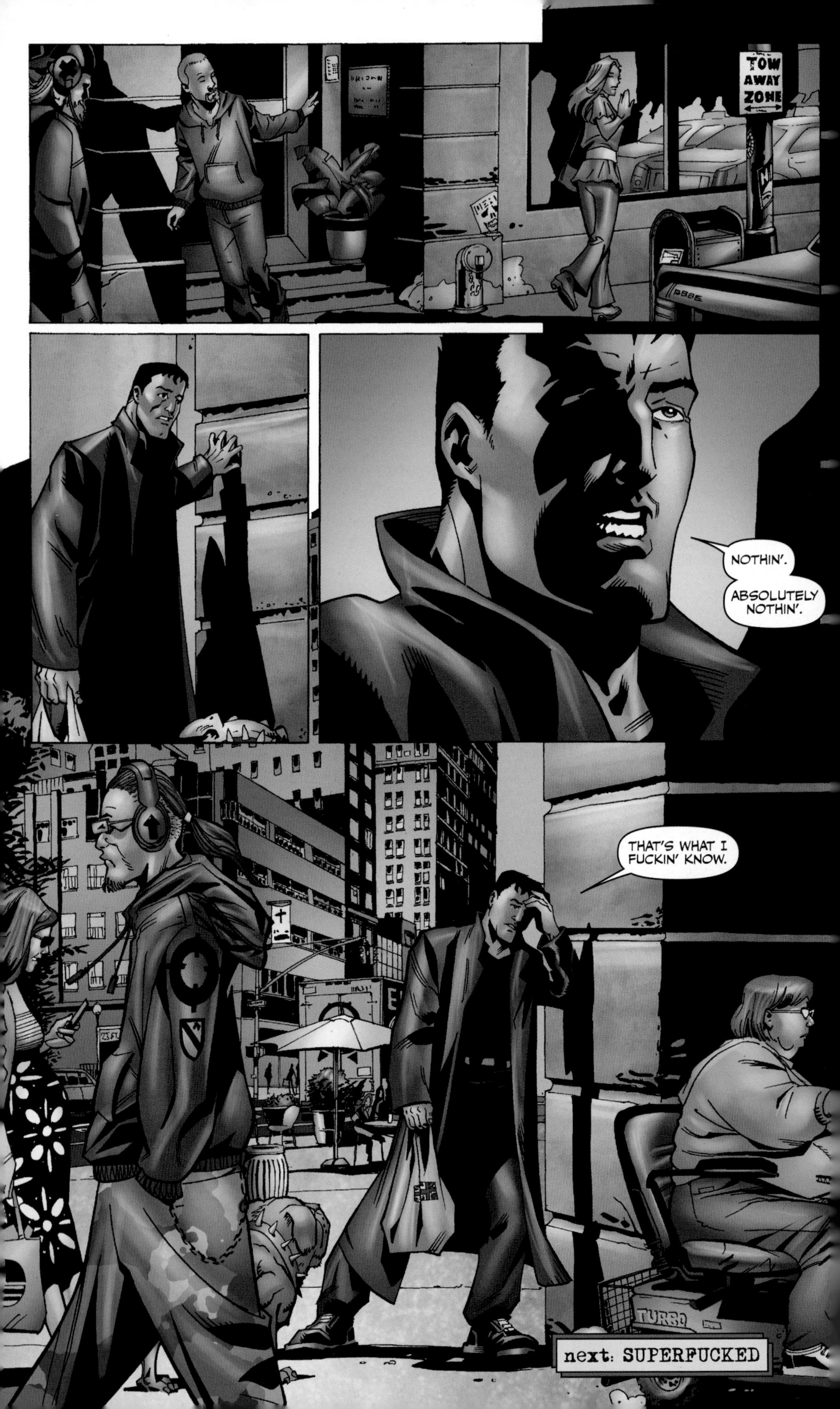
TOW AWAY ZONE
NOTHIN'.
ABSOLUTELY NOTHIN'.
THAT'S WHAT I FUCKIN' KNOW.
TURBO
next: SUPERFUCKED

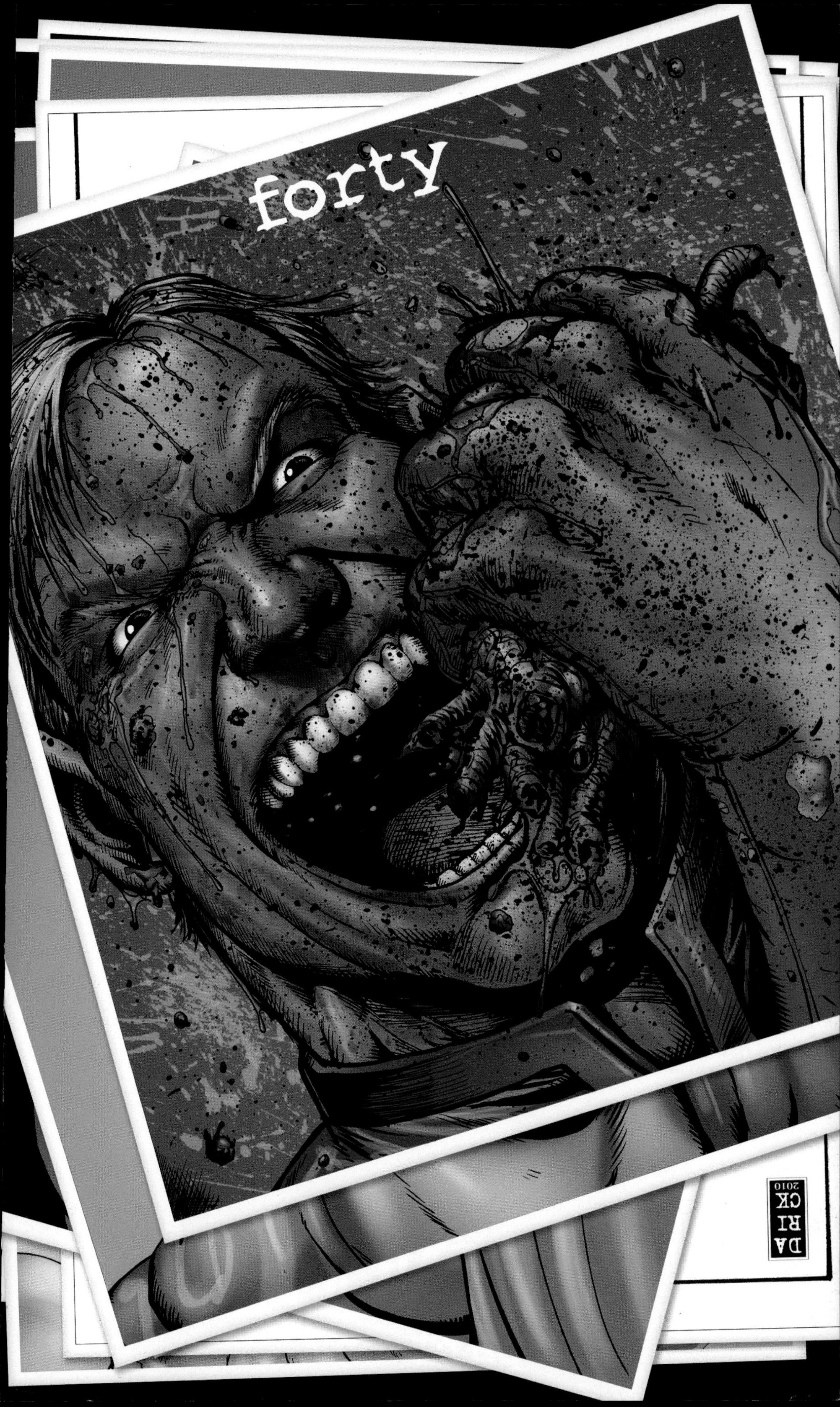
forty

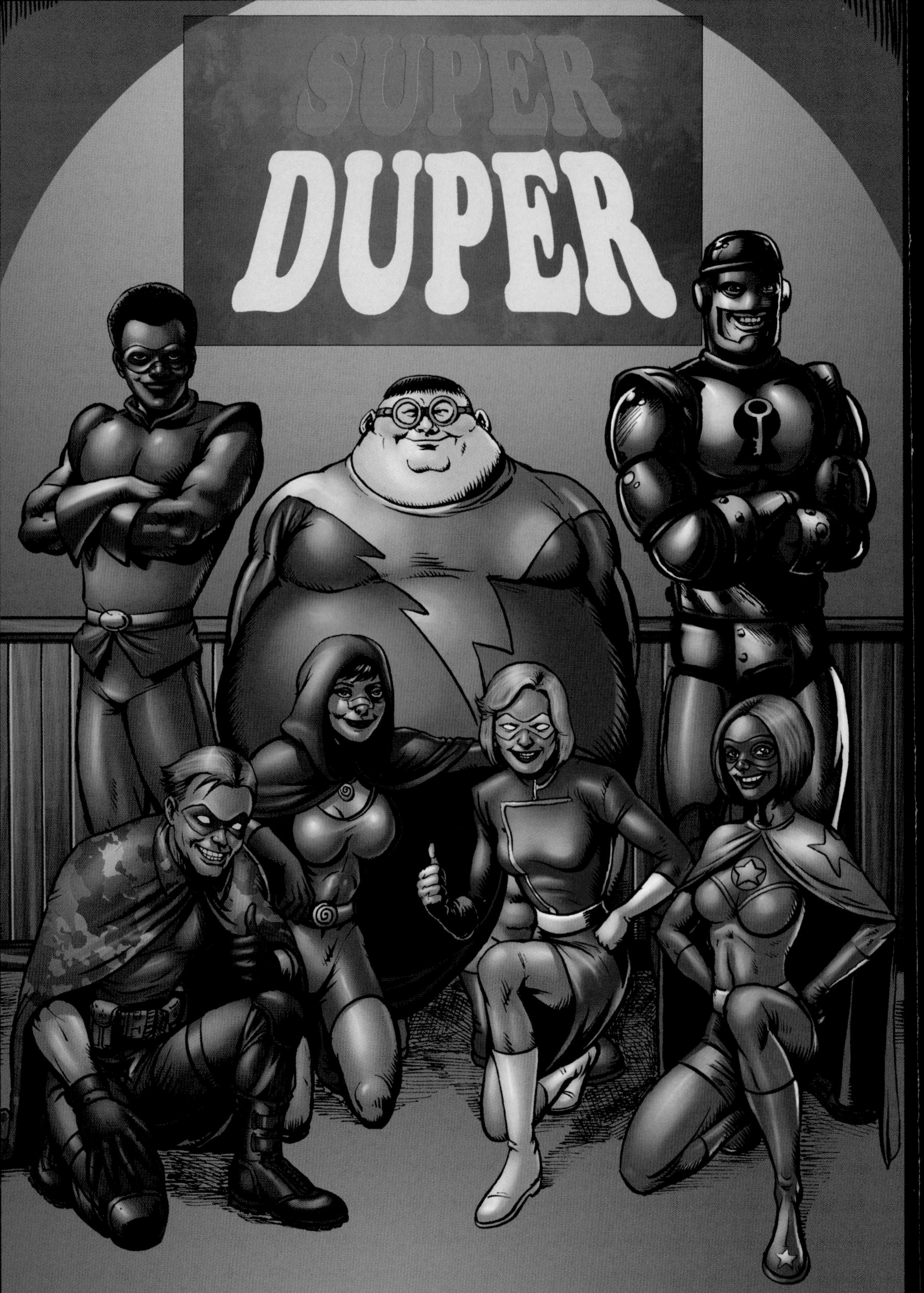
SUPER
DUPER

THE INNOCENTS
part one

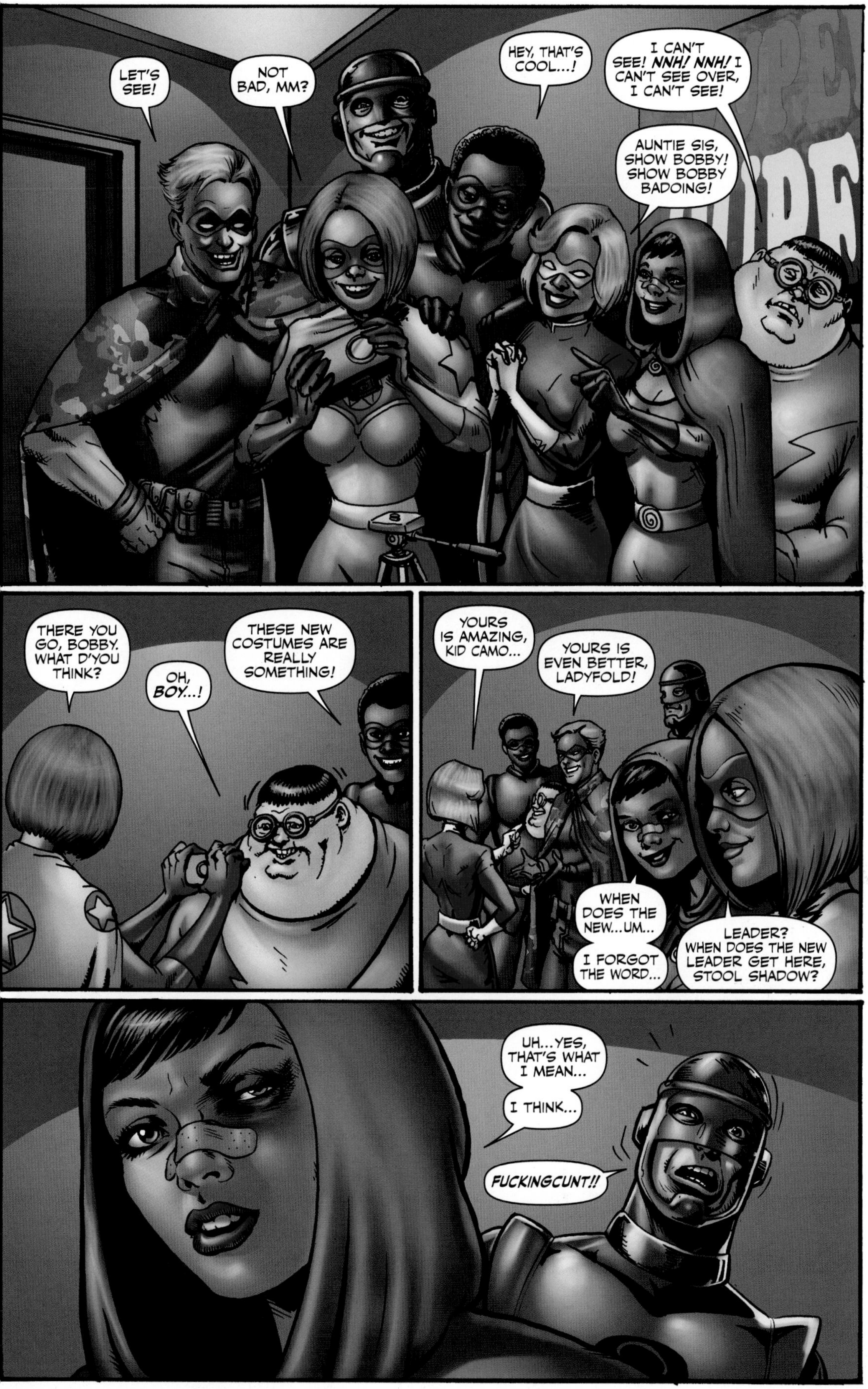
LET'S SEE!
NOT BAD, MM?
HEY, THAT'S COOL...!
I CAN'T SEE! NNH! NNH! I CAN'T SEE OVER, I CAN'T SEE!
AUNTIE SIS, SHOW BOBBY! SHOW BOBBY BADOING!
THERE YOU GO, BOBBY. WHAT D'YOU THINK?
OH, BOY...!
THESE NEW COSTUMES ARE REALLY SOMETHING!
YOURS IS AMAZING, KID CAMO...
YOURS IS EVEN BETTER, LADYFOLD!
WHEN DOES THE NEW...UM...
I FORGOT THE WORD...
LEADER? WHEN DOES THE NEW LEADER GET HERE, STOOL SHADOW?
UH...YES, THAT'S WHAT I MEAN...
I THINK...
FUCKINGCUNT!!

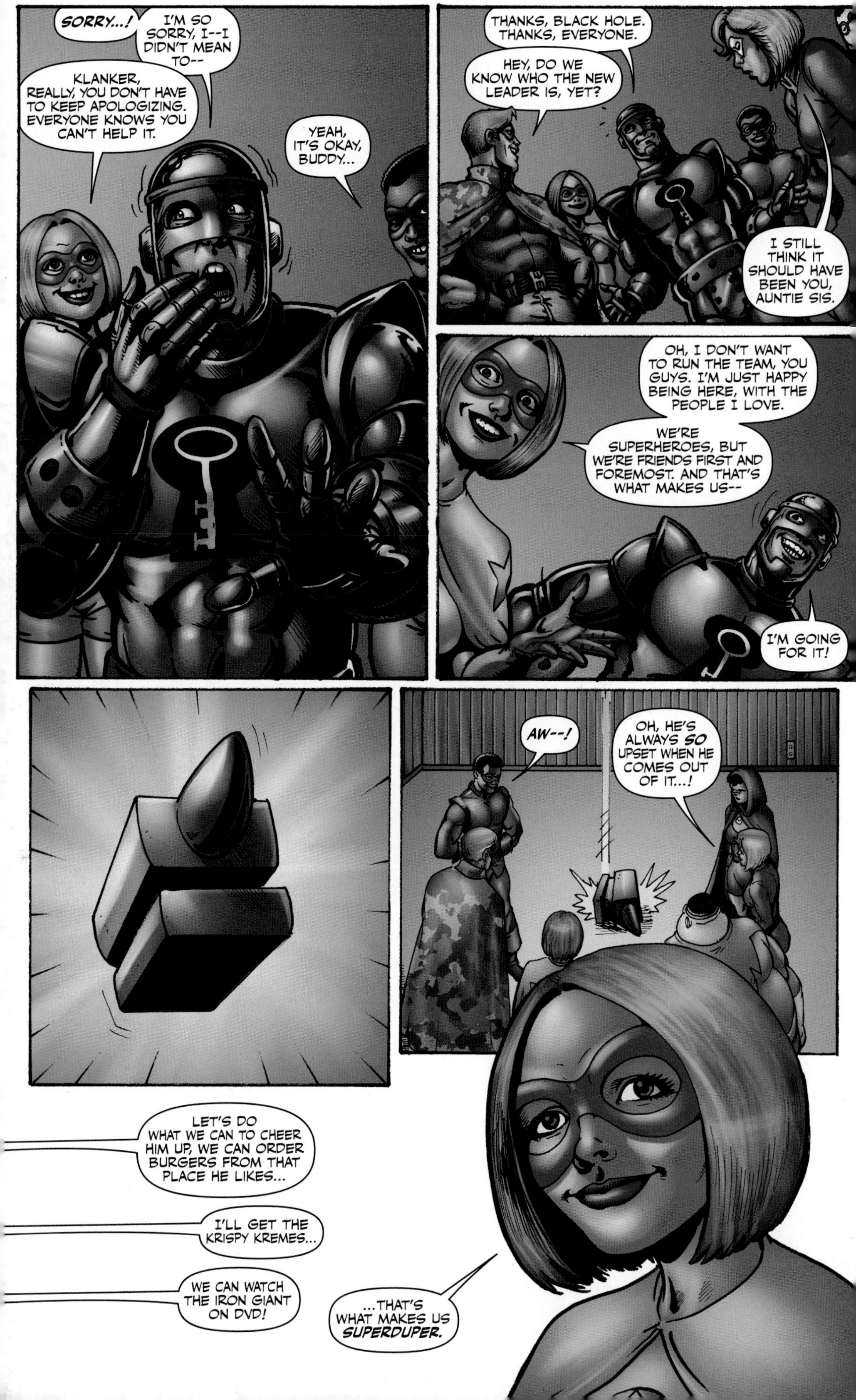
SORRY...!
I'M SO SORRY, I--I DIDN'T MEAN TO--
KLANKER, REALLY, YOU DON'T HAVE TO KEEP APOLOGIZING. EVERYONE KNOWS YOU CAN'T HELP IT.
YEAH, IT'S OKAY, BUDDY...
THANKS, BLACK HOLE. THANKS, EVERYONE.
HEY, DO WE KNOW WHO THE NEW LEADER IS, YET?
I STILL THINK IT SHOULD HAVE BEEN YOU, AUNTIE SIS.
OH, I DON'T WANT TO RUN THE TEAM, YOU GUYS. I'M JUST HAPPY BEING HERE, WITH THE PEOPLE I LOVE.
WE'RE SUPERHEROES, BUT WE'RE FRIENDS FIRST AND FOREMOST. AND THAT'S WHAT MAKES US--
I'M GOING FOR IT!
AW--!
OH, HE'S ALWAYS SO UPSET WHEN HE COMES OUT OF IT...!
LET'S DO WHAT WE CAN TO CHEER HIM UP, WE CAN ORDER BURGERS FROM THAT PLACE HE LIKES...
I'LL GET THE KRISPY KREMES...
WE CAN WATCH THE IRON GIANT ON DVD!
...THAT'S WHAT MAKES US SUPERDUPER.

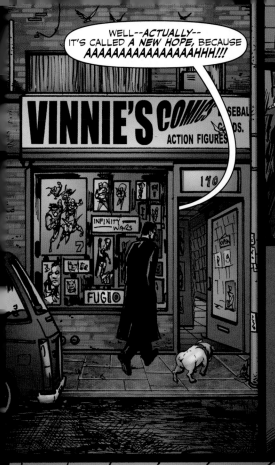

WELL--*ACTUALLY*--
IT'S CALLED *A NEW HOPE*, BECAUSE
AAAAAAAAAAAAAAAHHH!!!

VINNIE'S COMICS
ACTION FIGURES
SEBAL
DS.
INFINITY WARS
FUGIO

HEY,
BUTCHUH.

NNEEEEIIIIIGGGHH...!

YA CAN
GO ON DOWN,
HE KNOWS YA
COMIN'.

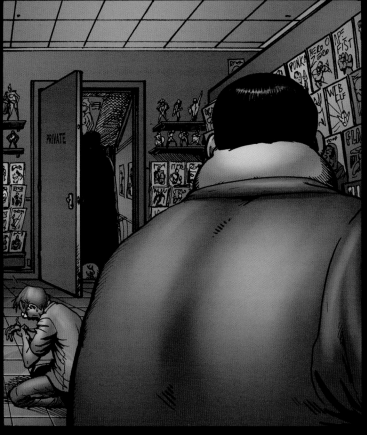

PRIVATE

FUCK
YOU TOO...

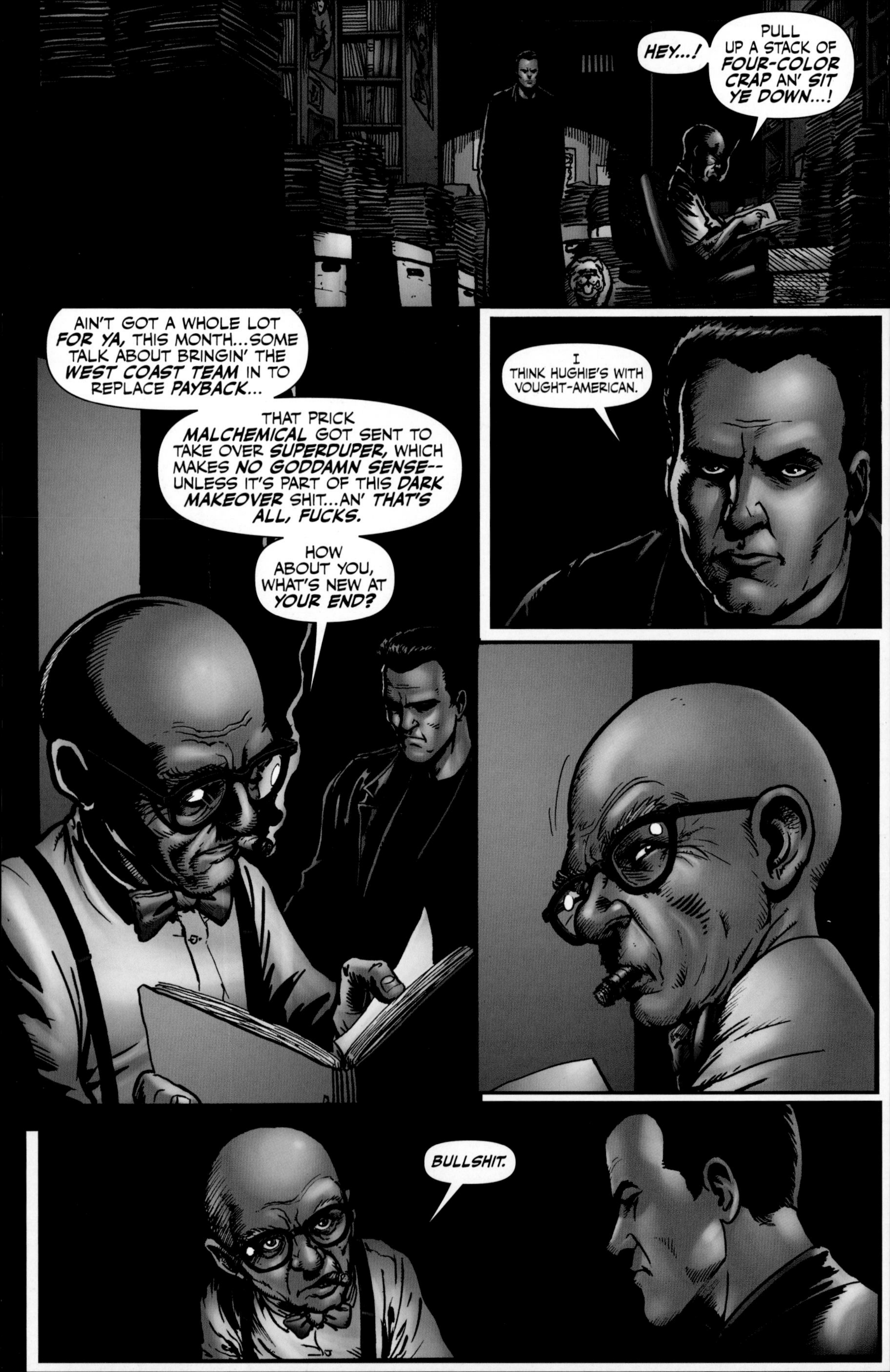
HEY...!
PULL UP A STACK OF FOUR-COLOR CRAP AN' SIT YE DOWN...!
AIN'T GOT A WHOLE LOT FOR YA, THIS MONTH...SOME TALK ABOUT BRINGIN' THE WEST COAST TEAM IN TO REPLACE PAYBACK...
THAT PRICK MALCHEMICAL GOT SENT TO TAKE OVER SUPERDUPER, WHICH MAKES NO GODDAMN SENSE--UNLESS IT'S PART OF THIS DARK MAKEOVER SHIT...AN' THAT'S ALL, FUCKS.
HOW ABOUT YOU, WHAT'S NEW AT YOUR END?
I THINK HUGHIE'S WITH VOUGHT-AMERICAN.
BULLSHIT.

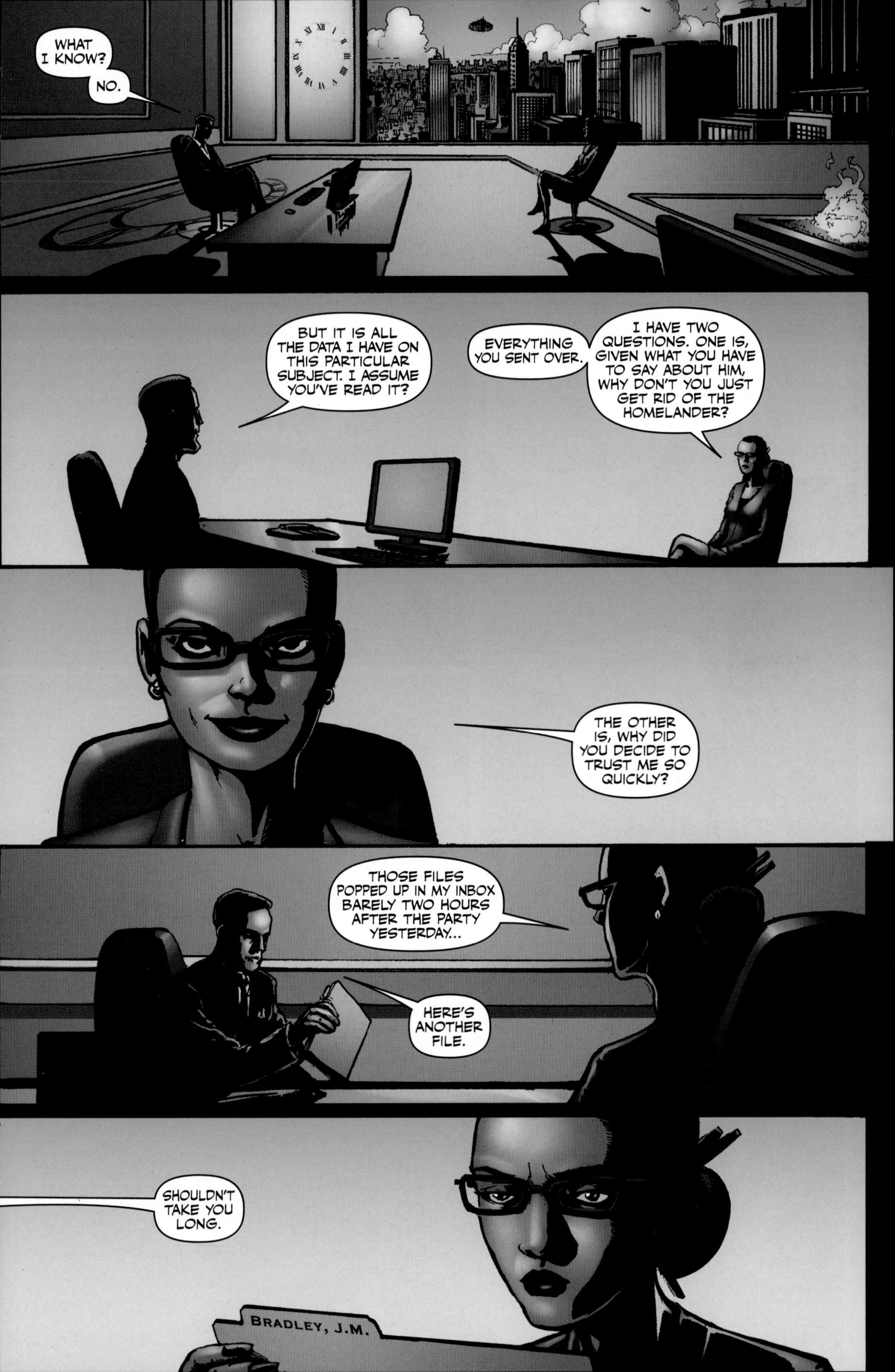
WHAT I KNOW?
NO.
BUT IT IS ALL THE DATA I HAVE ON THIS PARTICULAR SUBJECT. I ASSUME YOU'VE READ IT?
EVERYTHING YOU SENT OVER.
I HAVE TWO QUESTIONS. ONE IS, GIVEN WHAT YOU HAVE TO SAY ABOUT HIM, WHY DON'T YOU JUST GET RID OF THE HOMELANDER?
THE OTHER IS, WHY DID YOU DECIDE TO TRUST ME SO QUICKLY?
THOSE FILES POPPED UP IN MY INBOX BARELY TWO HOURS AFTER THE PARTY YESTERDAY...
HERE'S ANOTHER FILE.
SHOULDN'T TAKE YOU LONG.
BRADLEY, J.M.

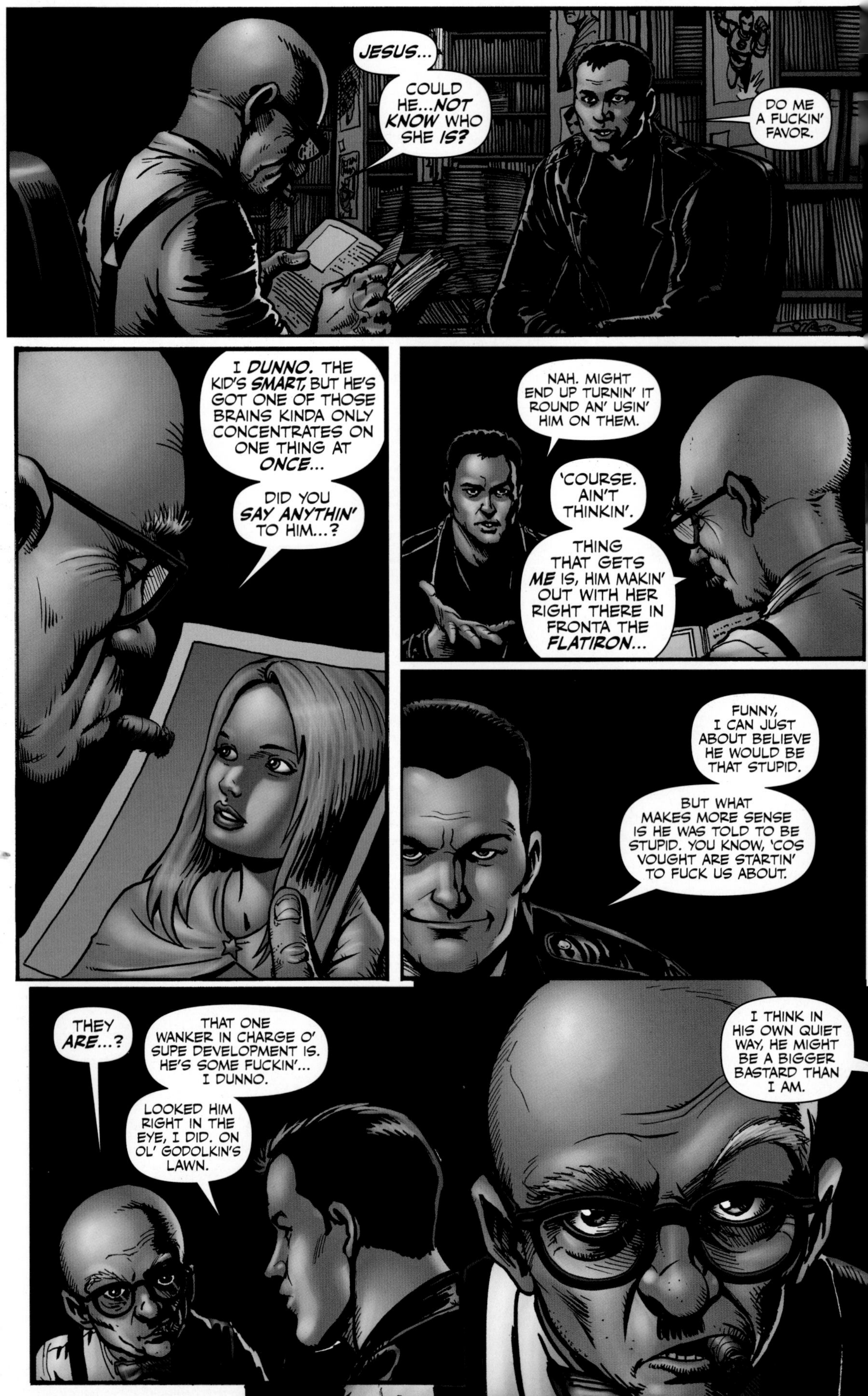
JESUS...
COULD HE...NOT KNOW WHO SHE IS?
DO ME A FUCKIN' FAVOR.
I DUNNO. THE KID'S SMART, BUT HE'S GOT ONE OF THOSE BRAINS KINDA ONLY CONCENTRATES ON ONE THING AT ONCE...
DID YOU SAY ANYTHIN' TO HIM...?
NAH. MIGHT END UP TURNIN' IT ROUND AN' USIN' HIM ON THEM.
'COURSE. AIN'T THINKIN'.
THING THAT GETS ME IS, HIM MAKIN' OUT WITH HER RIGHT THERE IN FRONTA THE FLATIRON...
FUNNY, I CAN JUST ABOUT BELIEVE HE WOULD BE THAT STUPID.
BUT WHAT MAKES MORE SENSE IS HE WAS TOLD TO BE STUPID. YOU KNOW, 'COS VOUGHT ARE STARTIN' TO FUCK US ABOUT.
THEY ARE...?
THAT ONE WANKER IN CHARGE O' SUPE DEVELOPMENT IS. HE'S SOME FUCKIN'... I DUNNO.
LOOKED HIM RIGHT IN THE EYE, I DID. ON OL' GODOLKIN'S LAWN.
I THINK IN HIS OWN QUIET WAY, HE MIGHT BE A BIGGER BASTARD THAN I AM.

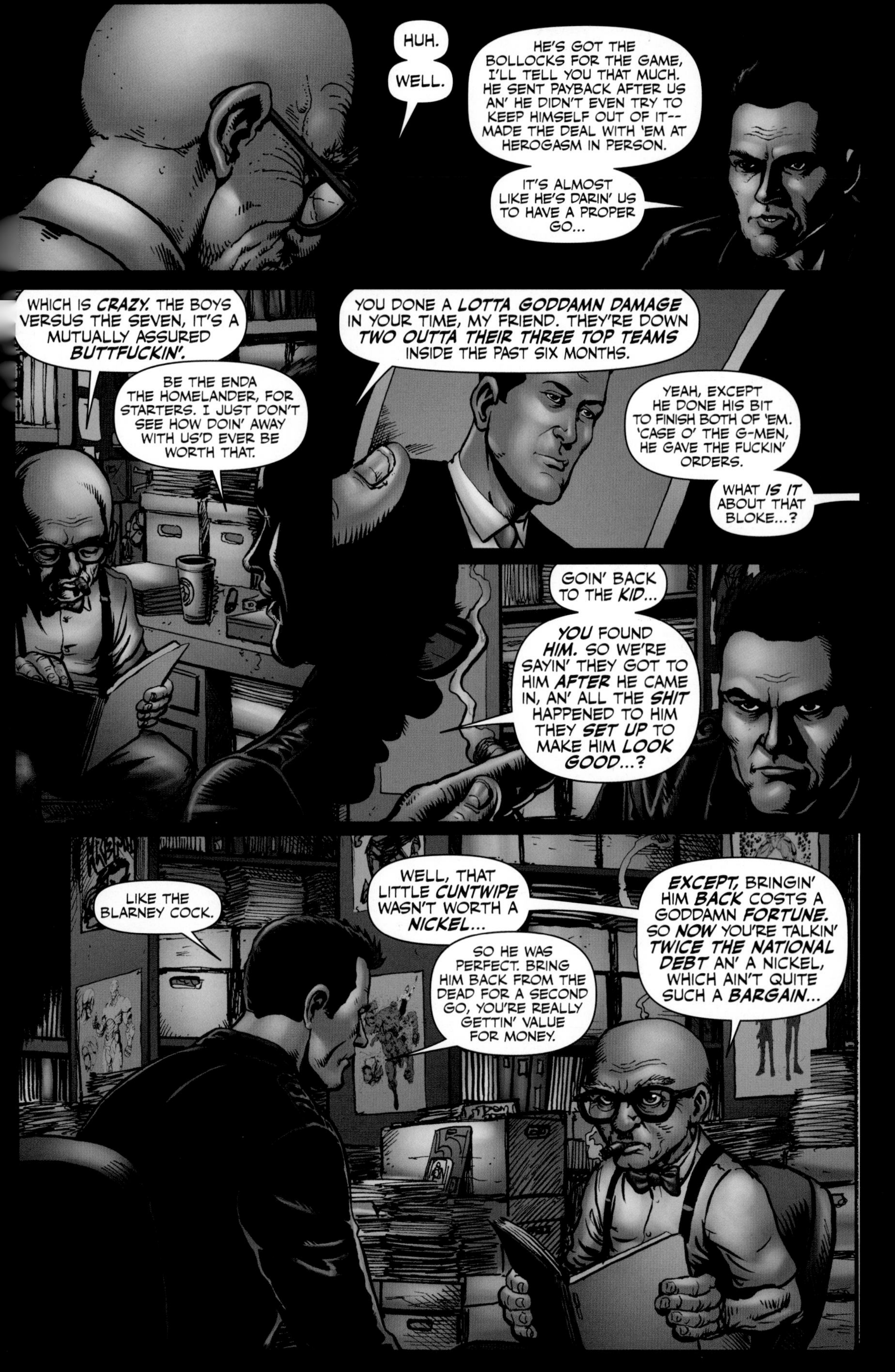

HUH.
WELL.
HE'S GOT THE BOLLOCKS FOR THE GAME, I'LL TELL YOU THAT MUCH. HE SENT PAYBACK AFTER US AN' HE DIDN'T EVEN TRY TO KEEP HIMSELF OUT OF IT-- MADE THE DEAL WITH 'EM AT HEROGASM IN PERSON.
IT'S ALMOST LIKE HE'S DARIN' US TO HAVE A PROPER GO...
WHICH IS CRAZY. THE BOYS VERSUS THE SEVEN, IT'S A MUTUALLY ASSURED BUTTFUCKIN'.
BE THE ENDA THE HOMELANDER, FOR STARTERS. I JUST DON'T SEE HOW DOIN' AWAY WITH US'D EVER BE WORTH THAT.
YOU DONE A LOTTA GODDAMN DAMAGE IN YOUR TIME, MY FRIEND. THEY'RE DOWN TWO OUTTA THEIR THREE TOP TEAMS INSIDE THE PAST SIX MONTHS.
YEAH, EXCEPT HE DONE HIS BIT TO FINISH BOTH OF 'EM. 'CASE O' THE G-MEN, HE GAVE THE FUCKIN' ORDERS.
WHAT IS IT ABOUT THAT BLOKE...?
GOIN' BACK TO THE KID...
YOU FOUND HIM. SO WE'RE SAYIN' THEY GOT TO HIM AFTER HE CAME IN, AN' ALL THE SHIT HAPPENED TO HIM THEY SET UP TO MAKE HIM LOOK GOOD...?
LIKE THE BLARNEY COCK.
WELL, THAT LITTLE CUNTWIPE WASN'T WORTH A NICKEL...
SO HE WAS PERFECT. BRING HIM BACK FROM THE DEAD FOR A SECOND GO, YOU'RE REALLY GETTIN' VALUE FOR MONEY.
EXCEPT, BRINGIN' HIM BACK COSTS A GODDAMN FORTUNE. SO NOW YOU'RE TALKIN' TWICE THE NATIONAL DEBT AN' A NICKEL, WHICH AIN'T QUITE SUCH A BARGAIN...

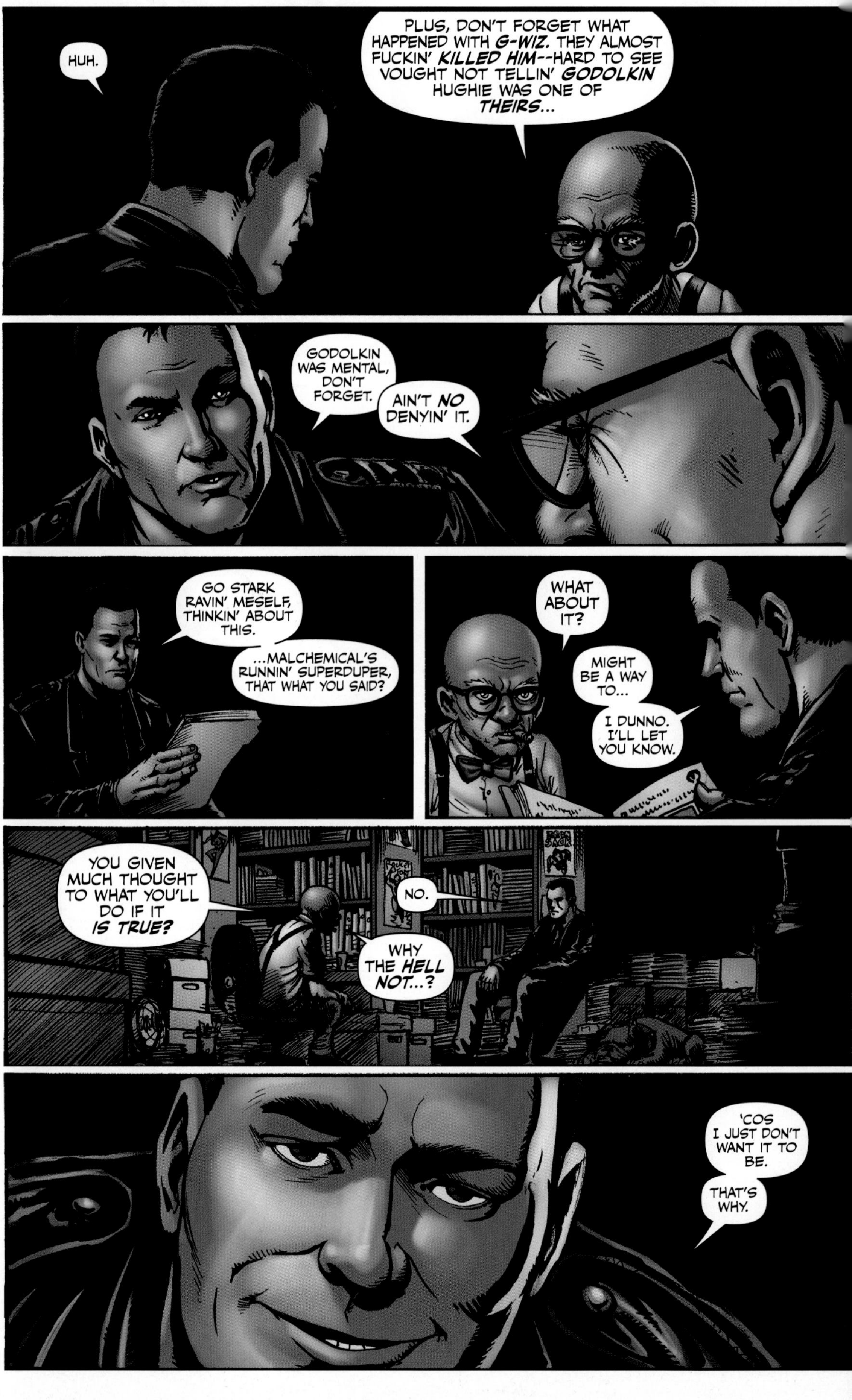
HUH.
PLUS, DON'T FORGET WHAT HAPPENED WITH G-WIZ. THEY ALMOST FUCKIN' KILLED HIM--HARD TO SEE VOUGHT NOT TELLIN' GODOLKIN HUGHIE WAS ONE OF THEIRS...
GODOLKIN WAS MENTAL, DON'T FORGET.
AIN'T NO DENYIN' IT.
GO STARK RAVIN' MESELF, THINKIN' ABOUT THIS.
...MALCHEMICAL'S RUNNIN' SUPERDUPER, THAT WHAT YOU SAID?
WHAT ABOUT IT?
MIGHT BE A WAY TO...
I DUNNO. I'LL LET YOU KNOW.
YOU GIVEN MUCH THOUGHT TO WHAT YOU'LL DO IF IT IS TRUE?
NO.
WHY THE HELL NOT...?
'COS I JUST DON'T WANT IT TO BE.
THAT'S WHY.

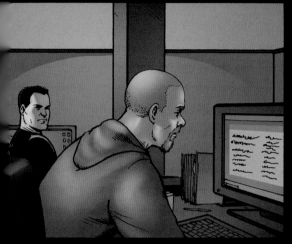

...IS THIS TRUE?

HE HAS TO MAKE A BIG GREEN HAND, AN' THEN THEY MAKE HIM *WANK OFF* THE GALAXIUS FELLA?

GOD, THAT'S SO HUMILIATIN'...

SO LISTEN, I THINK THAT'S ME UP TO DATE. D'YOU WANT ME TO GET BACK TO THE SEVEN TAPES, I THINK I'M UP TO ABOUT THE START OF OH-TWO...

NAH, YOU STAY AWAY FROM THEM FOR THE TIME BEIN'.

THIS IS YOUR NEW JOB HERE.

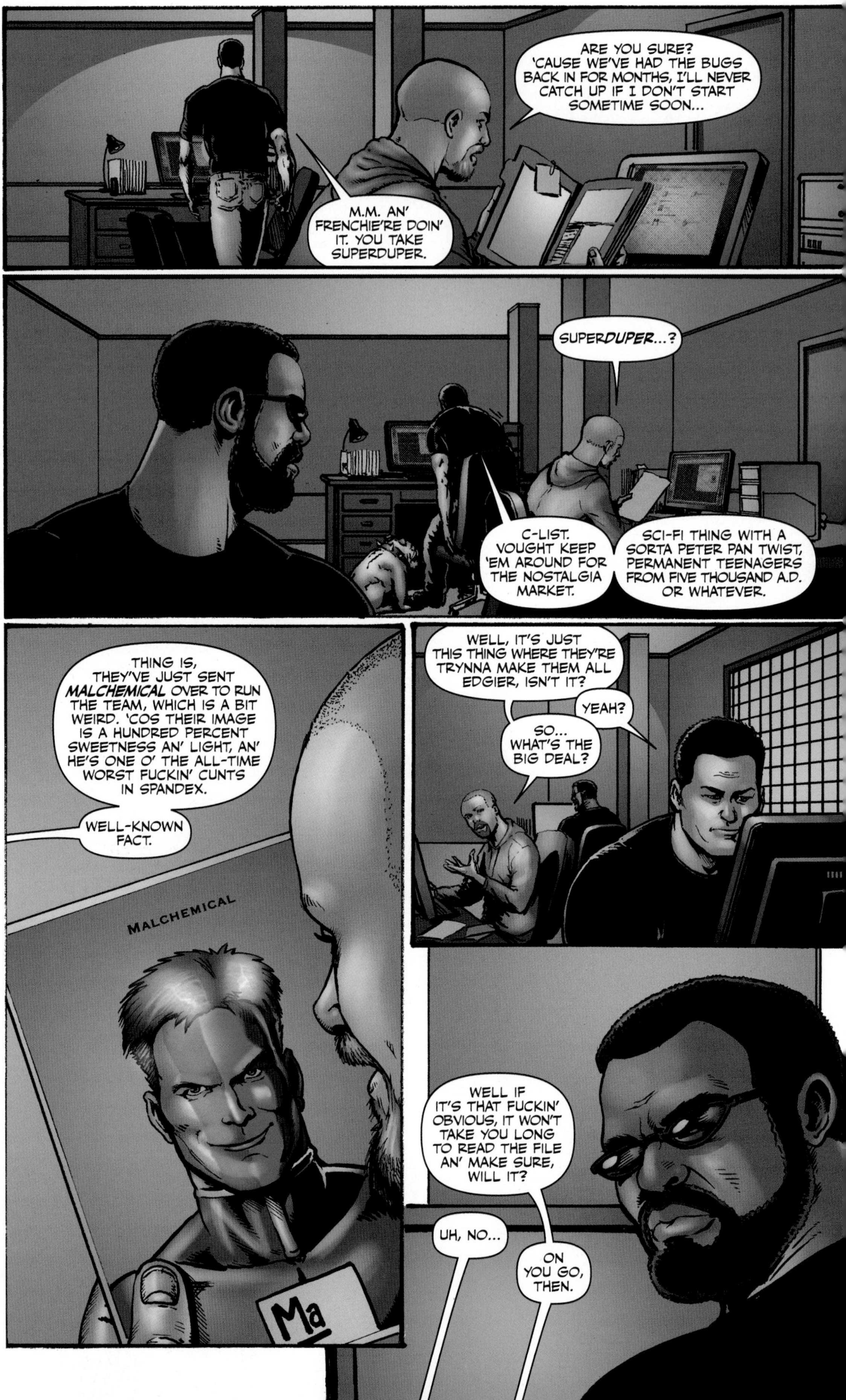
ARE YOU SURE? 'CAUSE WE'VE HAD THE BUGS BACK IN FOR MONTHS, I'LL NEVER CATCH UP IF I DON'T START SOMETIME SOON...
M.M. AN' FRENCHIE'RE DOIN' IT. YOU TAKE SUPERDUPER.
SUPERDUPER...?
C-LIST. VOUGHT KEEP 'EM AROUND FOR THE NOSTALGIA MARKET.
SCI-FI THING WITH A SORTA PETER PAN TWIST, PERMANENT TEENAGERS FROM FIVE THOUSAND A.D. OR WHATEVER.
THING IS, THEY'VE JUST SENT MALCHEMICAL OVER TO RUN THE TEAM, WHICH IS A BIT WEIRD. 'COS THEIR IMAGE IS A HUNDRED PERCENT SWEETNESS AN' LIGHT, AN' HE'S ONE O' THE ALL-TIME WORST FUCKIN' CUNTS IN SPANDEX.
WELL-KNOWN FACT.
MALCHEMICAL
Ma
WELL, IT'S JUST THIS THING WHERE THEY'RE TRYNNA MAKE THEM ALL EDGIER, ISN'T IT?
YEAH?
SO... WHAT'S THE BIG DEAL?
WELL IF IT'S THAT FUCKIN' OBVIOUS, IT WON'T TAKE YOU LONG TO READ THE FILE AN' MAKE SURE, WILL IT?
UH, NO...
ON YOU GO, THEN.

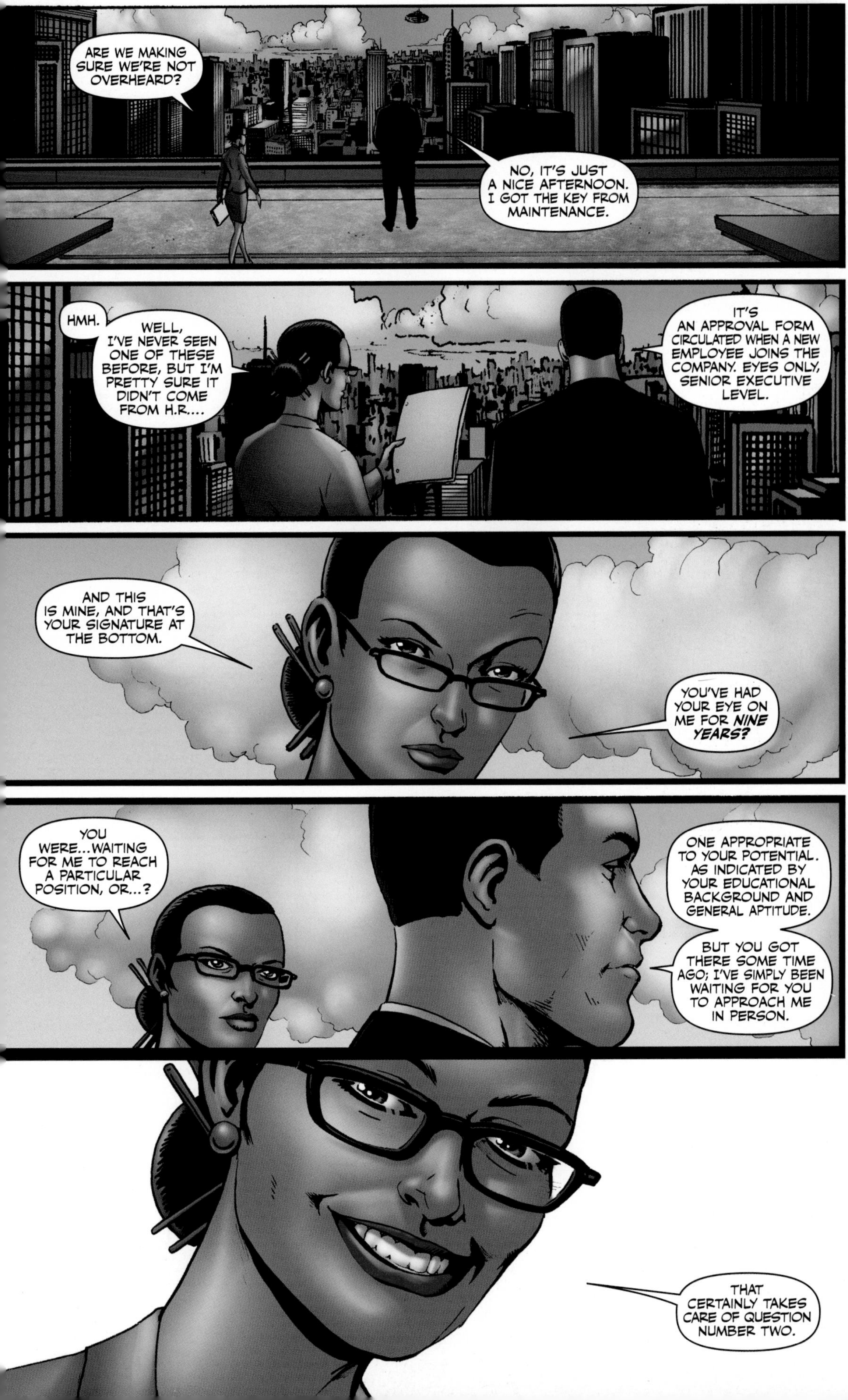

ARE WE MAKING SURE WE'RE NOT OVERHEARD?
NO, IT'S JUST A NICE AFTERNOON. I GOT THE KEY FROM MAINTENANCE.
HMH.
WELL, I'VE NEVER SEEN ONE OF THESE BEFORE, BUT I'M PRETTY SURE IT DIDN'T COME FROM H.R....
IT'S AN APPROVAL FORM CIRCULATED WHEN A NEW EMPLOYEE JOINS THE COMPANY. EYES ONLY, SENIOR EXECUTIVE LEVEL.
AND THIS IS MINE, AND THAT'S YOUR SIGNATURE AT THE BOTTOM.
YOU'VE HAD YOUR EYE ON ME FOR NINE YEARS?
YOU WERE...WAITING FOR ME TO REACH A PARTICULAR POSITION, OR...?
ONE APPROPRIATE TO YOUR POTENTIAL. AS INDICATED BY YOUR EDUCATIONAL BACKGROUND AND GENERAL APTITUDE.
BUT YOU GOT THERE SOME TIME AGO; I'VE SIMPLY BEEN WAITING FOR YOU TO APPROACH ME IN PERSON.
THAT CERTAINLY TAKES CARE OF QUESTION NUMBER TWO.

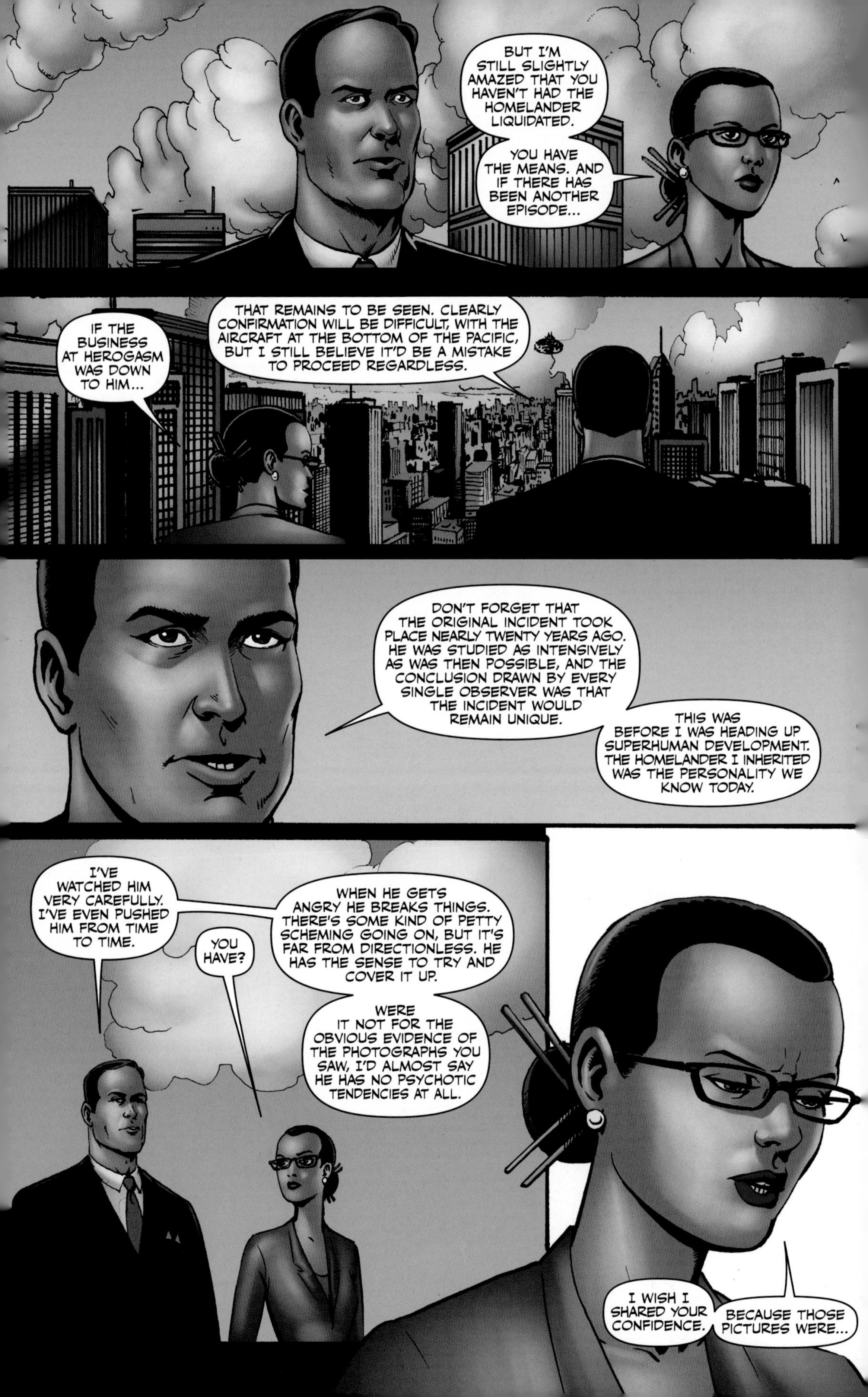
BUT I'M STILL SLIGHTLY AMAZED THAT YOU HAVEN'T HAD THE HOMELANDER LIQUIDATED.
YOU HAVE THE MEANS. AND IF THERE HAS BEEN ANOTHER EPISODE...
IF THE BUSINESS AT HEROGASM WAS DOWN TO HIM...
THAT REMAINS TO BE SEEN. CLEARLY CONFIRMATION WILL BE DIFFICULT, WITH THE AIRCRAFT AT THE BOTTOM OF THE PACIFIC, BUT I STILL BELIEVE IT'D BE A MISTAKE TO PROCEED REGARDLESS.
DON'T FORGET THAT THE ORIGINAL INCIDENT TOOK PLACE NEARLY TWENTY YEARS AGO. HE WAS STUDIED AS INTENSIVELY AS WAS THEN POSSIBLE, AND THE CONCLUSION DRAWN BY EVERY SINGLE OBSERVER WAS THAT THE INCIDENT WOULD REMAIN UNIQUE.
THIS WAS BEFORE I WAS HEADING UP SUPERHUMAN DEVELOPMENT. THE HOMELANDER I INHERITED WAS THE PERSONALITY WE KNOW TODAY.
I'VE WATCHED HIM VERY CAREFULLY. I'VE EVEN PUSHED HIM FROM TIME TO TIME.
YOU HAVE?
WHEN HE GETS ANGRY HE BREAKS THINGS. THERE'S SOME KIND OF PETTY SCHEMING GOING ON, BUT IT'S FAR FROM DIRECTIONLESS. HE HAS THE SENSE TO TRY AND COVER IT UP.
WERE IT NOT FOR THE OBVIOUS EVIDENCE OF THE PHOTOGRAPHS YOU SAW, I'D ALMOST SAY HE HAS NO PSYCHOTIC TENDENCIES AT ALL.
I WISH I SHARED YOUR CONFIDENCE.
BECAUSE THOSE PICTURES WERE...

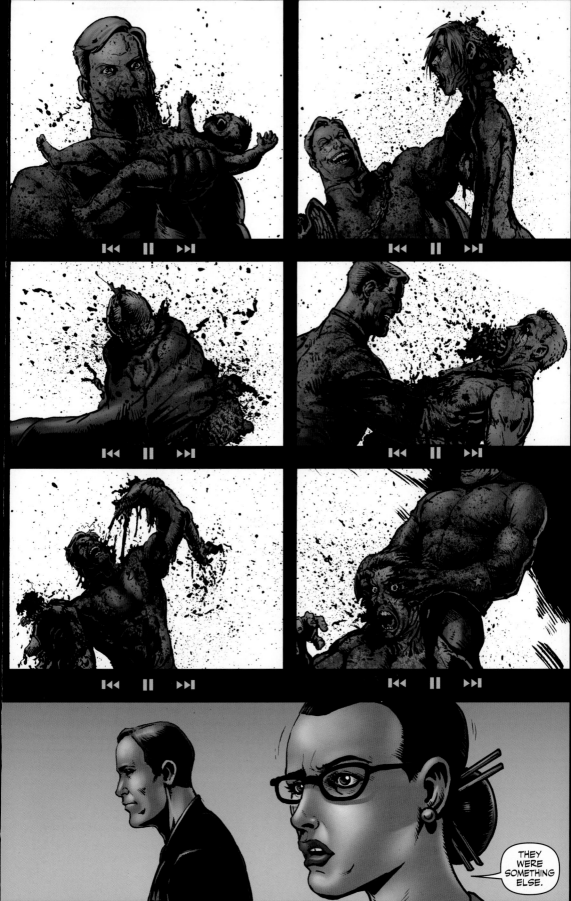

THEY WERE SOMETHING ELSE.

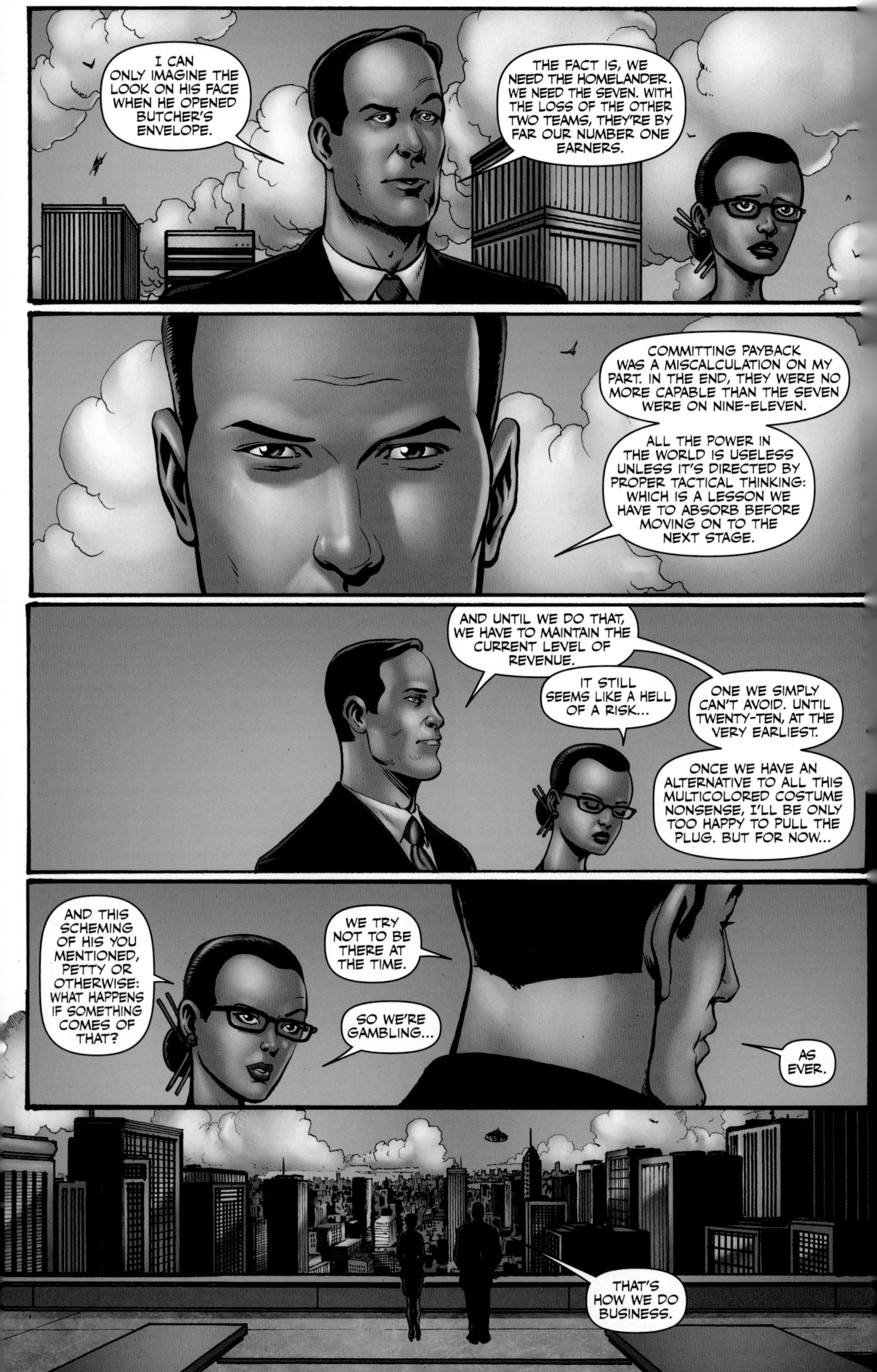

I CAN ONLY IMAGINE THE LOOK ON HIS FACE WHEN HE OPENED BUTCHER'S ENVELOPE.
THE FACT IS, WE NEED THE HOMELANDER. WE NEED THE SEVEN. WITH THE LOSS OF THE OTHER TWO TEAMS, THEY'RE BY FAR OUR NUMBER ONE EARNERS.
COMMITTING PAYBACK WAS A MISCALCULATION ON MY PART. IN THE END, THEY WERE NO MORE CAPABLE THAN THE SEVEN WERE ON NINE-ELEVEN.
ALL THE POWER IN THE WORLD IS USELESS UNLESS IT'S DIRECTED BY PROPER TACTICAL THINKING: WHICH IS A LESSON WE HAVE TO ABSORB BEFORE MOVING ON TO THE NEXT STAGE.
AND UNTIL WE DO THAT, WE HAVE TO MAINTAIN THE CURRENT LEVEL OF REVENUE.
IT STILL SEEMS LIKE A HELL OF A RISK...
ONE WE SIMPLY CAN'T AVOID. UNTIL TWENTY-TEN, AT THE VERY EARLIEST.
ONCE WE HAVE AN ALTERNATIVE TO ALL THIS MULTICOLORED COSTUME NONSENSE, I'LL BE ONLY TOO HAPPY TO PULL THE PLUG. BUT FOR NOW...
AND THIS SCHEMING OF HIS YOU MENTIONED, PETTY OR OTHERWISE: WHAT HAPPENS IF SOMETHING COMES OF THAT?
WE TRY NOT TO BE THERE AT THE TIME.
SO WE'RE GAMBLING...
AS EVER.
THAT'S HOW WE DO BUSINESS.

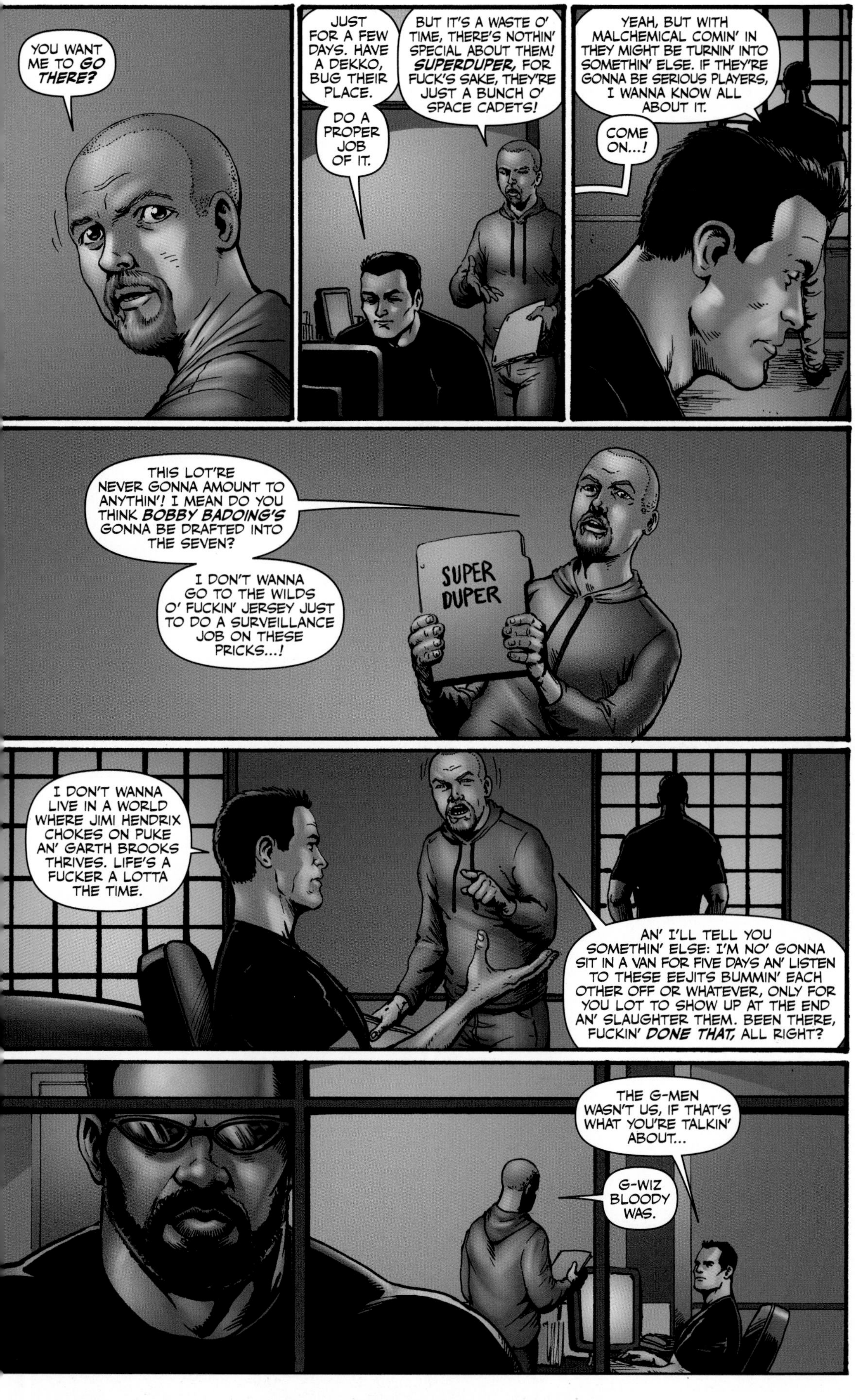
YOU WANT ME TO *GO THERE?*
JUST FOR A FEW DAYS. HAVE A DEKKO, BUG THEIR PLACE.
DO A PROPER JOB OF IT.
BUT IT'S A WASTE O' TIME, THERE'S NOTHIN' SPECIAL ABOUT THEM! ***SUPERDUPER,*** FOR FUCK'S SAKE, THEY'RE JUST A BUNCH O' SPACE CADETS!
YEAH, BUT WITH MALCHEMICAL COMIN' IN THEY MIGHT BE TURNIN' INTO SOMETHIN' ELSE. IF THEY'RE GONNA BE SERIOUS PLAYERS, I WANNA KNOW ALL ABOUT IT.
COME ON...!
THIS LOT'RE NEVER GONNA AMOUNT TO ANYTHIN'! I MEAN DO YOU THINK ***BOBBY BADOING'S*** GONNA BE DRAFTED INTO THE SEVEN?
I DON'T WANNA GO TO THE WILDS O' FUCKIN' JERSEY JUST TO DO A SURVEILLANCE JOB ON THESE PRICKS...!
SUPER DUPER
I DON'T WANNA LIVE IN A WORLD WHERE JIMI HENDRIX CHOKES ON PUKE AN' GARTH BROOKS THRIVES. LIFE'S A FUCKER A LOTTA THE TIME.
AN' I'LL TELL YOU SOMETHIN' ELSE: I'M NO' GONNA SIT IN A VAN FOR FIVE DAYS AN' LISTEN TO THESE EEJITS BUMMIN' EACH OTHER OFF OR WHATEVER, ONLY FOR YOU LOT TO SHOW UP AT THE END AN' SLAUGHTER THEM. BEEN THERE, FUCKIN' ***DONE THAT,*** ALL RIGHT?
THE G-MEN WASN'T US, IF THAT'S WHAT YOU'RE TALKIN' ABOUT...
G-WIZ BLOODY WAS.

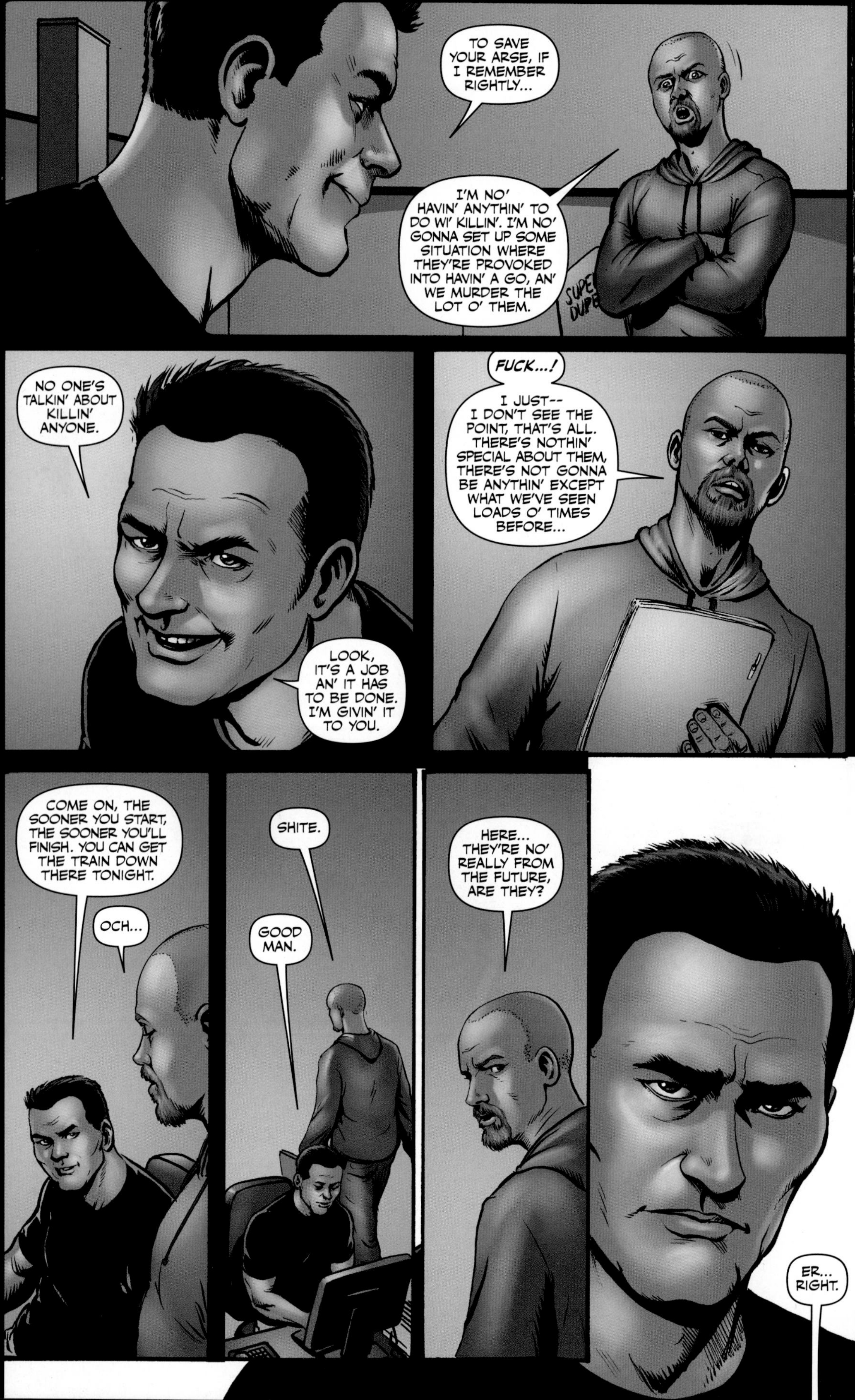
TO SAVE YOUR ARSE, IF I REMEMBER RIGHTLY...
I'M NO' HAVIN' ANYTHIN' TO DO WI' KILLIN'. I'M NO' GONNA SET UP SOME SITUATION WHERE THEY'RE PROVOKED INTO HAVIN' A GO, AN' WE MURDER THE LOT O' THEM.
NO ONE'S TALKIN' ABOUT KILLIN' ANYONE.
LOOK, IT'S A JOB AN' IT HAS TO BE DONE. I'M GIVIN' IT TO YOU.
FUCK...!
I JUST-- I DON'T SEE THE POINT, THAT'S ALL. THERE'S NOTHIN' SPECIAL ABOUT THEM, THERE'S NOT GONNA BE ANYTHIN' EXCEPT WHAT WE'VE SEEN LOADS O' TIMES BEFORE...
COME ON, THE SOONER YOU START, THE SOONER YOU'LL FINISH. YOU CAN GET THE TRAIN DOWN THERE TONIGHT.
OCH...
SHITE.
GOOD MAN.
HERE... THEY'RE NO' REALLY FROM THE FUTURE, ARE THEY?
ER... RIGHT.

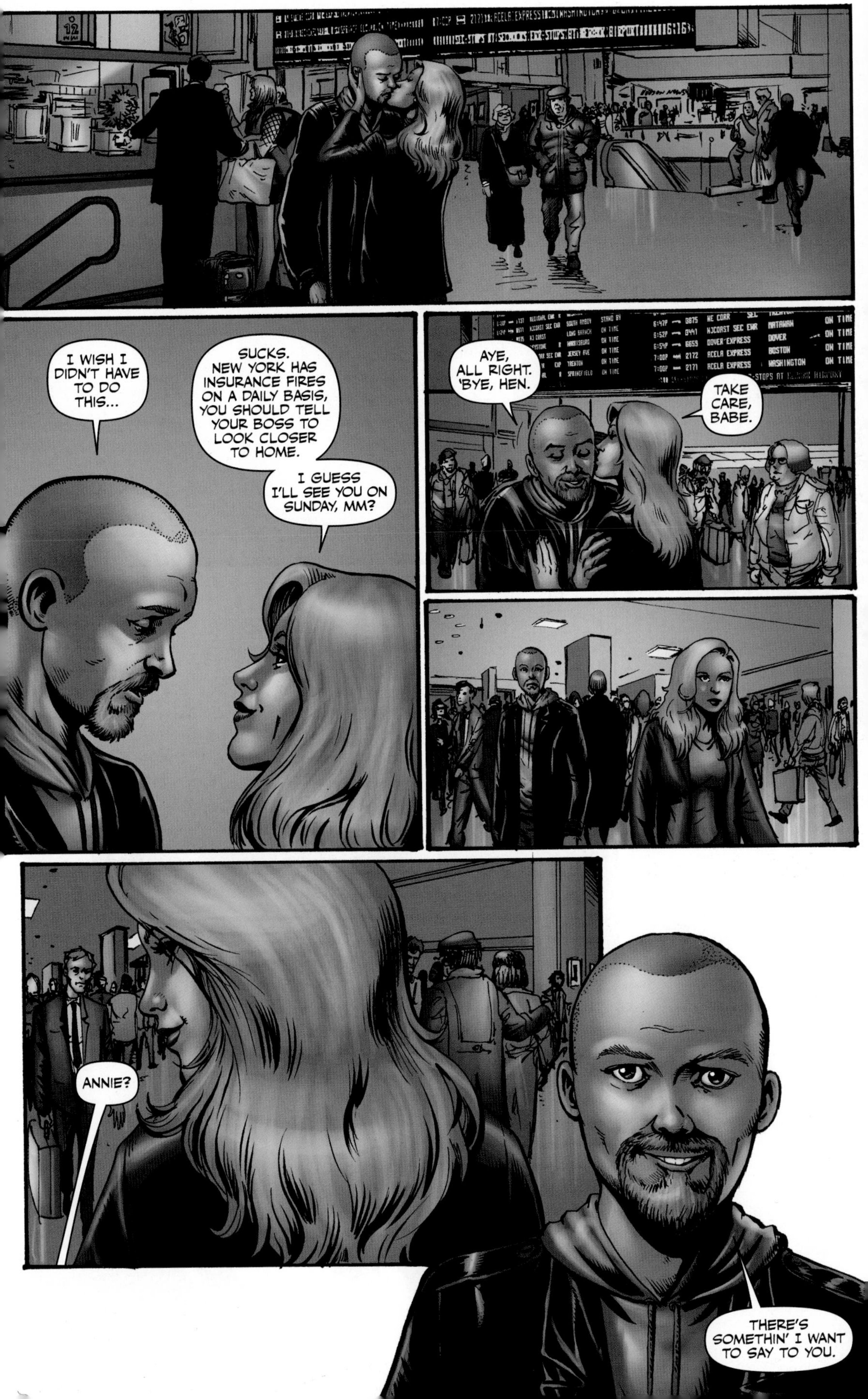
I WISH I DIDN'T HAVE TO DO THIS...
SUCKS. NEW YORK HAS INSURANCE FIRES ON A DAILY BASIS, YOU SHOULD TELL YOUR BOSS TO LOOK CLOSER TO HOME.
I GUESS I'LL SEE YOU ON SUNDAY, MM?
AYE, ALL RIGHT. 'BYE, HEN.
TAKE CARE, BABE.
ANNIE?
THERE'S SOMETHIN' I WANT TO SAY TO YOU.

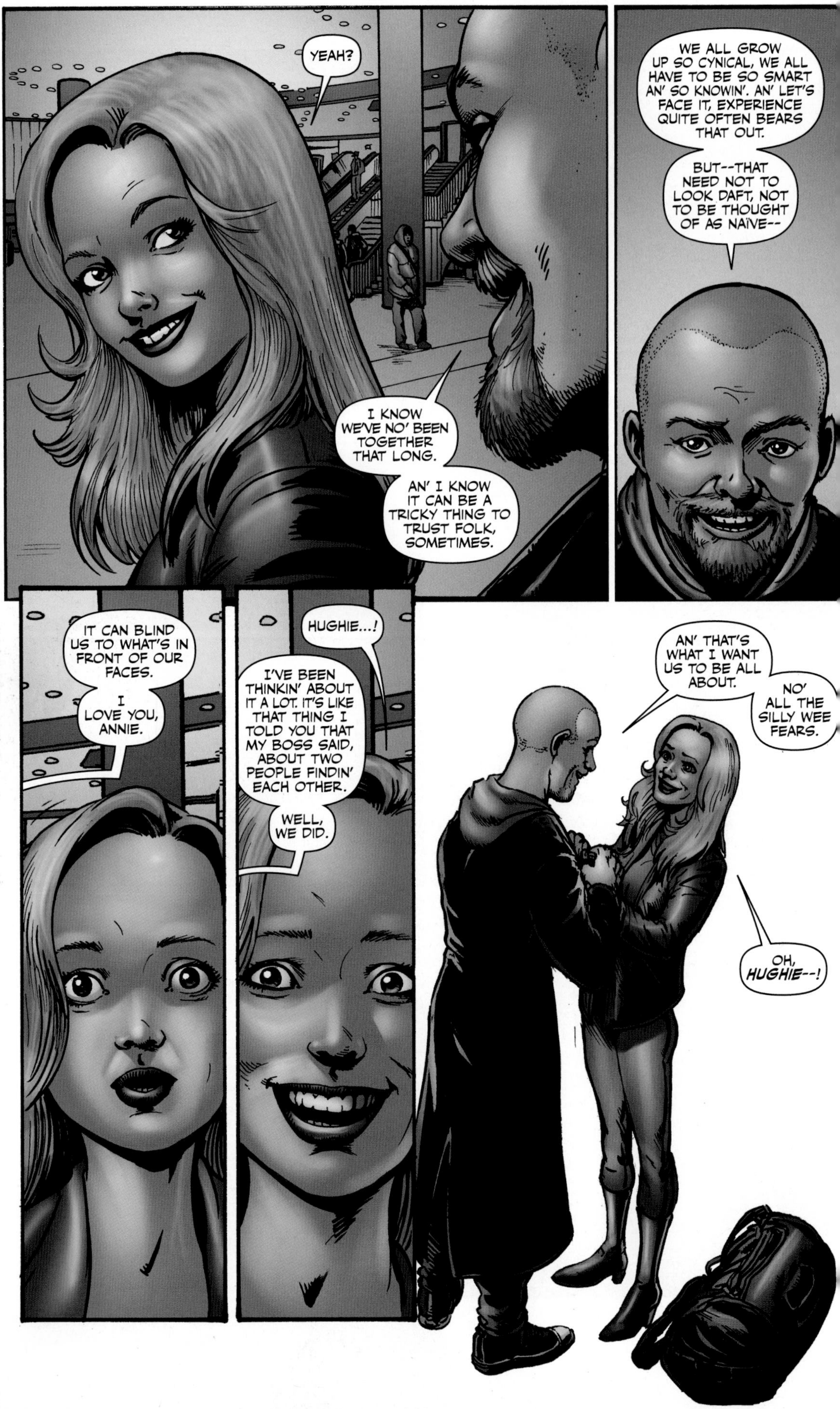
YEAH?
I KNOW WE'VE NO' BEEN TOGETHER THAT LONG.
AN' I KNOW IT CAN BE A TRICKY THING TO TRUST FOLK, SOMETIMES.
WE ALL GROW UP SO CYNICAL, WE ALL HAVE TO BE SO SMART AN' SO KNOWIN'. AN' LET'S FACE IT, EXPERIENCE QUITE OFTEN BEARS THAT OUT.
BUT--THAT NEED NOT TO LOOK DAFT, NOT TO BE THOUGHT OF AS NAÏVE--
IT CAN BLIND US TO WHAT'S IN FRONT OF OUR FACES.
I LOVE YOU, ANNIE.
HUGHIE...!
I'VE BEEN THINKIN' ABOUT IT A LOT. IT'S LIKE THAT THING I TOLD YOU THAT MY BOSS SAID, ABOUT TWO PEOPLE FINDIN' EACH OTHER.
WELL, WE DID.
AN' THAT'S WHAT I WANT US TO BE ALL ABOUT.
NO' ALL THE SILLY WEE FEARS.
OH, *HUGHIE*--!

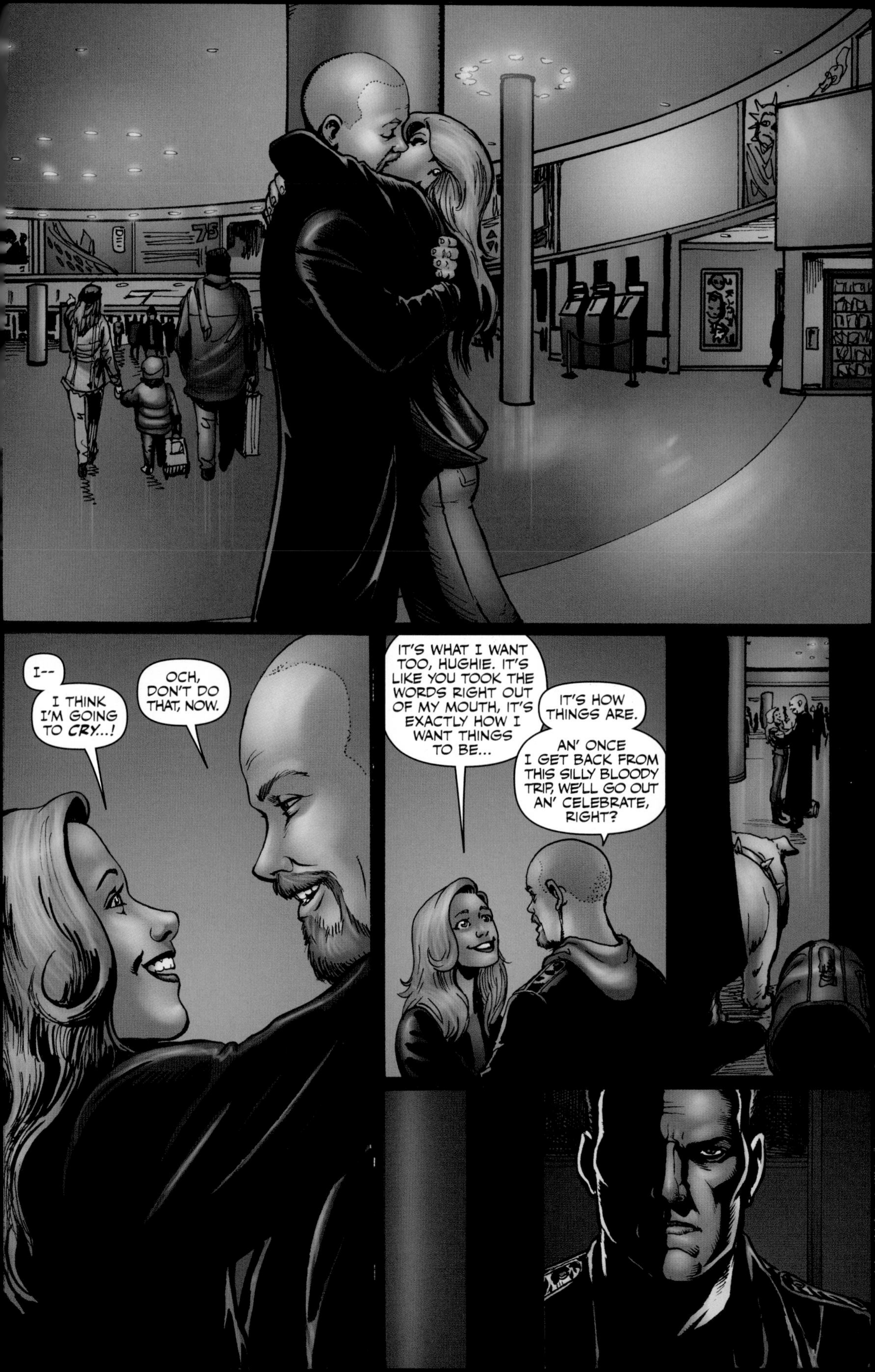
I--
I THINK I'M GOING TO CRY...!
OCH, DON'T DO THAT, NOW.
IT'S WHAT I WANT TOO, HUGHIE. IT'S LIKE YOU TOOK THE WORDS RIGHT OUT OF MY MOUTH, IT'S EXACTLY HOW I WANT THINGS TO BE...
IT'S HOW THINGS ARE.
AN' ONCE I GET BACK FROM THIS SILLY BLOODY TRIP, WE'LL GO OUT AN' CELEBRATE, RIGHT?

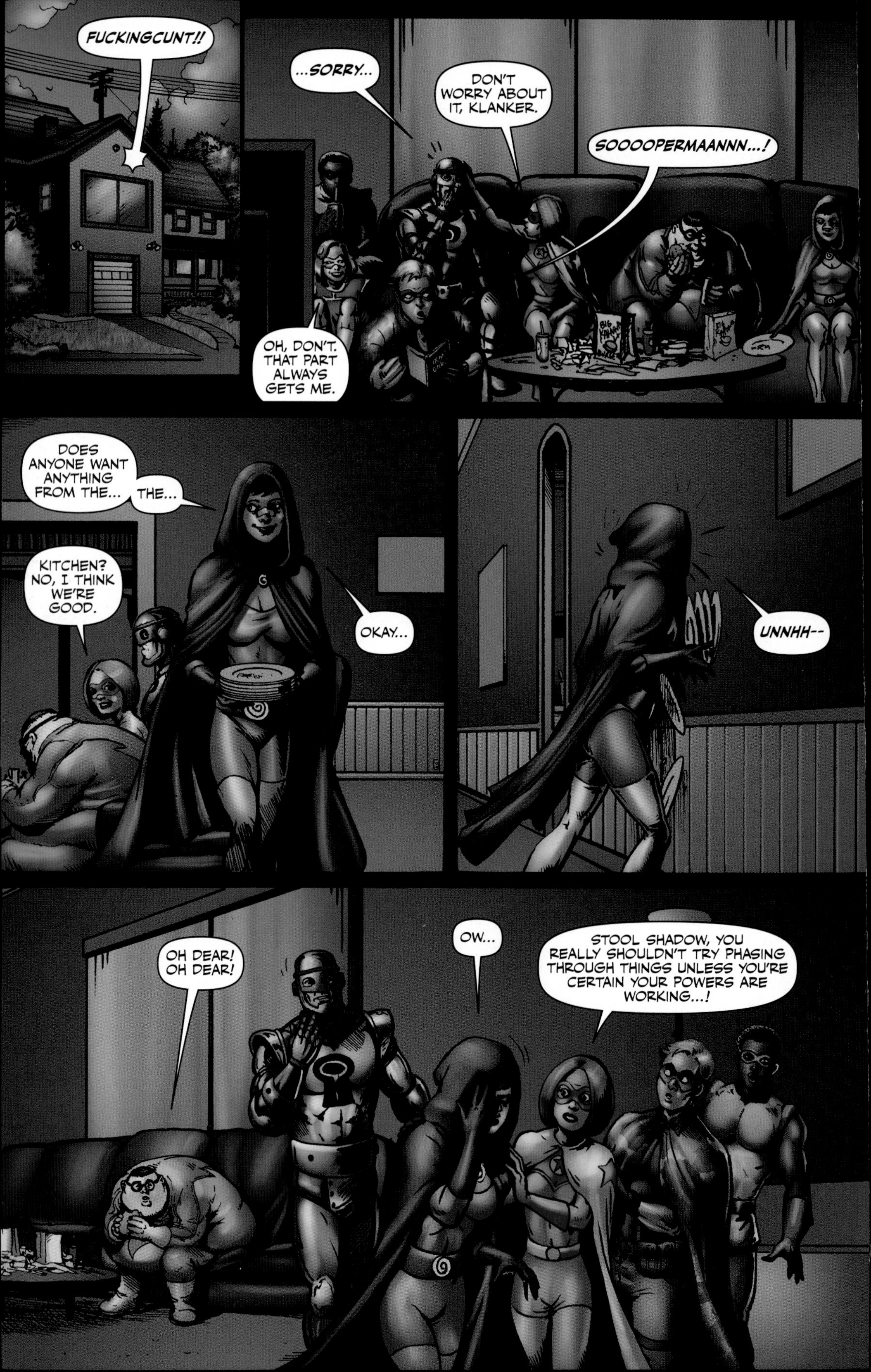
FUCKINGCUNT!!
...SORRY...
DON'T WORRY ABOUT IT, KLANKER.
SOOOOPERMAANNN...!
OH, DON'T. THAT PART ALWAYS GETS ME.
DOES ANYONE WANT ANYTHING FROM THE...
THE...
KITCHEN? NO, I THINK WE'RE GOOD.
OKAY...
UNNHH--
OH DEAR! OH DEAR!
OW...
STOOL SHADOW, YOU REALLY SHOULDN'T TRY PHASING THROUGH THINGS UNLESS YOU'RE CERTAIN YOUR POWERS ARE WORKING...!

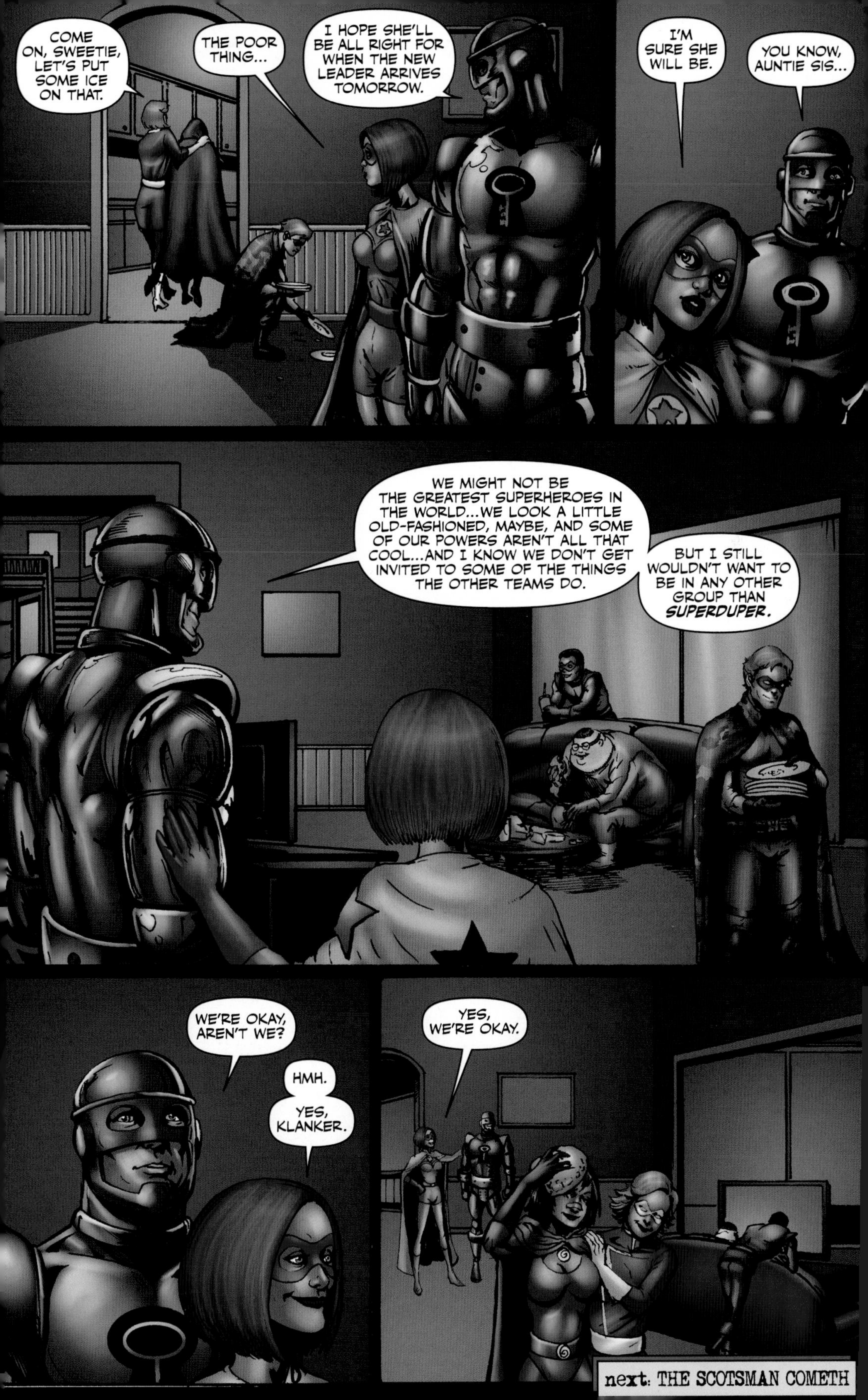
COME ON, SWEETIE, LET'S PUT SOME ICE ON THAT.
THE POOR THING...
I HOPE SHE'LL BE ALL RIGHT FOR WHEN THE NEW LEADER ARRIVES TOMORROW.
I'M SURE SHE WILL BE.
YOU KNOW, AUNTIE SIS...
WE MIGHT NOT BE THE GREATEST SUPERHEROES IN THE WORLD...WE LOOK A LITTLE OLD-FASHIONED, MAYBE, AND SOME OF OUR POWERS AREN'T ALL THAT COOL...AND I KNOW WE DON'T GET INVITED TO SOME OF THE THINGS THE OTHER TEAMS DO.
BUT I STILL WOULDN'T WANT TO BE IN ANY OTHER GROUP THAN *SUPERDUPER*.
WE'RE OKAY, AREN'T WE?
HMH.
YES, KLANKER.
YES, WE'RE OKAY.
next: THE SCOTSMAN COMETH

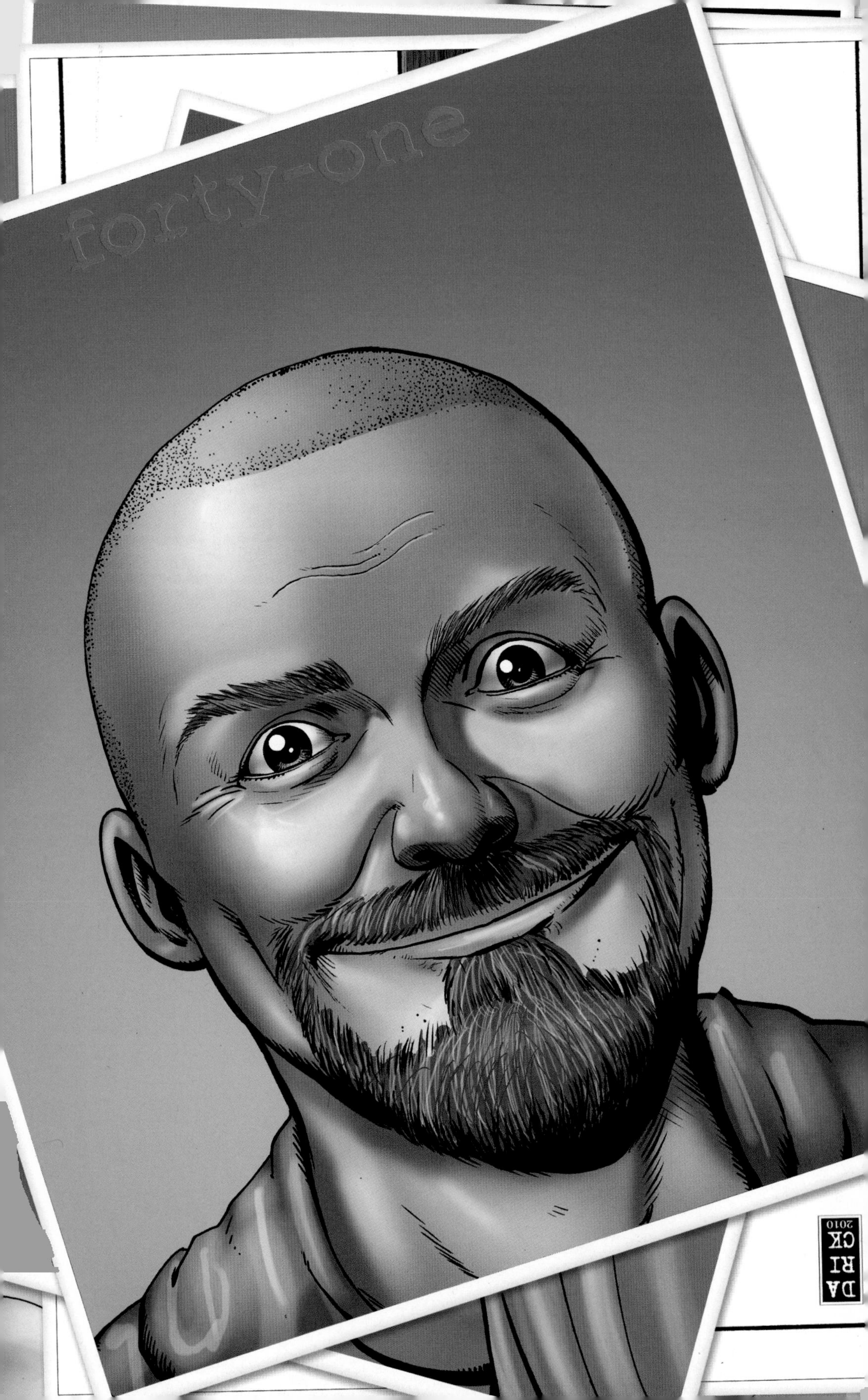
forty-one

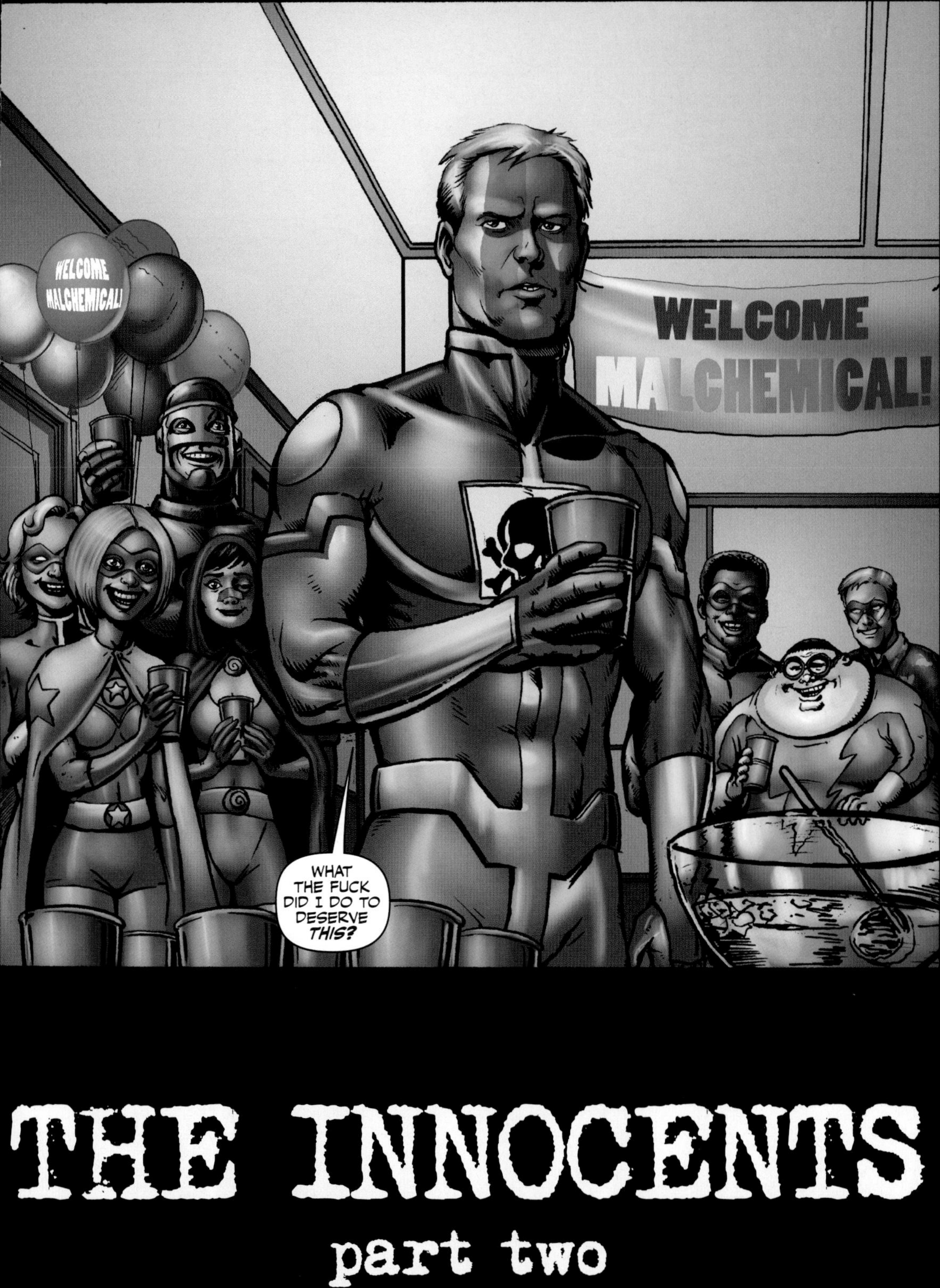
WELCOME MALCHEMICAL!
WELCOME MALCHEMICAL!
WHAT THE FUCK DID I DO TO DESERVE *THIS?*

THE INNOCENTS

part two

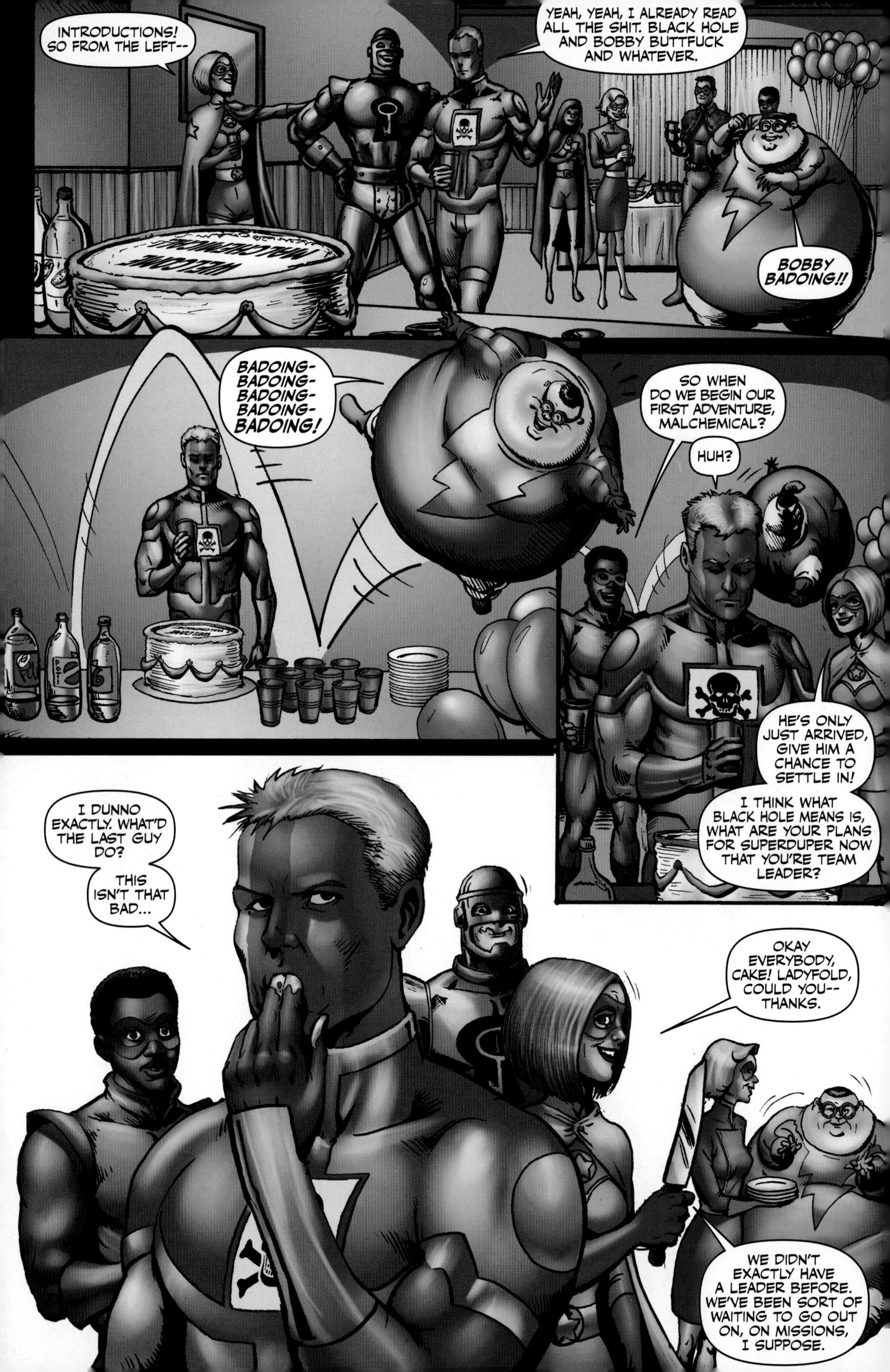
INTRODUCTIONS! SO FROM THE LEFT--
YEAH, YEAH, I ALREADY READ ALL THE SHIT. BLACK HOLE AND BOBBY BUTTFUCK AND WHATEVER.
BOBBY BADOING!!
BADOING- BADOING- BADOING- BADOING- BADOING!
SO WHEN DO WE BEGIN OUR FIRST ADVENTURE, MALCHEMICAL?
HUH?
HE'S ONLY JUST ARRIVED, GIVE HIM A CHANCE TO SETTLE IN!
I THINK WHAT BLACK HOLE MEANS IS, WHAT ARE YOUR PLANS FOR SUPERDUPER NOW THAT YOU'RE TEAM LEADER?
I DUNNO EXACTLY. WHAT'D THE LAST GUY DO?
THIS ISN'T THAT BAD...
OKAY EVERYBODY, CAKE! LADYFOLD, COULD YOU-- THANKS.
WE DIDN'T EXACTLY HAVE A LEADER BEFORE. WE'VE BEEN SORT OF WAITING TO GO OUT ON, ON MISSIONS, I SUPPOSE.

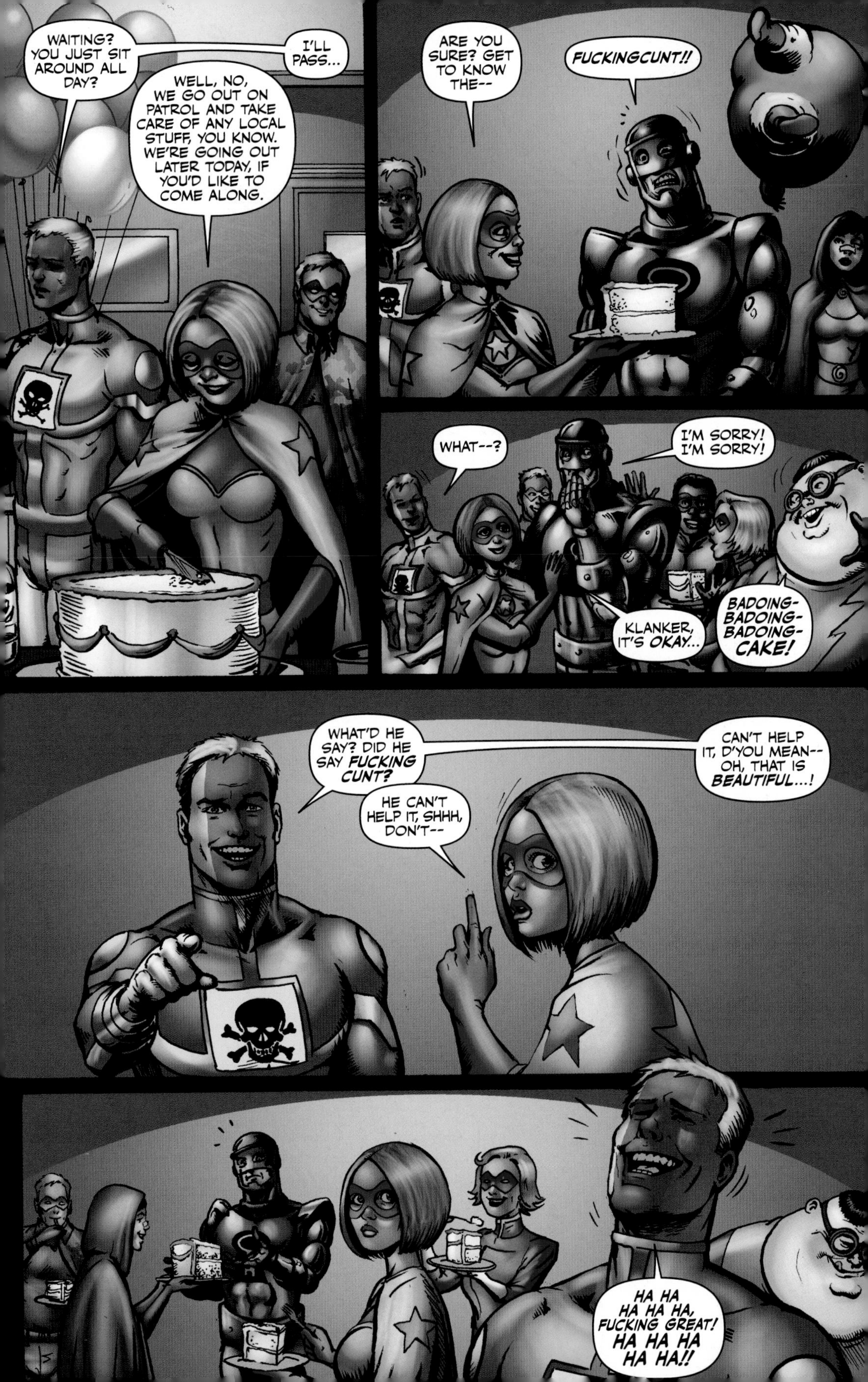
WAITING? YOU JUST SIT AROUND ALL DAY?
I'LL PASS...
WELL, NO, WE GO OUT ON PATROL AND TAKE CARE OF ANY LOCAL STUFF, YOU KNOW. WE'RE GOING OUT LATER TODAY, IF YOU'D LIKE TO COME ALONG.
ARE YOU SURE? GET TO KNOW THE--
FUCKINGCUNT!!
WHAT--?
I'M SORRY! I'M SORRY!
KLANKER, IT'S *OKAY*...
BADOING-BADOING-BADOING-CAKE!
WHAT'D HE SAY? DID HE SAY *FUCKING CUNT?*
HE CAN'T HELP IT, SHHH, DON'T--
CAN'T HELP IT, D'YOU MEAN--OH, THAT IS *BEAUTIFUL*...!
HA HA HA HA HA, FUCKING GREAT! HA HA HA HA HA!!

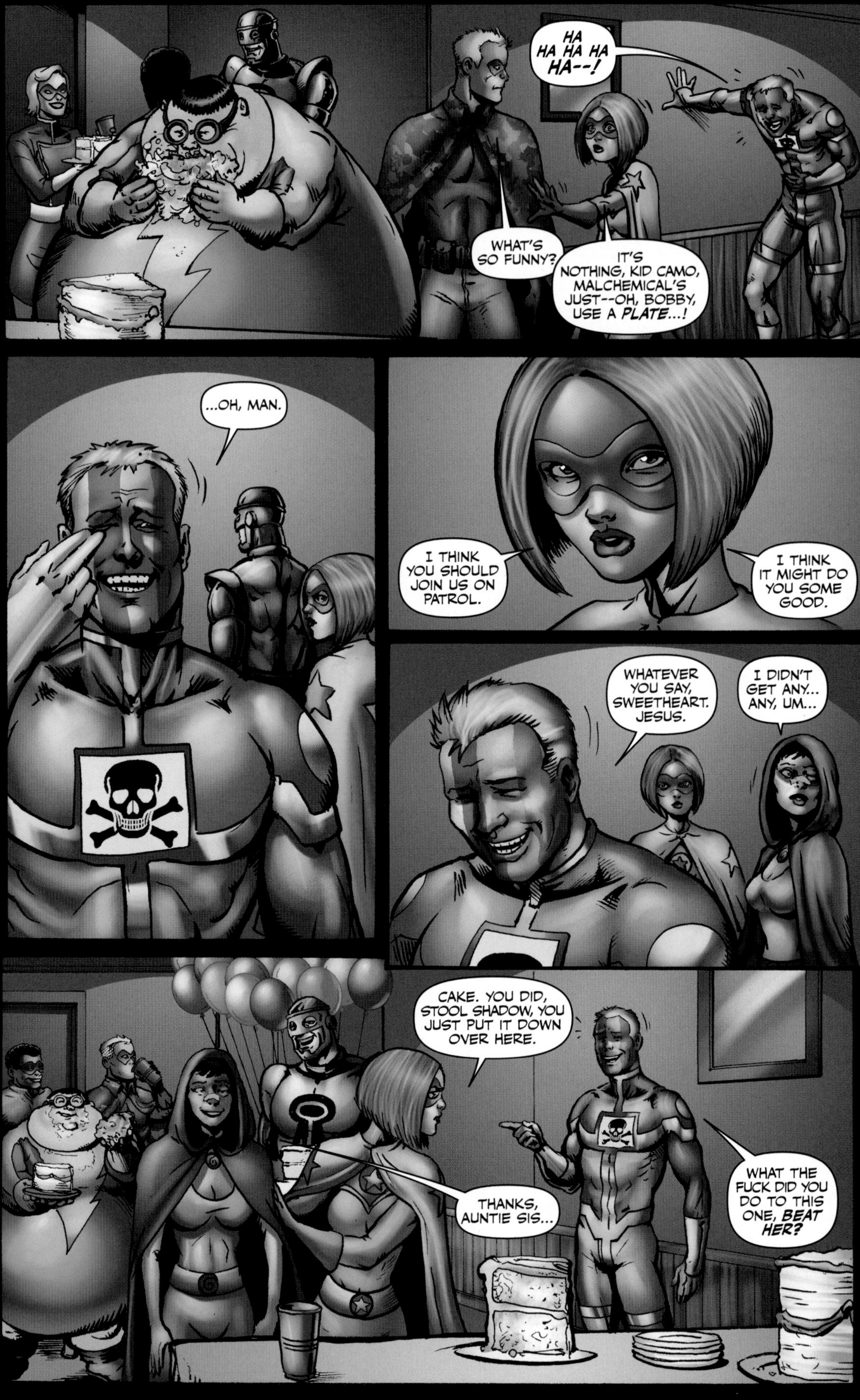
HA HA HA HA HA--!
WHAT'S SO FUNNY?
IT'S NOTHING, KID CAMO, MALCHEMICAL'S JUST--OH, BOBBY, USE A *PLATE*...!
...OH, MAN.
I THINK YOU SHOULD JOIN US ON PATROL.
I THINK IT MIGHT DO YOU SOME GOOD.
WHATEVER YOU SAY, SWEETHEART. JESUS.
I DIDN'T GET ANY... ANY, UM...
CAKE. YOU DID, STOOL SHADOW, YOU JUST PUT IT DOWN OVER HERE.
THANKS, AUNTIE SIS...
WHAT THE FUCK DID YOU DO TO THIS ONE, *BEAT HER?*

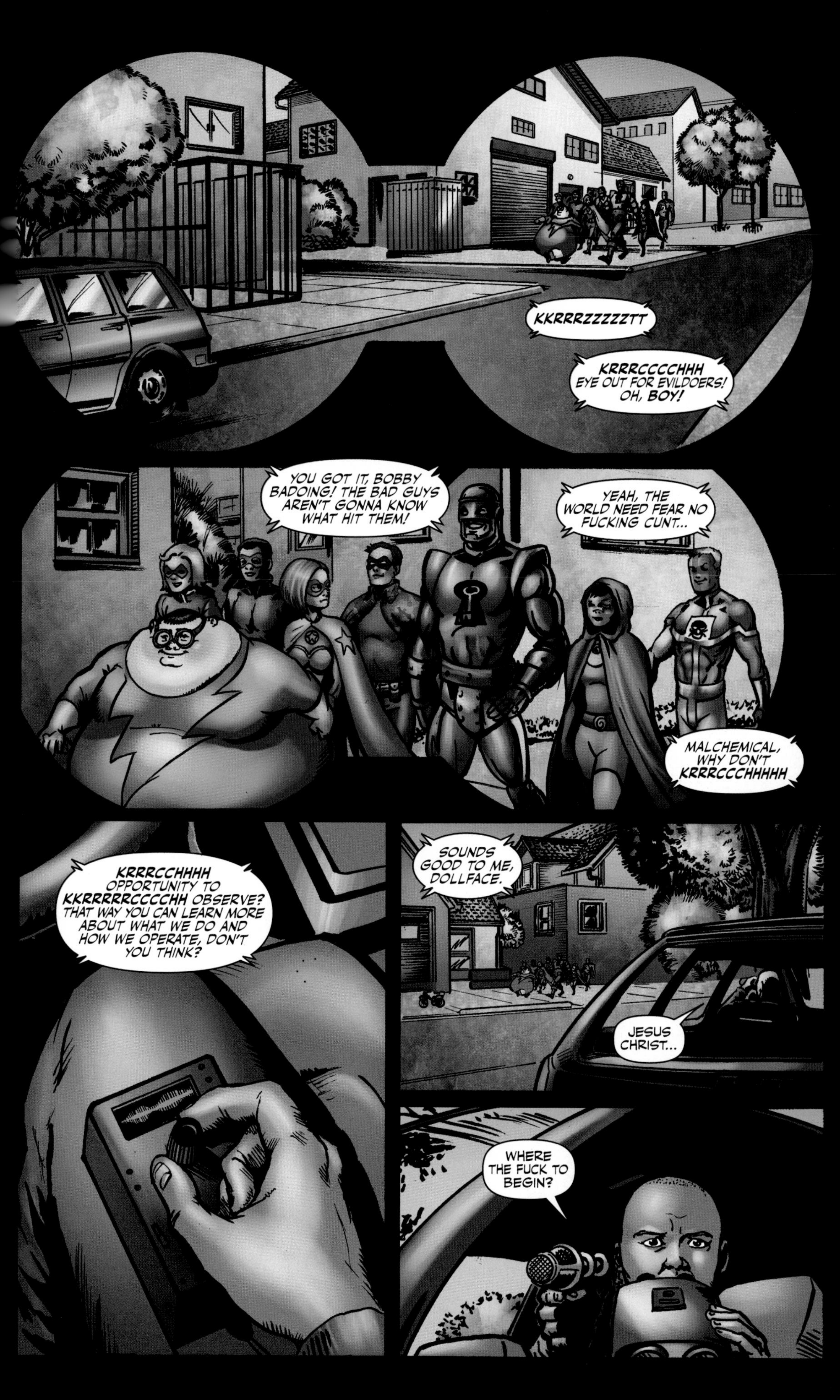
KKRRRZZZZZTT
KRRRCCCCHHH EYE OUT FOR EVILDOERS! OH, BOY!
YOU GOT IT, BOBBY BADOING! THE BAD GUYS AREN'T GONNA KNOW WHAT HIT THEM!
YEAH, THE WORLD NEED FEAR NO FUCKING CUNT...
MALCHEMICAL, WHY DON'T KRRRCCCHHHHH
KRRRCCHHHH OPPORTUNITY TO KKRRRRRCCCCHH OBSERVE? THAT WAY YOU CAN LEARN MORE ABOUT WHAT WE DO AND HOW WE OPERATE, DON'T YOU THINK?
SOUNDS GOOD TO ME, DOLLFACE.
JESUS CHRIST...
WHERE THE FUCK TO BEGIN?

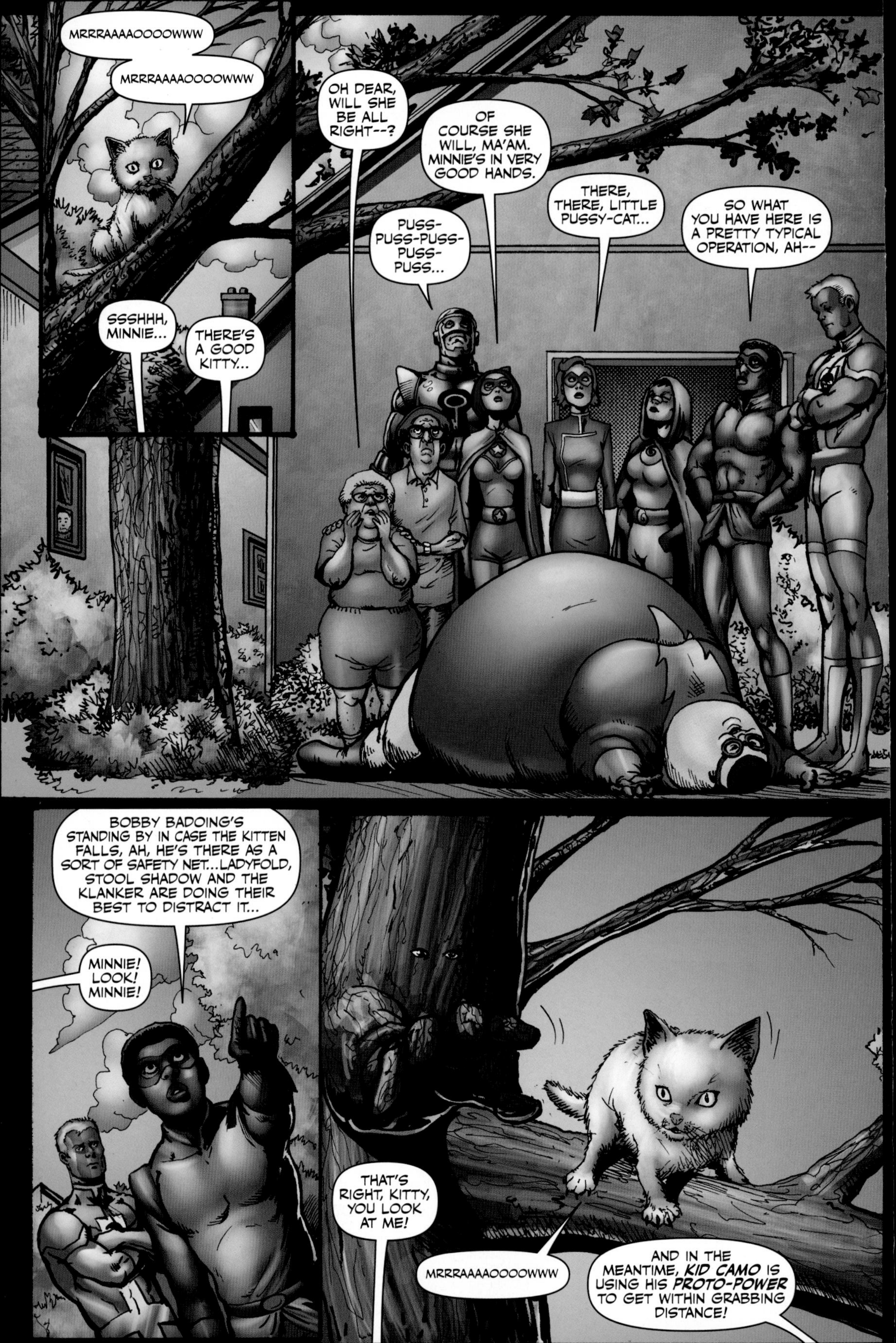
MRRRAAAAOOOOWWW
MRRRAAAAOOOOWWW
SSSHHH, MINNIE...
THERE'S A GOOD KITTY...
OH DEAR, WILL SHE BE ALL RIGHT--?
OF COURSE SHE WILL, MA'AM. MINNIE'S IN VERY GOOD HANDS.
PUSS-PUSS-PUSS-PUSS-PUSS...
THERE, THERE, LITTLE PUSSY-CAT...
SO WHAT YOU HAVE HERE IS A PRETTY TYPICAL OPERATION, AH--
BOBBY BADOING'S STANDING BY IN CASE THE KITTEN FALLS, AH, HE'S THERE AS A SORT OF SAFETY NET...LADYFOLD, STOOL SHADOW AND THE KLANKER ARE DOING THEIR BEST TO DISTRACT IT...
MINNIE! LOOK! MINNIE!
THAT'S RIGHT, KITTY, YOU LOOK AT ME!
MRRRAAAAOOOOWWW
AND IN THE MEANTIME, KID CAMO IS USING HIS PROTO-POWER TO GET WITHIN GRABBING DISTANCE!

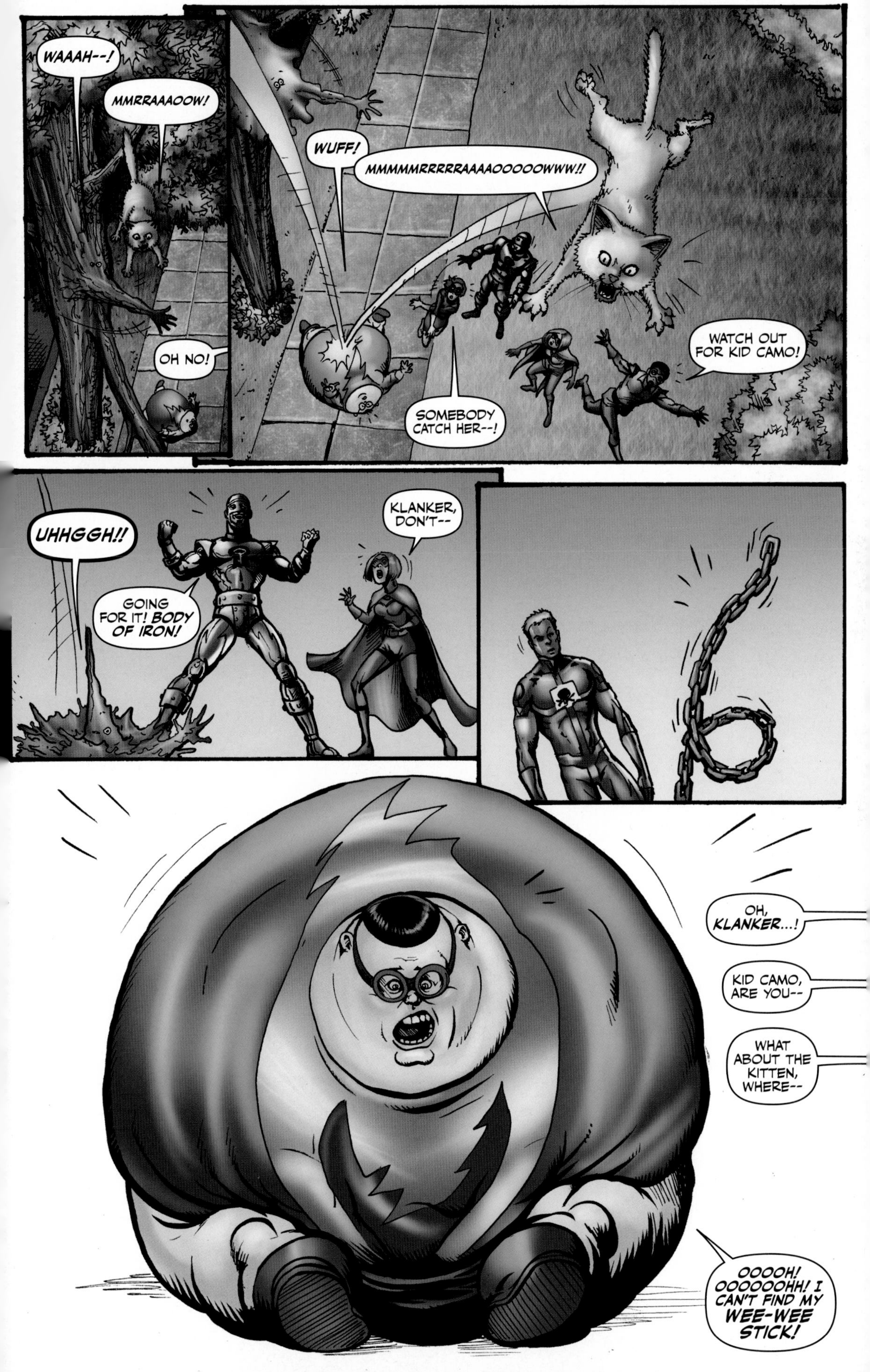

WAAAH--!
MMRRAAAOOW!
OH NO!
WUFF!
MMMMMRRRRRAAAAOOOOOWWW!!
SOMEBODY CATCH HER--!
WATCH OUT FOR KID CAMO!
UHHGGH!!
GOING FOR IT! BODY OF IRON!
KLANKER, DON'T--
OH, KLANKER...!
KID CAMO, ARE YOU--
WHAT ABOUT THE KITTEN, WHERE--
OOOOH! OOOOOOHH! I CAN'T FIND MY WEE-WEE STICK!

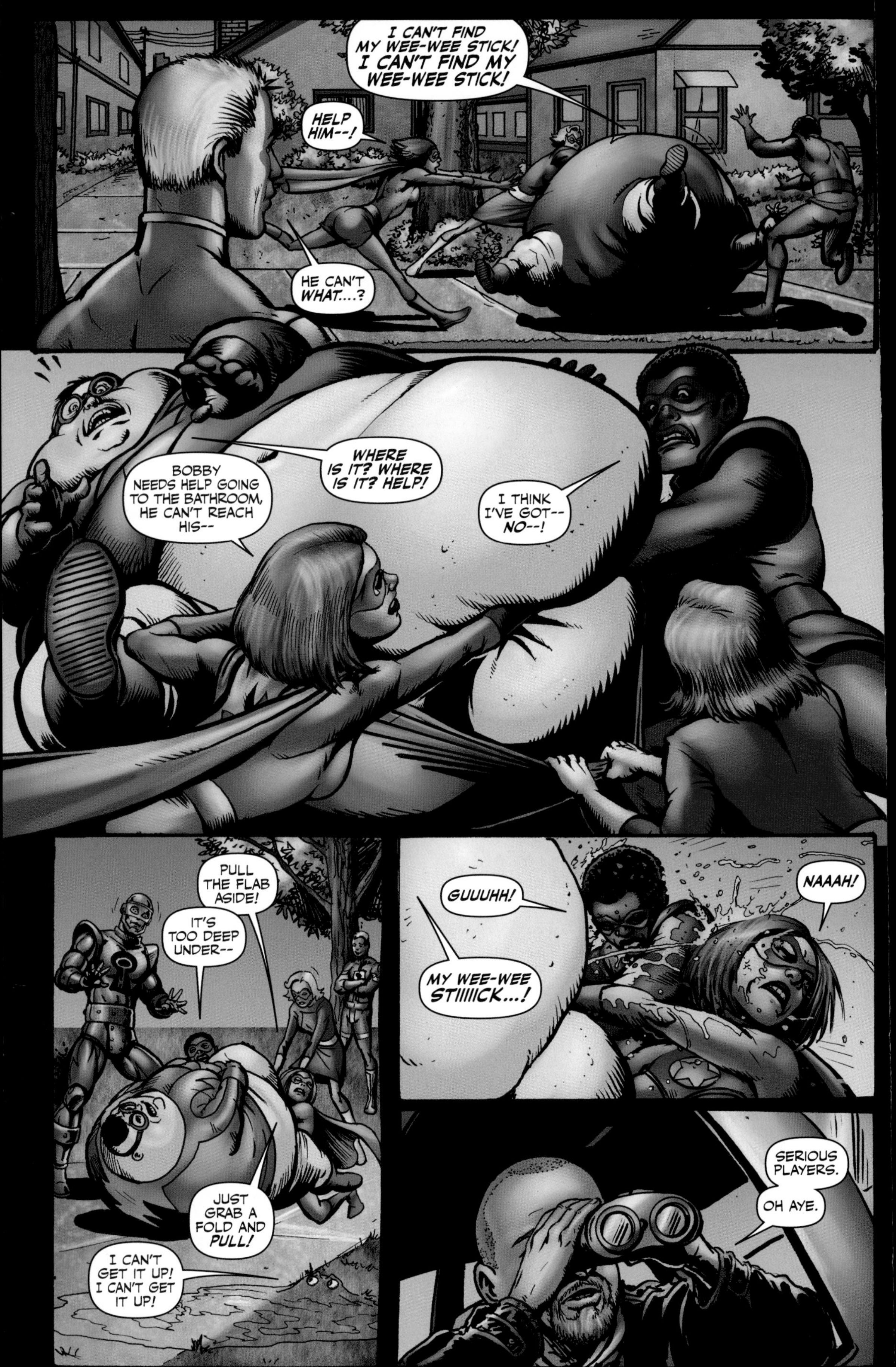
I CAN'T FIND MY WEE-WEE STICK! I CAN'T FIND MY WEE-WEE STICK!
HELP HIM--!
HE CAN'T WHAT...?
WHERE IS IT? WHERE IS IT? HELP!
BOBBY NEEDS HELP GOING TO THE BATHROOM, HE CAN'T REACH HIS--
I THINK I'VE GOT-- NO--!
PULL THE FLAB ASIDE!
IT'S TOO DEEP UNDER--
JUST GRAB A FOLD AND PULL!
I CAN'T GET IT UP! I CAN'T GET IT UP!
GUUUHH!
MY WEE-WEE STIIIICK...!
NAAAH!
SERIOUS PLAYERS.
OH AYE.

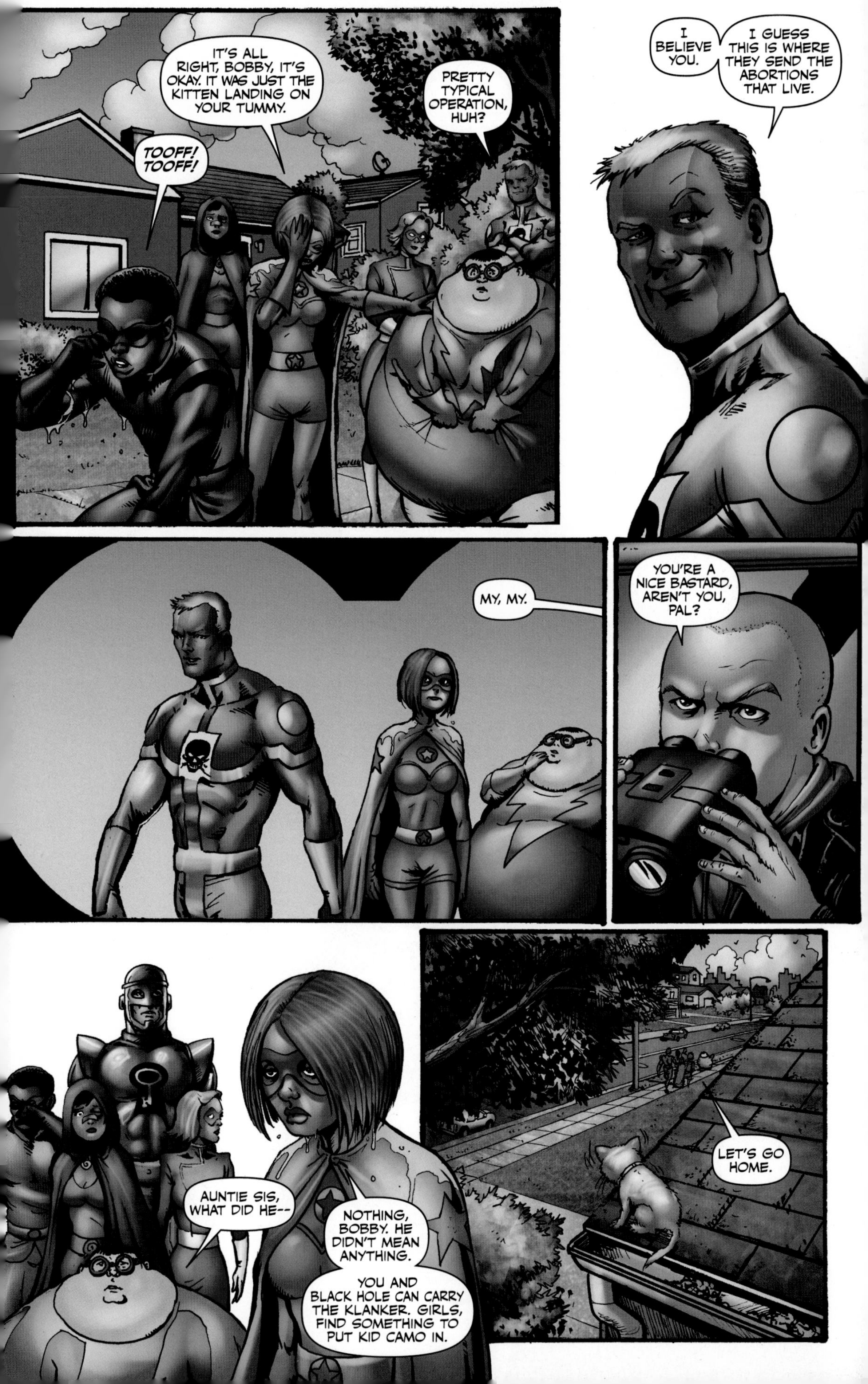
TOOFF! TOOFF!
IT'S ALL RIGHT, BOBBY, IT'S OKAY. IT WAS JUST THE KITTEN LANDING ON YOUR TUMMY.
PRETTY TYPICAL OPERATION, HUH?
I BELIEVE YOU.
I GUESS THIS IS WHERE THEY SEND THE ABORTIONS THAT LIVE.
MY, MY.
YOU'RE A NICE BASTARD, AREN'T YOU, PAL?
AUNTIE SIS, WHAT DID HE--
NOTHING, BOBBY. HE DIDN'T MEAN ANYTHING.
YOU AND BLACK HOLE CAN CARRY THE KLANKER. GIRLS, FIND SOMETHING TO PUT KID CAMO IN.
LET'S GO HOME.

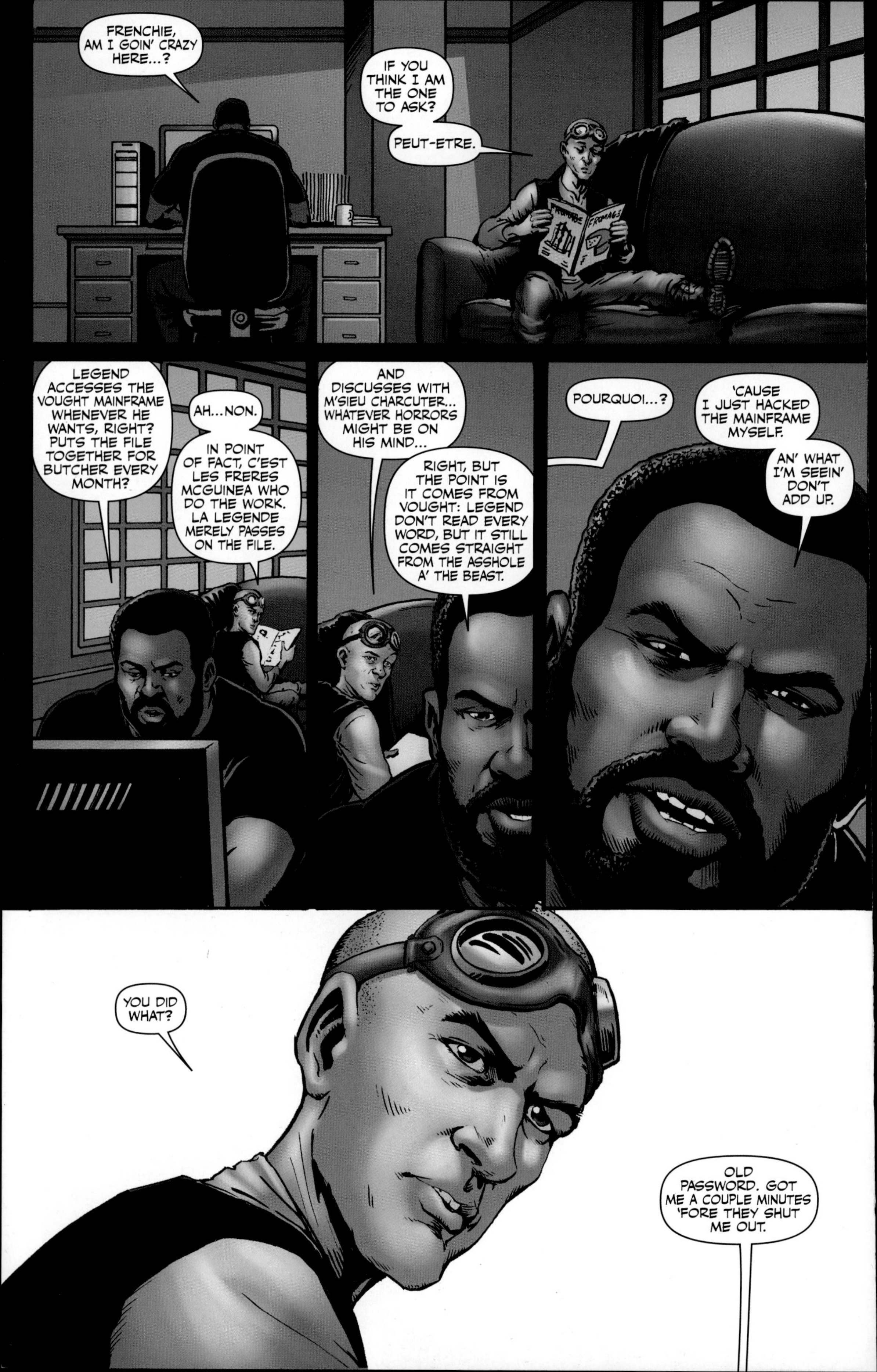

FRENCHIE, AM I GOIN' CRAZY HERE...?
IF YOU THINK I AM THE ONE TO ASK?
PEUT-ETRE.
FROMAGE
LEGEND ACCESSES THE VOUGHT MAINFRAME WHENEVER HE WANTS, RIGHT? PUTS THE FILE TOGETHER FOR BUTCHER EVERY MONTH?
AH...NON.
IN POINT OF FACT, C'EST LES FRERES MCGUINEA WHO DO THE WORK. LA LEGENDE MERELY PASSES ON THE FILE.
AND DISCUSSES WITH M'SIEU CHARCUTER... WHATEVER HORRORS MIGHT BE ON HIS MIND...
RIGHT, BUT THE POINT IS IT COMES FROM VOUGHT: LEGEND DON'T READ EVERY WORD, BUT IT STILL COMES STRAIGHT FROM THE ASSHOLE A' THE BEAST.
POURQUOI...?
'CAUSE I JUST HACKED THE MAINFRAME MYSELF.
AN' WHAT I'M SEEIN' DON'T ADD UP.
YOU DID WHAT?
OLD PASSWORD. GOT ME A COUPLE MINUTES 'FORE THEY SHUT ME OUT.

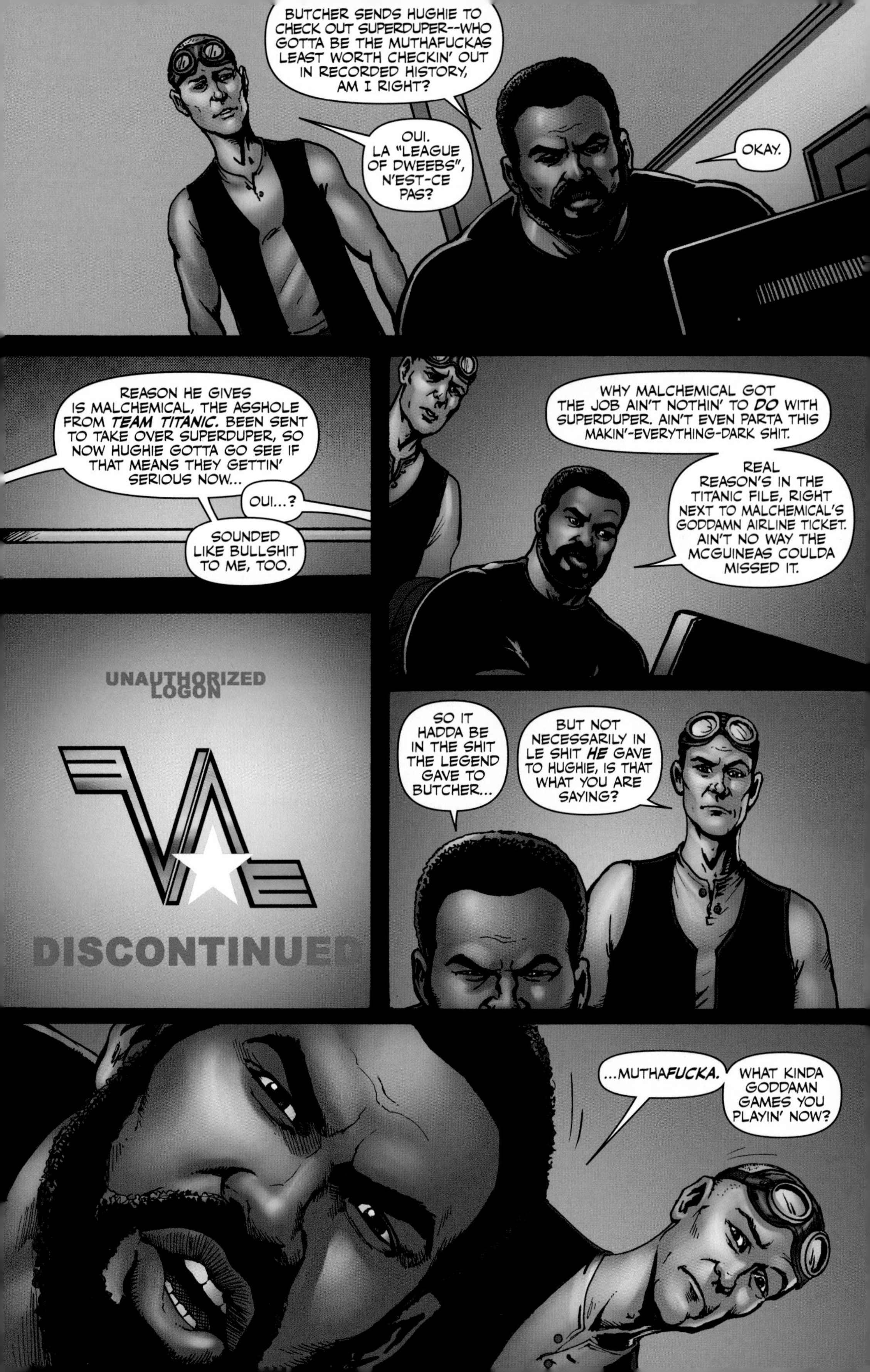
BUTCHER SENDS HUGHIE TO CHECK OUT SUPERDUPER--WHO GOTTA BE THE MUTHAFUCKAS LEAST WORTH CHECKIN' OUT IN RECORDED HISTORY, AM I RIGHT?
OUI. LA "LEAGUE OF DWEEBS", N'EST-CE PAS?
OKAY.
REASON HE GIVES IS MALCHEMICAL, THE ASSHOLE FROM *TEAM TITANIC.* BEEN SENT TO TAKE OVER SUPERDUPER, SO NOW HUGHIE GOTTA GO SEE IF THAT MEANS THEY GETTIN' SERIOUS NOW...
OUI...?
SOUNDED LIKE BULLSHIT TO ME, TOO.
WHY MALCHEMICAL GOT THE JOB AIN'T NOTHIN' TO ***DO*** WITH SUPERDUPER. AIN'T EVEN PARTA THIS MAKIN'-EVERYTHING-DARK SHIT.
REAL REASON'S IN THE TITANIC FILE, RIGHT NEXT TO MALCHEMICAL'S GODDAMN AIRLINE TICKET. AIN'T NO WAY THE MCGUINEAS COULDA MISSED IT.
UNAUTHORIZED LOGON
DISCONTINUED
SO IT HADDA BE IN THE SHIT THE LEGEND GAVE TO BUTCHER...
BUT NOT NECESSARILY IN LE SHIT ***HE*** GAVE TO HUGHIE, IS THAT WHAT YOU ARE SAYING?
...MUTHA**FUCKA.**
WHAT KINDA GODDAMN GAMES YOU PLAYIN' NOW?

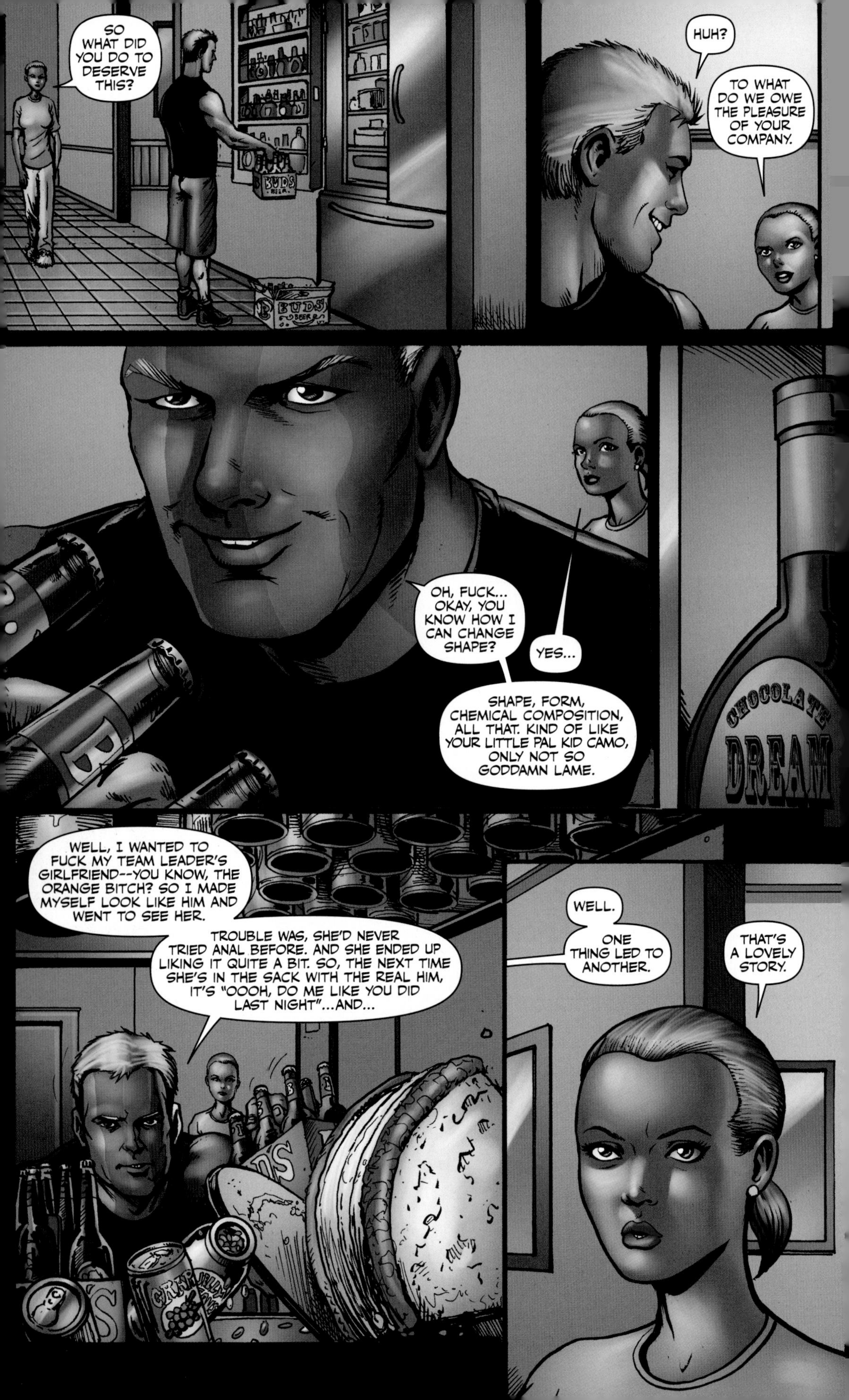
SO WHAT DID YOU DO TO DESERVE THIS?
BUDS BEER
HUH?
TO WHAT DO WE OWE THE PLEASURE OF YOUR COMPANY.
OH, FUCK... OKAY, YOU KNOW HOW I CAN CHANGE SHAPE?
YES...
SHAPE, FORM, CHEMICAL COMPOSITION, ALL THAT. KIND OF LIKE YOUR LITTLE PAL KID CAMO, ONLY NOT SO GODDAMN LAME.
CHOCOLATE DREAM
WELL, I WANTED TO FUCK MY TEAM LEADER'S GIRLFRIEND--YOU KNOW, THE ORANGE BITCH? SO I MADE MYSELF LOOK LIKE HIM AND WENT TO SEE HER.
TROUBLE WAS, SHE'D NEVER TRIED ANAL BEFORE. AND SHE ENDED UP LIKING IT QUITE A BIT. SO, THE NEXT TIME SHE'S IN THE SACK WITH THE REAL HIM, IT'S "OOOH, DO ME LIKE YOU DID LAST NIGHT"...AND...
WELL.
ONE THING LED TO ANOTHER.
THAT'S A LOVELY STORY.

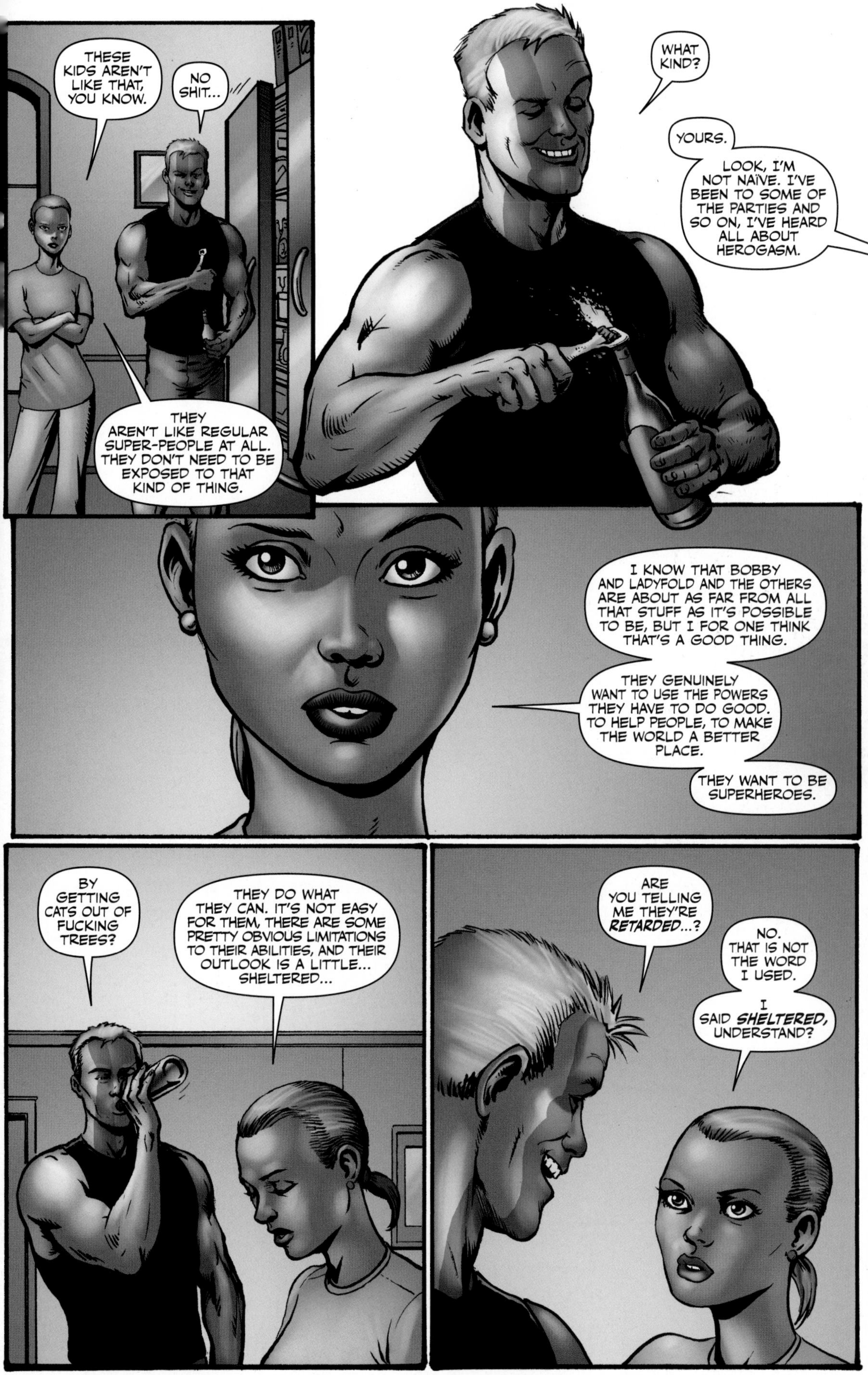
THESE KIDS AREN'T LIKE THAT, YOU KNOW.
NO SHIT...
THEY AREN'T LIKE REGULAR SUPER-PEOPLE AT ALL. THEY DON'T NEED TO BE EXPOSED TO THAT KIND OF THING.
WHAT KIND?
YOURS.
LOOK, I'M NOT NAÏVE. I'VE BEEN TO SOME OF THE PARTIES AND SO ON, I'VE HEARD ALL ABOUT HEROGASM.
I KNOW THAT BOBBY AND LADYFOLD AND THE OTHERS ARE ABOUT AS FAR FROM ALL THAT STUFF AS IT'S POSSIBLE TO BE, BUT I FOR ONE THINK THAT'S A GOOD THING.
THEY GENUINELY WANT TO USE THE POWERS THEY HAVE TO DO GOOD. TO HELP PEOPLE, TO MAKE THE WORLD A BETTER PLACE.
THEY WANT TO BE SUPERHEROES.
BY GETTING CATS OUT OF FUCKING TREES?
THEY DO WHAT THEY CAN. IT'S NOT EASY FOR THEM, THERE ARE SOME PRETTY OBVIOUS LIMITATIONS TO THEIR ABILITIES, AND THEIR OUTLOOK IS A LITTLE... SHELTERED...
ARE YOU TELLING ME THEY'RE RETARDED...?
NO. THAT IS NOT THE WORD I USED.
I SAID SHELTERED, UNDERSTAND?

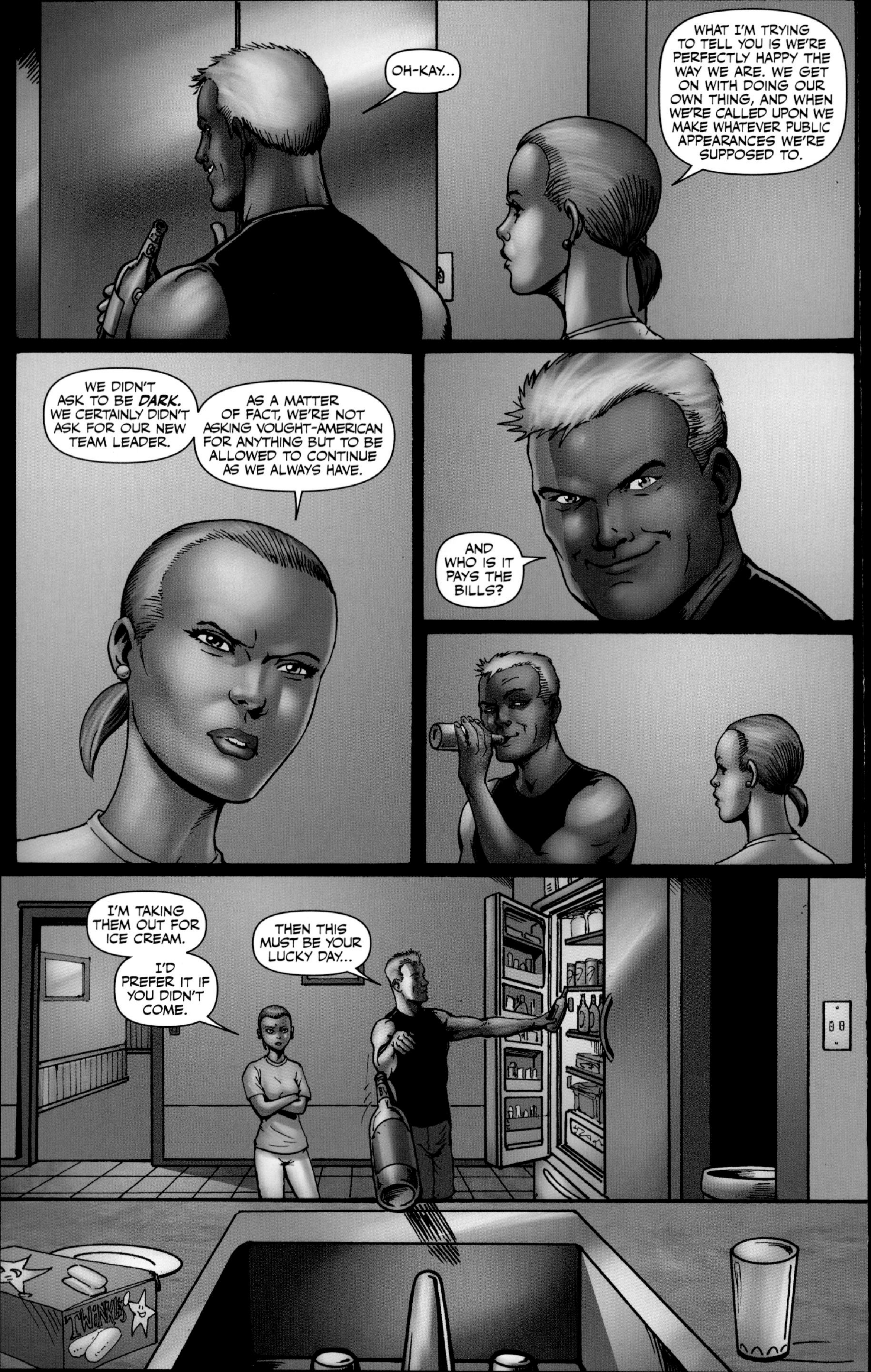
OH-KAY...
WHAT I'M TRYING TO TELL YOU IS WE'RE PERFECTLY HAPPY THE WAY WE ARE. WE GET ON WITH DOING OUR OWN THING, AND WHEN WE'RE CALLED UPON WE MAKE WHATEVER PUBLIC APPEARANCES WE'RE SUPPOSED TO.
WE DIDN'T ASK TO BE DARK. WE CERTAINLY DIDN'T ASK FOR OUR NEW TEAM LEADER.
AS A MATTER OF FACT, WE'RE NOT ASKING VOUGHT-AMERICAN FOR ANYTHING BUT TO BE ALLOWED TO CONTINUE AS WE ALWAYS HAVE.
AND WHO IS IT PAYS THE BILLS?
I'M TAKING THEM OUT FOR ICE CREAM.
I'D PREFER IT IF YOU DIDN'T COME.
THEN THIS MUST BE YOUR LUCKY DAY...
TWINKIES

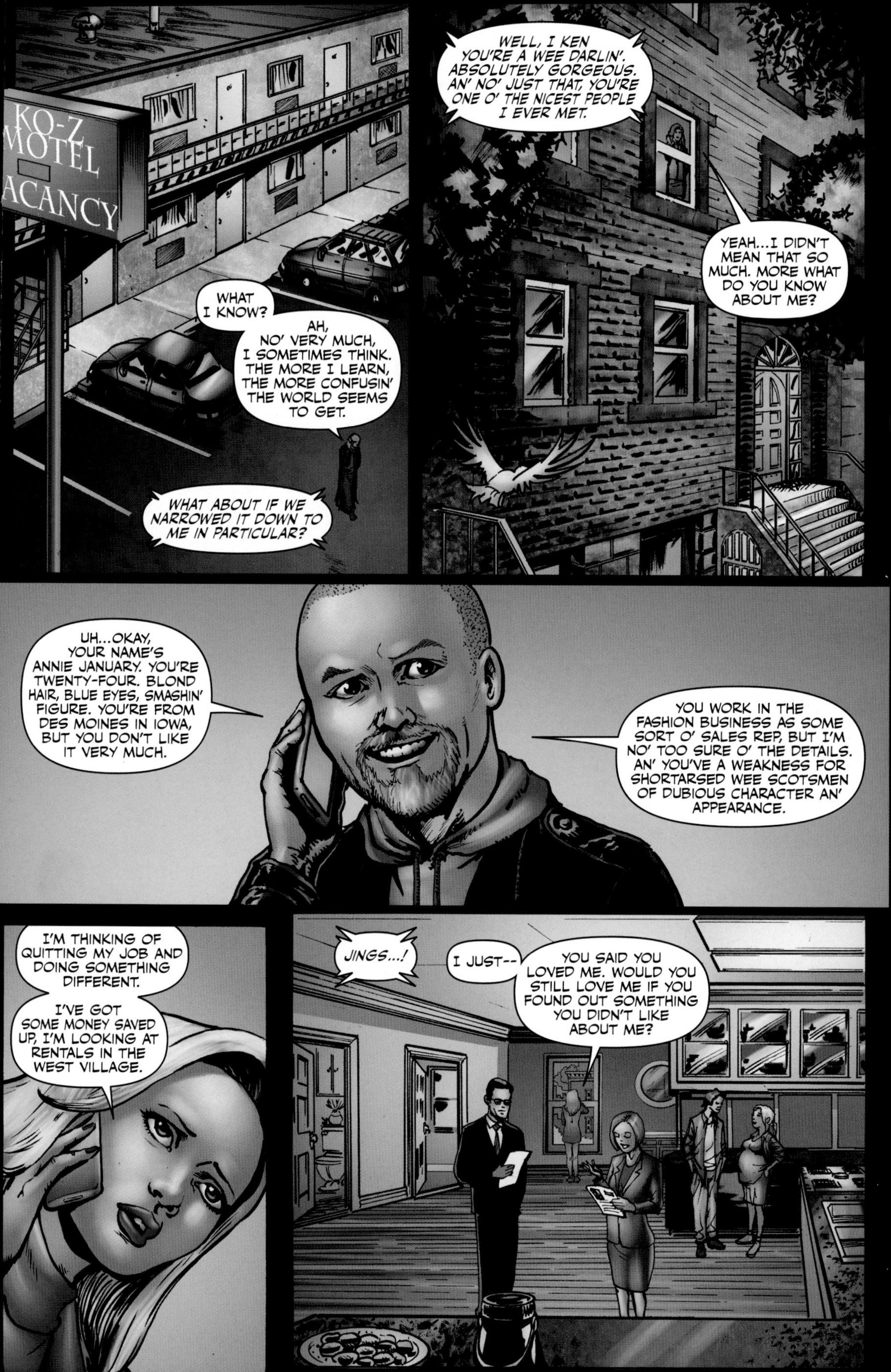
KO-Z MOTEL
ACANCY
WHAT I KNOW?
AH, NO' VERY MUCH, I SOMETIMES THINK. THE MORE I LEARN, THE MORE CONFUSIN' THE WORLD SEEMS TO GET.
WHAT ABOUT IF WE NARROWED IT DOWN TO ME IN PARTICULAR?
WELL, I KEN YOU'RE A WEE DARLIN'. ABSOLUTELY GORGEOUS. AN' NO' JUST THAT, YOU'RE ONE O' THE NICEST PEOPLE I EVER MET.
YEAH...I DIDN'T MEAN THAT SO MUCH. MORE WHAT DO YOU KNOW ABOUT ME?
UH...OKAY, YOUR NAME'S ANNIE JANUARY. YOU'RE TWENTY-FOUR. BLOND HAIR, BLUE EYES, SMASHIN' FIGURE. YOU'RE FROM DES MOINES IN IOWA, BUT YOU DON'T LIKE IT VERY MUCH.
YOU WORK IN THE FASHION BUSINESS AS SOME SORT O' SALES REP, BUT I'M NO' TOO SURE O' THE DETAILS. AN' YOU'VE A WEAKNESS FOR SHORTARSED WEE SCOTSMEN OF DUBIOUS CHARACTER AN' APPEARANCE.
I'M THINKING OF QUITTING MY JOB AND DOING SOMETHING DIFFERENT.
I'VE GOT SOME MONEY SAVED UP, I'M LOOKING AT RENTALS IN THE WEST VILLAGE.
JINGS...!
I JUST--
YOU SAID YOU LOVED ME. WOULD YOU STILL LOVE ME IF YOU FOUND OUT SOMETHING YOU DIDN'T LIKE ABOUT ME?

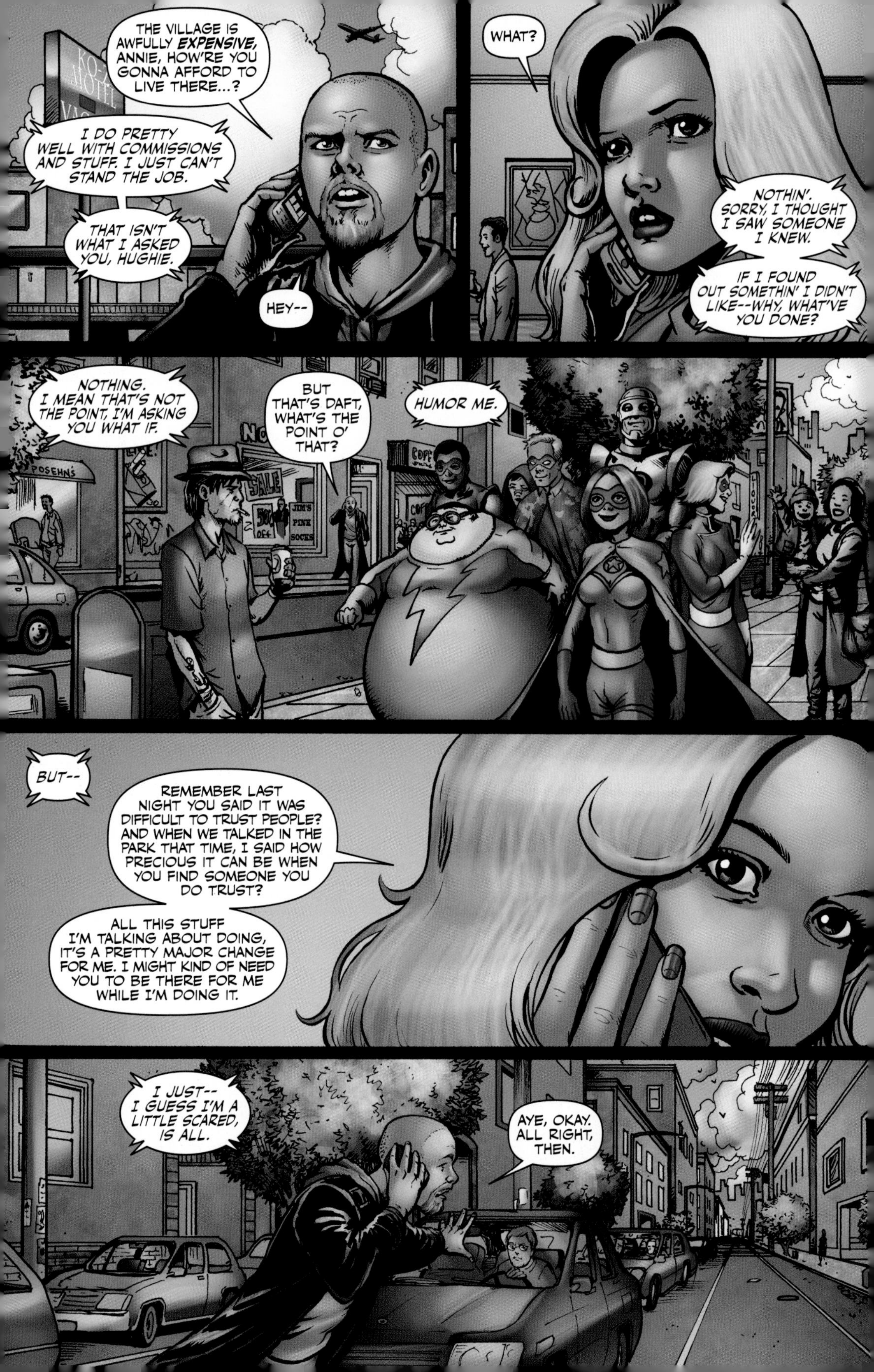
THE VILLAGE IS AWFULLY *EXPENSIVE,* ANNIE, HOW'RE YOU GONNA AFFORD TO LIVE THERE...?
I DO PRETTY WELL WITH COMMISSIONS AND STUFF. I JUST CAN'T STAND THE JOB.
THAT ISN'T WHAT I ASKED YOU, HUGHIE.
HEY--
WHAT?
NOTHIN'. SORRY, I THOUGHT I SAW SOMEONE I KNEW.
IF I FOUND OUT SOMETHIN' I DIDN'T LIKE--WHY, WHAT'VE YOU DONE?
NOTHING. I MEAN THAT'S NOT THE POINT, I'M ASKING YOU WHAT IF.
BUT THAT'S DAFT, WHAT'S THE POINT O' THAT?
HUMOR ME.
POSEHN'S
SALE
JIM'S PINK SOCKS
BUT--
REMEMBER LAST NIGHT YOU SAID IT WAS DIFFICULT TO TRUST PEOPLE? AND WHEN WE TALKED IN THE PARK THAT TIME, I SAID HOW PRECIOUS IT CAN BE WHEN YOU FIND SOMEONE YOU DO TRUST?
ALL THIS STUFF I'M TALKING ABOUT DOING, IT'S A PRETTY MAJOR CHANGE FOR ME. I MIGHT KIND OF NEED YOU TO BE THERE FOR ME WHILE I'M DOING IT.
I JUST-- I GUESS I'M A LITTLE SCARED, IS ALL.
AYE, OKAY. ALL RIGHT, THEN.

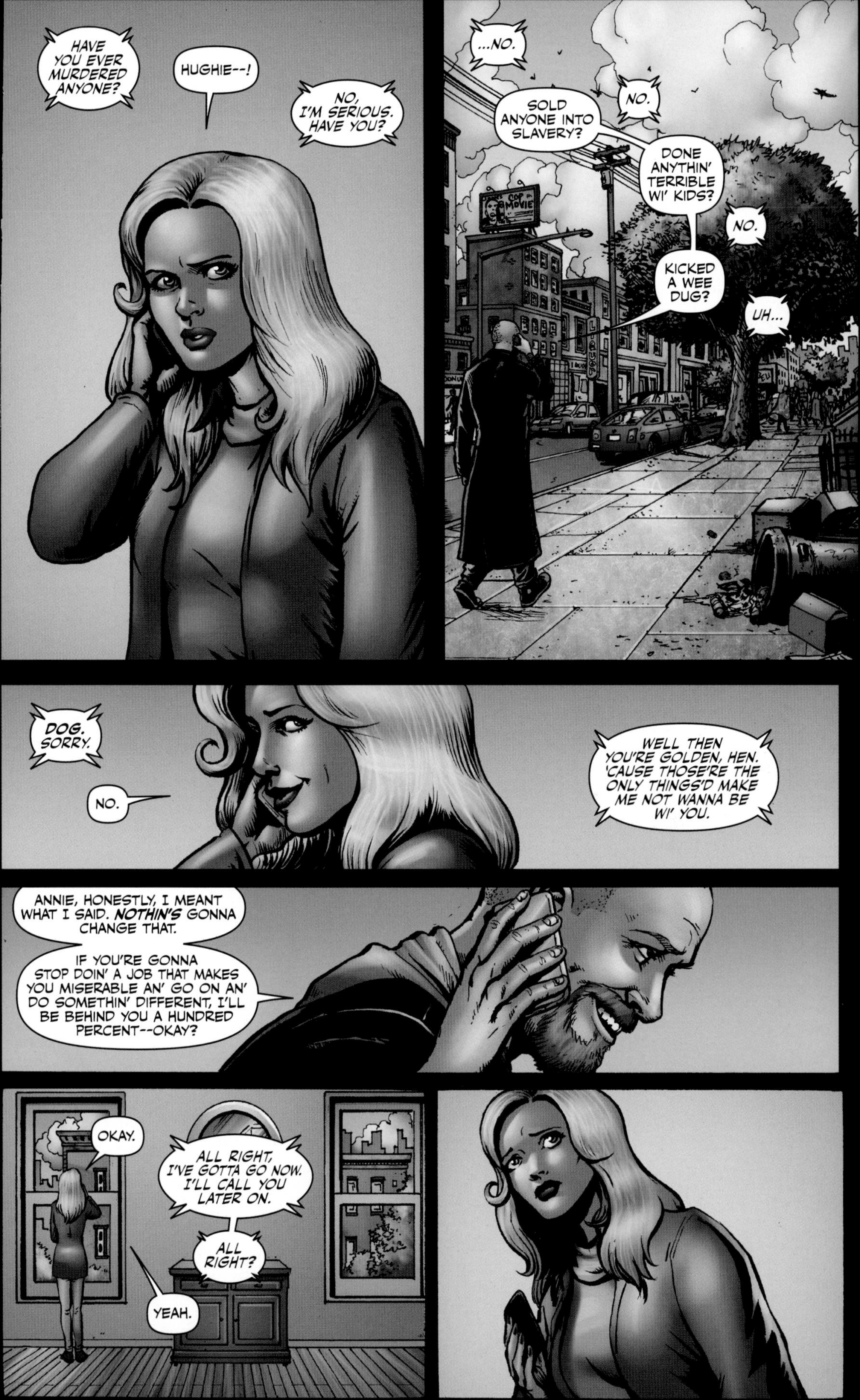
HAVE YOU EVER MURDERED ANYONE?
HUGHIE--!
NO, I'M SERIOUS. HAVE YOU?
...NO.
SOLD ANYONE INTO SLAVERY?
NO.
DONE ANYTHIN' TERRIBLE WI' KIDS?
NO.
KICKED A WEE DUG?
UH...
DOG. SORRY.
NO.
WELL THEN YOU'RE GOLDEN, HEN. 'CAUSE THOSE'RE THE ONLY THINGS'D MAKE ME NOT WANNA BE WI' YOU.
ANNIE, HONESTLY, I MEANT WHAT I SAID. NOTHIN'S GONNA CHANGE THAT.
IF YOU'RE GONNA STOP DOIN' A JOB THAT MAKES YOU MISERABLE AN' GO ON AN' DO SOMETHIN' DIFFERENT, I'LL BE BEHIND YOU A HUNDRED PERCENT--OKAY?
OKAY.
ALL RIGHT, I'VE GOTTA GO NOW. I'LL CALL YOU LATER ON.
ALL RIGHT?
YEAH.

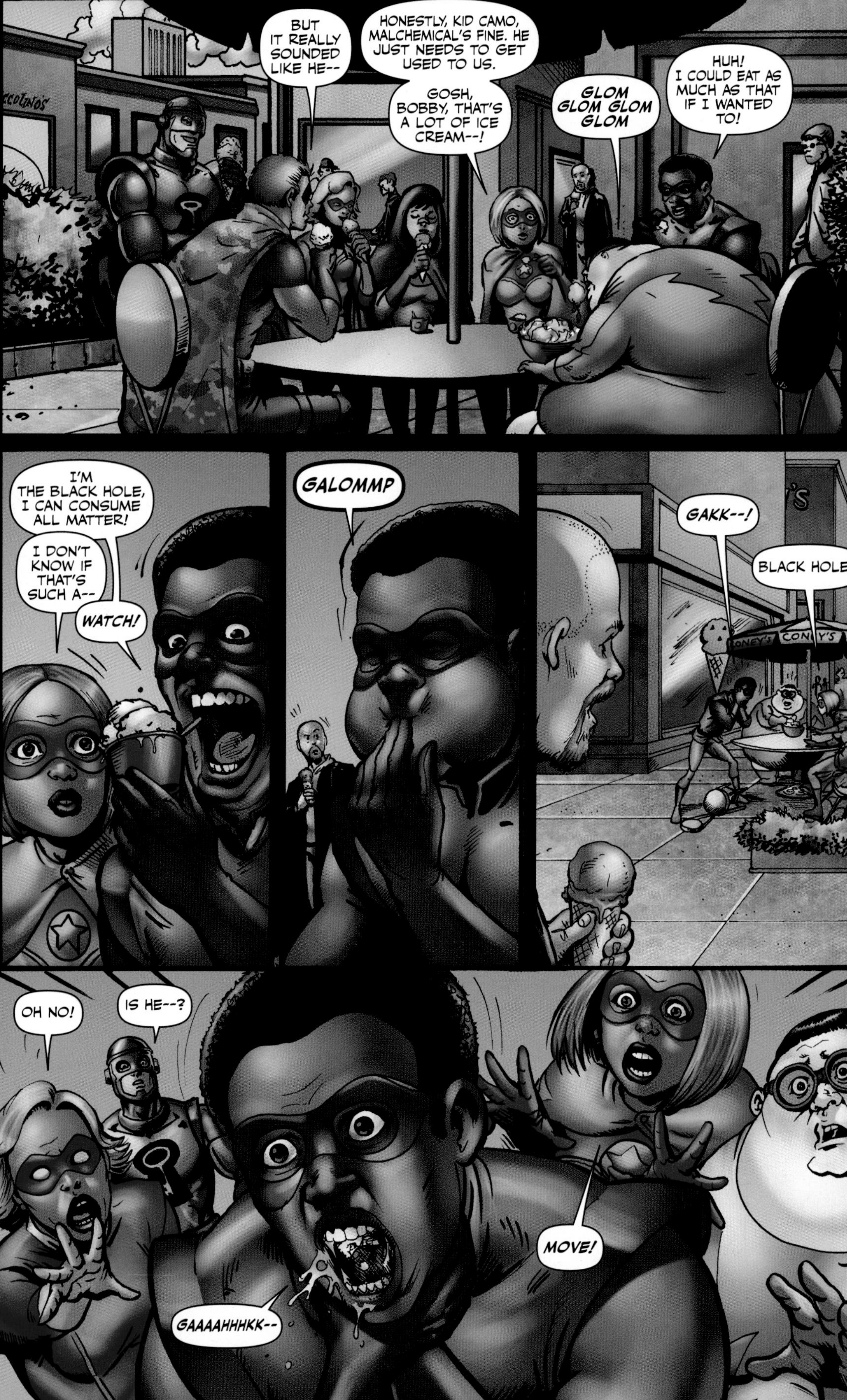
BUT IT REALLY SOUNDED LIKE HE--
HONESTLY, KID CAMO, MALCHEMICAL'S FINE. HE JUST NEEDS TO GET USED TO US.
GOSH, BOBBY, THAT'S A LOT OF ICE CREAM--!
GLOM GLOM GLOM GLOM
HUH! I COULD EAT AS MUCH AS THAT IF I WANTED TO!
I'M THE BLACK HOLE, I CAN CONSUME ALL MATTER!
I DON'T KNOW IF THAT'S SUCH A--
WATCH!
GALOMMP
GAKK--!
BLACK HOLE?
OH NO!
IS HE--?
MOVE!
GAAAAHHHKK--

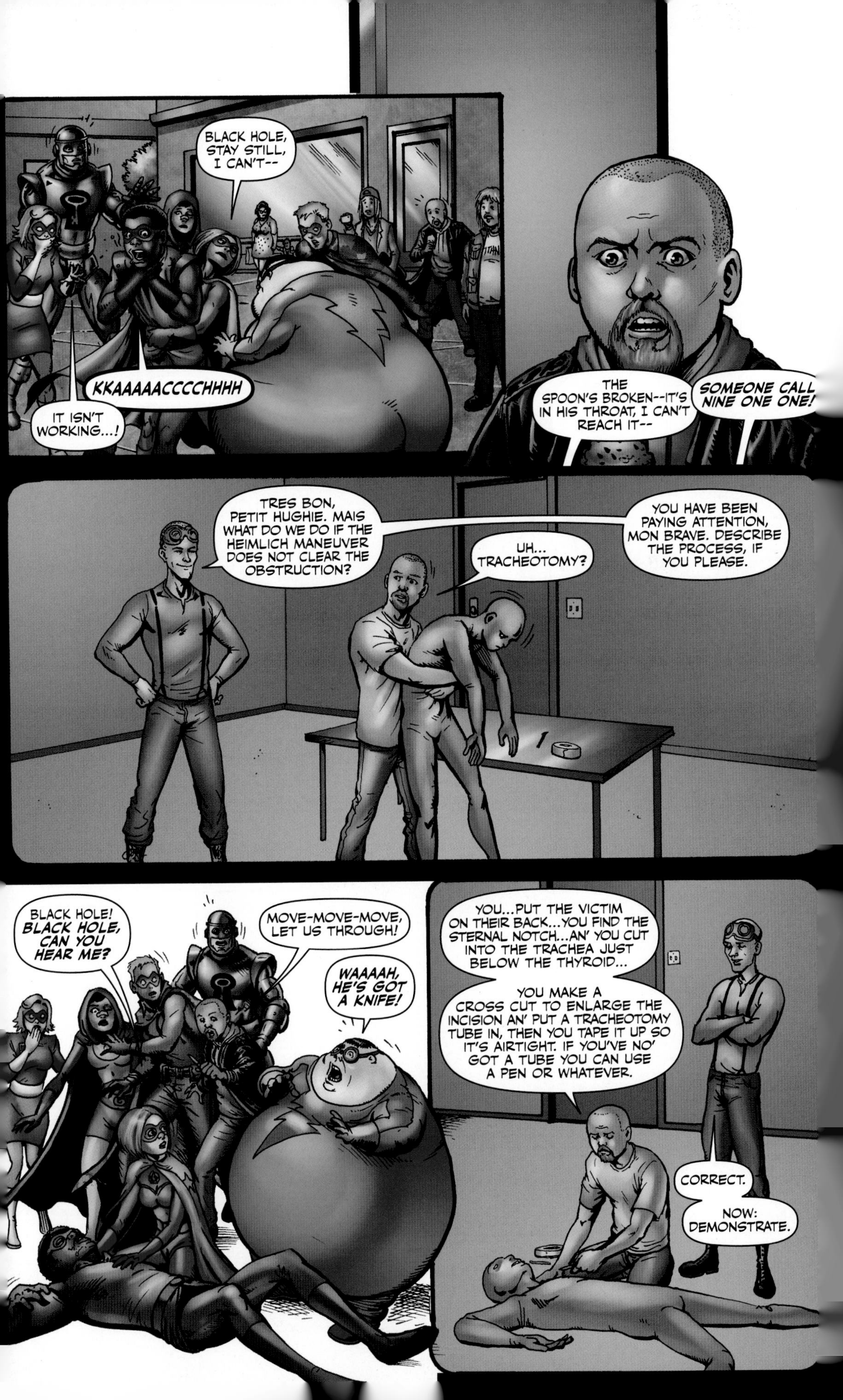

BLACK HOLE, STAY STILL, I CAN'T--
KKAAAAACCCCHHHH
IT ISN'T WORKING...!
THE SPOON'S BROKEN--IT'S IN HIS THROAT, I CAN'T REACH IT--
SOMEONE CALL NINE ONE ONE!
TRES BON, PETIT HUGHIE. MAIS WHAT DO WE DO IF THE HEIMLICH MANEUVER DOES NOT CLEAR THE OBSTRUCTION?
UH... TRACHEOTOMY?
YOU HAVE BEEN PAYING ATTENTION, MON BRAVE. DESCRIBE THE PROCESS, IF YOU PLEASE.
BLACK HOLE! BLACK HOLE, CAN YOU HEAR ME?
MOVE-MOVE-MOVE, LET US THROUGH!
WAAAAH, HE'S GOT A KNIFE!
YOU...PUT THE VICTIM ON THEIR BACK...YOU FIND THE STERNAL NOTCH...AN' YOU CUT INTO THE TRACHEA JUST BELOW THE THYROID...
YOU MAKE A CROSS CUT TO ENLARGE THE INCISION AN' PUT A TRACHEOTOMY TUBE IN, THEN YOU TAPE IT UP SO IT'S AIRTIGHT. IF YOU'VE NO' GOT A TUBE YOU CAN USE A PEN OR WHATEVER.
CORRECT.
NOW: DEMONSTRATE.

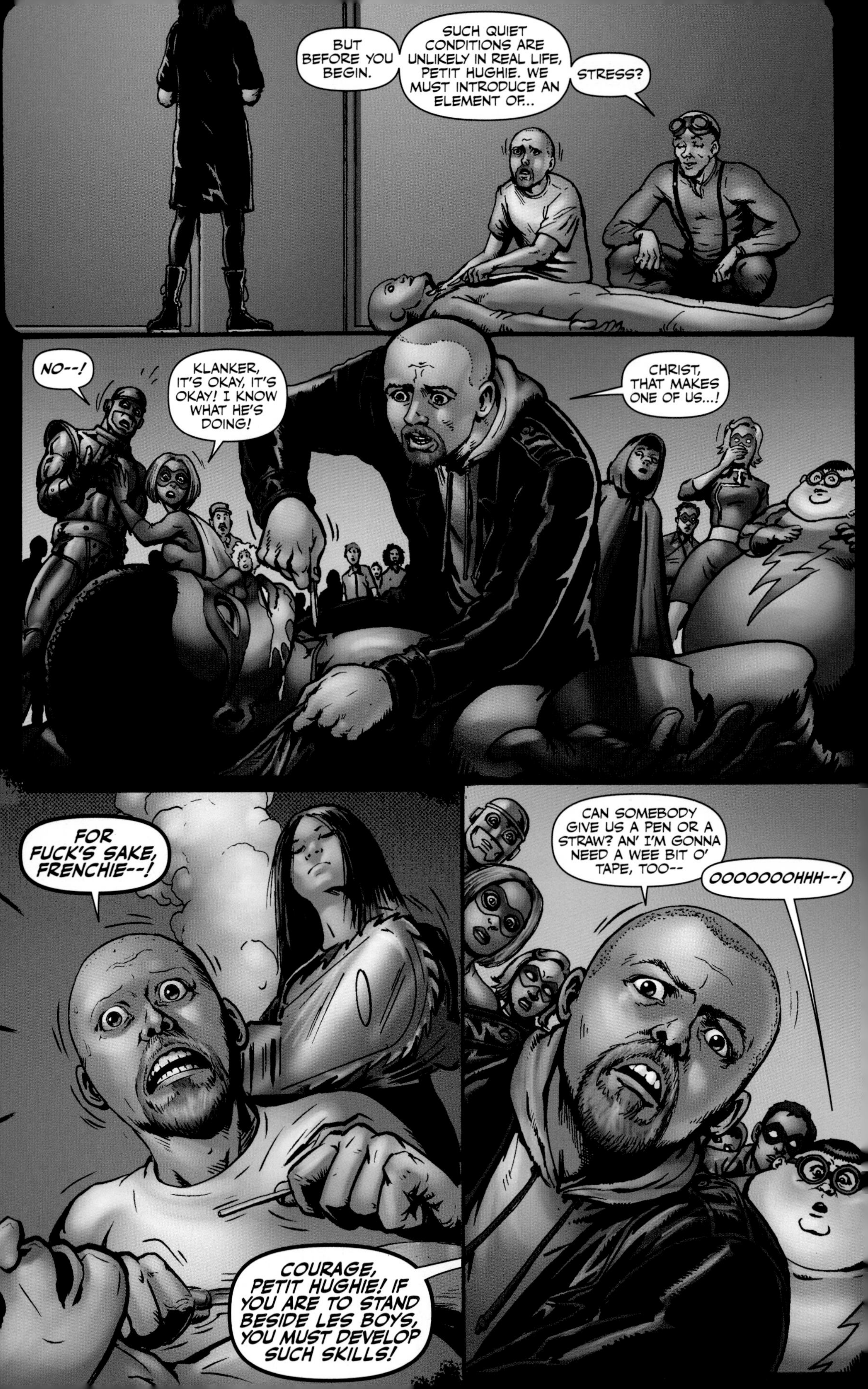
BUT BEFORE YOU BEGIN.
SUCH QUIET CONDITIONS ARE UNLIKELY IN REAL LIFE, PETIT HUGHIE. WE MUST INTRODUCE AN ELEMENT OF...
STRESS?
NO--!
KLANKER, IT'S OKAY, IT'S OKAY! I KNOW WHAT HE'S DOING!
CHRIST, THAT MAKES ONE OF US...!
FOR FUCK'S SAKE, FRENCHIE--!
COURAGE, PETIT HUGHIE! IF YOU ARE TO STAND BESIDE LES BOYS, YOU MUST DEVELOP SUCH SKILLS!
CAN SOMEBODY GIVE US A PEN OR A STRAW? AN' I'M GONNA NEED A WEE BIT O' TAPE, TOO--
OOOOOOOHHH--!

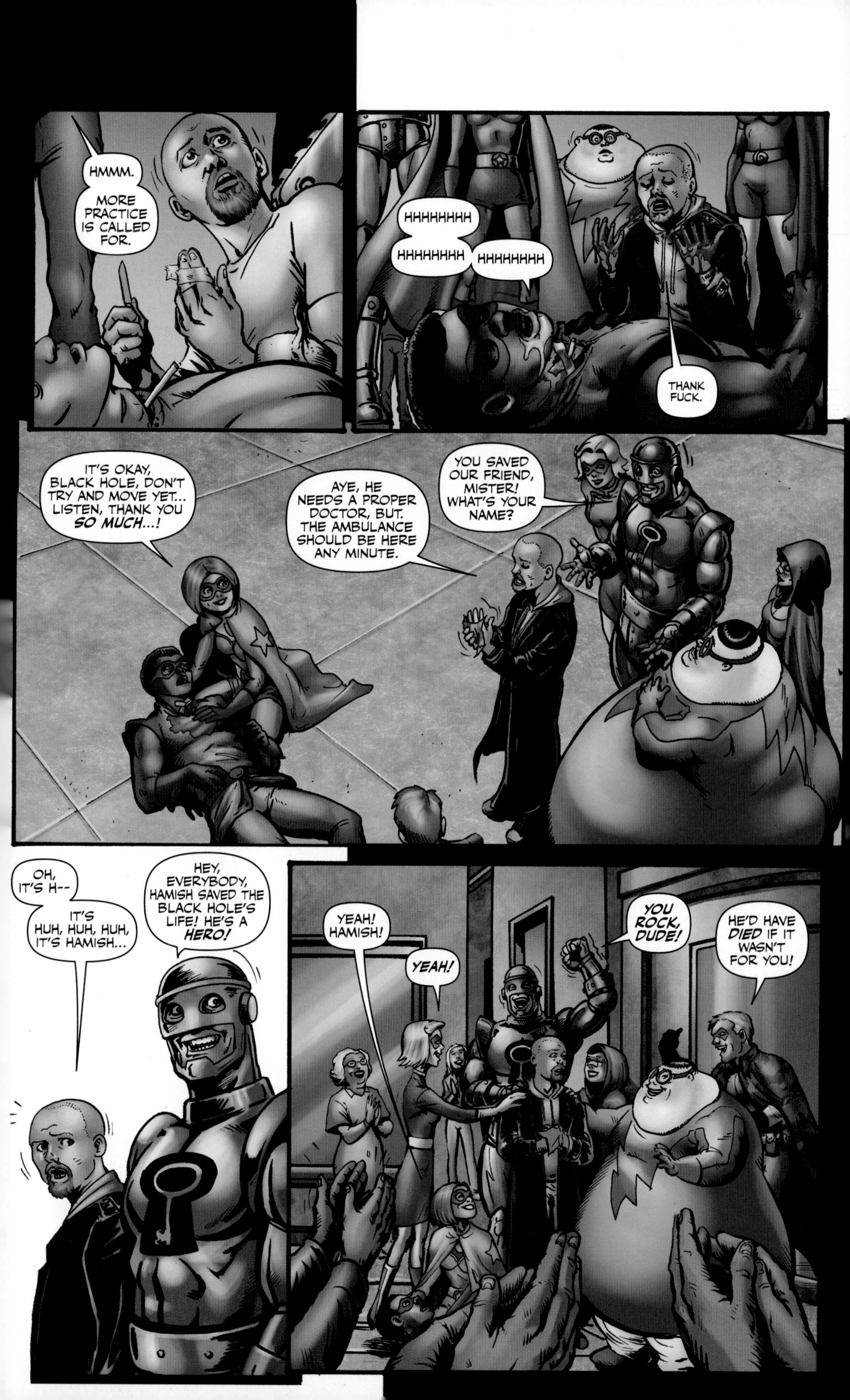
HMMM.
MORE PRACTICE IS CALLED FOR.
HHHHHHHH
HHHHHHHH
HHHHHHHH
THANK FUCK.
IT'S OKAY, BLACK HOLE, DON'T TRY AND MOVE YET... LISTEN, THANK YOU *SO MUCH*...!
AYE, HE NEEDS A PROPER DOCTOR, BUT. THE AMBULANCE SHOULD BE HERE ANY MINUTE.
YOU SAVED OUR FRIEND, MISTER! WHAT'S YOUR NAME?
OH, IT'S H--
IT'S HUH, HUH, HUH, IT'S HAMISH...
HEY, EVERYBODY, HAMISH SAVED THE BLACK HOLE'S LIFE! HE'S A *HERO!*
YEAH! HAMISH!
YEAH!
YOU ROCK, DUDE!
HE'D HAVE *DIED* IF IT WASN'T FOR YOU!

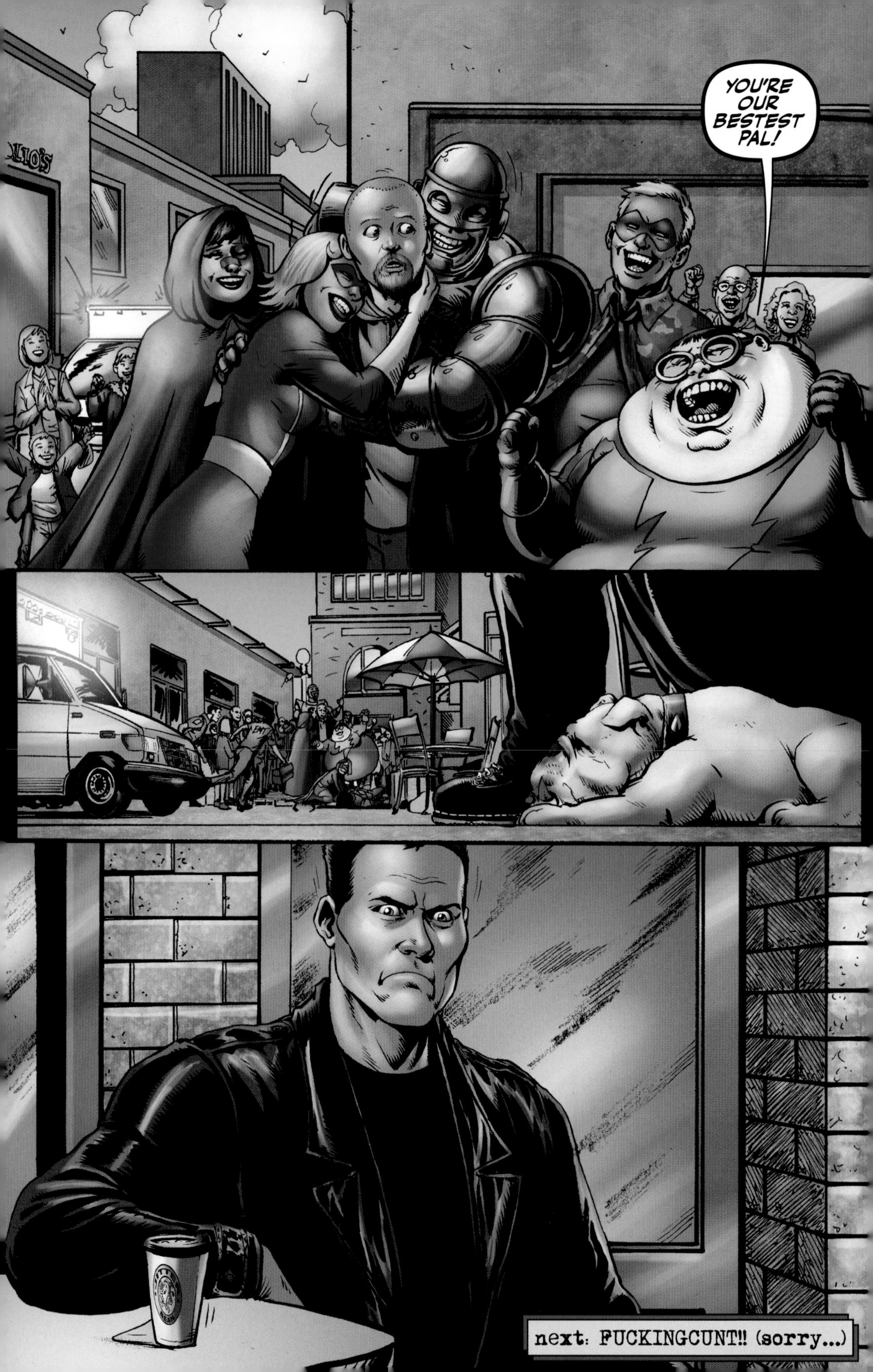
YOU'RE OUR BESTEST PAL!
next: FUCKINGCUNT!! (sorry...)

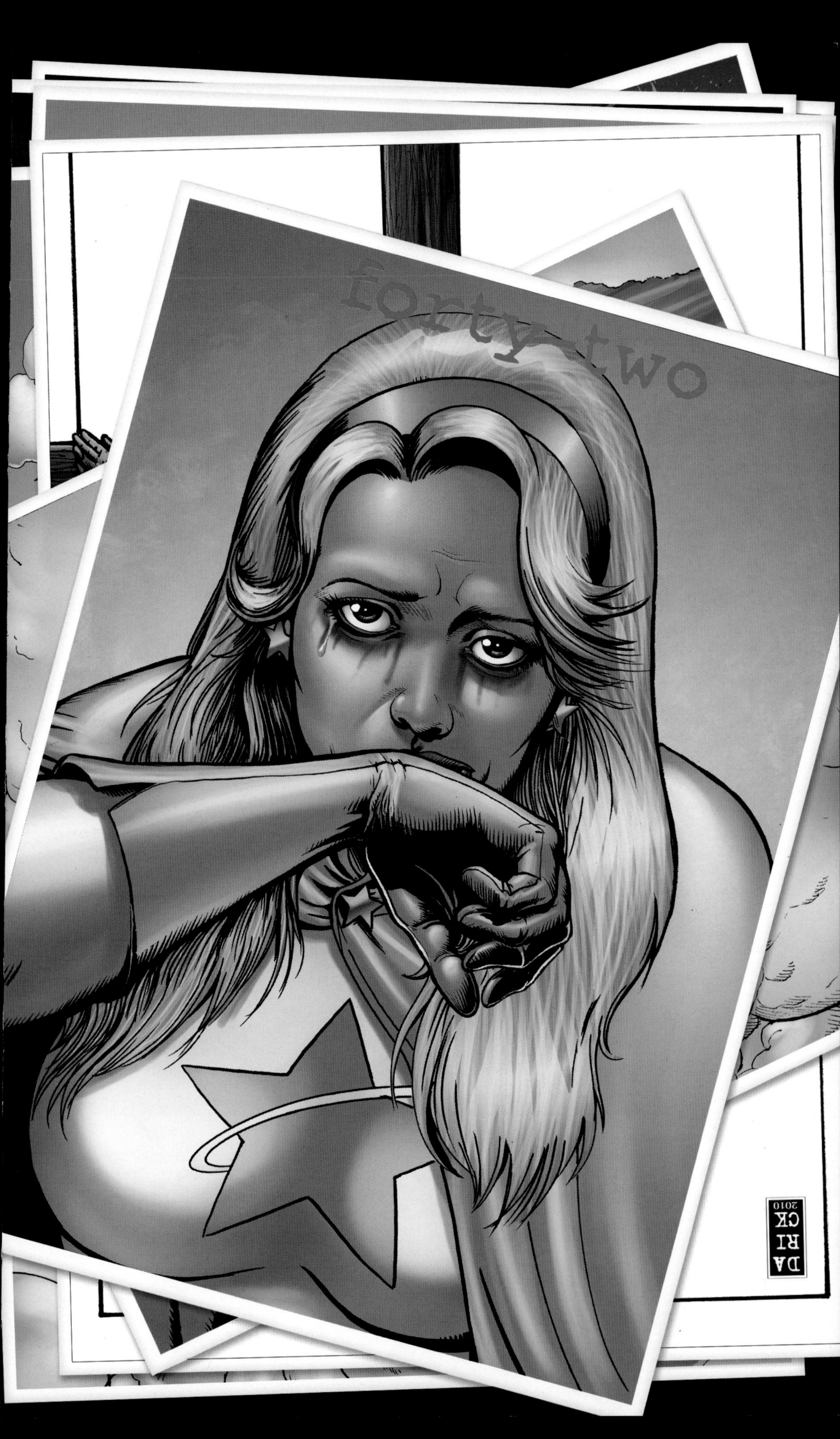
forty-two

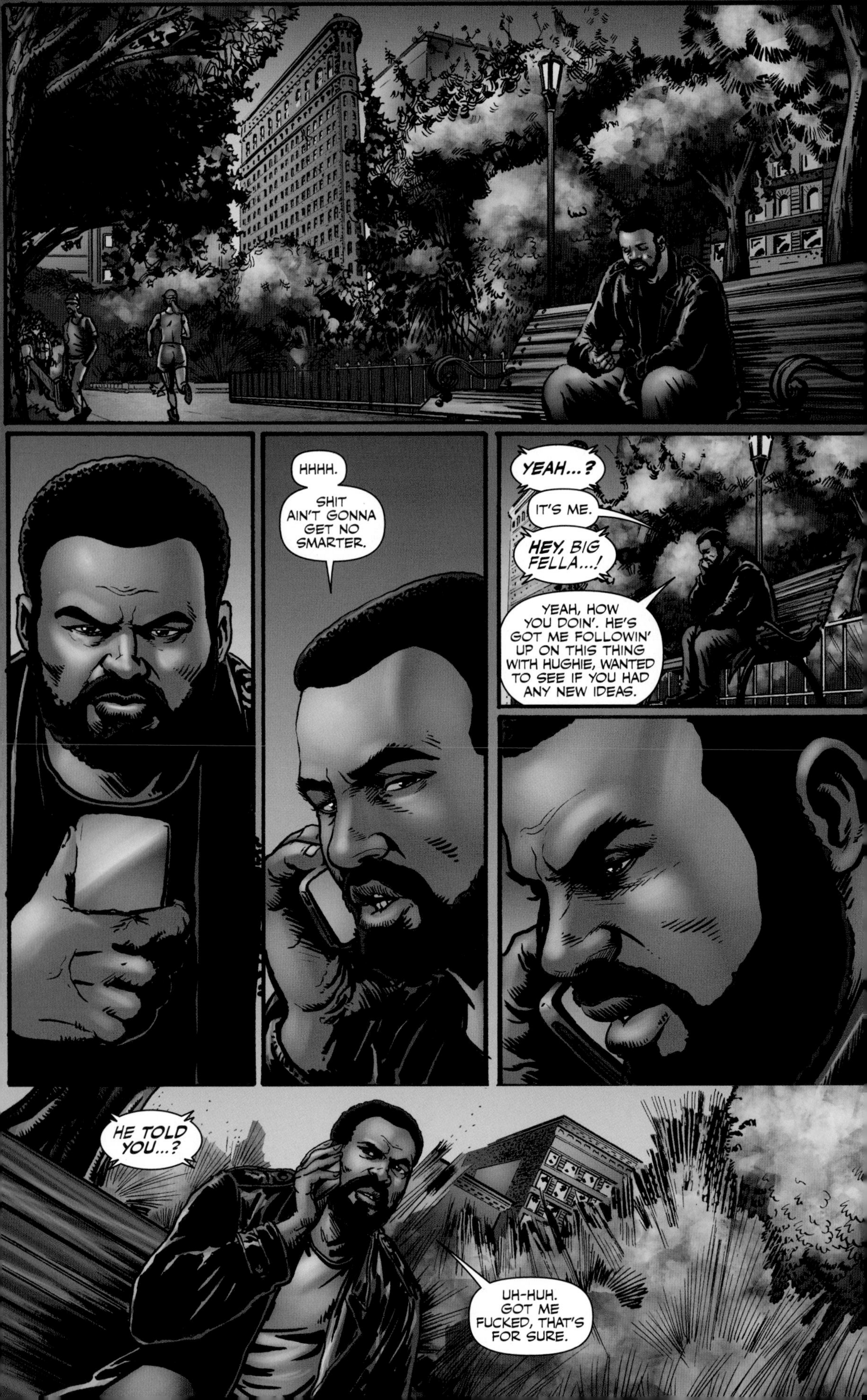
HHHH.
SHIT AIN'T GONNA GET NO SMARTER.
YEAH...?
IT'S ME.
HEY, BIG FELLA...!
YEAH, HOW YOU DOIN'. HE'S GOT ME FOLLOWIN' UP ON THIS THING WITH HUGHIE, WANTED TO SEE IF YOU HAD ANY NEW IDEAS.
HE TOLD YOU...?
UH-HUH. GOT ME FUCKED, THAT'S FOR SURE.

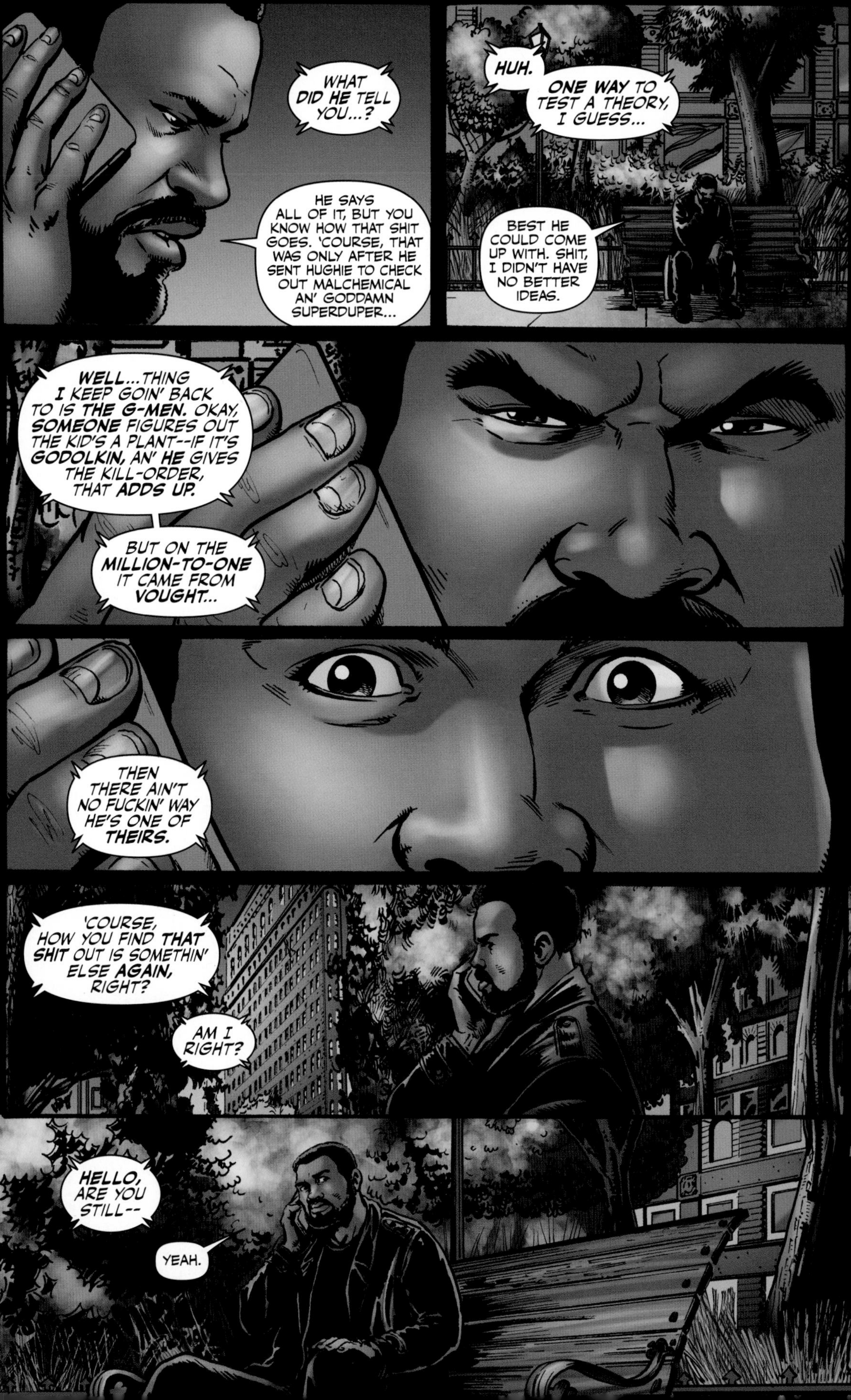
WHAT DID HE TELL YOU...?
HE SAYS ALL OF IT, BUT YOU KNOW HOW THAT SHIT GOES. 'COURSE, THAT WAS ONLY AFTER HE SENT HUGHIE TO CHECK OUT MALCHEMICAL AN' GODDAMN SUPERDUPER...
HUH.
ONE WAY TO TEST A THEORY, I GUESS...
BEST HE COULD COME UP WITH. SHIT, I DIDN'T HAVE NO BETTER IDEAS.
WELL...THING I KEEP GOIN' BACK TO IS THE G-MEN. OKAY, SOMEONE FIGURES OUT THE KID'S A PLANT--IF IT'S GODOLKIN, AN' HE GIVES THE KILL-ORDER, THAT ADDS UP.
BUT ON THE MILLION-TO-ONE IT CAME FROM VOUGHT...
THEN THERE AIN'T NO FUCKIN' WAY HE'S ONE OF THEIRS.
'COURSE, HOW YOU FIND THAT SHIT OUT IS SOMETHIN' ELSE AGAIN, RIGHT?
AM I RIGHT?
HELLO, ARE YOU STILL--
YEAH.

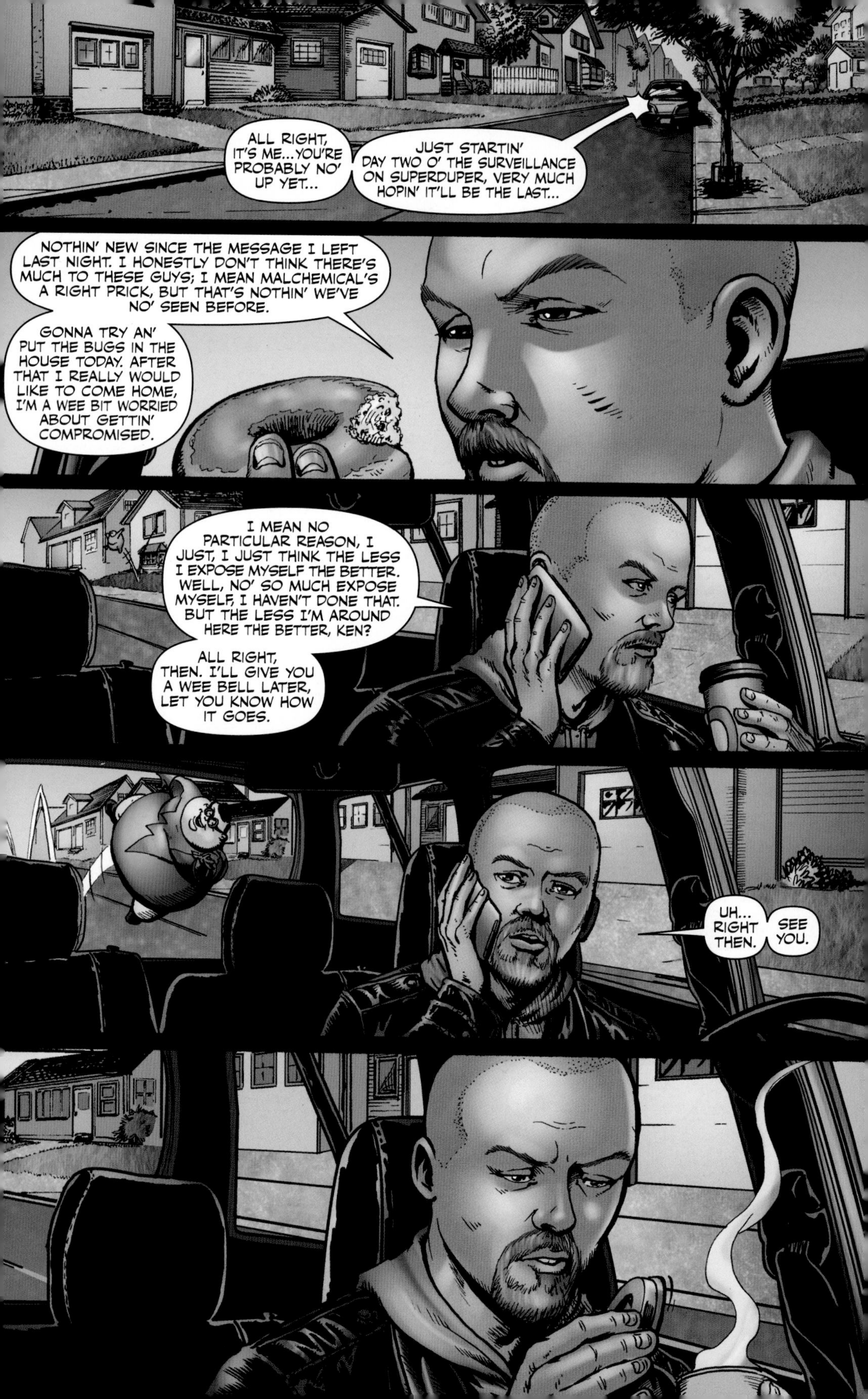
ALL RIGHT, IT'S ME...YOU'RE PROBABLY NO' UP YET...
JUST STARTIN' DAY TWO O' THE SURVEILLANCE ON SUPERDUPER, VERY MUCH HOPIN' IT'LL BE THE LAST...
NOTHIN' NEW SINCE THE MESSAGE I LEFT LAST NIGHT. I HONESTLY DON'T THINK THERE'S MUCH TO THESE GUYS; I MEAN MALCHEMICAL'S A RIGHT PRICK, BUT THAT'S NOTHIN' WE'VE NO' SEEN BEFORE.
GONNA TRY AN' PUT THE BUGS IN THE HOUSE TODAY. AFTER THAT I REALLY WOULD LIKE TO COME HOME, I'M A WEE BIT WORRIED ABOUT GETTIN' COMPROMISED.
I MEAN NO PARTICULAR REASON, I JUST, I JUST THINK THE LESS I EXPOSE MYSELF THE BETTER. WELL, NO' SO MUCH EXPOSE MYSELF, I HAVEN'T DONE THAT. BUT THE LESS I'M AROUND HERE THE BETTER, KEN?
ALL RIGHT, THEN. I'LL GIVE YOU A WEE BELL LATER, LET YOU KNOW HOW IT GOES.
UH... RIGHT THEN.
SEE YOU.

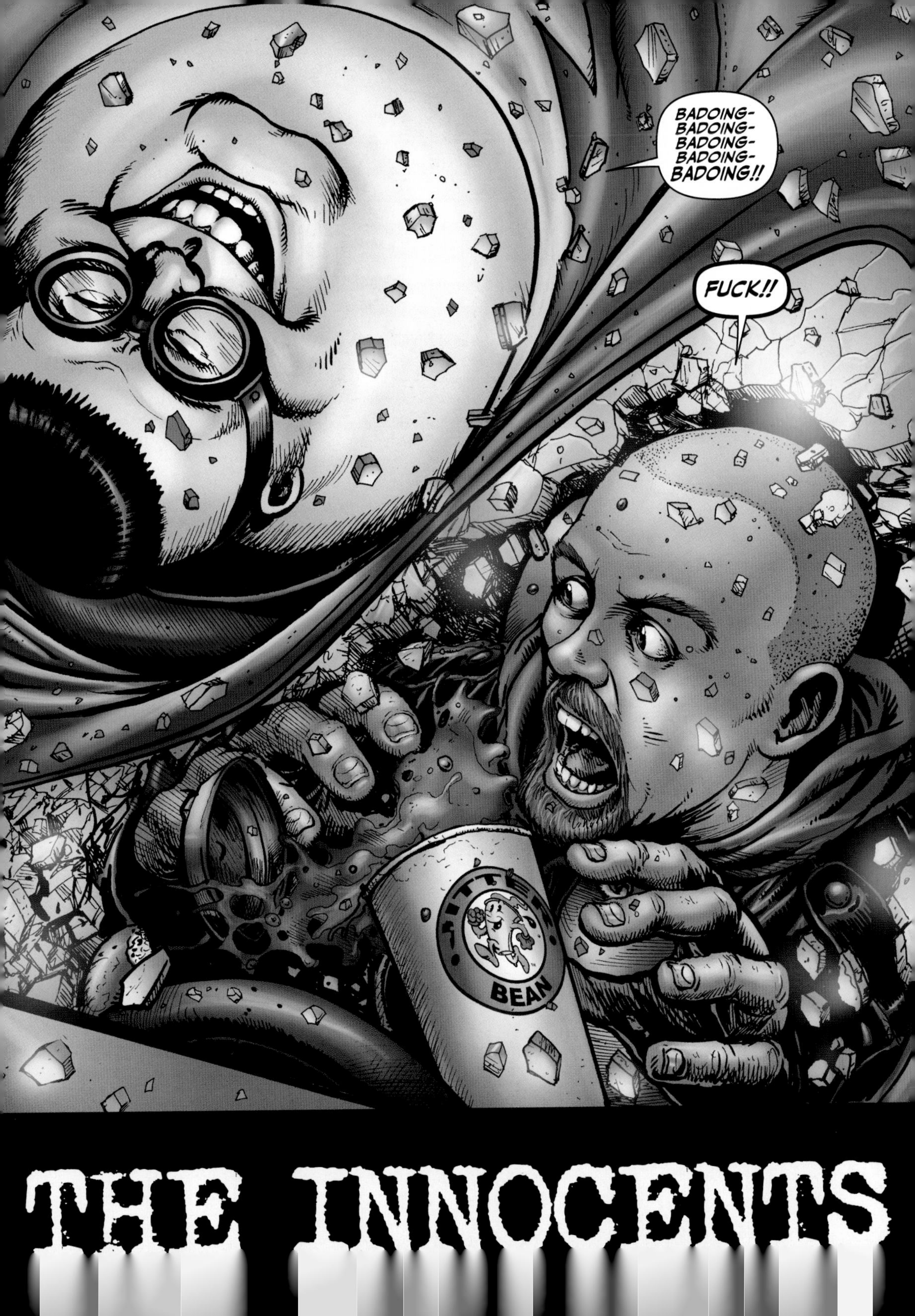
BADOING-
BADOING-
BADOING-
BADOING-
BADOING!!
FUCK!!
BEAN

THE INNOCENTS

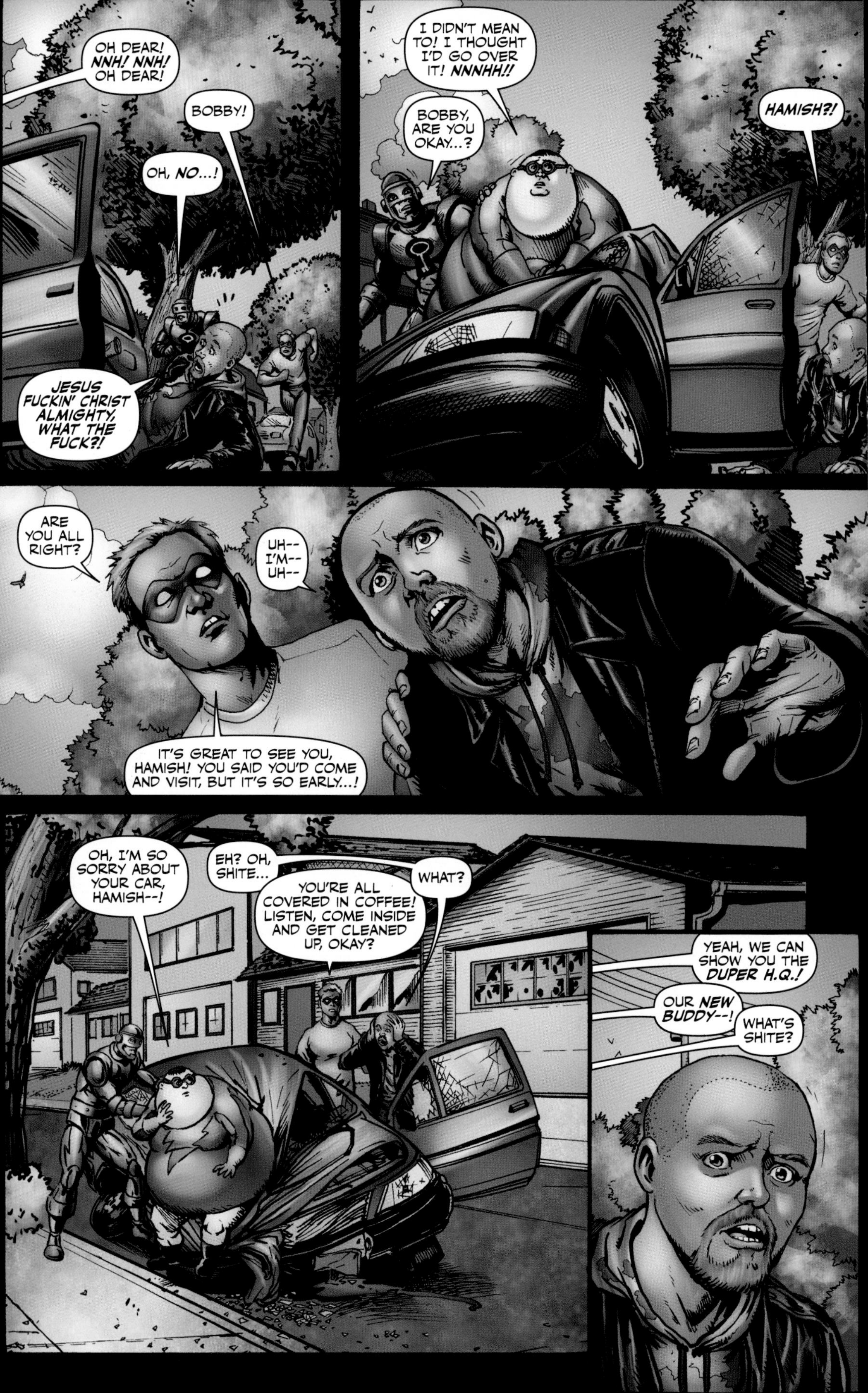
OH DEAR! NNH! NNH! OH DEAR!
BOBBY!
OH, NO...!
JESUS FUCKIN' CHRIST ALMIGHTY, WHAT THE FUCK?!
I DIDN'T MEAN TO! I THOUGHT I'D GO OVER IT! NNNHH!!
BOBBY, ARE YOU OKAY...?
HAMISH?!
ARE YOU ALL RIGHT?
UH-- I'M-- UH--
IT'S GREAT TO SEE YOU, HAMISH! YOU SAID YOU'D COME AND VISIT, BUT IT'S SO EARLY...!
OH, I'M SO SORRY ABOUT YOUR CAR, HAMISH--!
EH? OH, SHITE...
WHAT?
YOU'RE ALL COVERED IN COFFEE! LISTEN, COME INSIDE AND GET CLEANED UP, OKAY?
YEAH, WE CAN SHOW YOU THE DUPER H.Q.!
OUR NEW BUDDY--!
WHAT'S SHITE?

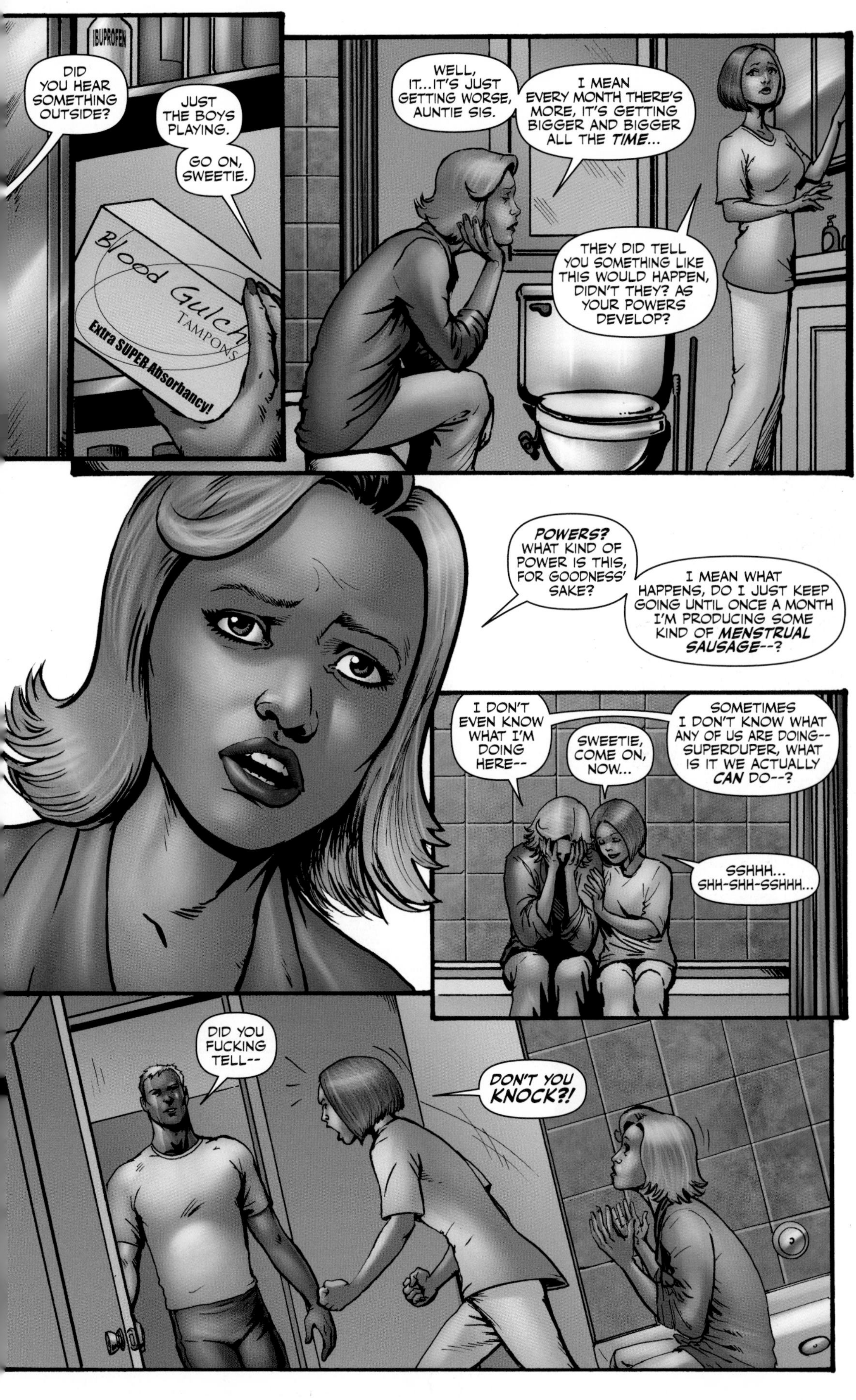
IBUPROFEN
DID YOU HEAR SOMETHING OUTSIDE?
JUST THE BOYS PLAYING.
GO ON, SWEETIE.
Blood Gulch TAMPONS Extra SUPER Absorbancy!
WELL, IT...IT'S JUST GETTING WORSE, AUNTIE SIS.
I MEAN EVERY MONTH THERE'S MORE, IT'S GETTING BIGGER AND BIGGER ALL THE TIME...
THEY DID TELL YOU SOMETHING LIKE THIS WOULD HAPPEN, DIDN'T THEY? AS YOUR POWERS DEVELOP?
POWERS? WHAT KIND OF POWER IS THIS, FOR GOODNESS' SAKE?
I MEAN WHAT HAPPENS, DO I JUST KEEP GOING UNTIL ONCE A MONTH I'M PRODUCING SOME KIND OF MENSTRUAL SAUSAGE--?
I DON'T EVEN KNOW WHAT I'M DOING HERE--
SWEETIE, COME ON, NOW...
SOMETIMES I DON'T KNOW WHAT ANY OF US ARE DOING-- SUPERDUPER, WHAT IS IT WE ACTUALLY CAN DO--?
SSHHH... SHH-SHH-SSHHH...
DID YOU FUCKING TELL--
DON'T YOU KNOCK?!

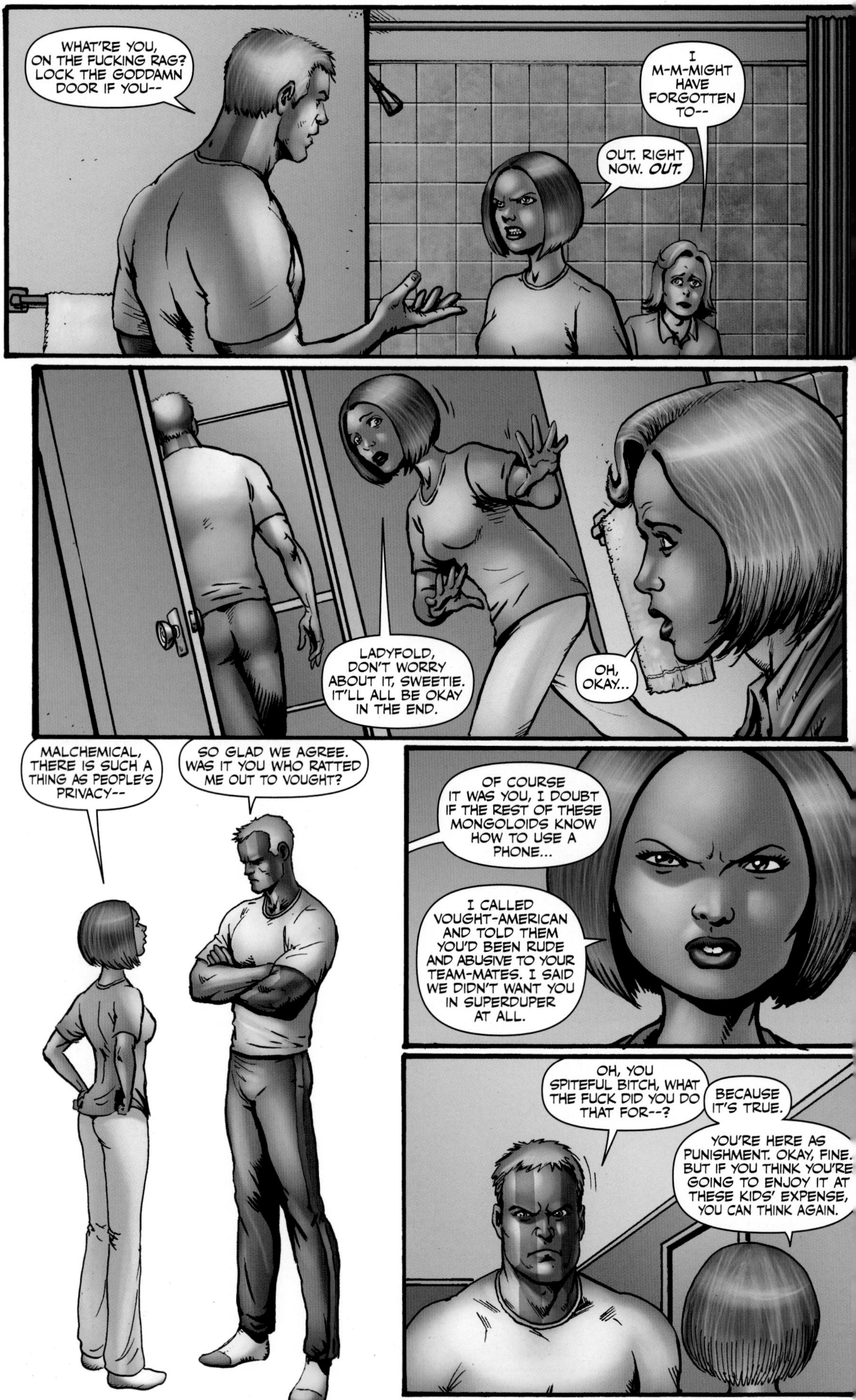
WHAT'RE YOU, ON THE FUCKING RAG? LOCK THE GODDAMN DOOR IF YOU--
I M-M-MIGHT HAVE FORGOTTEN TO--
OUT. RIGHT NOW. OUT.
LADYFOLD, DON'T WORRY ABOUT IT, SWEETIE. IT'LL ALL BE OKAY IN THE END.
OH, OKAY...
MALCHEMICAL, THERE IS SUCH A THING AS PEOPLE'S PRIVACY--
SO GLAD WE AGREE. WAS IT YOU WHO RATTED ME OUT TO VOUGHT?
OF COURSE IT WAS YOU, I DOUBT IF THE REST OF THESE MONGOLOIDS KNOW HOW TO USE A PHONE...
I CALLED VOUGHT-AMERICAN AND TOLD THEM YOU'D BEEN RUDE AND ABUSIVE TO YOUR TEAM-MATES. I SAID WE DIDN'T WANT YOU IN SUPERDUPER AT ALL.
OH, YOU SPITEFUL BITCH, WHAT THE FUCK DID YOU DO THAT FOR--?
BECAUSE IT'S TRUE.
YOU'RE HERE AS PUNISHMENT. OKAY, FINE. BUT IF YOU THINK YOU'RE GOING TO ENJOY IT AT THESE KIDS' EXPENSE, YOU CAN THINK AGAIN.

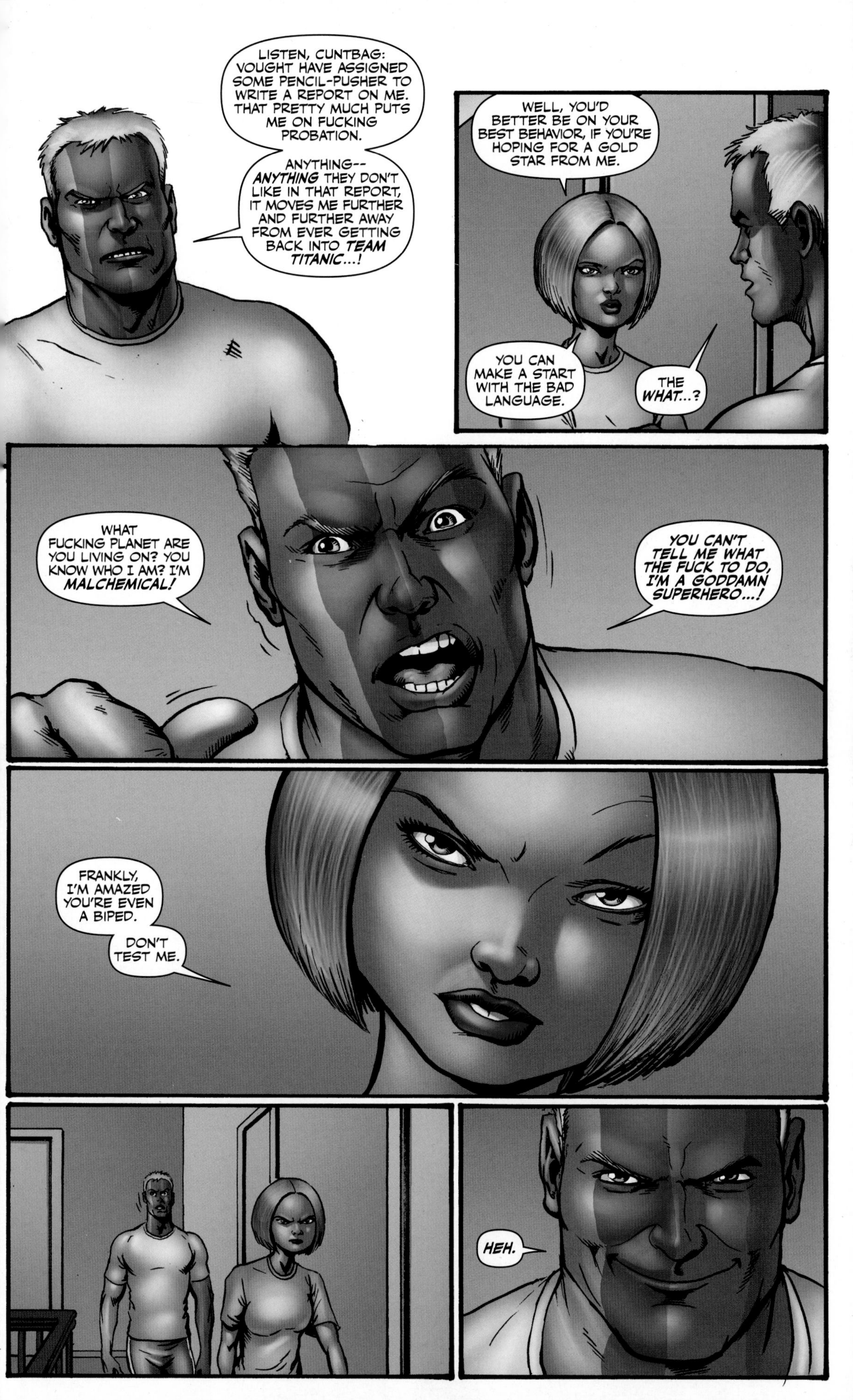

LISTEN, CUNTBAG: VOUGHT HAVE ASSIGNED SOME PENCIL-PUSHER TO WRITE A REPORT ON ME. THAT PRETTY MUCH PUTS ME ON FUCKING PROBATION.
ANYTHING-- *ANYTHING* THEY DON'T LIKE IN THAT REPORT, IT MOVES ME FURTHER AND FURTHER AWAY FROM EVER GETTING BACK INTO *TEAM TITANIC*...!
WELL, YOU'D BETTER BE ON YOUR BEST BEHAVIOR, IF YOU'RE HOPING FOR A GOLD STAR FROM ME.
YOU CAN MAKE A START WITH THE BAD LANGUAGE.
THE *WHAT*...?
WHAT FUCKING PLANET ARE YOU LIVING ON? YOU KNOW WHO I AM? I'M *MALCHEMICAL!*
YOU CAN'T TELL ME WHAT THE FUCK TO DO, I'M A GODDAMN SUPERHERO...!
FRANKLY, I'M AMAZED YOU'RE EVEN A BIPED.
DON'T TEST ME.
HEH.

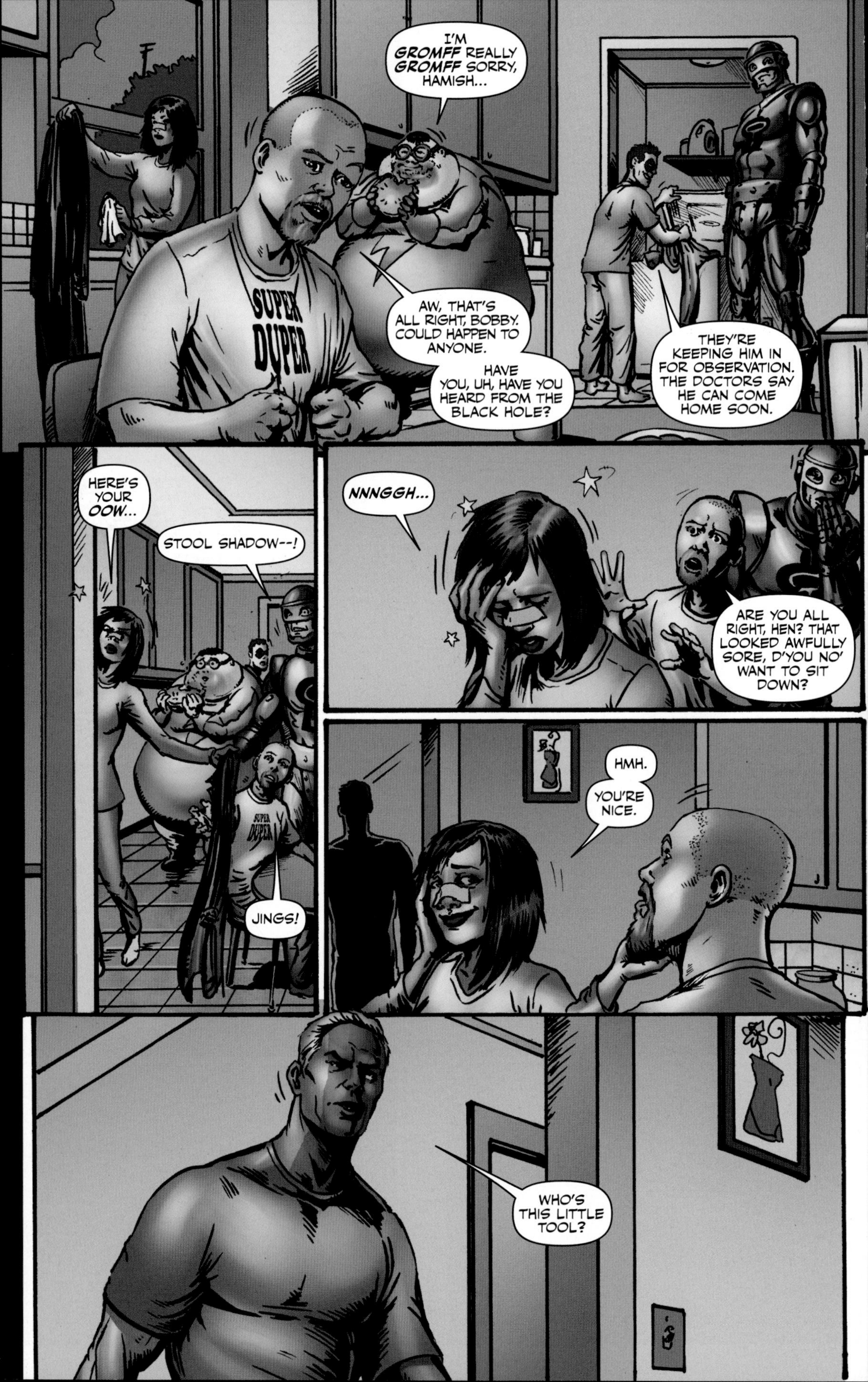
I'M GROMFF REALLY GROMFF SORRY, HAMISH...
AW, THAT'S ALL RIGHT, BOBBY. COULD HAPPEN TO ANYONE.
HAVE YOU, UH, HAVE YOU HEARD FROM THE BLACK HOLE?
THEY'RE KEEPING HIM IN FOR OBSERVATION. THE DOCTORS SAY HE CAN COME HOME SOON.
SUPER DUPER
HERE'S YOUR OOW...
STOOL SHADOW--!
JINGS!
NNNGGH...
ARE YOU ALL RIGHT, HEN? THAT LOOKED AWFULLY SORE, D'YOU NO' WANT TO SIT DOWN?
HMH.
YOU'RE NICE.
WHO'S THIS LITTLE TOOL?

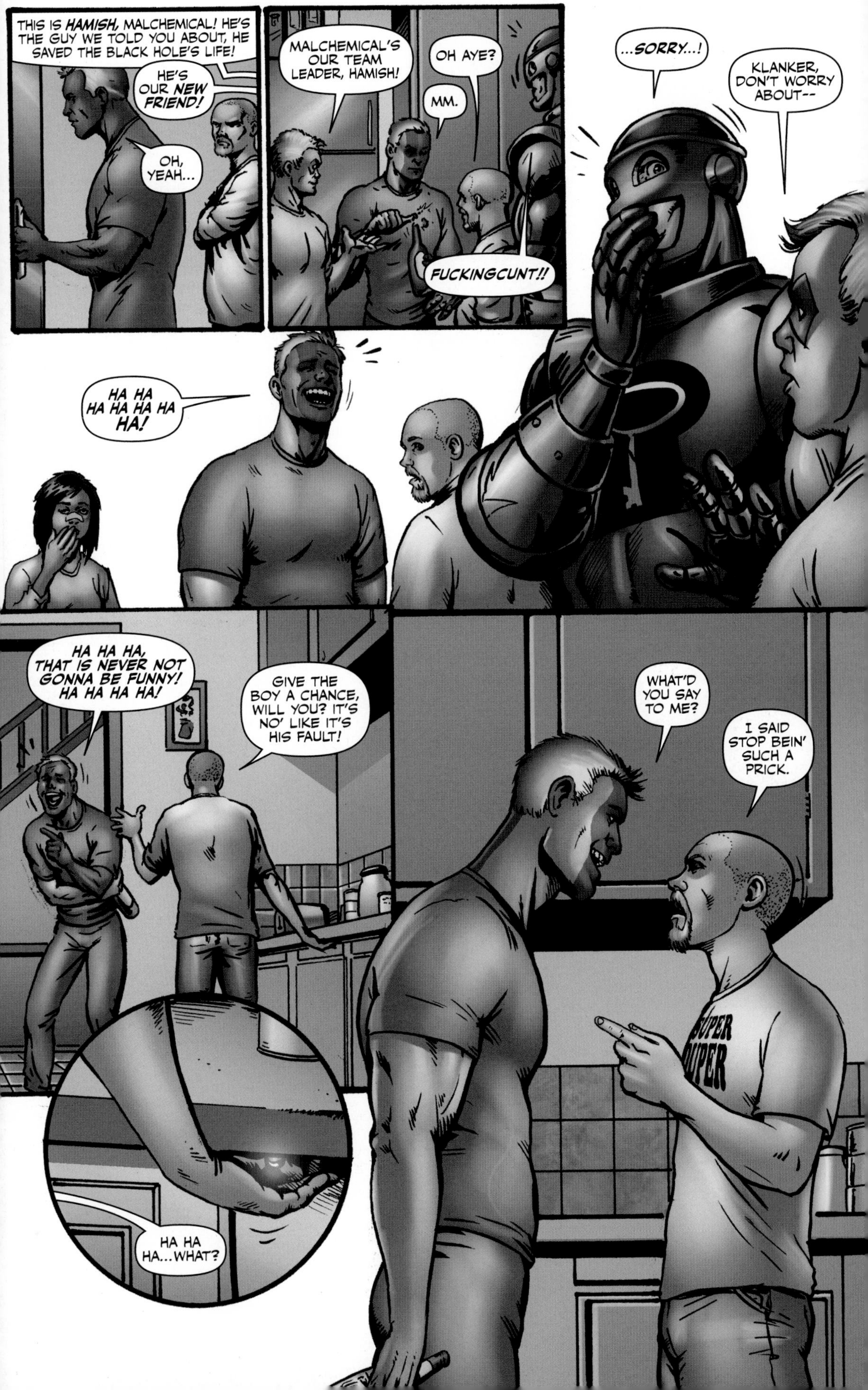
THIS IS HAMISH, MALCHEMICAL! HE'S THE GUY WE TOLD YOU ABOUT, HE SAVED THE BLACK HOLE'S LIFE!
HE'S OUR NEW FRIEND!
OH, YEAH...
MALCHEMICAL'S OUR TEAM LEADER, HAMISH!
OH AYE?
MM.
FUCKINGCUNT!!
...SORRY...!
KLANKER, DON'T WORRY ABOUT--
HA HA HA HA HA HA HA!
HA HA HA, THAT IS NEVER NOT GONNA BE FUNNY! HA HA HA HA!
GIVE THE BOY A CHANCE, WILL YOU? IT'S NO' LIKE IT'S HIS FAULT!
WHAT'D YOU SAY TO ME?
I SAID STOP BEIN' SUCH A PRICK.
SUPER DUPER
HA HA HA...WHAT?

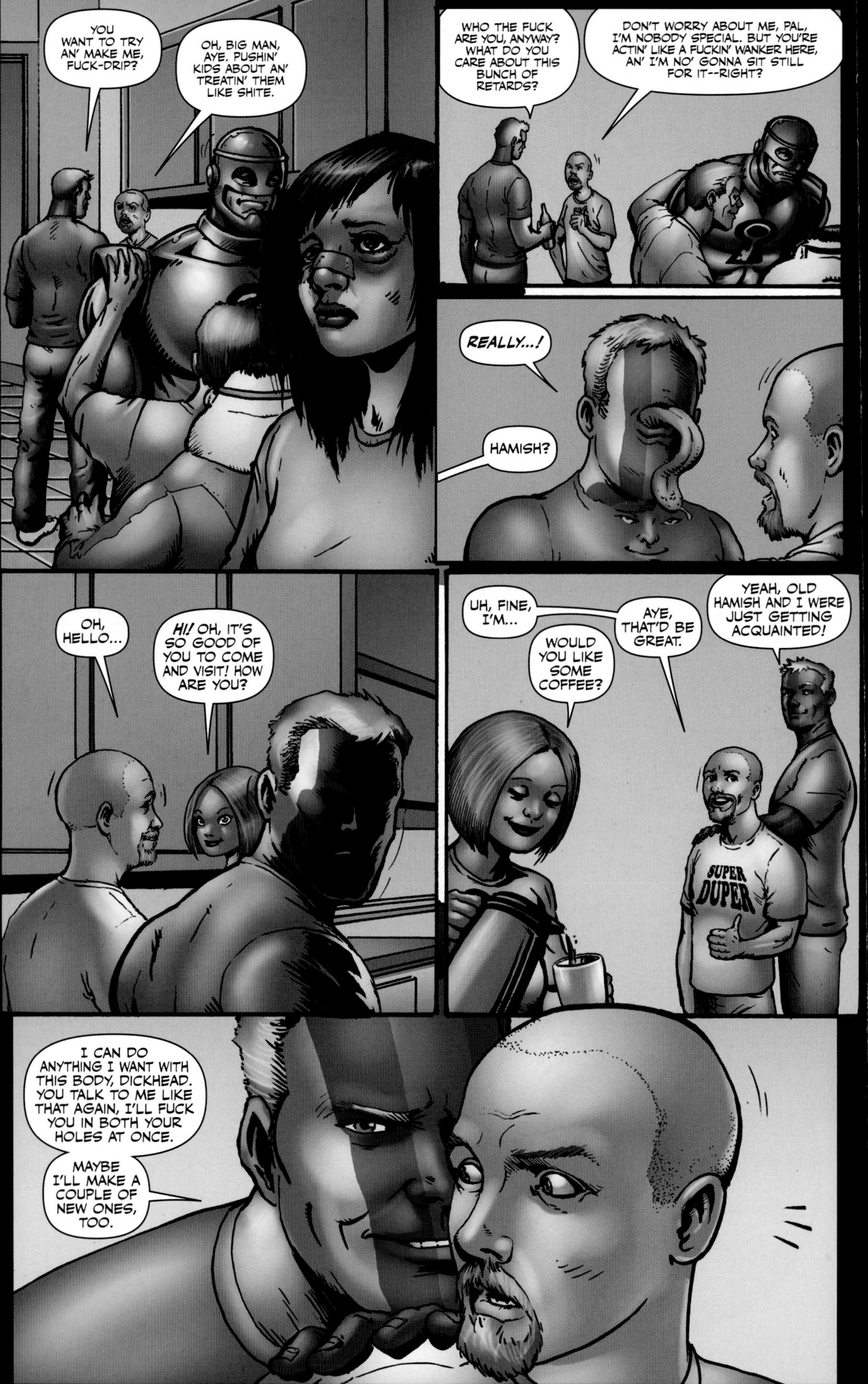
YOU WANT TO TRY AN' MAKE ME, FUCK-DRIP?
OH, BIG MAN, AYE. PUSHIN' KIDS ABOUT AN' TREATIN' THEM LIKE SHITE.
WHO THE FUCK ARE YOU, ANYWAY? WHAT DO YOU CARE ABOUT THIS BUNCH OF RETARDS?
DON'T WORRY ABOUT ME, PAL, I'M NOBODY SPECIAL. BUT YOU'RE ACTIN' LIKE A FUCKIN' WANKER HERE, AN' I'M NO' GONNA SIT STILL FOR IT--RIGHT?
REALLY...!
HAMISH?
OH, HELLO...
HI! OH, IT'S SO GOOD OF YOU TO COME AND VISIT! HOW ARE YOU?
UH, FINE, I'M...
WOULD YOU LIKE SOME COFFEE?
AYE, THAT'D BE GREAT.
YEAH, OLD HAMISH AND I WERE JUST GETTING ACQUAINTED!
SUPER DUPER
I CAN DO ANYTHING I WANT WITH THIS BODY, DICKHEAD. YOU TALK TO ME LIKE THAT AGAIN, I'LL FUCK YOU IN BOTH YOUR HOLES AT ONCE.
MAYBE I'LL MAKE A COUPLE OF NEW ONES, TOO.

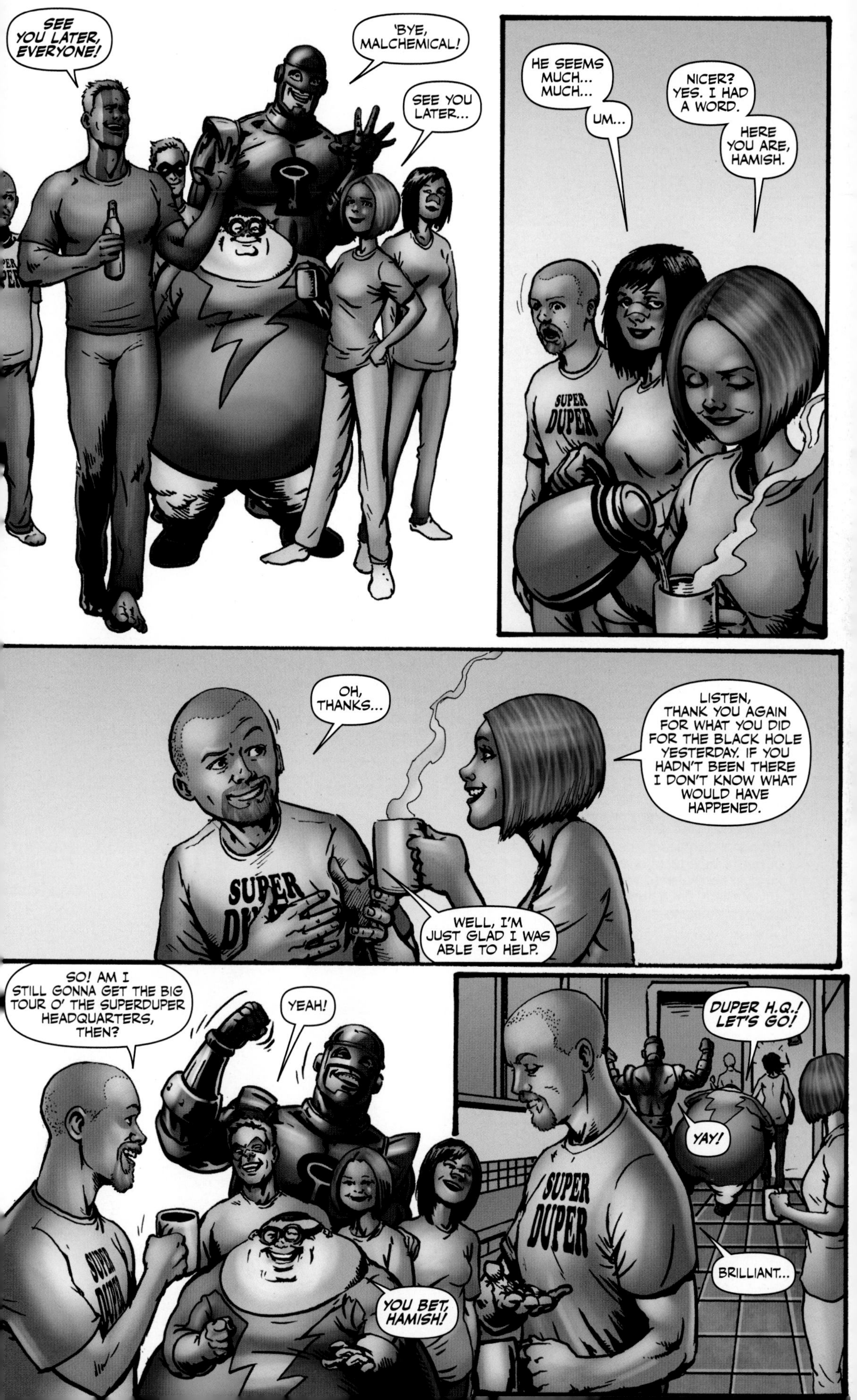
SEE YOU LATER, EVERYONE!
'BYE, MALCHEMICAL!
SEE YOU LATER...
HE SEEMS MUCH... MUCH...
UM...
NICER? YES. I HAD A WORD.
HERE YOU ARE, HAMISH.
OH, THANKS...
LISTEN, THANK YOU AGAIN FOR WHAT YOU DID FOR THE BLACK HOLE YESTERDAY. IF YOU HADN'T BEEN THERE I DON'T KNOW WHAT WOULD HAVE HAPPENED.
WELL, I'M JUST GLAD I WAS ABLE TO HELP.
SO! AM I STILL GONNA GET THE BIG TOUR O' THE SUPERDUPER HEADQUARTERS, THEN?
YEAH!
YOU BET, HAMISH!
DUPER H.Q.! LET'S GO!
YAY!
BRILLIANT...

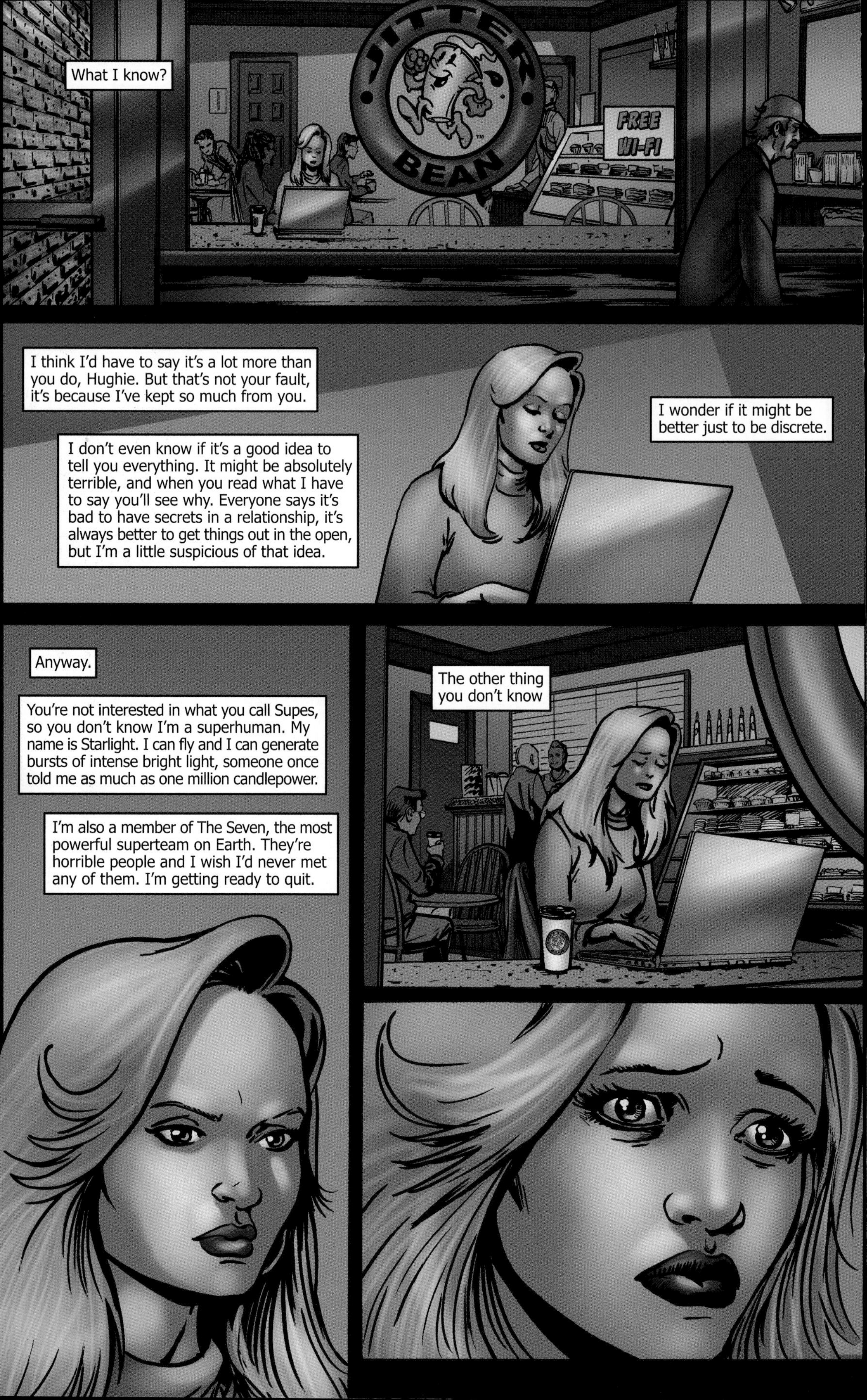
What I know?
JITTER BEAN
FREE WI-FI
I think I'd have to say it's a lot more than you do, Hughie. But that's not your fault, it's because I've kept so much from you.
I don't even know if it's a good idea to tell you everything. It might be absolutely terrible, and when you read what I have to say you'll see why. Everyone says it's bad to have secrets in a relationship, it's always better to get things out in the open, but I'm a little suspicious of that idea.
I wonder if it might be better just to be discrete.
Anyway.
You're not interested in what you call Supes, so you don't know I'm a superhuman. My name is Starlight. I can fly and I can generate bursts of intense bright light, someone once told me as much as one million candlepower.
I'm also a member of The Seven, the most powerful superteam on Earth. They're horrible people and I wish I'd never met any of them. I'm getting ready to quit.
The other thing you don't know

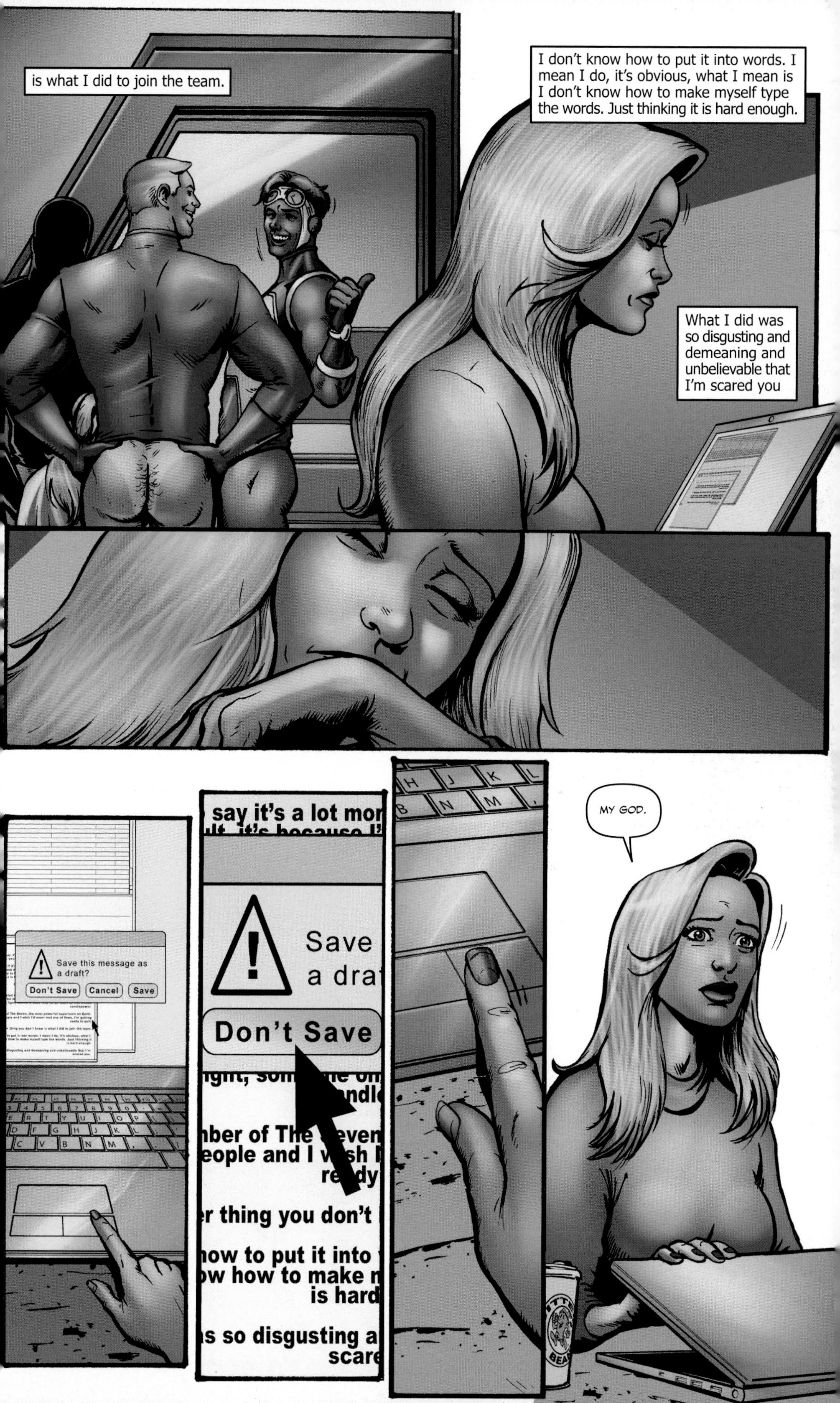
is what I did to join the team.
I don't know how to put it into words. I mean I do, it's obvious, what I mean is I don't know how to make myself type the words. Just thinking it is hard enough.
What I did was so disgusting and demeaning and unbelievable that I'm scared you
Save this message as a draft?
Don't Save
Cancel
Save
Don't Save
MY GOD.

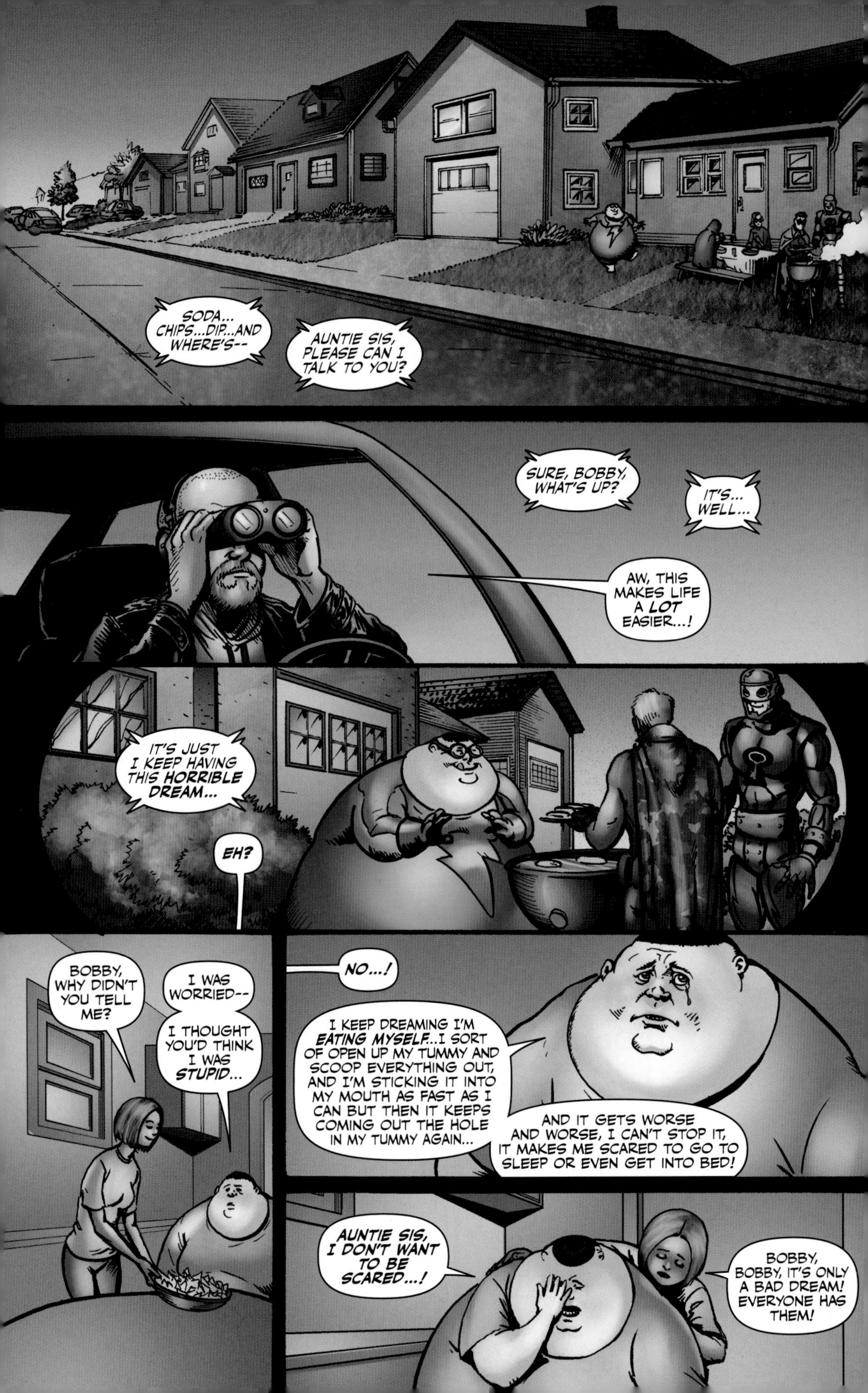
SODA... CHIPS...DIP...AND WHERE'S--
AUNTIE SIS, PLEASE CAN I TALK TO YOU?
SURE, BOBBY, WHAT'S UP?
IT'S... WELL...
AW, THIS MAKES LIFE A LOT EASIER...!
IT'S JUST I KEEP HAVING THIS HORRIBLE DREAM...
EH?
BOBBY, WHY DIDN'T YOU TELL ME?
I WAS WORRIED--
I THOUGHT YOU'D THINK I WAS STUPID...
NO...!
I KEEP DREAMING I'M EATING MYSELF...I SORT OF OPEN UP MY TUMMY AND SCOOP EVERYTHING OUT, AND I'M STICKING IT INTO MY MOUTH AS FAST AS I CAN BUT THEN IT KEEPS COMING OUT THE HOLE IN MY TUMMY AGAIN...
AND IT GETS WORSE AND WORSE, I CAN'T STOP IT, IT MAKES ME SCARED TO GO TO SLEEP OR EVEN GET INTO BED!
AUNTIE SIS, I DON'T WANT TO BE SCARED...!
BOBBY, BOBBY, IT'S ONLY A BAD DREAM! EVERYONE HAS THEM!

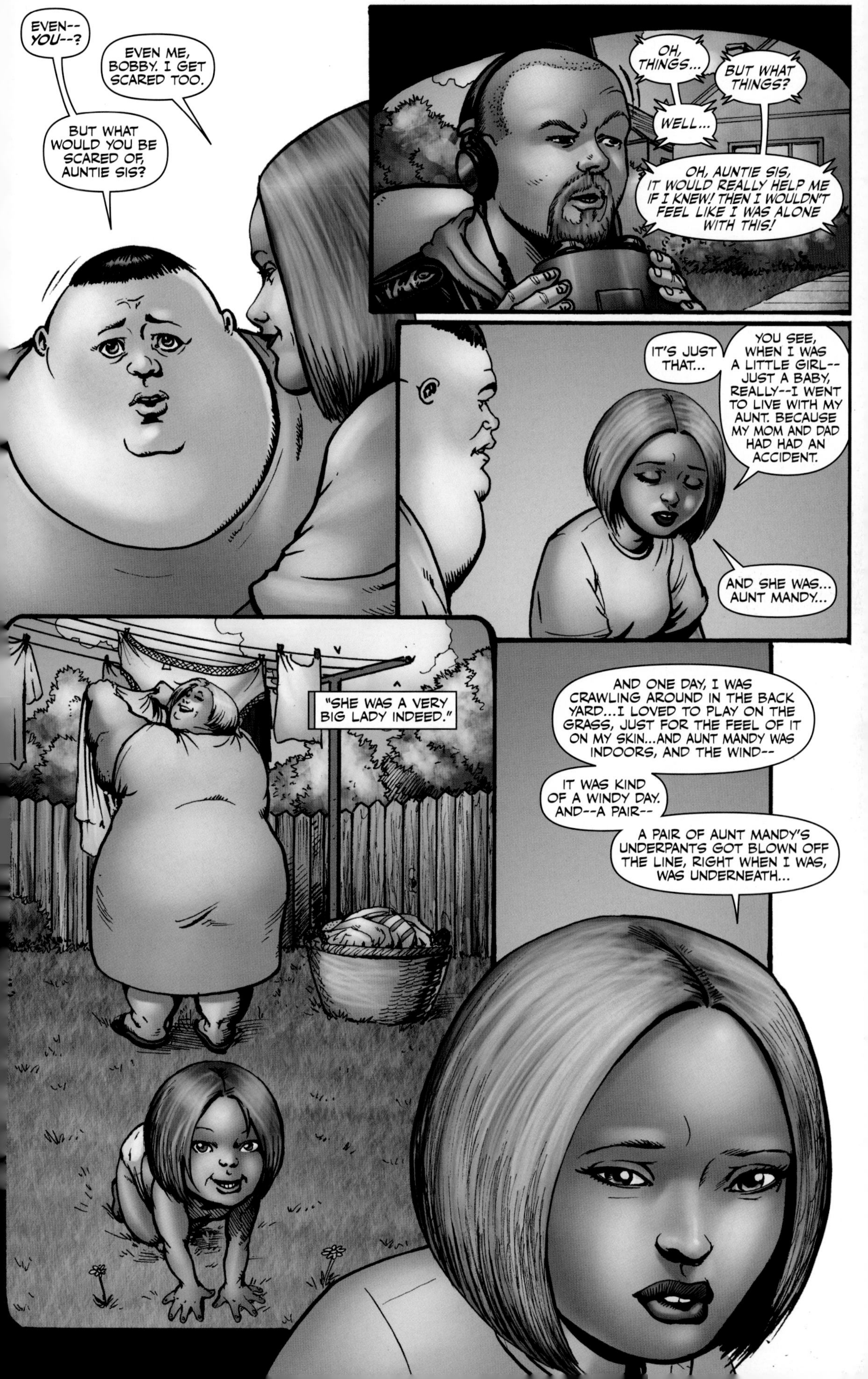
EVEN--
YOU--?
EVEN ME, BOBBY. I GET SCARED TOO.
BUT WHAT WOULD YOU BE SCARED OF, AUNTIE SIS?
OH, THINGS...
BUT WHAT THINGS?
WELL...
OH, AUNTIE SIS, IT WOULD REALLY HELP ME IF I KNEW! THEN I WOULDN'T FEEL LIKE I WAS ALONE WITH THIS!
IT'S JUST THAT...
YOU SEE, WHEN I WAS A LITTLE GIRL-- JUST A BABY, REALLY--I WENT TO LIVE WITH MY AUNT. BECAUSE MY MOM AND DAD HAD HAD AN ACCIDENT.
AND SHE WAS... AUNT MANDY...
"SHE WAS A VERY BIG LADY INDEED."
AND ONE DAY, I WAS CRAWLING AROUND IN THE BACK YARD...I LOVED TO PLAY ON THE GRASS, JUST FOR THE FEEL OF IT ON MY SKIN...AND AUNT MANDY WAS INDOORS, AND THE WIND--
IT WAS KIND OF A WINDY DAY. AND--A PAIR--
A PAIR OF AUNT MANDY'S UNDERPANTS GOT BLOWN OFF THE LINE, RIGHT WHEN I WAS, WAS UNDERNEATH...

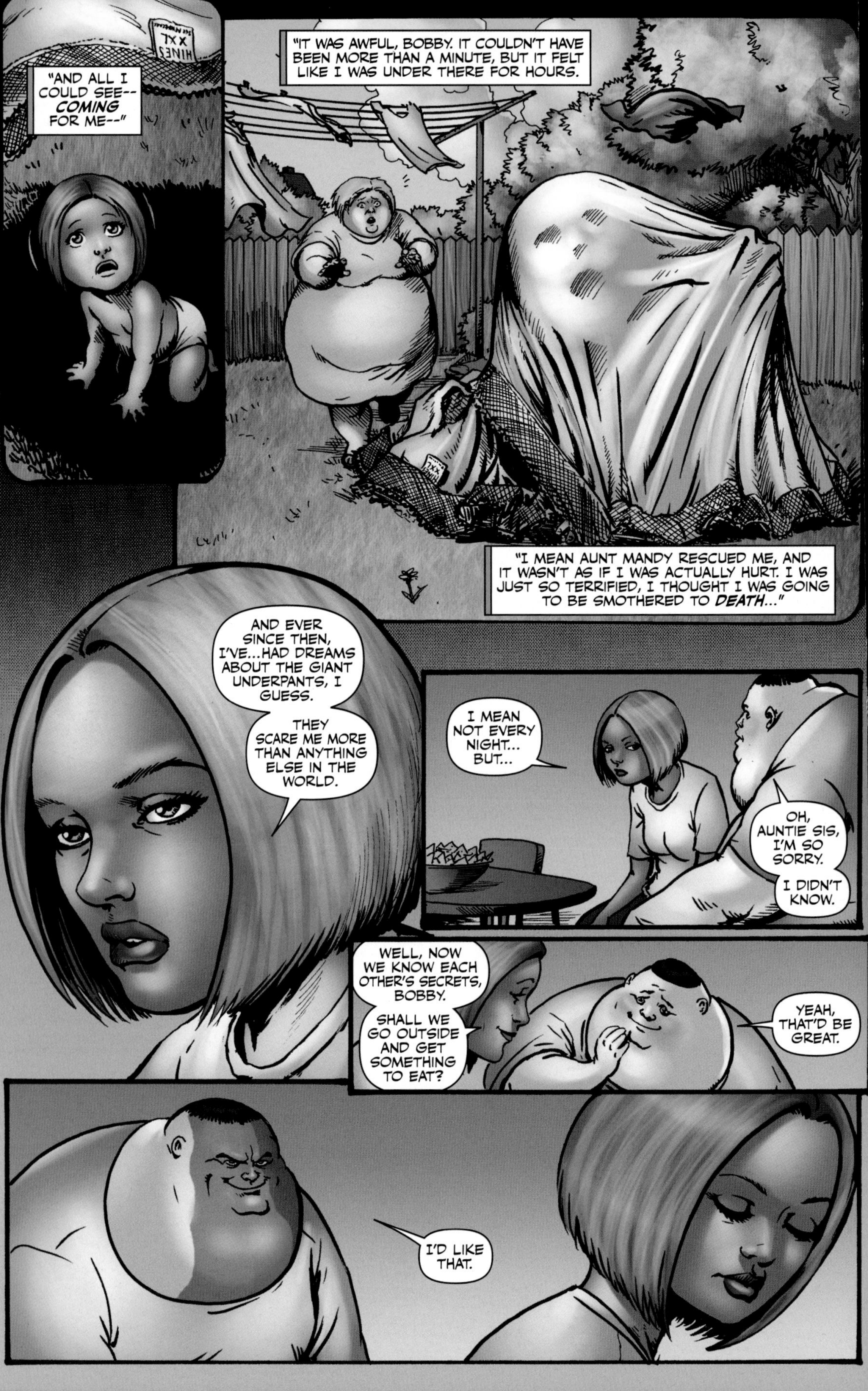
"AND ALL I COULD SEE-- *COMING* FOR ME--"
"IT WAS AWFUL, BOBBY. IT COULDN'T HAVE BEEN MORE THAN A MINUTE, BUT IT FELT LIKE I WAS UNDER THERE FOR HOURS.
"I MEAN AUNT MANDY RESCUED ME, AND IT WASN'T AS IF I WAS ACTUALLY HURT. I WAS JUST SO TERRIFIED, I THOUGHT I WAS GOING TO BE SMOTHERED TO *DEATH*..."
AND EVER SINCE THEN, I'VE...HAD DREAMS ABOUT THE GIANT UNDERPANTS, I GUESS.
THEY SCARE ME MORE THAN ANYTHING ELSE IN THE WORLD.
I MEAN NOT EVERY NIGHT... BUT...
OH, AUNTIE SIS, I'M SO SORRY.
I DIDN'T KNOW.
WELL, NOW WE KNOW EACH OTHER'S SECRETS, BOBBY.
SHALL WE GO OUTSIDE AND GET SOMETHING TO EAT?
YEAH, THAT'D BE GREAT.
I'D LIKE THAT.

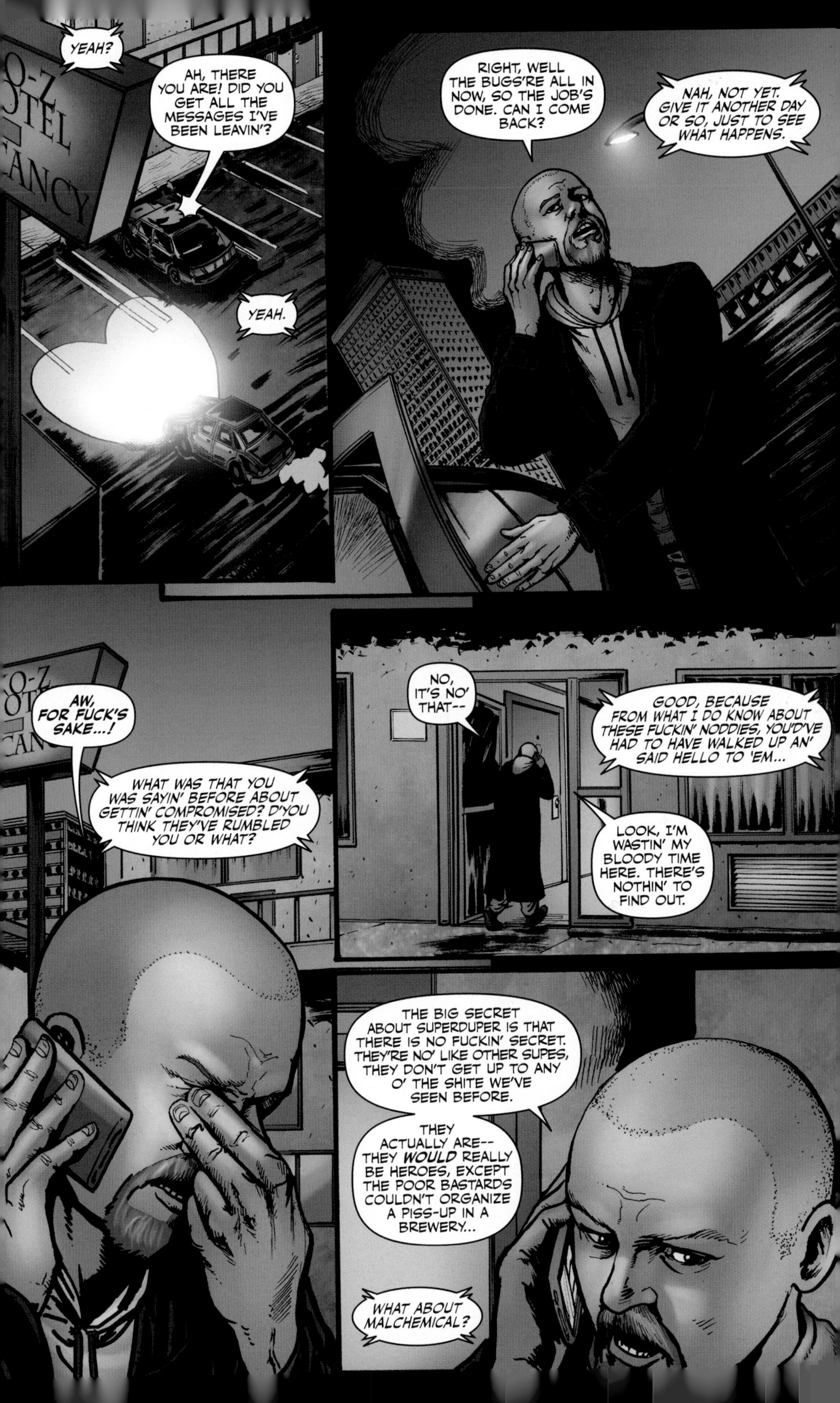
YEAH?
AH, THERE YOU ARE! DID YOU GET ALL THE MESSAGES I'VE BEEN LEAVIN'?
YEAH.
RIGHT, WELL THE BUGS'RE ALL IN NOW, SO THE JOB'S DONE. CAN I COME BACK?
NAH, NOT YET. GIVE IT ANOTHER DAY OR SO, JUST TO SEE WHAT HAPPENS.
AW, FOR FUCK'S SAKE...!
WHAT WAS THAT YOU WAS SAYIN' BEFORE ABOUT GETTIN' COMPROMISED? D'YOU THINK THEY'VE RUMBLED YOU OR WHAT?
NO, IT'S NO' THAT--
GOOD, BECAUSE FROM WHAT I DO KNOW ABOUT THESE FUCKIN' NODDIES, YOU'D'VE HAD TO HAVE WALKED UP AN' SAID HELLO TO 'EM...
LOOK, I'M WASTIN' MY BLOODY TIME HERE. THERE'S NOTHIN' TO FIND OUT.
THE BIG SECRET ABOUT SUPERDUPER IS THAT THERE IS NO FUCKIN' SECRET. THEY'RE NO' LIKE OTHER SUPES, THEY DON'T GET UP TO ANY O' THE SHITE WE'VE SEEN BEFORE.
THEY ACTUALLY ARE-- THEY *WOULD* REALLY BE HEROES, EXCEPT THE POOR BASTARDS COULDN'T ORGANIZE A PISS-UP IN A BREWERY...
WHAT ABOUT MALCHEMICAL?

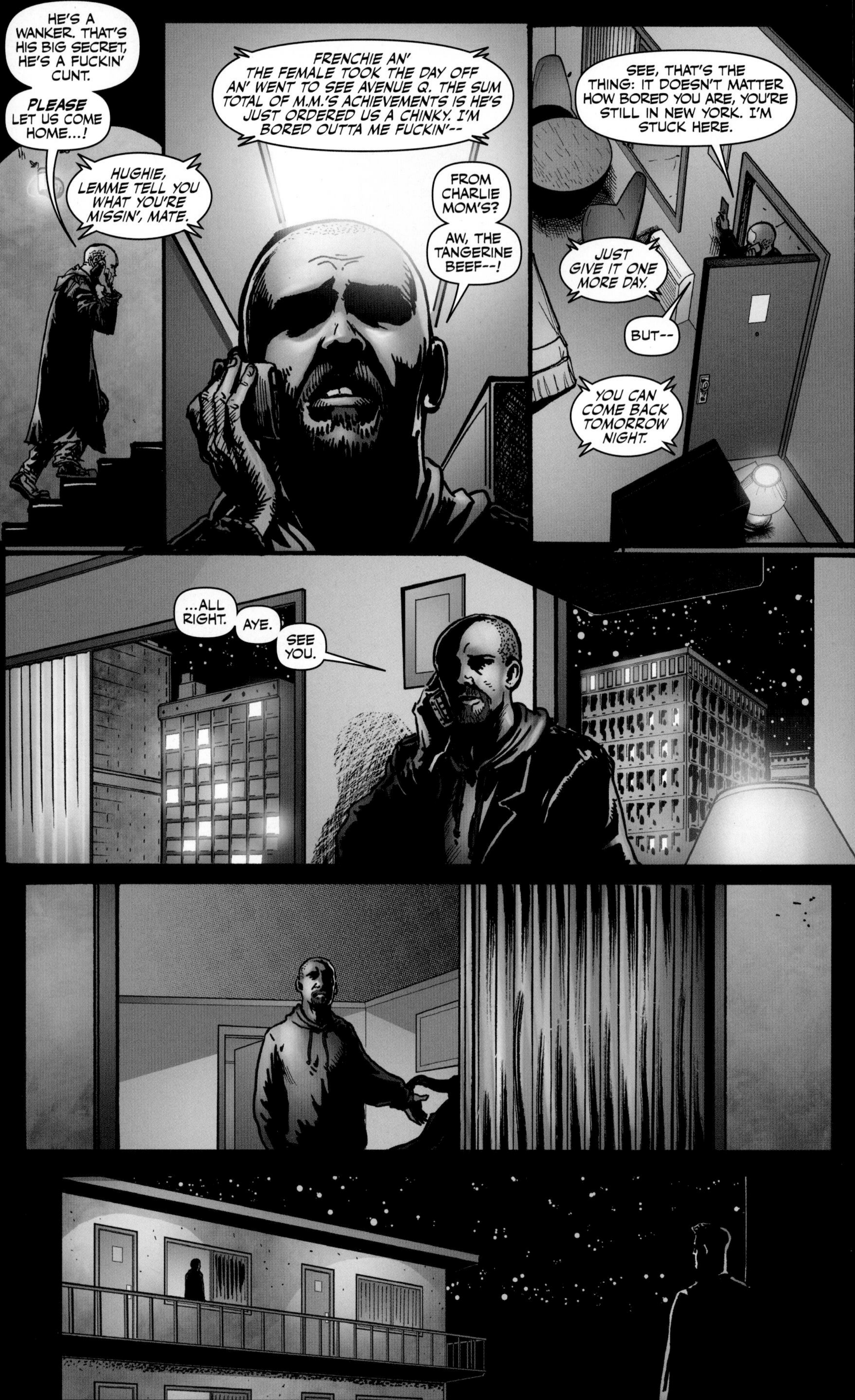

HE'S A WANKER. THAT'S HIS BIG SECRET, HE'S A FUCKIN' CUNT.
PLEASE LET US COME HOME...!
HUGHIE, LEMME TELL YOU WHAT YOU'RE MISSIN', MATE.
FRENCHIE AN' THE FEMALE TOOK THE DAY OFF AN' WENT TO SEE AVENUE Q. THE SUM TOTAL OF M.M.'S ACHIEVEMENTS IS HE'S JUST ORDERED US A CHINKY. I'M BORED OUTTA ME FUCKIN'--
FROM CHARLIE MOM'S?
AW, THE TANGERINE BEEF--!
SEE, THAT'S THE THING: IT DOESN'T MATTER HOW BORED YOU ARE, YOU'RE STILL IN NEW YORK. I'M STUCK HERE.
JUST GIVE IT ONE MORE DAY.
BUT--
YOU CAN COME BACK TOMORROW NIGHT.
...ALL RIGHT.
AYE.
SEE YOU.

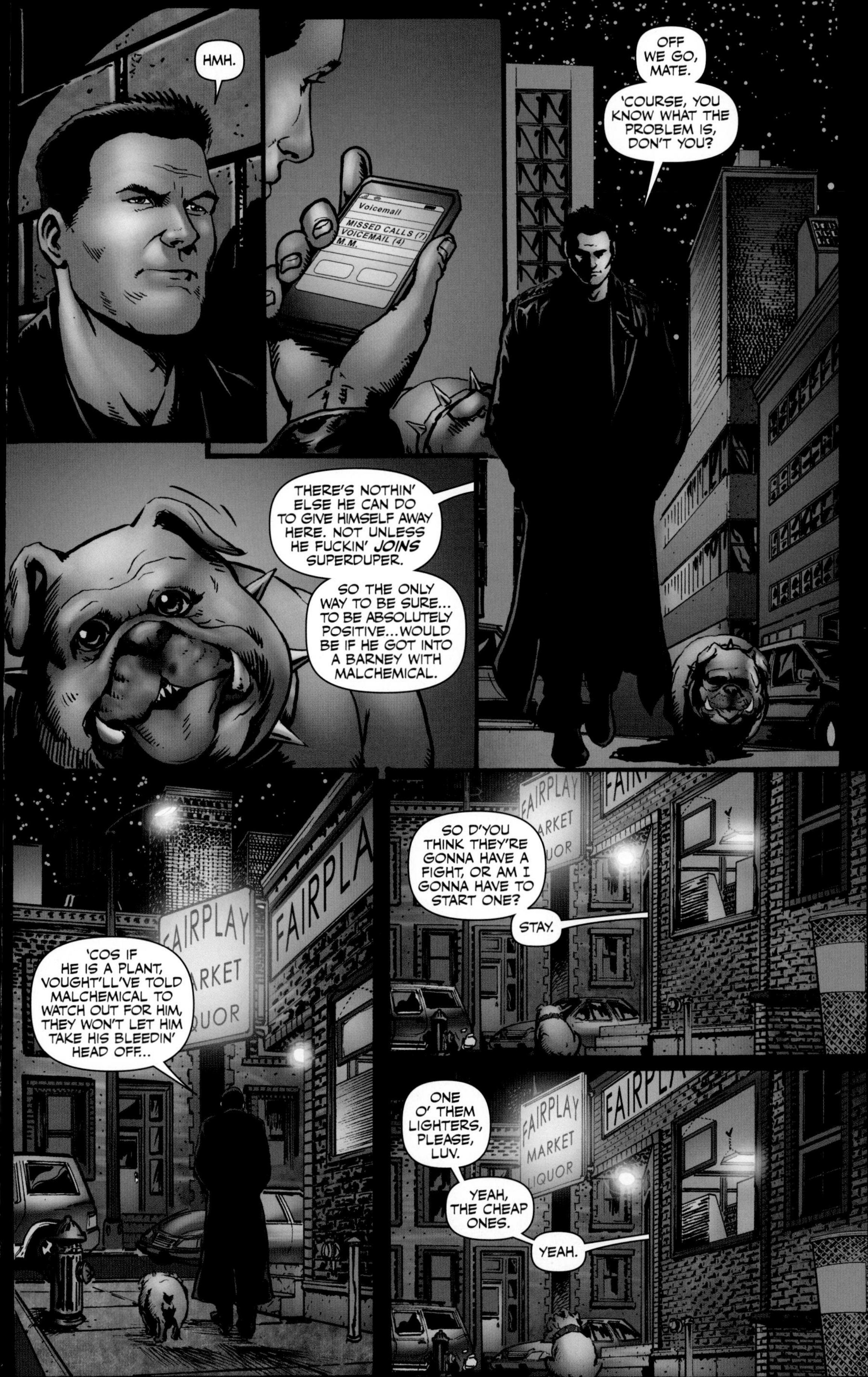
HMH.
Voicemail
MISSED CALLS (7)
VOICEMAIL (4)
M.M.
OFF WE GO, MATE.
'COURSE, YOU KNOW WHAT THE PROBLEM IS, DON'T YOU?
THERE'S NOTHIN' ELSE HE CAN DO TO GIVE HIMSELF AWAY HERE. NOT UNLESS HE FUCKIN' *JOINS* SUPERDUPER.
SO THE ONLY WAY TO BE SURE... TO BE ABSOLUTELY POSITIVE...WOULD BE IF HE GOT INTO A BARNEY WITH MALCHEMICAL.
FAIRPLAY
FAIRPLAY MARKET LIQUOR
'COS IF HE IS A PLANT, VOUGHT'LL'VE TOLD MALCHEMICAL TO WATCH OUT FOR HIM, THEY WON'T LET HIM TAKE HIS BLEEDIN' HEAD OFF...
SO D'YOU THINK THEY'RE GONNA HAVE A FIGHT, OR AM I GONNA HAVE TO START ONE?
STAY.
ONE O' THEM LIGHTERS, PLEASE, LUV.
YEAH, THE CHEAP ONES.
YEAH.

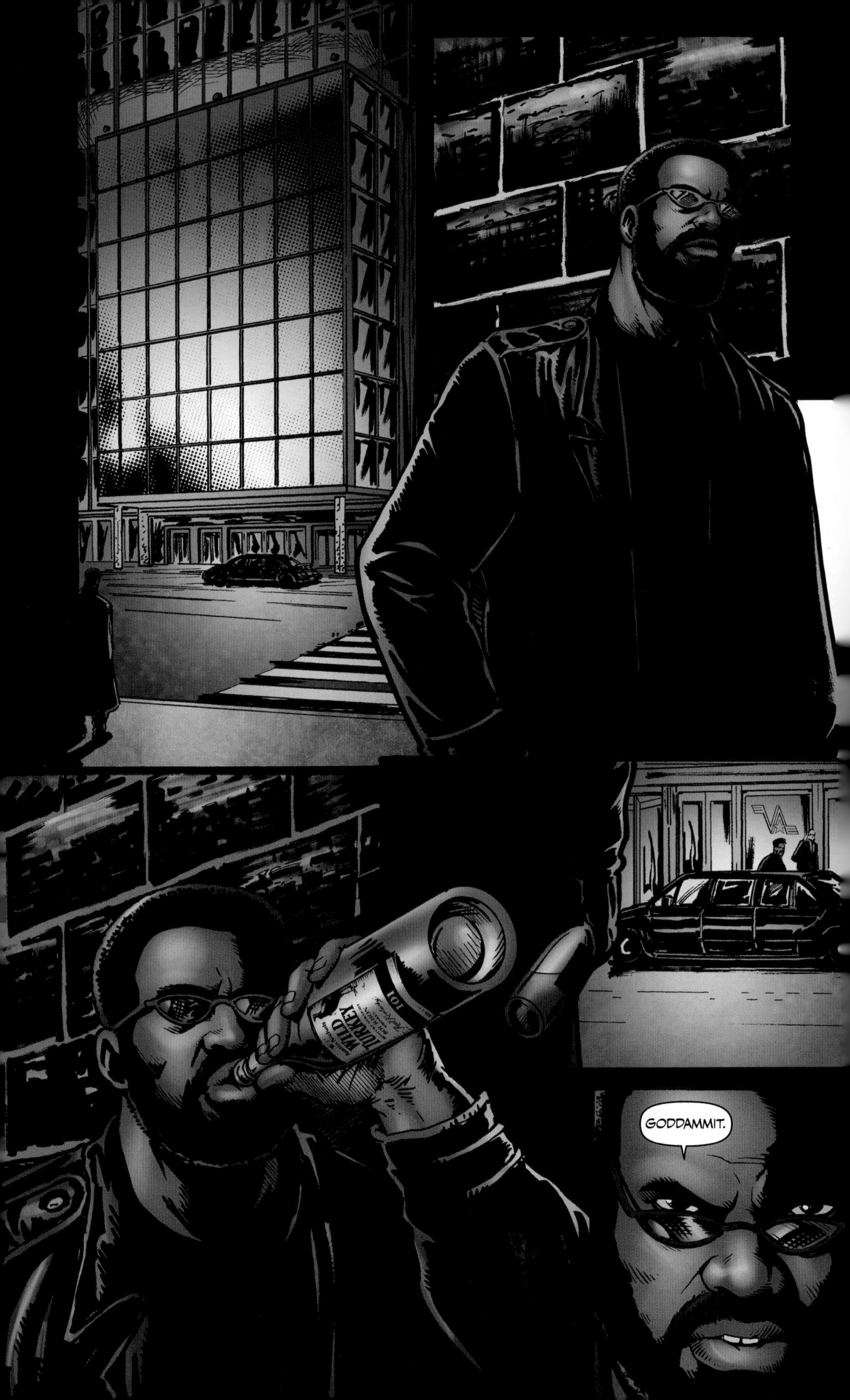
WILD
TURKEY
101
GODDAMMIT.

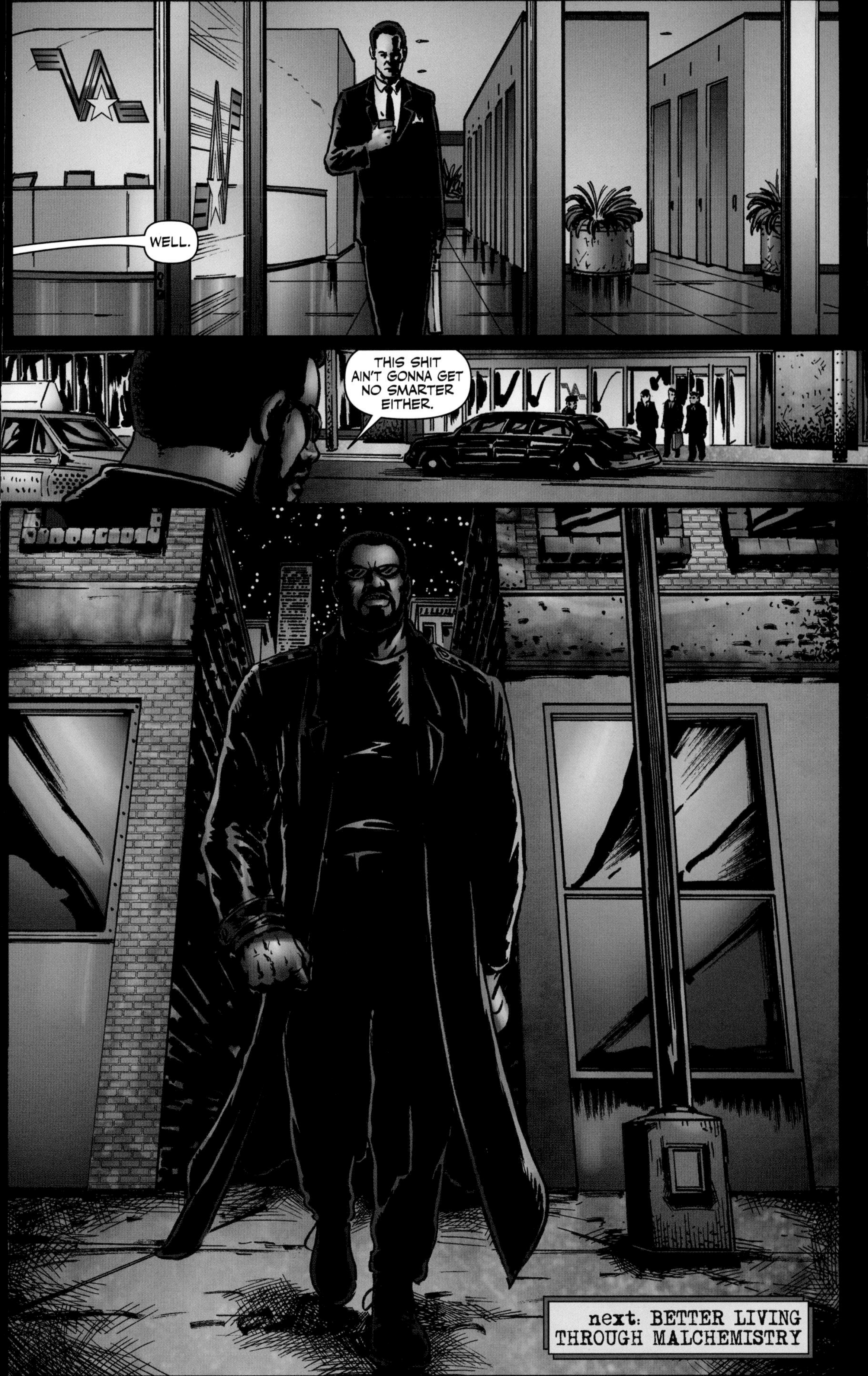
WELL.
THIS SHIT AIN'T GONNA GET NO SMARTER EITHER.
next: BETTER LIVING THROUGH MALCHEMISTRY

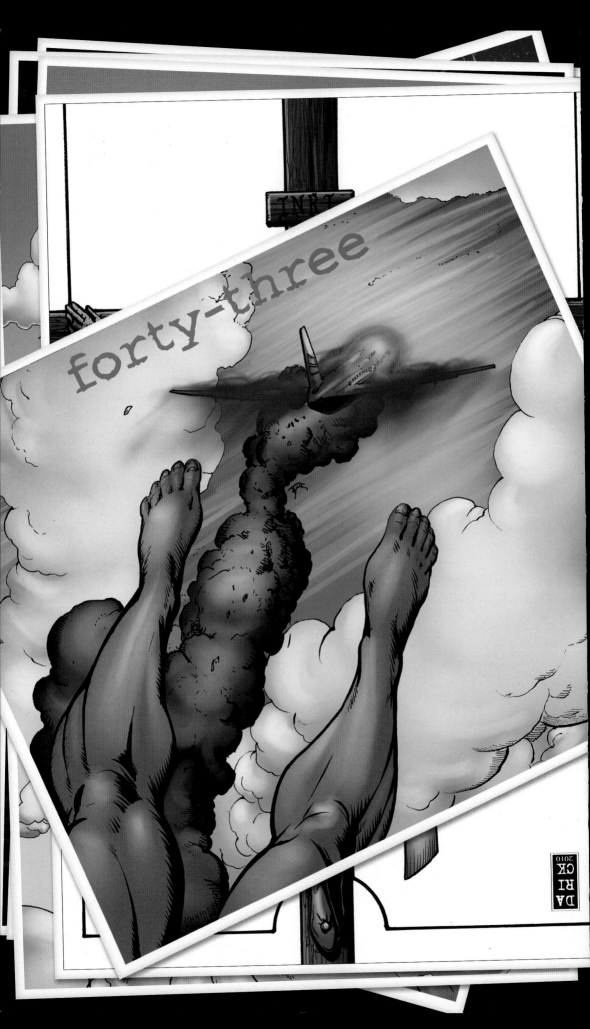

forty-three

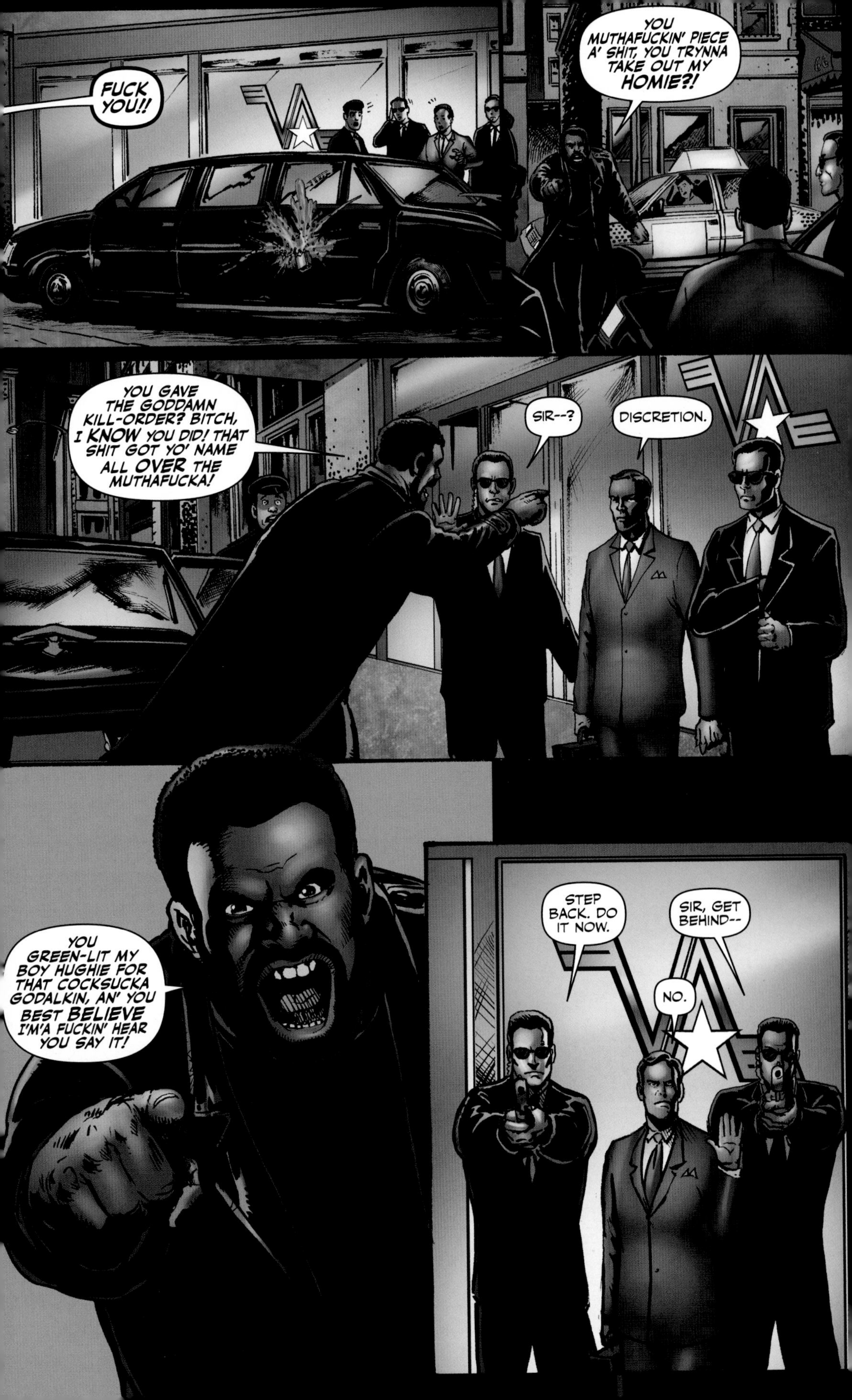
FUCK YOU!!
YOU MUTHAFUCKIN' PIECE A' SHIT, YOU TRYNNA TAKE OUT MY HOMIE?!
YOU GAVE THE GODDAMN KILL-ORDER? BITCH, I KNOW YOU DID! THAT SHIT GOT YO' NAME ALL OVER THE MUTHAFUCKA!
SIR--?
DISCRETION.
YOU GREEN-LIT MY BOY HUGHIE FOR THAT COCKSUCKA GODALKIN, AN' YOU BEST BELIEVE I'M'A FUCKIN' HEAR YOU SAY IT!
STEP BACK. DO IT NOW.
SIR, GET BEHIND--
NO.

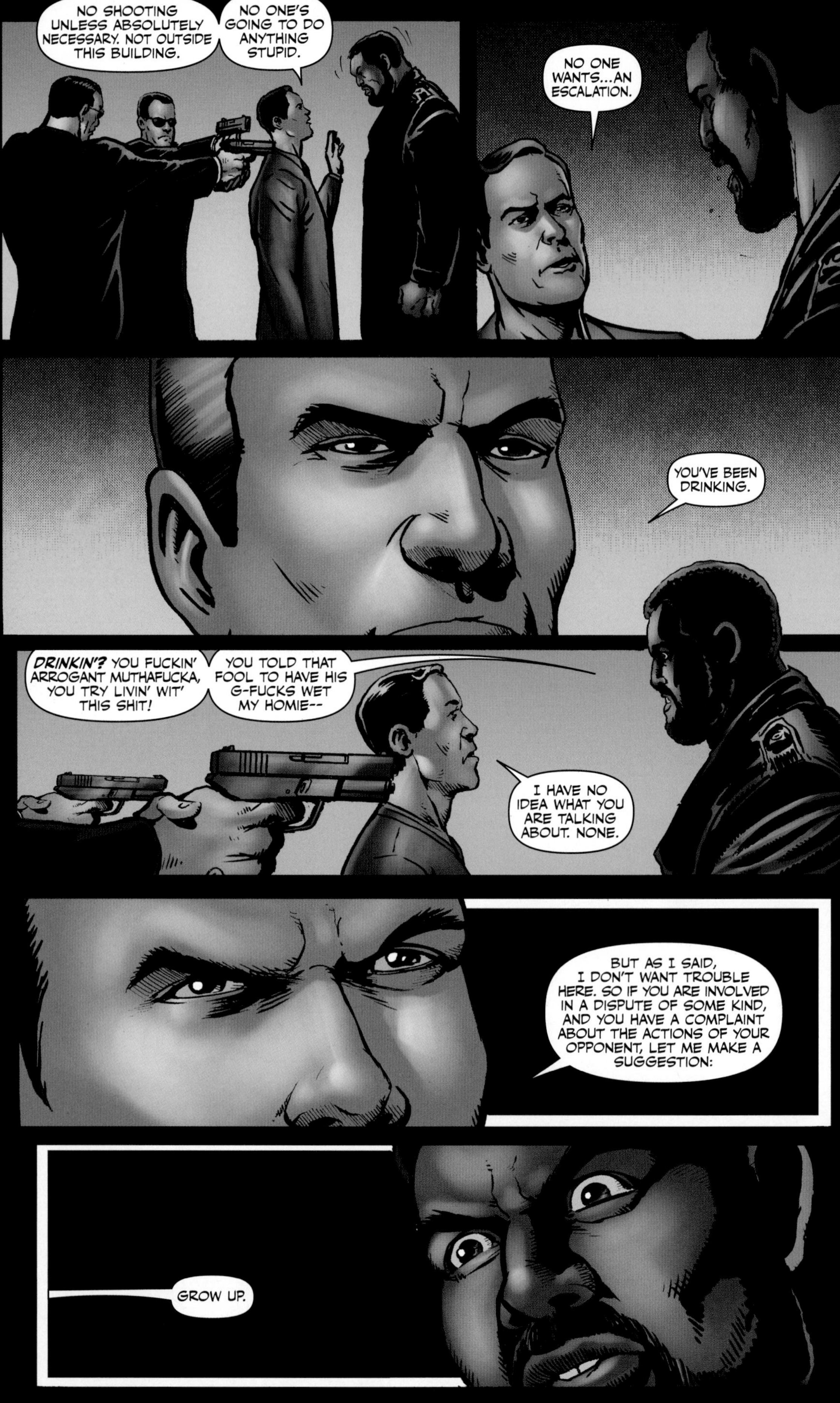
NO SHOOTING UNLESS ABSOLUTELY NECESSARY. NOT OUTSIDE THIS BUILDING.
NO ONE'S GOING TO DO ANYTHING STUPID.
NO ONE WANTS...AN ESCALATION.
YOU'VE BEEN DRINKING.
DRINKIN'? YOU FUCKIN' ARROGANT MUTHAFUCKA, YOU TRY LIVIN' WIT' THIS SHIT!
YOU TOLD THAT FOOL TO HAVE HIS G-FUCKS WET MY HOMIE--
I HAVE NO IDEA WHAT YOU ARE TALKING ABOUT. NONE.
BUT AS I SAID, I DON'T WANT TROUBLE HERE. SO IF YOU ARE INVOLVED IN A DISPUTE OF SOME KIND, AND YOU HAVE A COMPLAINT ABOUT THE ACTIONS OF YOUR OPPONENT, LET ME MAKE A SUGGESTION:
GROW UP.

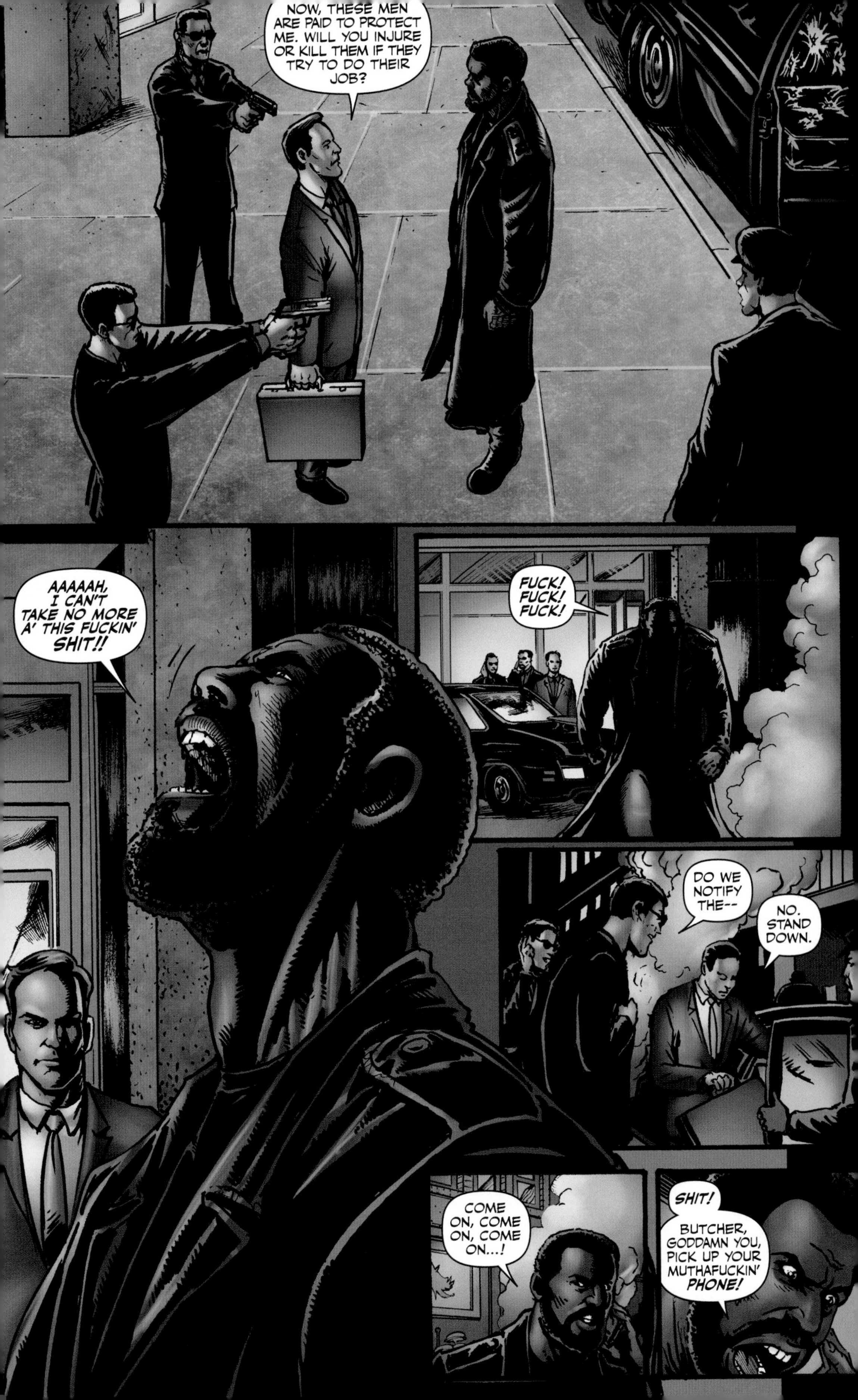
NOW, THESE MEN ARE PAID TO PROTECT ME. WILL YOU INJURE OR KILL THEM IF THEY TRY TO DO THEIR JOB?
AAAAAH, I CAN'T TAKE NO MORE A' THIS FUCKIN' SHIT!!
FUCK! FUCK! FUCK!
DO WE NOTIFY THE--
NO. STAND DOWN.
COME ON, COME ON, COME ON...!
SHIT!
BUTCHER, GODDAMN YOU, PICK UP YOUR MUTHAFUCKIN' PHONE!

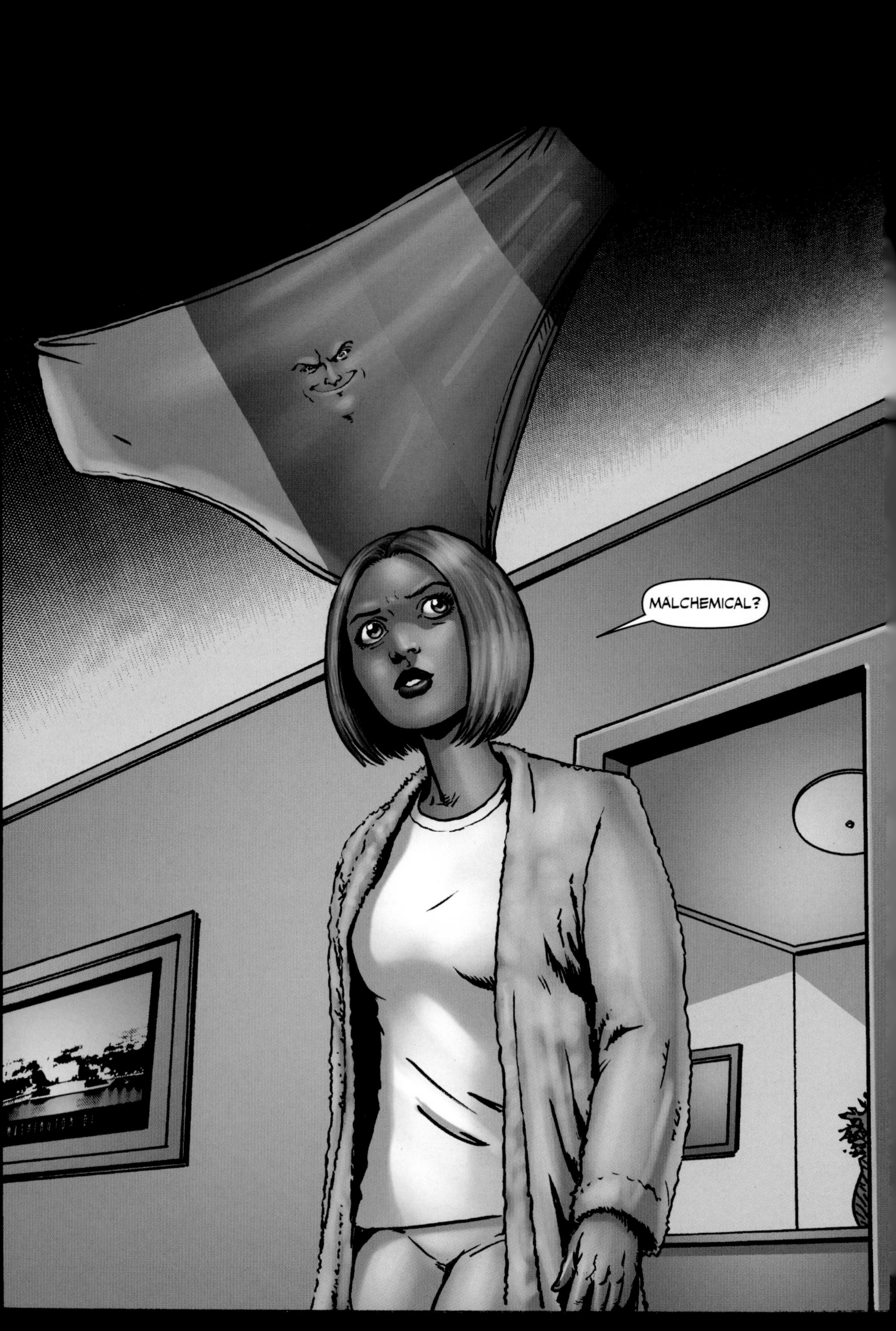
MALCHEMICAL?

THE INNOCENTS
conclusion

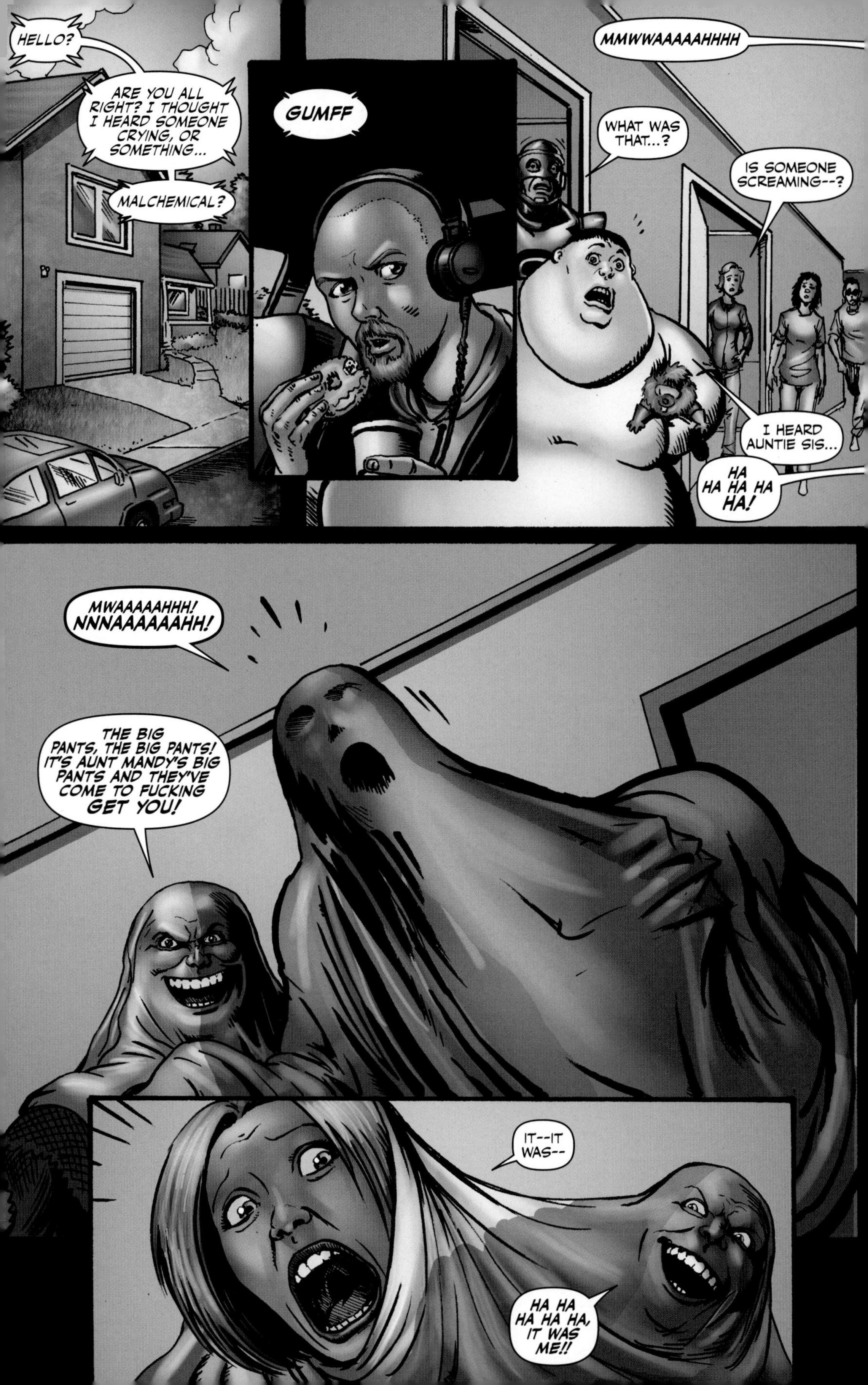
HELLO?
ARE YOU ALL RIGHT? I THOUGHT I HEARD SOMEONE CRYING, OR SOMETHING...
MALCHEMICAL?
GUMFF
MMWWAAAAAHHHH
WHAT WAS THAT...?
IS SOMEONE SCREAMING--?
I HEARD AUNTIE SIS...
HA HA HA HA HA!
MWAAAAAHHH! NNNAAAAAAHH!
THE BIG PANTS, THE BIG PANTS! IT'S AUNT MANDY'S BIG PANTS AND THEY'VE COME TO FUCKING GET YOU!
IT--IT WAS--
HA HA HA HA HA, IT WAS ME!!

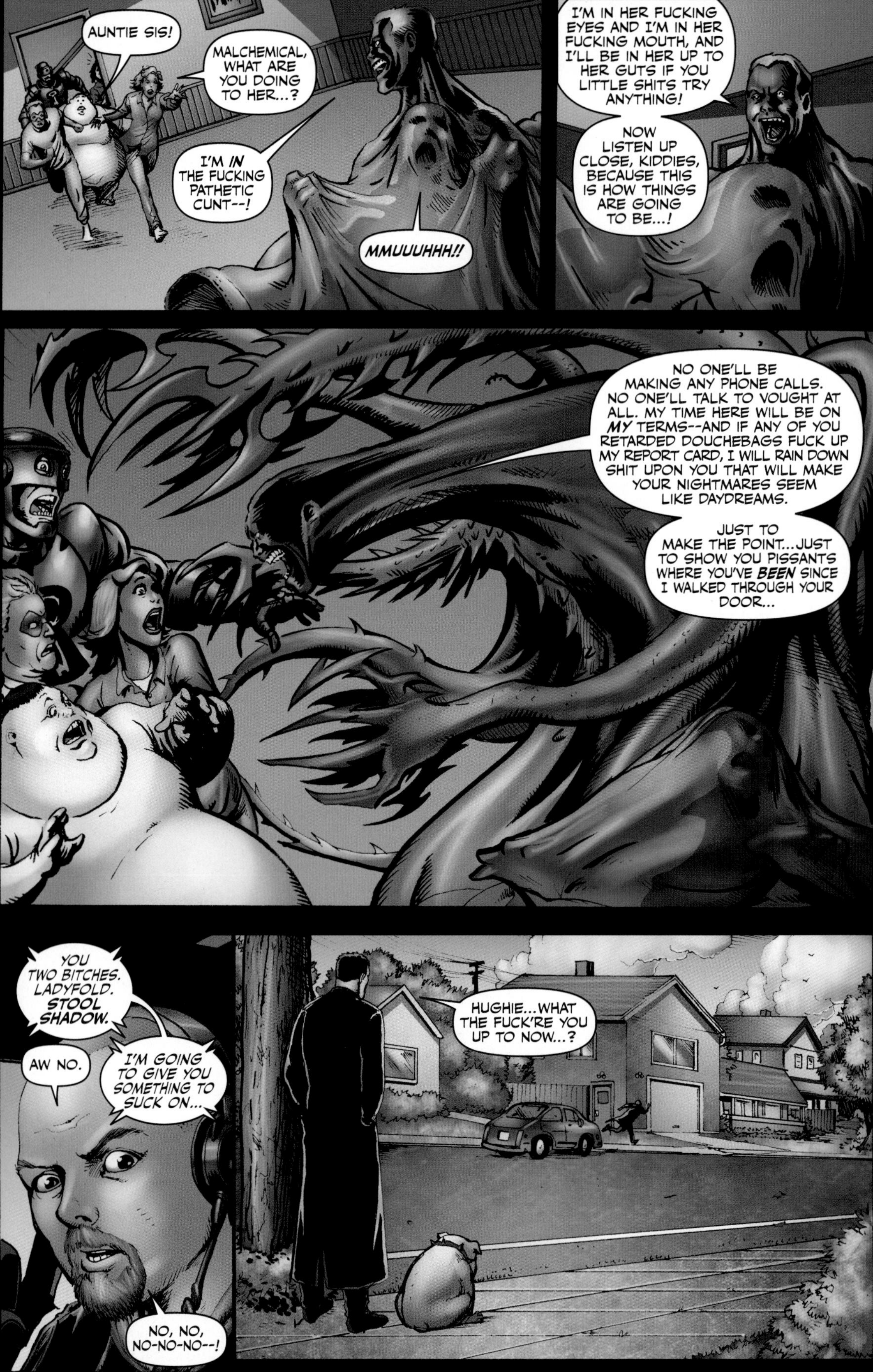
AUNTIE SIS!
MALCHEMICAL, WHAT ARE YOU DOING TO HER...?
I'M IN THE FUCKING PATHETIC CUNT--!
MMUUUHHH!!
I'M IN HER FUCKING EYES AND I'M IN HER FUCKING MOUTH, AND I'LL BE IN HER UP TO HER GUTS IF YOU LITTLE SHITS TRY ANYTHING!
NOW LISTEN UP CLOSE, KIDDIES, BECAUSE THIS IS HOW THINGS ARE GOING TO BE...!
NO ONE'LL BE MAKING ANY PHONE CALLS. NO ONE'LL TALK TO VOUGHT AT ALL. MY TIME HERE WILL BE ON MY TERMS--AND IF ANY OF YOU RETARDED DOUCHEBAGS FUCK UP MY REPORT CARD, I WILL RAIN DOWN SHIT UPON YOU THAT WILL MAKE YOUR NIGHTMARES SEEM LIKE DAYDREAMS.
JUST TO MAKE THE POINT...JUST TO SHOW YOU PISSANTS WHERE YOU'VE BEEN SINCE I WALKED THROUGH YOUR DOOR...
YOU TWO BITCHES. LADYFOLD. STOOL SHADOW.
AW NO.
I'M GOING TO GIVE YOU SOMETHING TO SUCK ON...
NO, NO, NO-NO-NO--!
HUGHIE...WHAT THE FUCK'RE YOU UP TO NOW...?

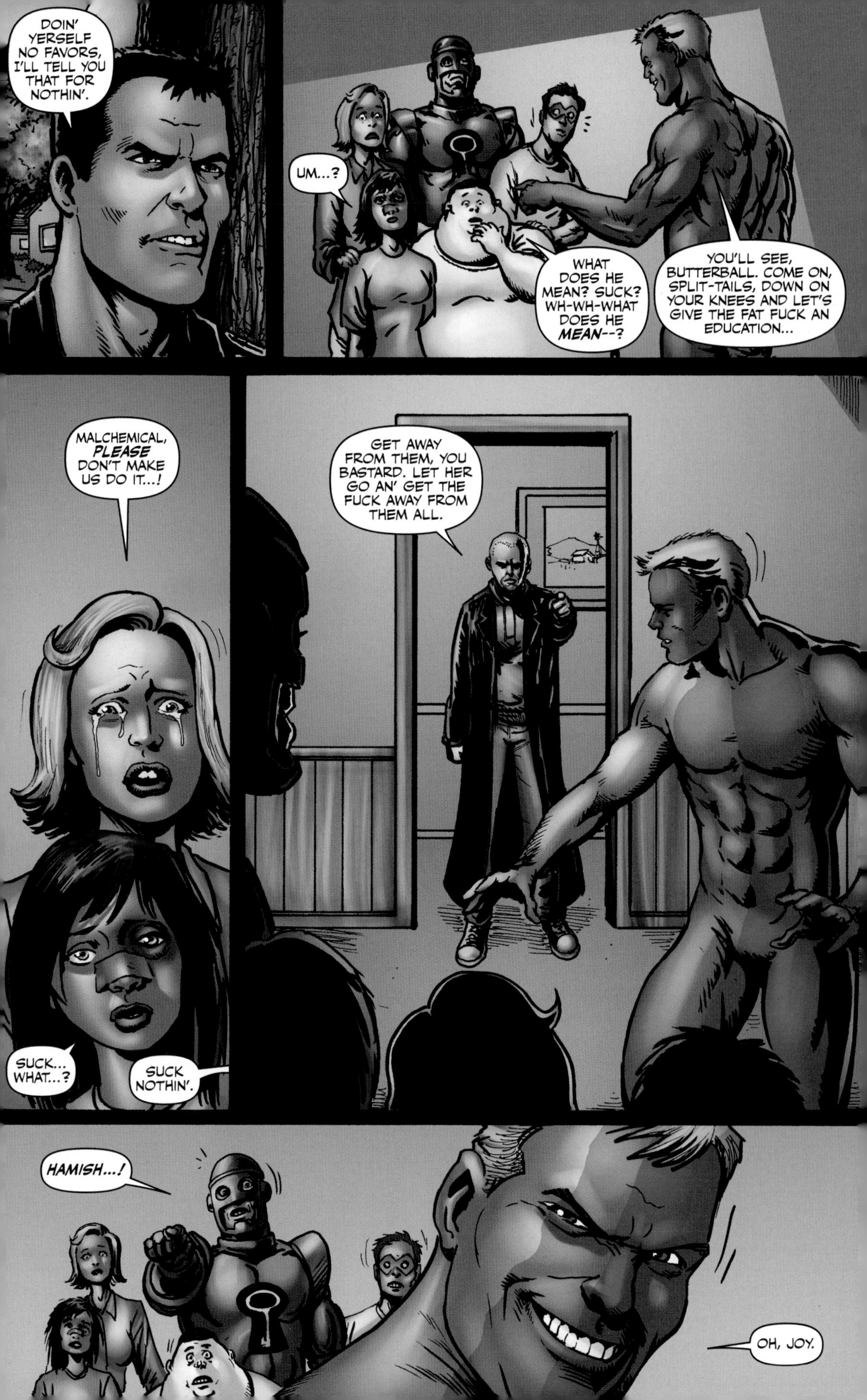
DOIN' YERSELF NO FAVORS, I'LL TELL YOU THAT FOR NOTHIN'.
UM...?
WHAT DOES HE MEAN? SUCK? WH-WH-WHAT DOES HE *MEAN*--?
YOU'LL SEE, BUTTERBALL. COME ON, SPLIT-TAILS, DOWN ON YOUR KNEES AND LET'S GIVE THE FAT FUCK AN EDUCATION...
MALCHEMICAL, *PLEASE* DON'T MAKE US DO IT...!
SUCK... WHAT...?
SUCK NOTHIN'.
GET AWAY FROM THEM, YOU BASTARD. LET HER GO AN' GET THE FUCK AWAY FROM THEM ALL.
HAMISH...!
OH, JOY.

BLOODY HELL...

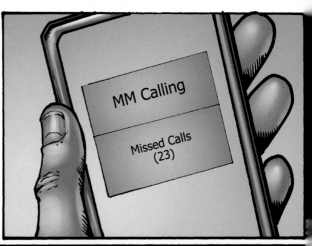

MM Calling

Missed Calls (23)

YEAH?

GODDAMMIT, WHERE THE FUCK YOU AT, I BEEN CALLIN' ALL MUTHAFUCKIN' NIGHT!

OH, YEAH, THE RECEPTION'S SHIT AROUND HERE, YOU--

FUCK ALL THAT! I KNOW WHAT YOU DOIN'! HUGHIE AIN'T FUCKIN' WORKIN' FOR VOUGHT!!

YOU-- YOU TALKED TO THE LEGEND.

YOU WENT TO THE LEGEND BEHIND MY FUCKIN' BACK...

AN' WHAT ABOUT WHAT YOU DID? YOU SENT HUGHIE INTO SOME SHIT WIT' FUCKIN' MALCHEMICAL! YOU DIDN'T TELL THE REST OF US!

YOU TOOK SUPERDUPER'S FUCKIN' ADDRESS OUTTA THEIR FILE SO I COULDN'T FIND YOU, MUTHAFUCKA, YOU GODDAMN RIGHT I WENT TO THE FUCKIN' LEGEND!

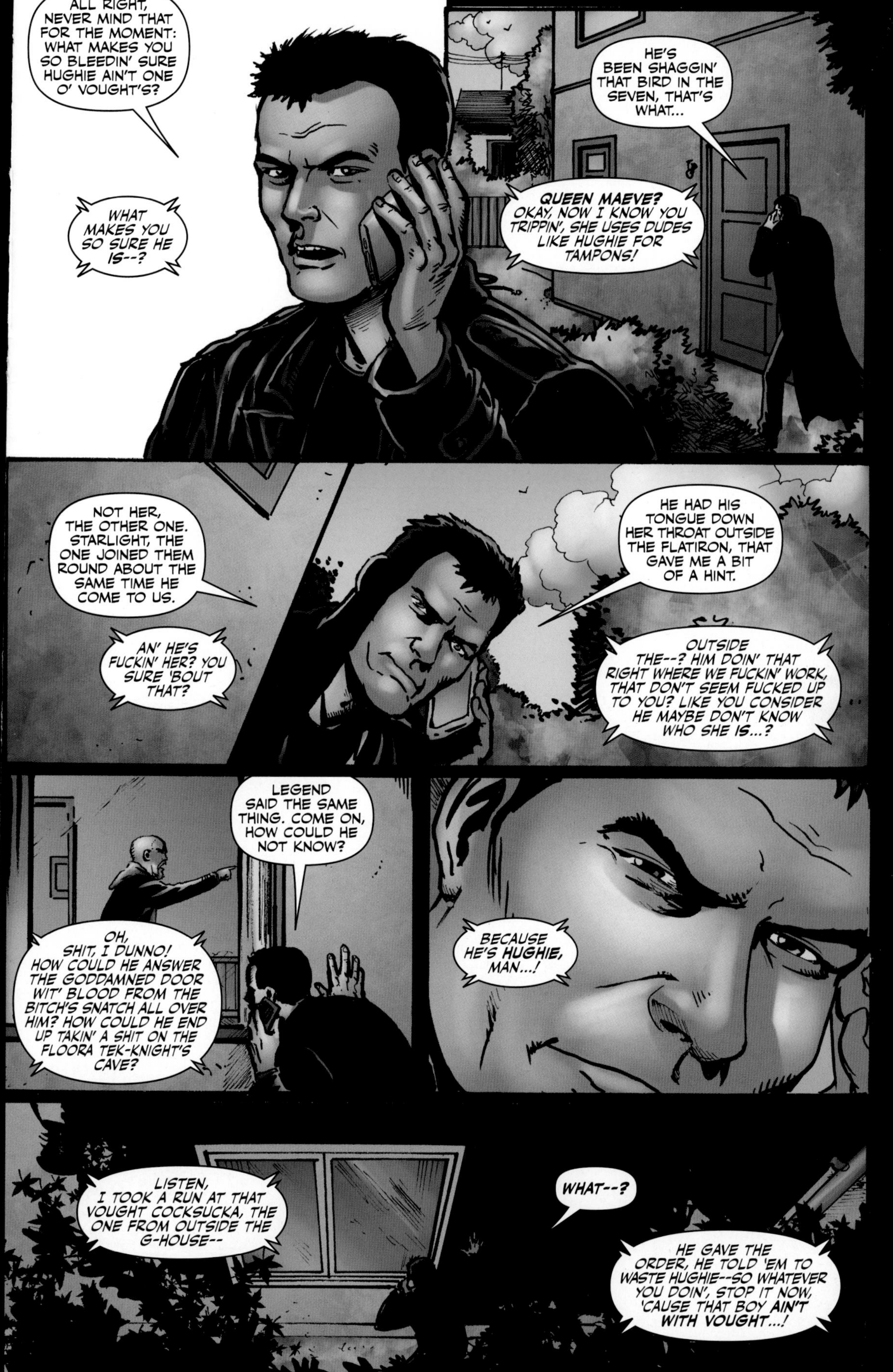
ALL RIGHT, NEVER MIND THAT FOR THE MOMENT: WHAT MAKES YOU SO BLEEDIN' SURE HUGHIE AIN'T ONE O' VOUGHT'S?
WHAT MAKES YOU SO SURE HE IS--?
HE'S BEEN SHAGGIN' THAT BIRD IN THE SEVEN, THAT'S WHAT...
QUEEN MAEVE? OKAY, NOW I KNOW YOU TRIPPIN', SHE USES DUDES LIKE HUGHIE FOR TAMPONS!
NOT HER, THE OTHER ONE. STARLIGHT, THE ONE JOINED THEM ROUND ABOUT THE SAME TIME HE COME TO US.
AN' HE'S FUCKIN' HER? YOU SURE 'BOUT THAT?
HE HAD HIS TONGUE DOWN HER THROAT OUTSIDE THE FLATIRON, THAT GAVE ME A BIT OF A HINT.
OUTSIDE THE--? HIM DOIN' THAT RIGHT WHERE WE FUCKIN' WORK, THAT DON'T SEEM FUCKED UP TO YOU? LIKE YOU CONSIDER HE MAYBE DON'T KNOW WHO SHE IS...?
LEGEND SAID THE SAME THING. COME ON, HOW COULD HE NOT KNOW?
OH, SHIT, I DUNNO! HOW COULD HE ANSWER THE GODDAMNED DOOR WIT' BLOOD FROM THE BITCH'S SNATCH ALL OVER HIM? HOW COULD HE END UP TAKIN' A SHIT ON THE FLOORA TEK-KNIGHT'S CAVE?
BECAUSE HE'S HUGHIE, MAN...!
LISTEN, I TOOK A RUN AT THAT VOUGHT COCKSUCKA, THE ONE FROM OUTSIDE THE G-HOUSE--
WHAT--?
HE GAVE THE ORDER, HE TOLD 'EM TO WASTE HUGHIE--SO WHATEVER YOU DOIN', STOP IT NOW, 'CAUSE THAT BOY AIN'T WITH VOUGHT...!

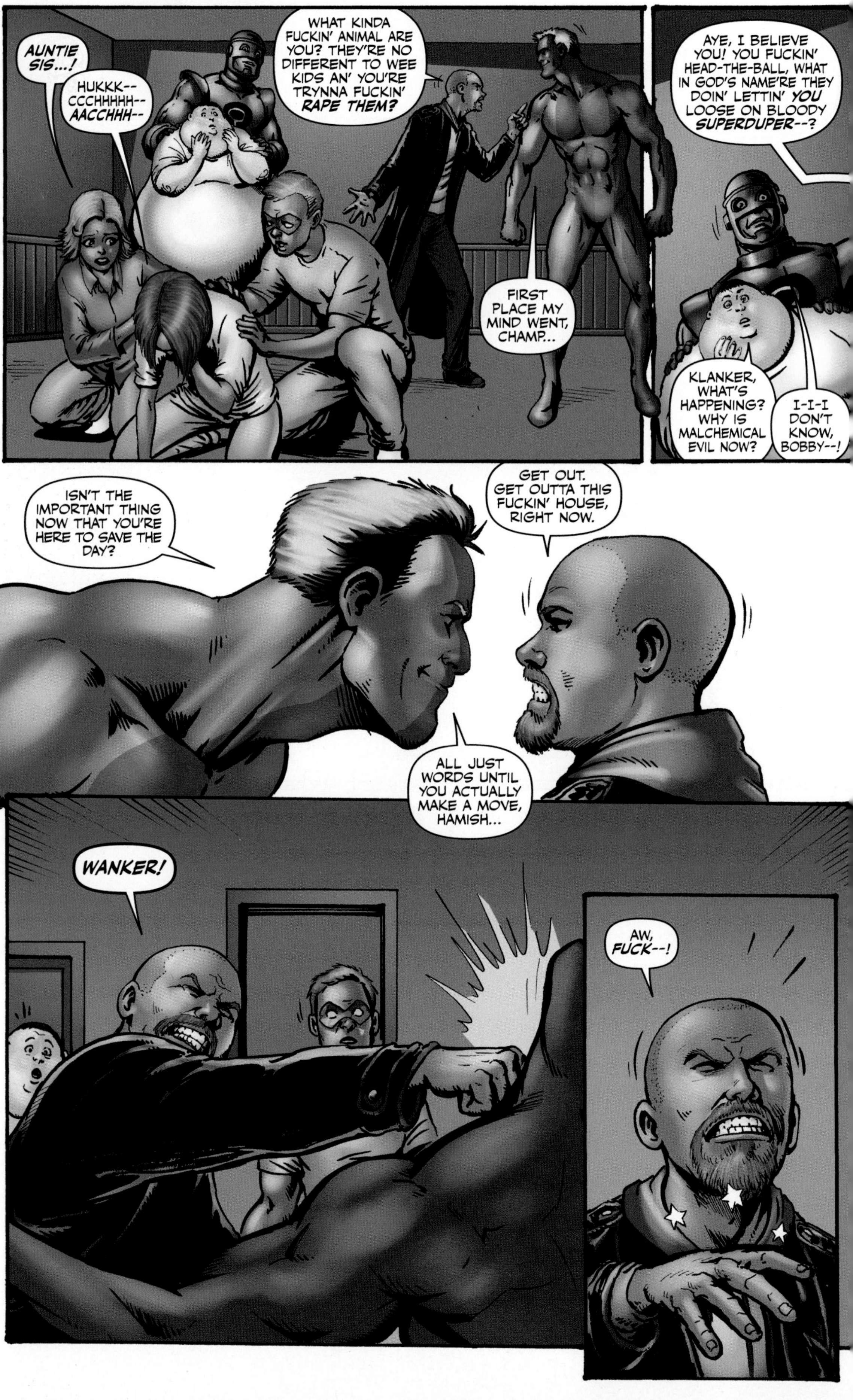
AUNTIE SIS...!
HUKKK-- CCCHHHHH-- AACCHHH--
WHAT KINDA FUCKIN' ANIMAL ARE YOU? THEY'RE NO DIFFERENT TO WEE KIDS AN' YOU'RE TRYNNA FUCKIN' RAPE THEM?
FIRST PLACE MY MIND WENT, CHAMP...
AYE, I BELIEVE YOU! YOU FUCKIN' HEAD-THE-BALL, WHAT IN GOD'S NAME'RE THEY DOIN' LETTIN' YOU LOOSE ON BLOODY SUPERDUPER--?
KLANKER, WHAT'S HAPPENING? WHY IS MALCHEMICAL EVIL NOW?
I-I-I DON'T KNOW, BOBBY--!
ISN'T THE IMPORTANT THING NOW THAT YOU'RE HERE TO SAVE THE DAY?
GET OUT. GET OUTTA THIS FUCKIN' HOUSE, RIGHT NOW.
ALL JUST WORDS UNTIL YOU ACTUALLY MAKE A MOVE, HAMISH...
WANKER!
AW, FUCK--!

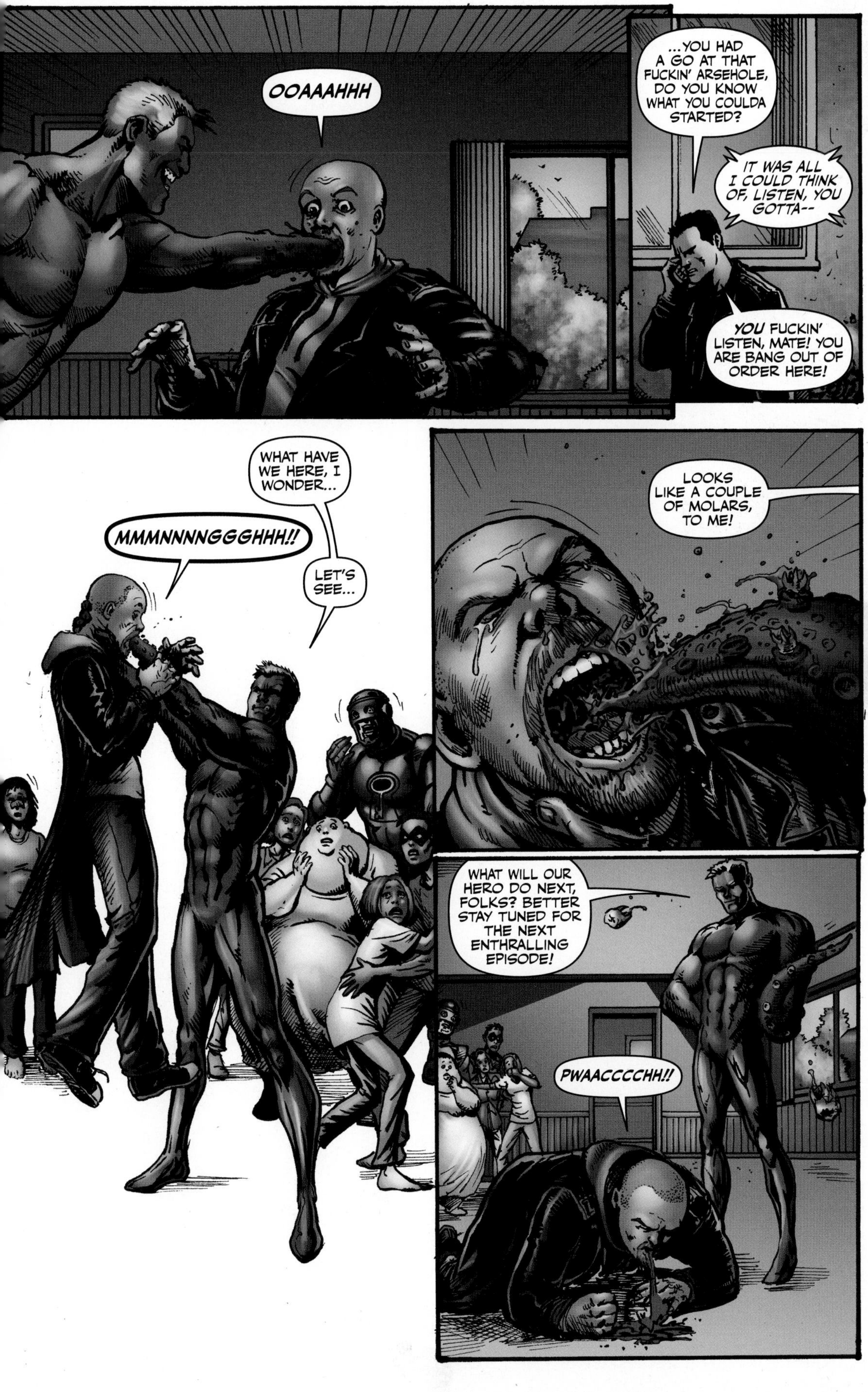
OOAAAHHH
...YOU HAD A GO AT THAT FUCKIN' ARSEHOLE, DO YOU KNOW WHAT YOU COULDA STARTED?
IT WAS ALL I COULD THINK OF, LISTEN, YOU GOTTA--
YOU FUCKIN' LISTEN, MATE! YOU ARE BANG OUT OF ORDER HERE!
WHAT HAVE WE HERE, I WONDER...
MMMNNNNGGGHHH!!
LET'S SEE...
LOOKS LIKE A COUPLE OF MOLARS, TO ME!
WHAT WILL OUR HERO DO NEXT, FOLKS? BETTER STAY TUNED FOR THE NEXT ENTHRALLING EPISODE!
PWAACCCCHH!!

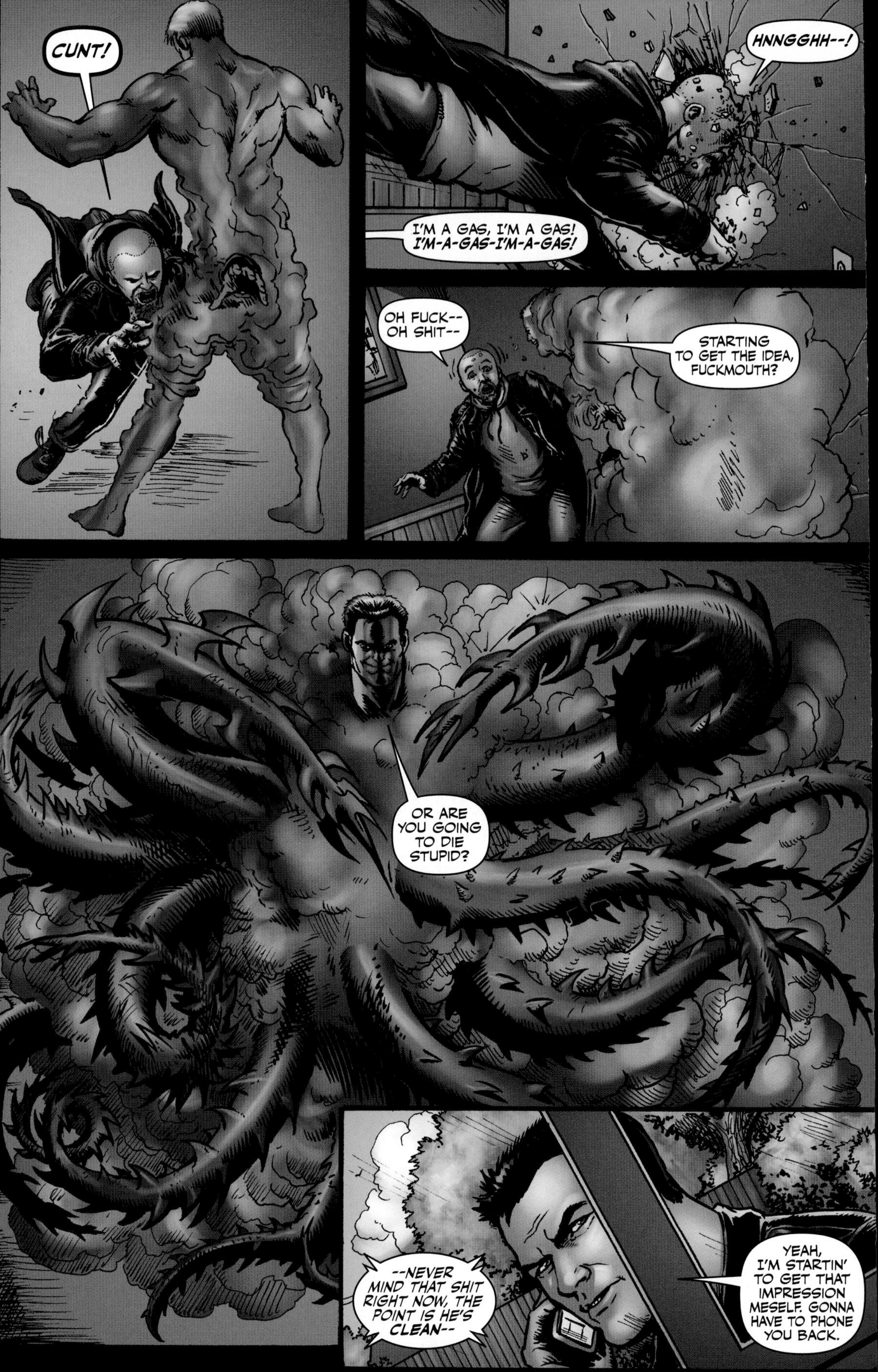
CUNT!
HNNGGHH--!
I'M A GAS, I'M A GAS! I'M-A-GAS-I'M-A-GAS!
OH FUCK-- OH SHIT--
STARTING TO GET THE IDEA, FUCKMOUTH?
OR ARE YOU GOING TO DIE STUPID?
--NEVER MIND THAT SHIT RIGHT NOW, THE POINT IS HE'S CLEAN--
YEAH, I'M STARTIN' TO GET THAT IMPRESSION MESELF. GONNA HAVE TO PHONE YOU BACK.

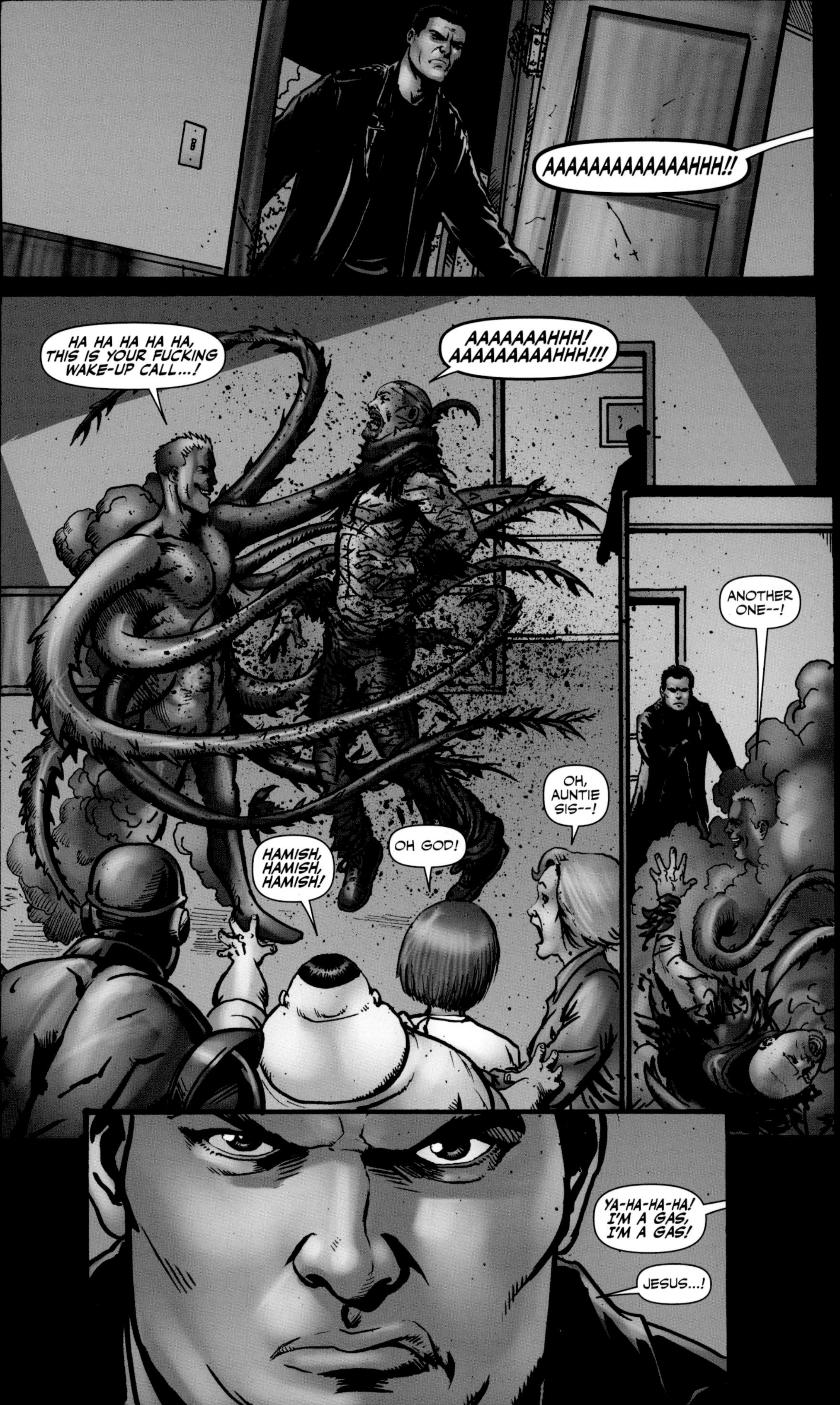

AAAAAAAAAAAAAAHHH!!
HA HA HA HA HA, THIS IS YOUR FUCKING WAKE-UP CALL...!
AAAAAAAAHHH! AAAAAAAAAAHHH!!!
ANOTHER ONE--!
OH, AUNTIE SIS--!
OH GOD!
HAMISH, HAMISH, HAMISH!
YA-HA-HA-HA! I'M A GAS, I'M A GAS!
JESUS...!

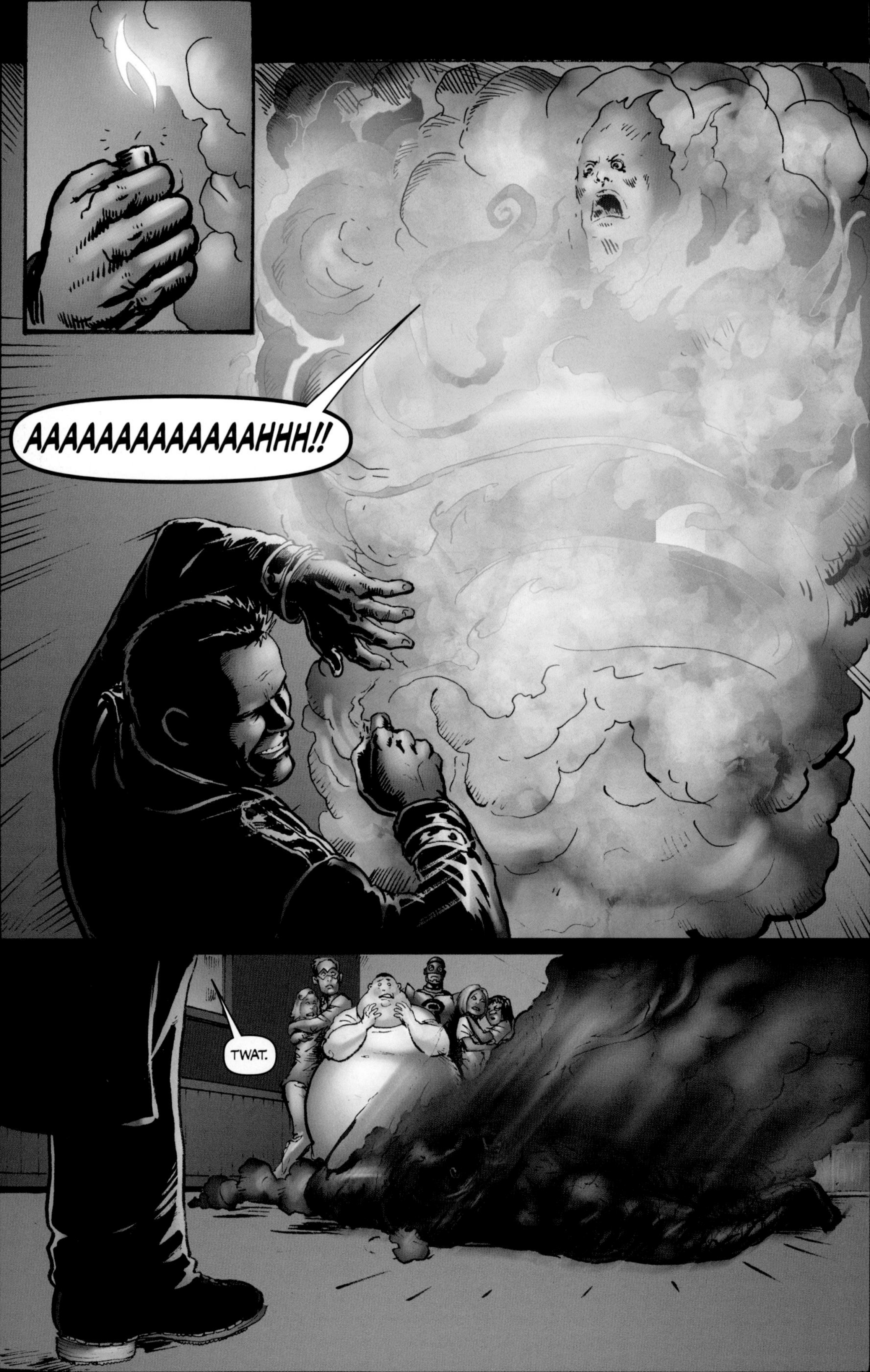
AAAAAAAAAAAAAAHHH!!
TWAT.

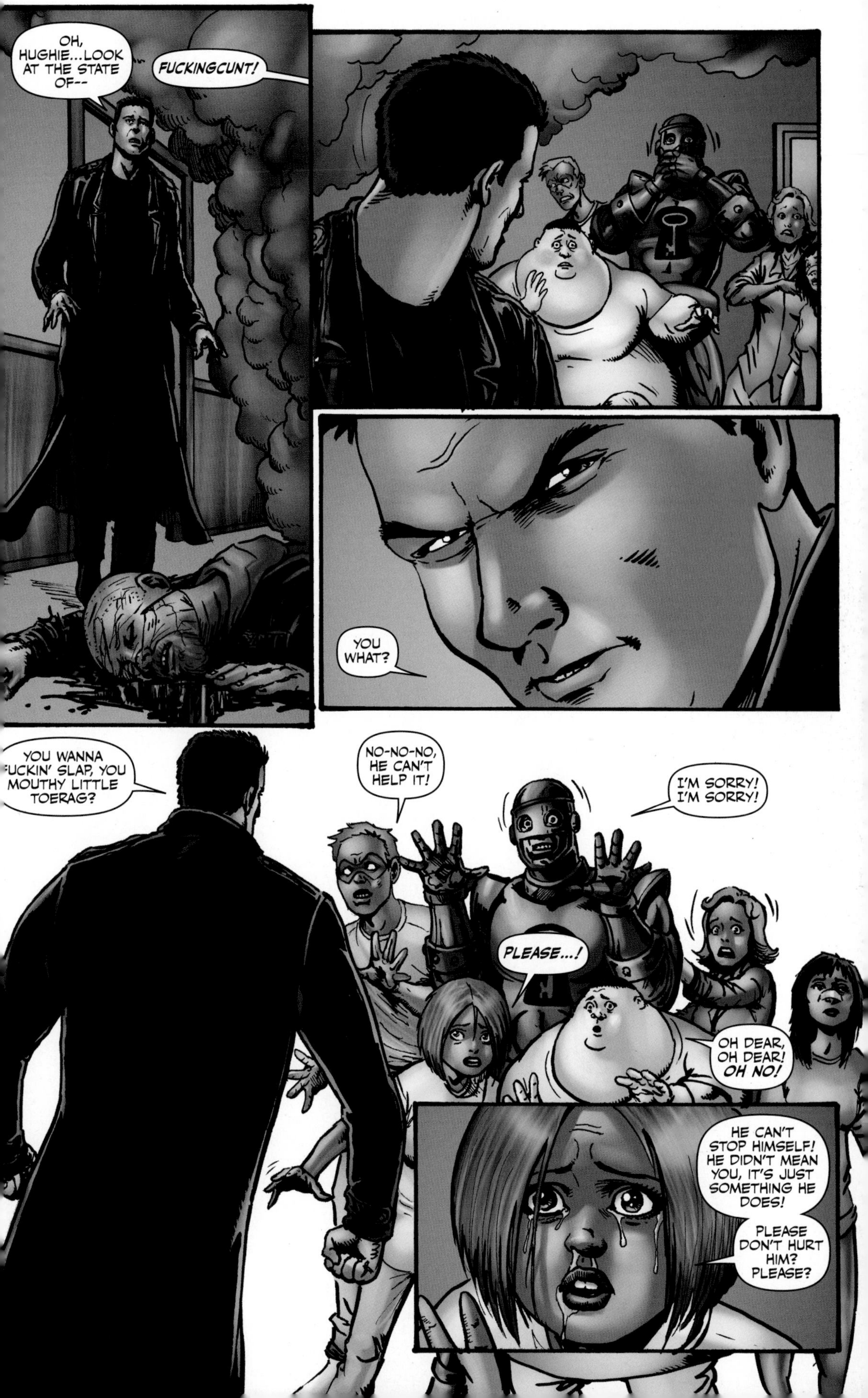
OH, HUGHIE...LOOK AT THE STATE OF--
FUCKINGCUNT!
YOU WHAT?
YOU WANNA FUCKIN' SLAP, YOU MOUTHY LITTLE TOERAG?
NO-NO-NO, HE CAN'T HELP IT!
I'M SORRY! I'M SORRY!
PLEASE...!
OH DEAR, OH DEAR! OH NO!
HE CAN'T STOP HIMSELF! HE DIDN'T MEAN YOU, IT'S JUST SOMETHING HE DOES!
PLEASE DON'T HURT HIM? PLEASE?

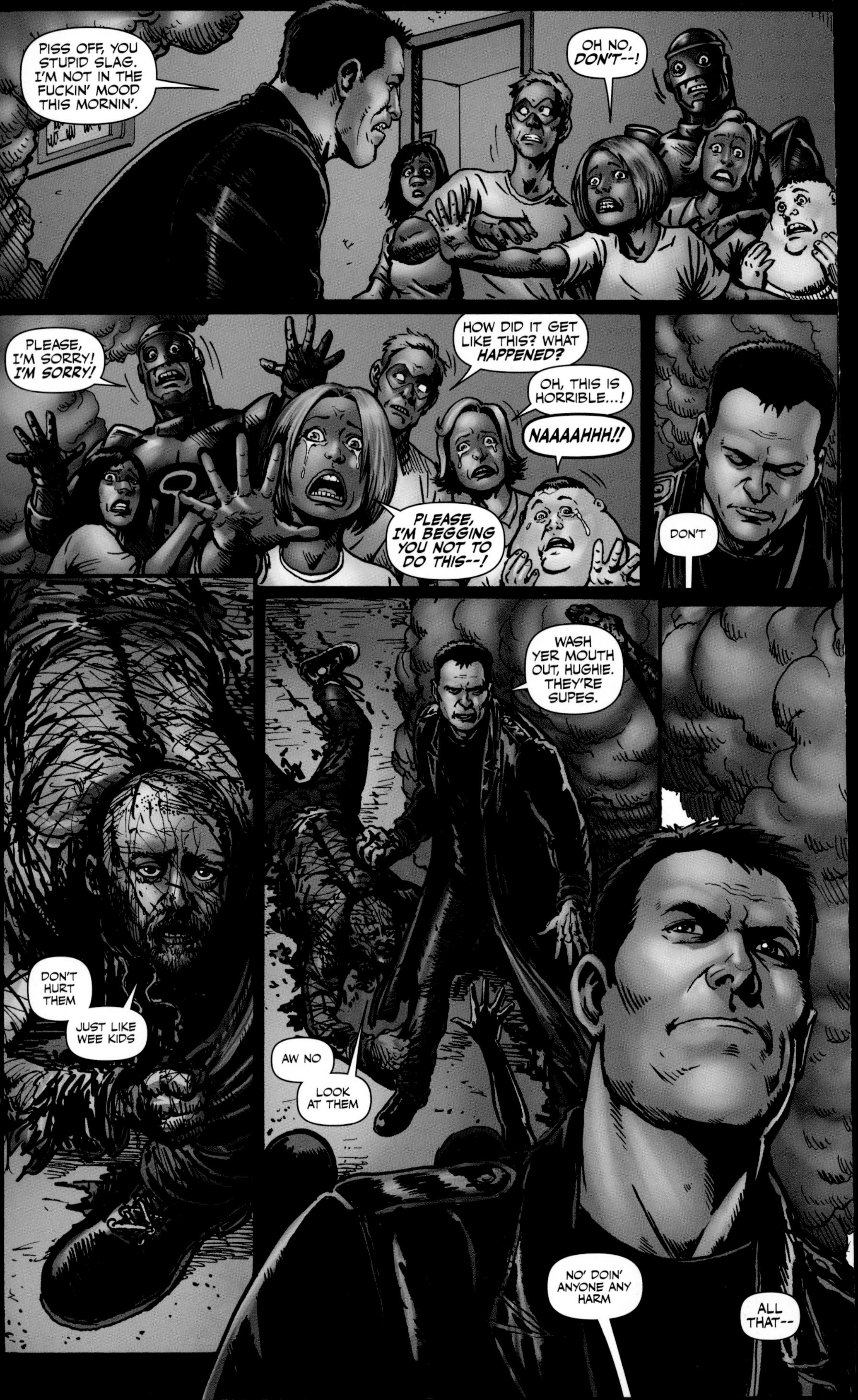
PISS OFF, YOU STUPID SLAG. I'M NOT IN THE FUCKIN' MOOD THIS MORNIN'.
OH NO, DON'T--!
PLEASE, I'M SORRY! I'M SORRY!
HOW DID IT GET LIKE THIS? WHAT HAPPENED?
OH, THIS IS HORRIBLE...!
NAAAAHHH!!
PLEASE, I'M BEGGING YOU NOT TO DO THIS--!
DON'T
DON'T HURT THEM
JUST LIKE WEE KIDS
WASH YER MOUTH OUT, HUGHIE. THEY'RE SUPES.
AW NO
LOOK AT THEM
NO' DOIN' ANYONE ANY HARM
ALL THAT--

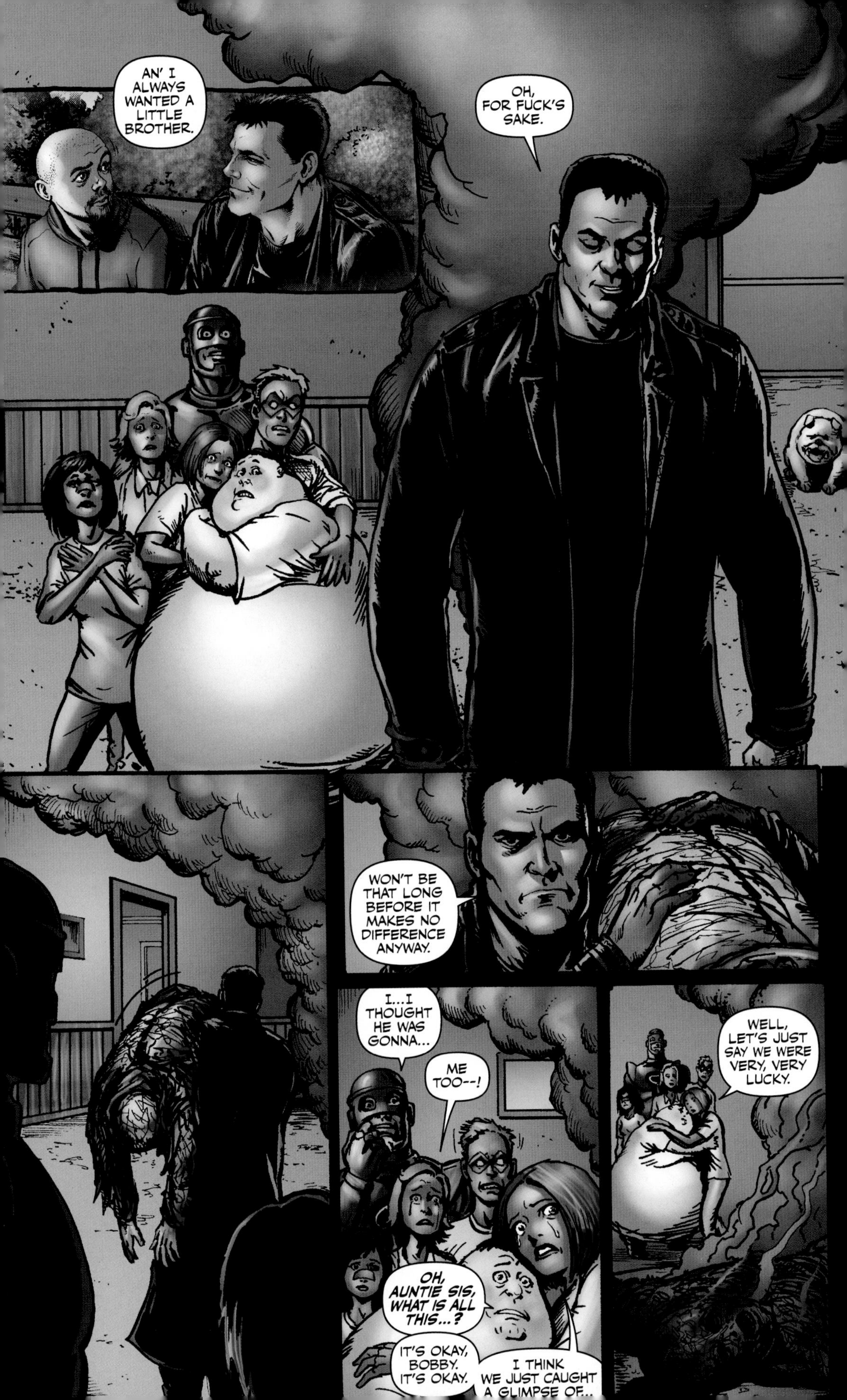
AN' I ALWAYS WANTED A LITTLE BROTHER.
OH, FOR FUCK'S SAKE.
WON'T BE THAT LONG BEFORE IT MAKES NO DIFFERENCE ANYWAY.
I...I THOUGHT HE WAS GONNA...
ME TOO--!
OH, AUNTIE SIS, WHAT IS ALL THIS...?
IT'S OKAY, BOBBY. IT'S OKAY.
I THINK WE JUST CAUGHT A GLIMPSE OF..
WELL, LET'S JUST SAY WE WERE VERY, VERY LUCKY.

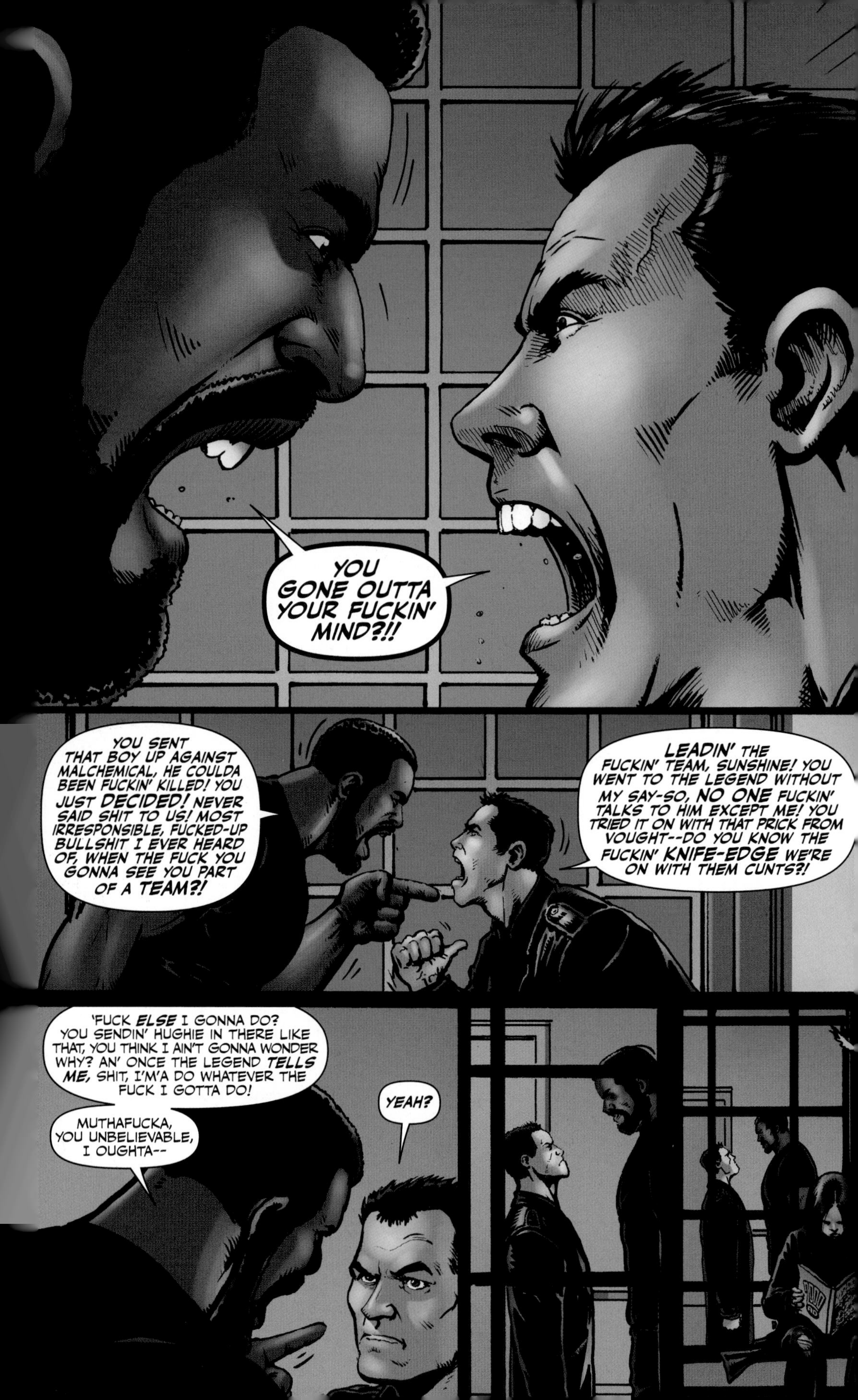
YOU GONE OUTTA YOUR FUCKIN' MIND?!!
YOU SENT THAT BOY UP AGAINST MALCHEMICAL, HE COULDA BEEN FUCKIN' KILLED! YOU JUST DECIDED! NEVER SAID SHIT TO US! MOST IRRESPONSIBLE, FUCKED-UP BULLSHIT I EVER HEARD OF, WHEN THE FUCK YOU GONNA SEE YOU PART OF A TEAM?!
LEADIN' THE FUCKIN' TEAM, SUNSHINE! YOU WENT TO THE LEGEND WITHOUT MY SAY-SO, NO ONE FUCKIN' TALKS TO HIM EXCEPT ME! YOU TRIED IT ON WITH THAT PRICK FROM VOUGHT--DO YOU KNOW THE FUCKIN' KNIFE-EDGE WE'RE ON WITH THEM CUNTS?!
'FUCK ELSE I GONNA DO? YOU SENDIN' HUGHIE IN THERE LIKE THAT, YOU THINK I AIN'T GONNA WONDER WHY? AN' ONCE THE LEGEND TELLS ME, SHIT, I'M'A DO WHATEVER THE FUCK I GOTTA DO!
MUTHAFUCKA, YOU UNBELIEVABLE, I OUGHTA--
YEAH?

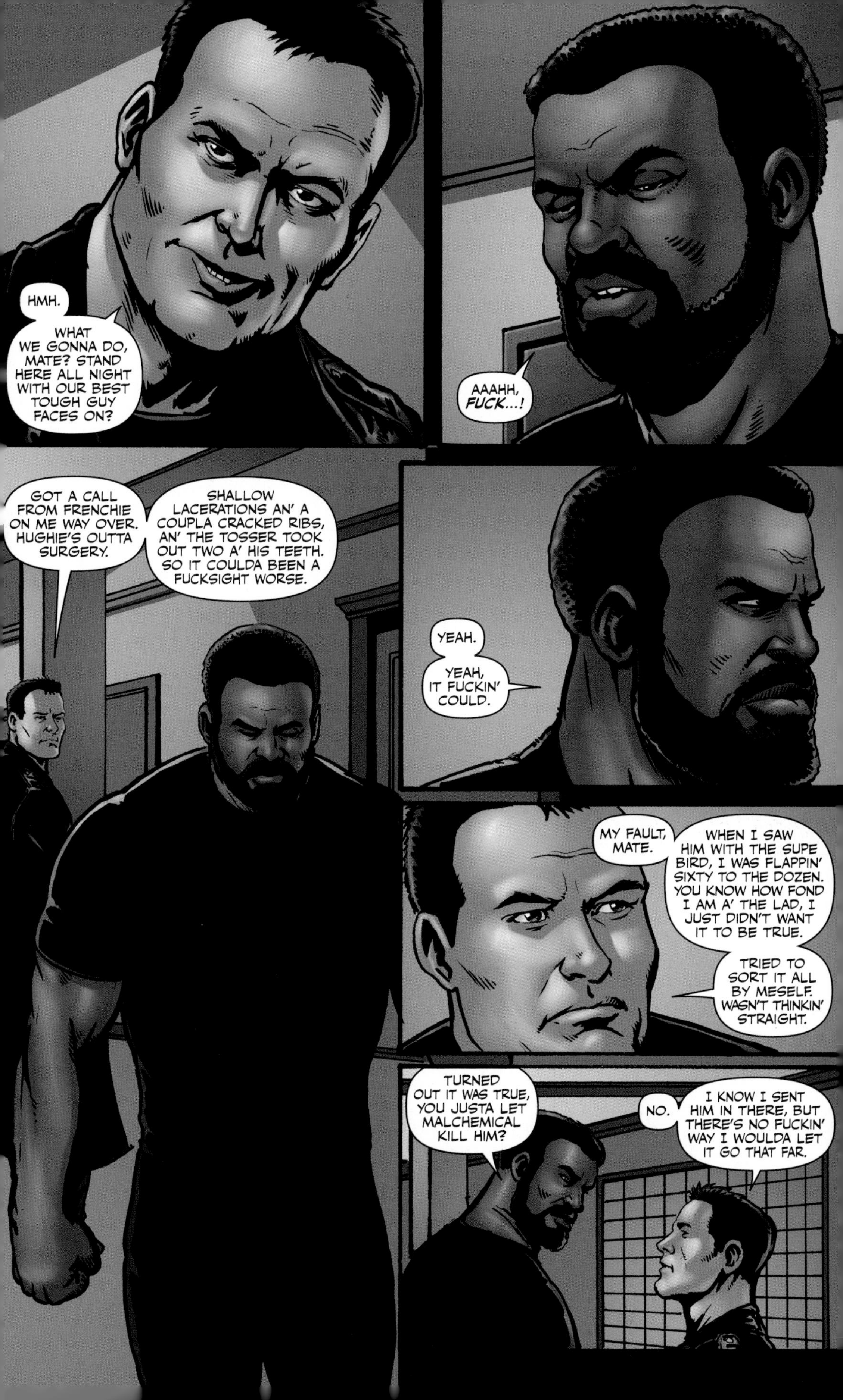
HMH.
WHAT WE GONNA DO, MATE? STAND HERE ALL NIGHT WITH OUR BEST TOUGH GUY FACES ON?
AAAHH, FUCK...!
GOT A CALL FROM FRENCHIE ON ME WAY OVER. HUGHIE'S OUTTA SURGERY.
SHALLOW LACERATIONS AN' A COUPLA CRACKED RIBS, AN' THE TOSSER TOOK OUT TWO A' HIS TEETH. SO IT COULDA BEEN A FUCKSIGHT WORSE.
YEAH.
YEAH, IT FUCKIN' COULD.
MY FAULT, MATE.
WHEN I SAW HIM WITH THE SUPE BIRD, I WAS FLAPPIN' SIXTY TO THE DOZEN. YOU KNOW HOW FOND I AM A' THE LAD, I JUST DIDN'T WANT IT TO BE TRUE.
TRIED TO SORT IT ALL BY MESELF. WASN'T THINKIN' STRAIGHT.
TURNED OUT IT WAS TRUE, YOU JUSTA LET MALCHEMICAL KILL HIM?
NO.
I KNOW I SENT HIM IN THERE, BUT THERE'S NO FUCKIN' WAY I WOULDA LET IT GO THAT FAR.

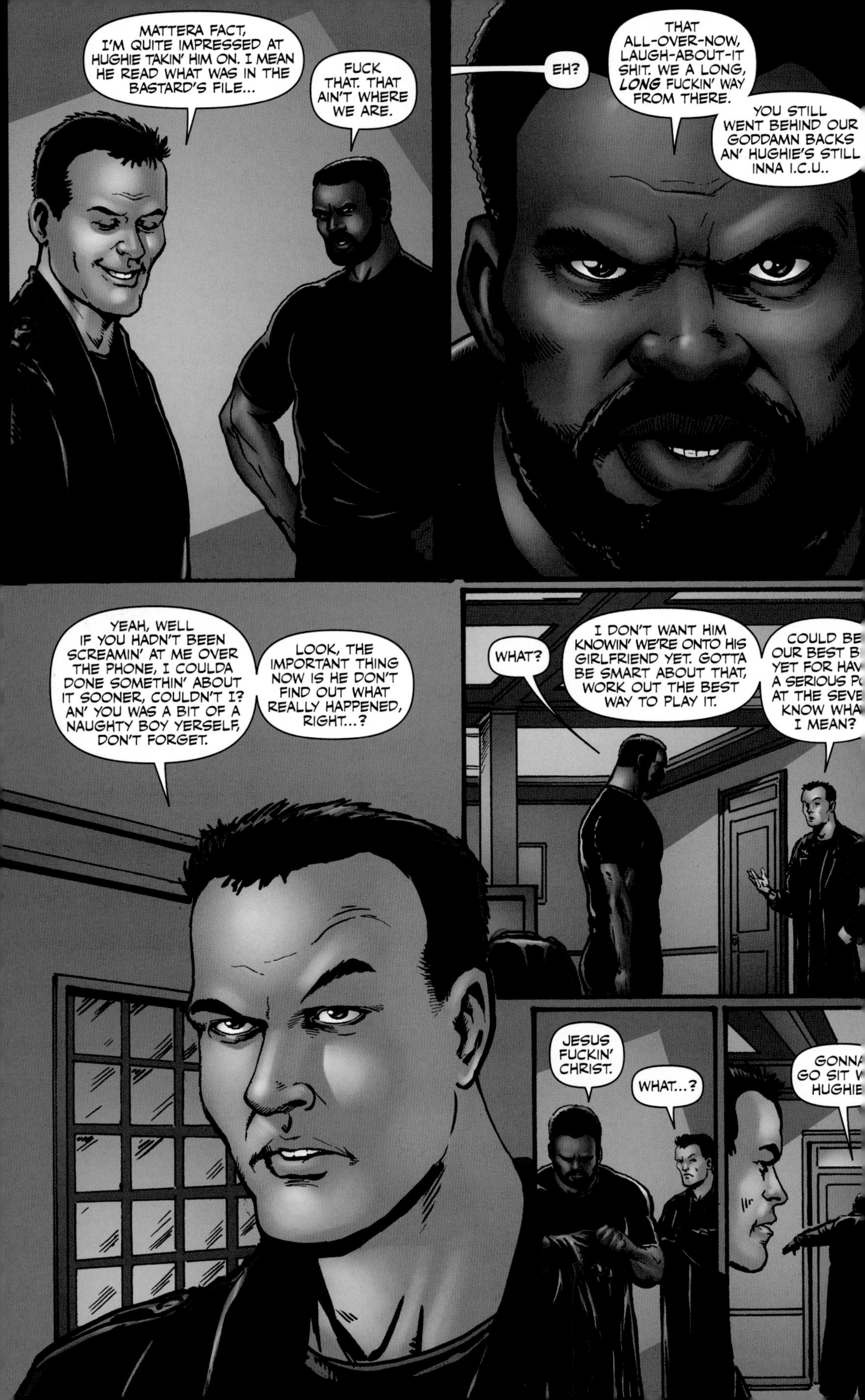
MATTERA FACT, I'M QUITE IMPRESSED AT HUGHIE TAKIN' HIM ON. I MEAN HE READ WHAT WAS IN THE BASTARD'S FILE...
FUCK THAT. THAT AIN'T WHERE WE ARE.
EH?
THAT ALL-OVER-NOW, LAUGH-ABOUT-IT SHIT. WE A LONG, *LONG* FUCKIN' WAY FROM THERE.
YOU STILL WENT BEHIND OUR GODDAMN BACKS AN' HUGHIE'S STILL INNA I.C.U..
YEAH, WELL IF YOU HADN'T BEEN SCREAMIN' AT ME OVER THE PHONE, I COULDA DONE SOMETHIN' ABOUT IT SOONER, COULDN'T I? AN' YOU WAS A BIT OF A NAUGHTY BOY YERSELF, DON'T FORGET.
LOOK, THE IMPORTANT THING NOW IS HE DON'T FIND OUT WHAT REALLY HAPPENED, RIGHT...?
WHAT?
I DON'T WANT HIM KNOWIN' WE'RE ONTO HIS GIRLFRIEND YET. GOTTA BE SMART ABOUT THAT, WORK OUT THE BEST WAY TO PLAY IT.
JESUS FUCKIN' CHRIST.
WHAT...?

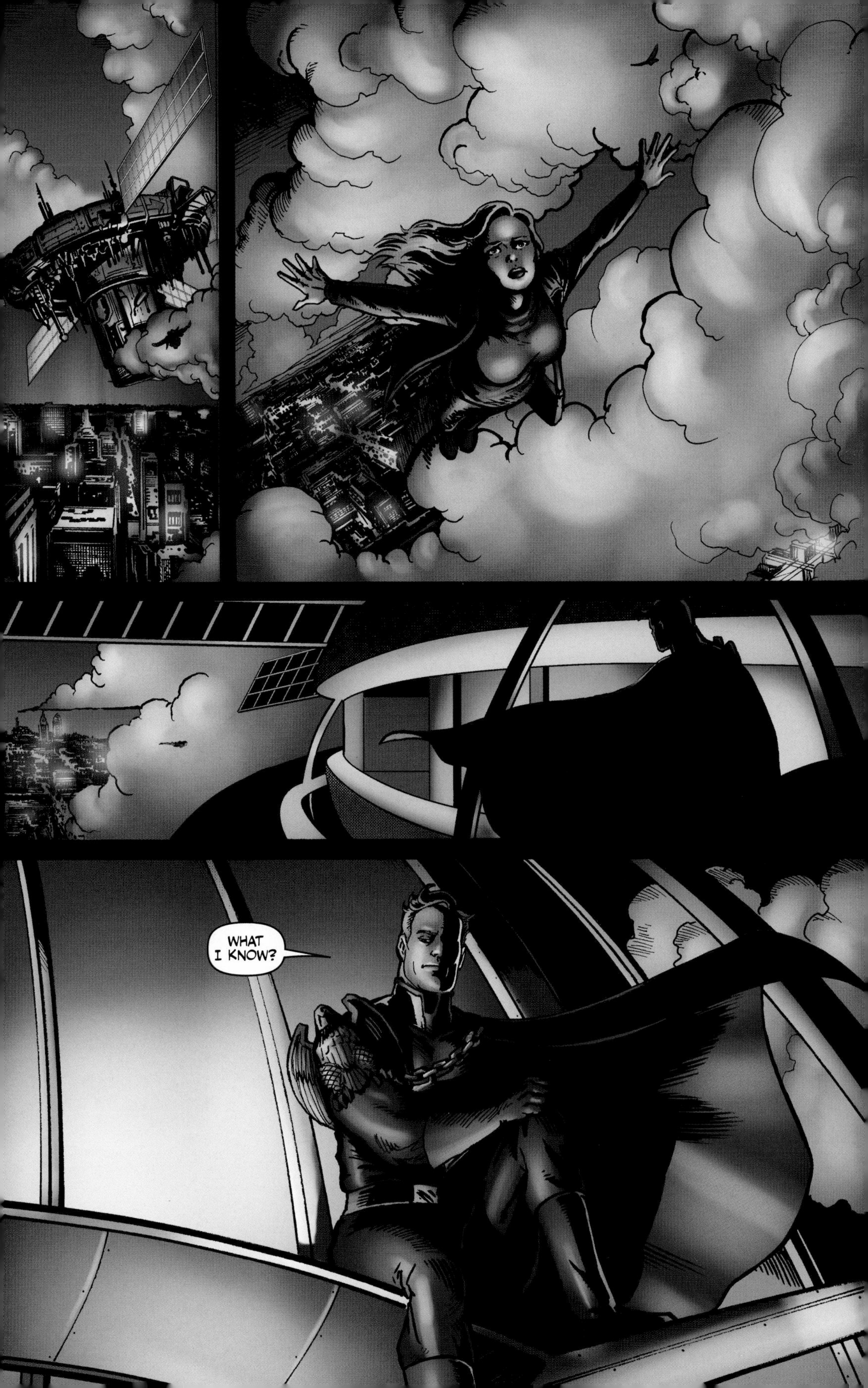
WHAT I KNOW?

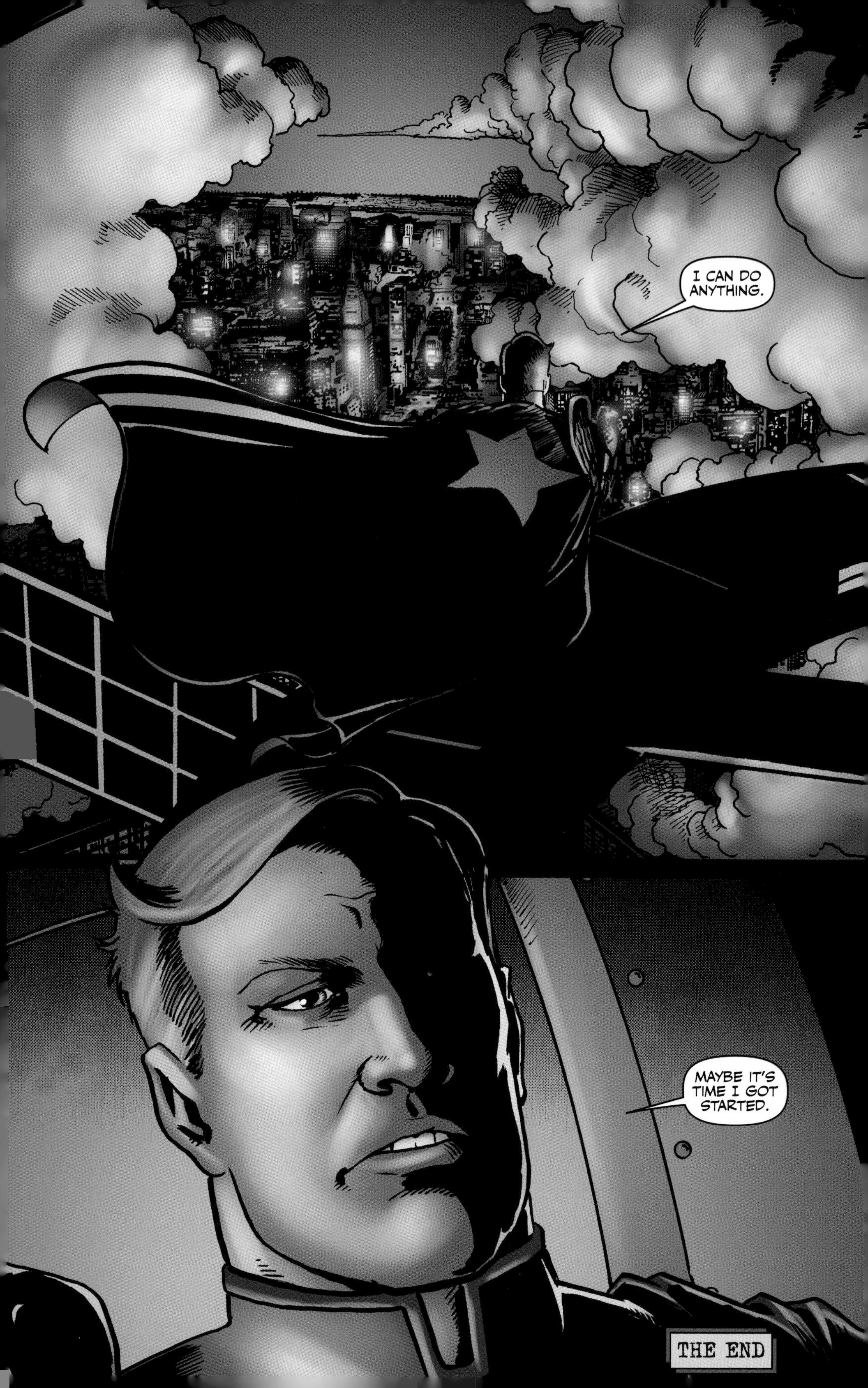
I CAN DO ANYTHING.
MAYBE IT'S TIME I GOT STARTED.
THE END

forty-four

INRI

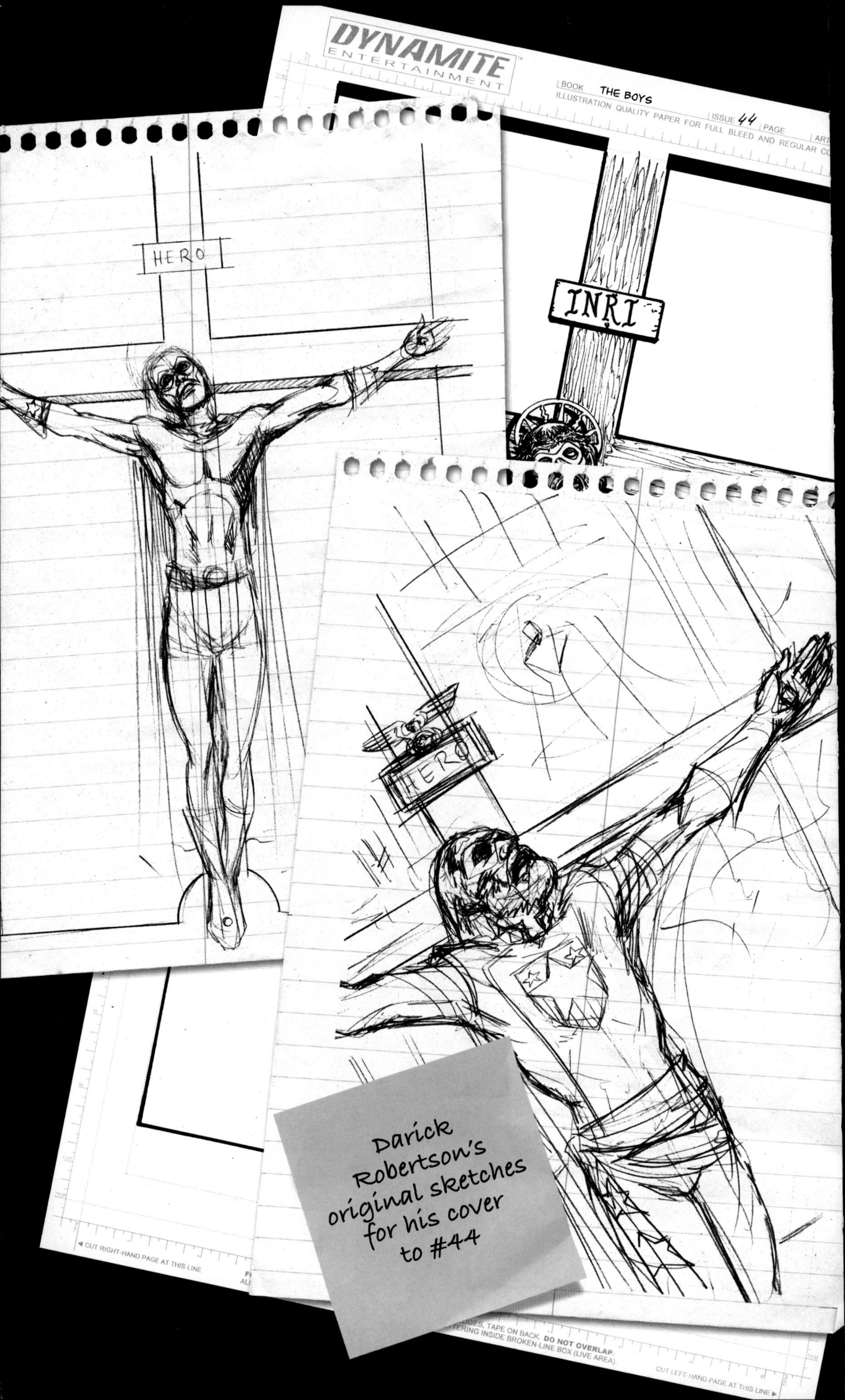
DYNAMITE
ENTERTAINMENT
BOOK THE BOYS
ISSUE 44
PAGE
HERO
INRI
HERO
CUT RIGHT-HAND PAGE AT THIS LINE
DO NOT OVERLAP.
CUT LEFT-HAND PAGE AT THIS LINE
Darick Robertson's original sketches for his cover to #44

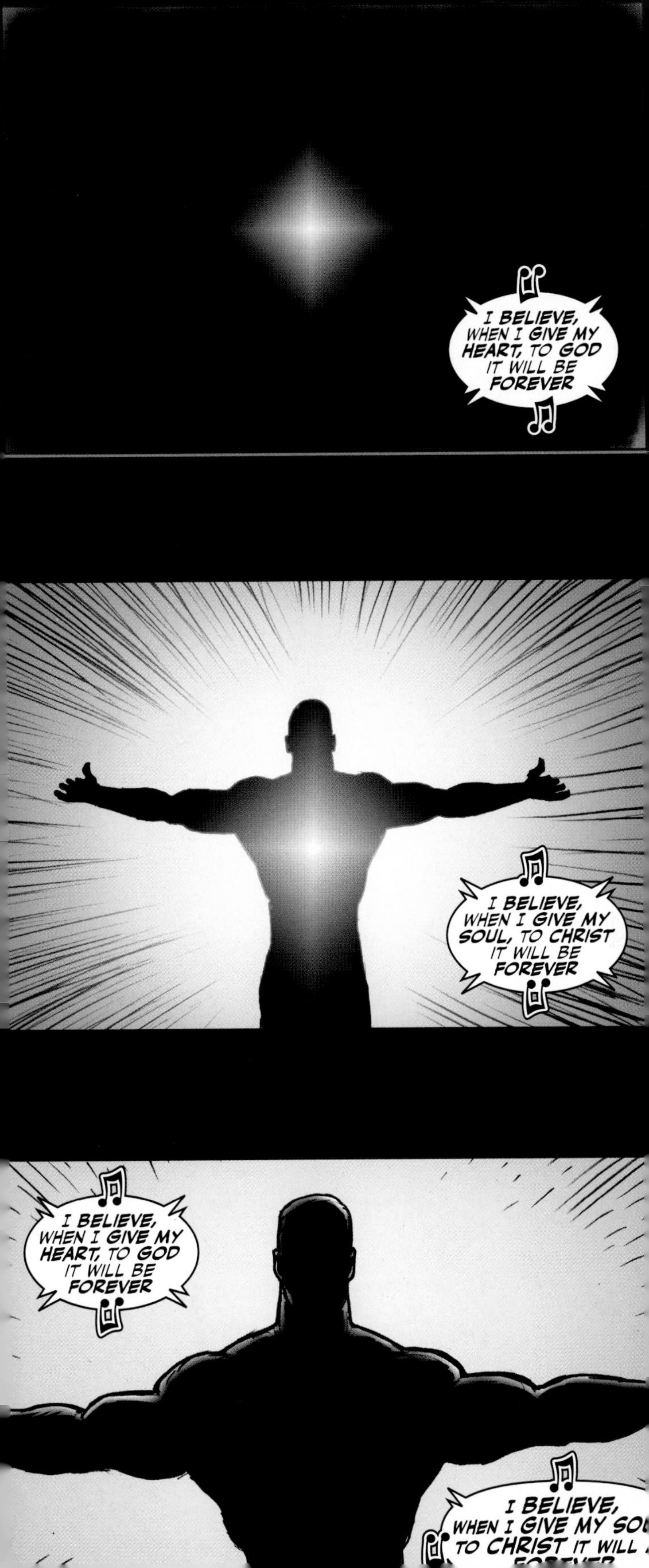
I BELIEVE, WHEN I GIVE MY HEART, TO GOD IT WILL BE FOREVER
I BELIEVE, WHEN I GIVE MY SOUL, TO CHRIST IT WILL BE FOREVER
I BELIEVE, WHEN I GIVE MY HEART, TO GOD IT WILL BE FOREVER
I BELIEVE, WHEN I GIVE MY
TO CHRIST IT WILL

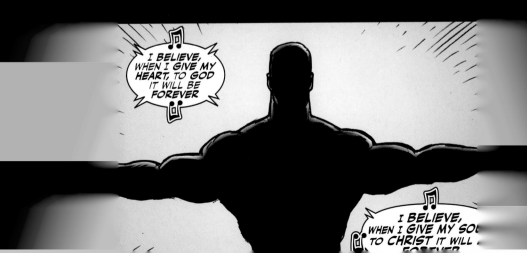

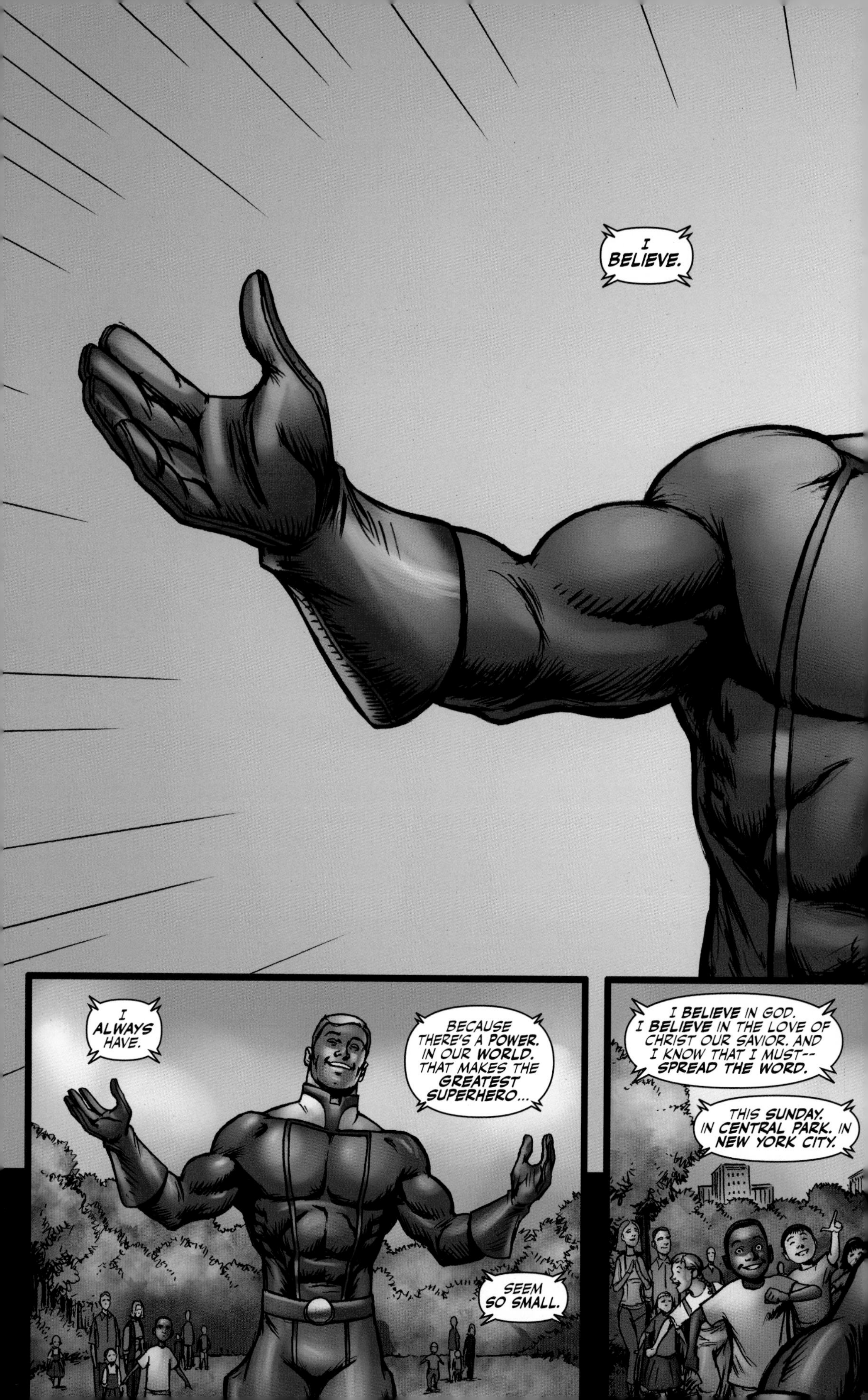
I BELIEVE.
I ALWAYS HAVE.
BECAUSE THERE'S A POWER. IN OUR WORLD. THAT MAKES THE GREATEST SUPERHERO...
SEEM SO SMALL.
I BELIEVE IN GOD. I BELIEVE IN THE LOVE OF CHRIST OUR SAVIOR. AND I KNOW THAT I MUST-- SPREAD THE WORD.
THIS SUNDAY. IN CENTRAL PARK. IN NEW YORK CITY.

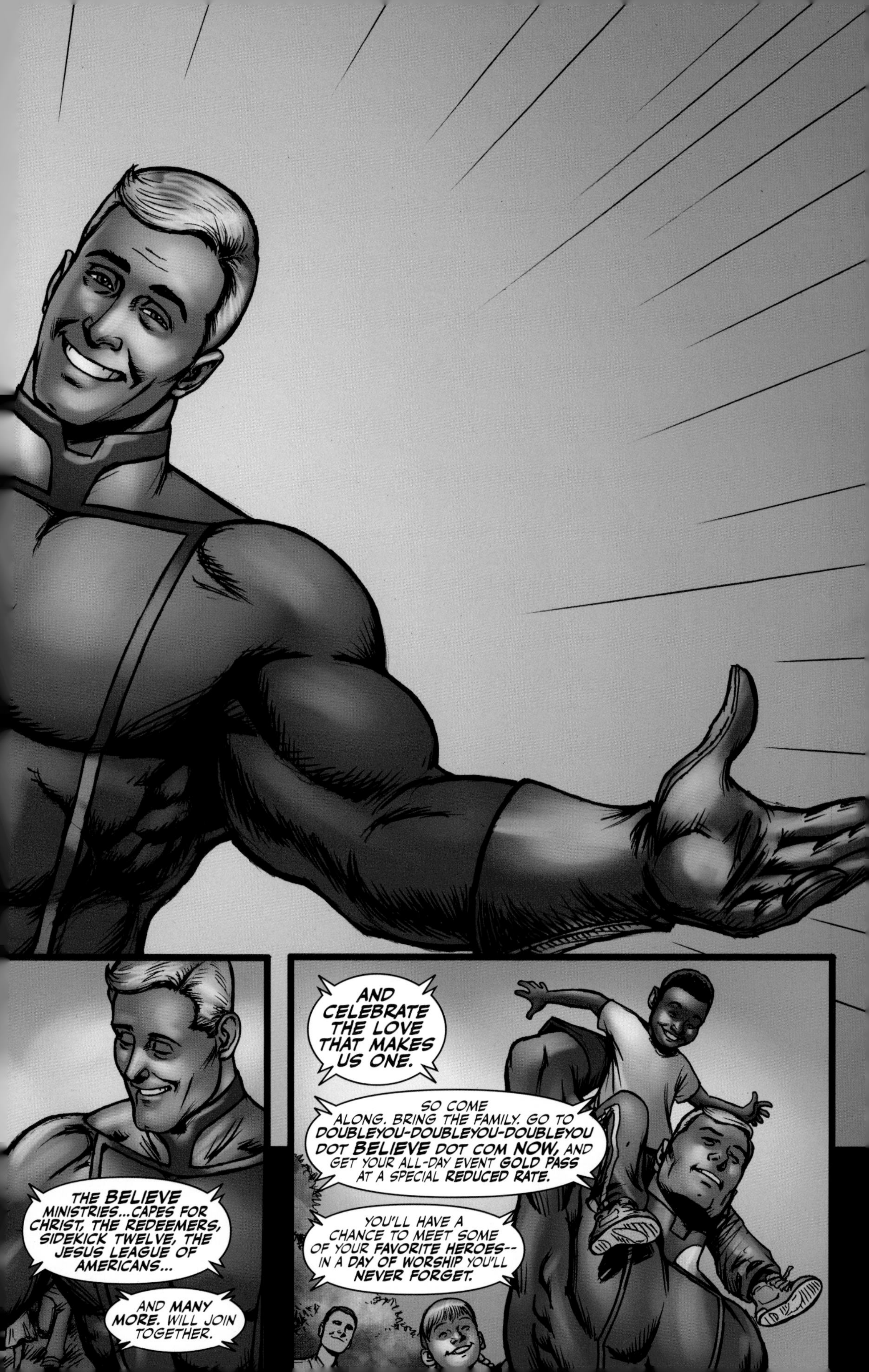
THE BELIEVE MINISTRIES...CAPES FOR CHRIST, THE REDEEMERS, SIDEKICK TWELVE, THE JESUS LEAGUE OF AMERICANS...
AND MANY MORE. WILL JOIN TOGETHER.
AND CELEBRATE THE LOVE THAT MAKES US ONE.
SO COME ALONG. BRING THE FAMILY. GO TO DOUBLEYOU-DOUBLEYOU-DOUBLEYOU DOT BELIEVE DOT COM NOW, AND GET YOUR ALL-DAY EVENT GOLD PASS AT A SPECIAL REDUCED RATE.
YOU'LL HAVE A CHANCE TO MEET SOME OF YOUR FAVORITE HEROES-- IN A DAY OF WORSHIP YOU'LL NEVER FORGET.

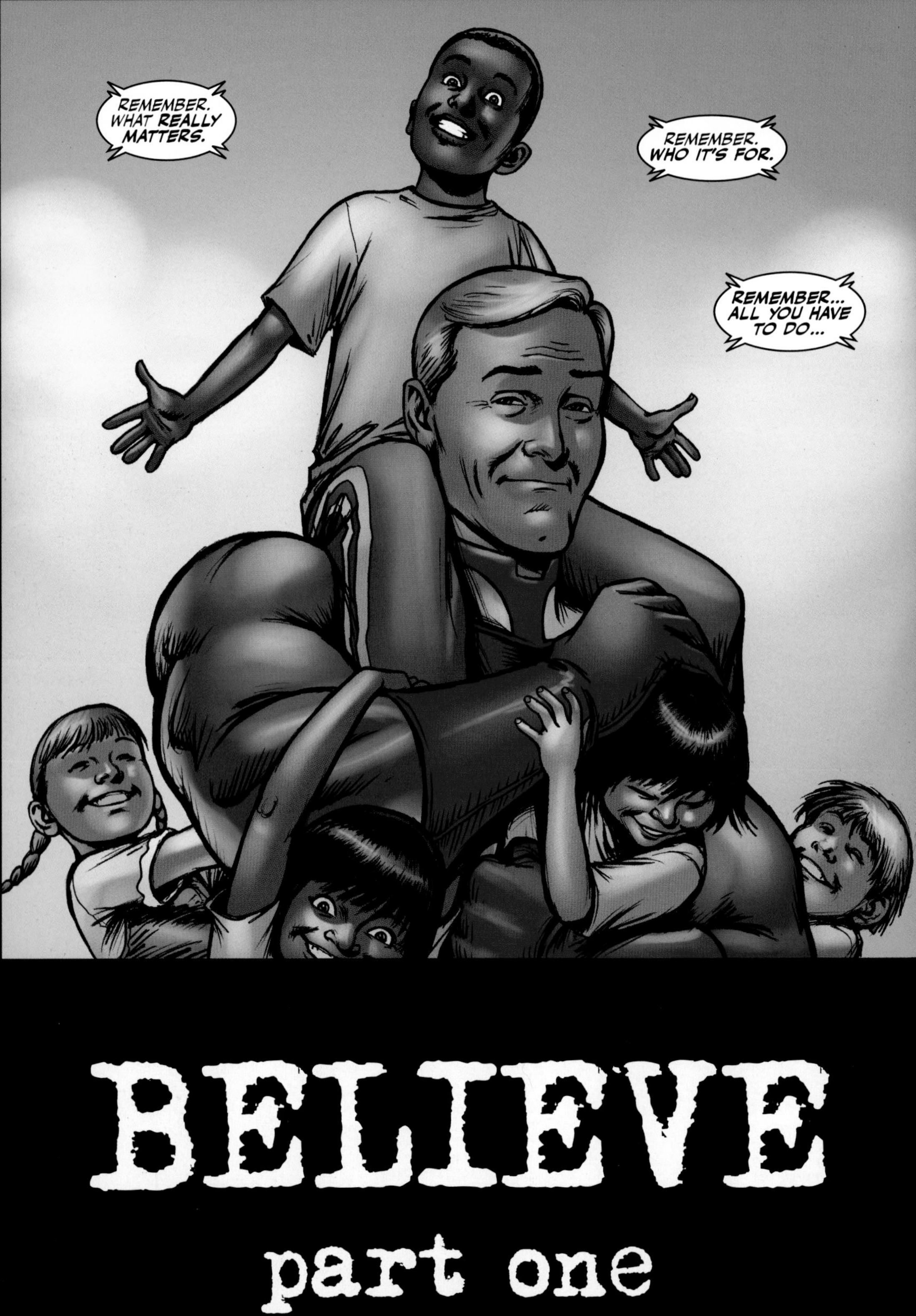
REMEMBER. WHAT REALLY MATTERS.
REMEMBER. WHO IT'S FOR.
REMEMBER... ALL YOU HAVE TO DO...

BELIEVE
part one

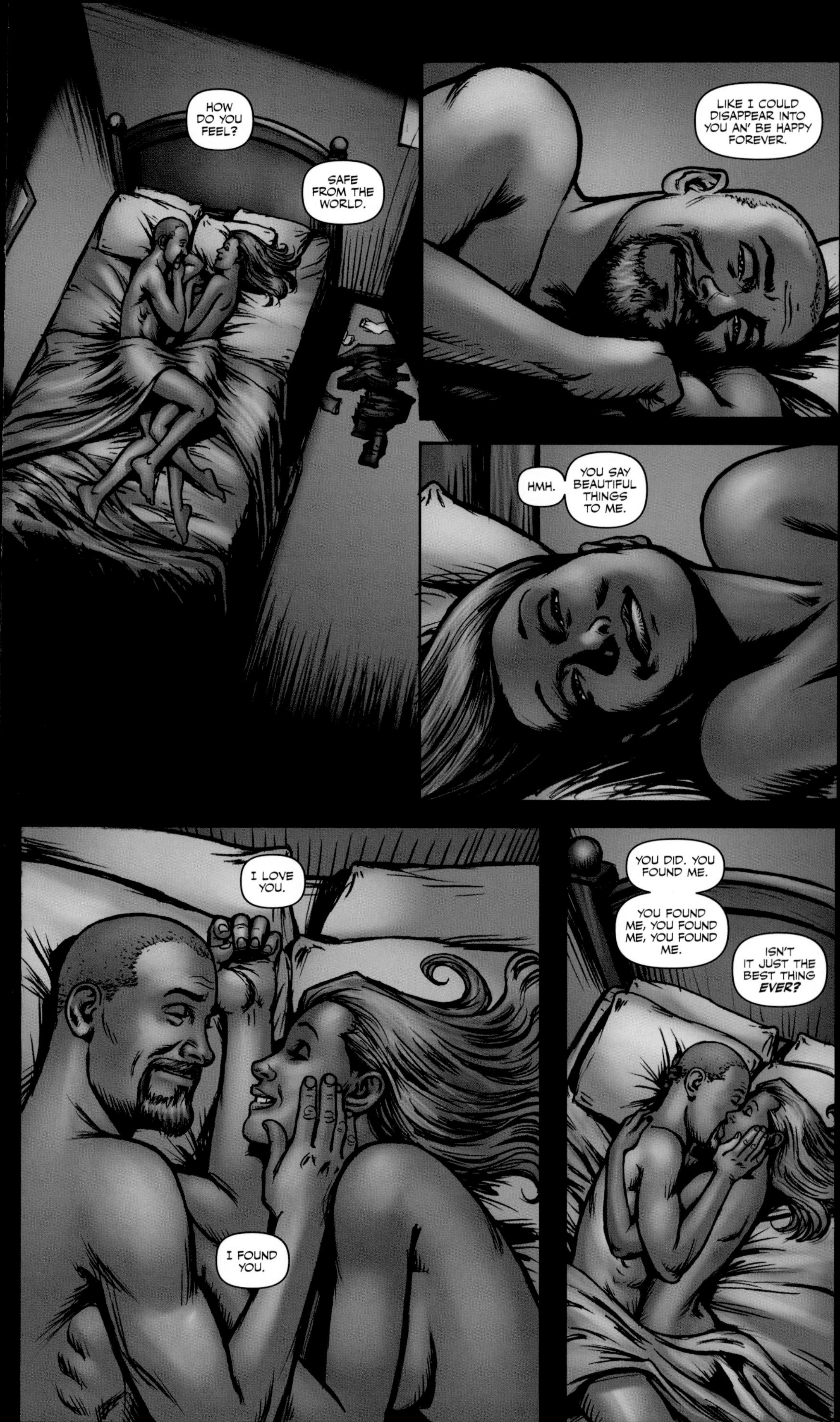
HOW DO YOU FEEL?
SAFE FROM THE WORLD.
LIKE I COULD DISAPPEAR INTO YOU AN' BE HAPPY FOREVER.
HMH.
YOU SAY BEAUTIFUL THINGS TO ME.
I LOVE YOU.
I FOUND YOU.
YOU DID. YOU FOUND ME.
YOU FOUND ME, YOU FOUND ME, YOU FOUND ME.
ISN'T IT JUST THE BEST THING *EVER?*

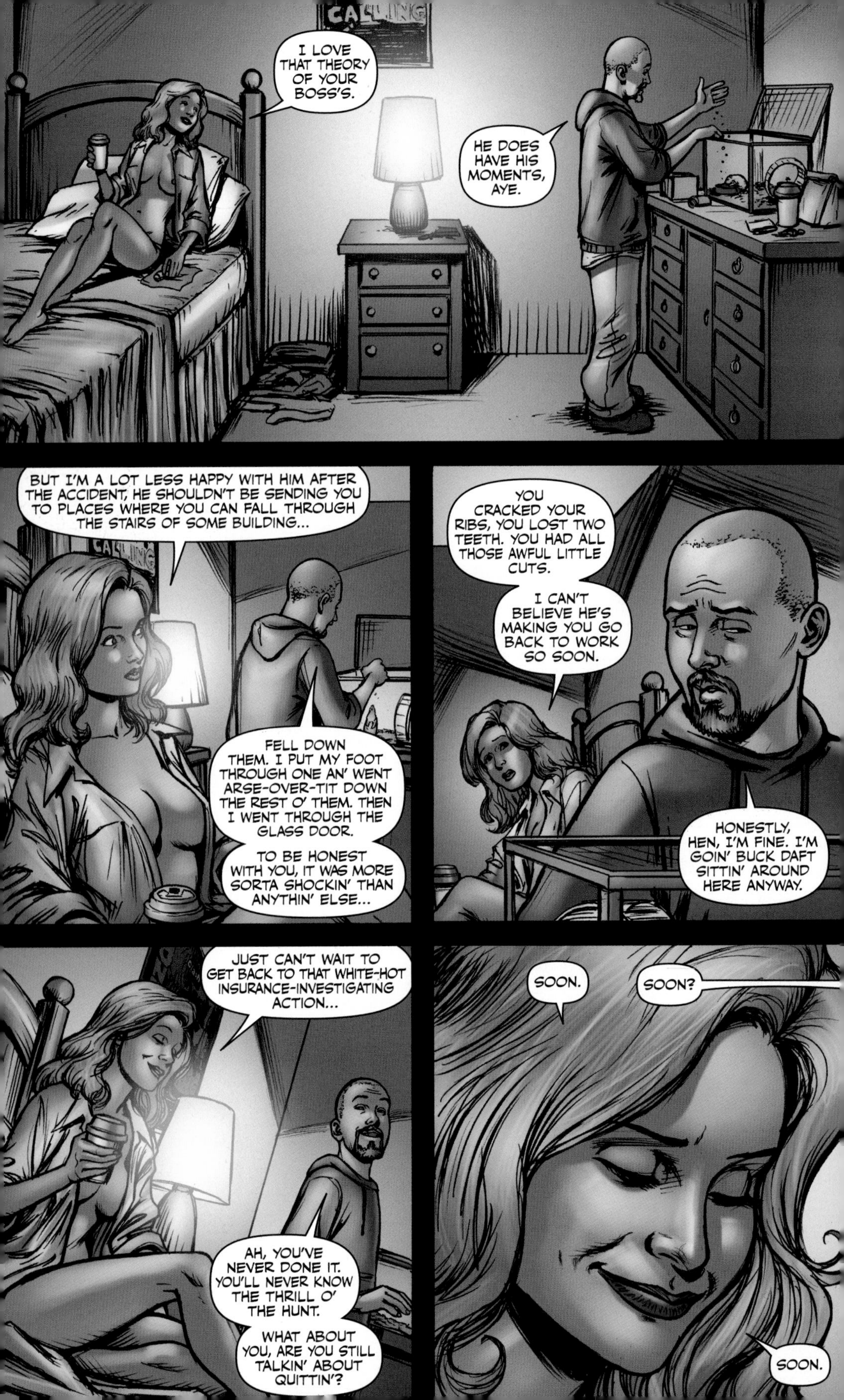
CALLING
I LOVE THAT THEORY OF YOUR BOSS'S.
HE DOES HAVE HIS MOMENTS, AYE.
BUT I'M A LOT LESS HAPPY WITH HIM AFTER THE ACCIDENT, HE SHOULDN'T BE SENDING YOU TO PLACES WHERE YOU CAN FALL THROUGH THE STAIRS OF SOME BUILDING...
FELL DOWN THEM. I PUT MY FOOT THROUGH ONE AN' WENT ARSE-OVER-TIT DOWN THE REST O' THEM. THEN I WENT THROUGH THE GLASS DOOR.
TO BE HONEST WITH YOU, IT WAS MORE SORTA SHOCKIN' THAN ANYTHIN' ELSE...
YOU CRACKED YOUR RIBS, YOU LOST TWO TEETH. YOU HAD ALL THOSE AWFUL LITTLE CUTS.
I CAN'T BELIEVE HE'S MAKING YOU GO BACK TO WORK SO SOON.
HONESTLY, HEN, I'M FINE. I'M GOIN' BUCK DAFT SITTIN' AROUND HERE ANYWAY.
JUST CAN'T WAIT TO GET BACK TO THAT WHITE-HOT INSURANCE-INVESTIGATING ACTION...
AH, YOU'VE NEVER DONE IT. YOU'LL NEVER KNOW THE THRILL O' THE HUNT.
WHAT ABOUT YOU, ARE YOU STILL TALKIN' ABOUT QUITTIN'?
SOON.
SOON?
SOON.

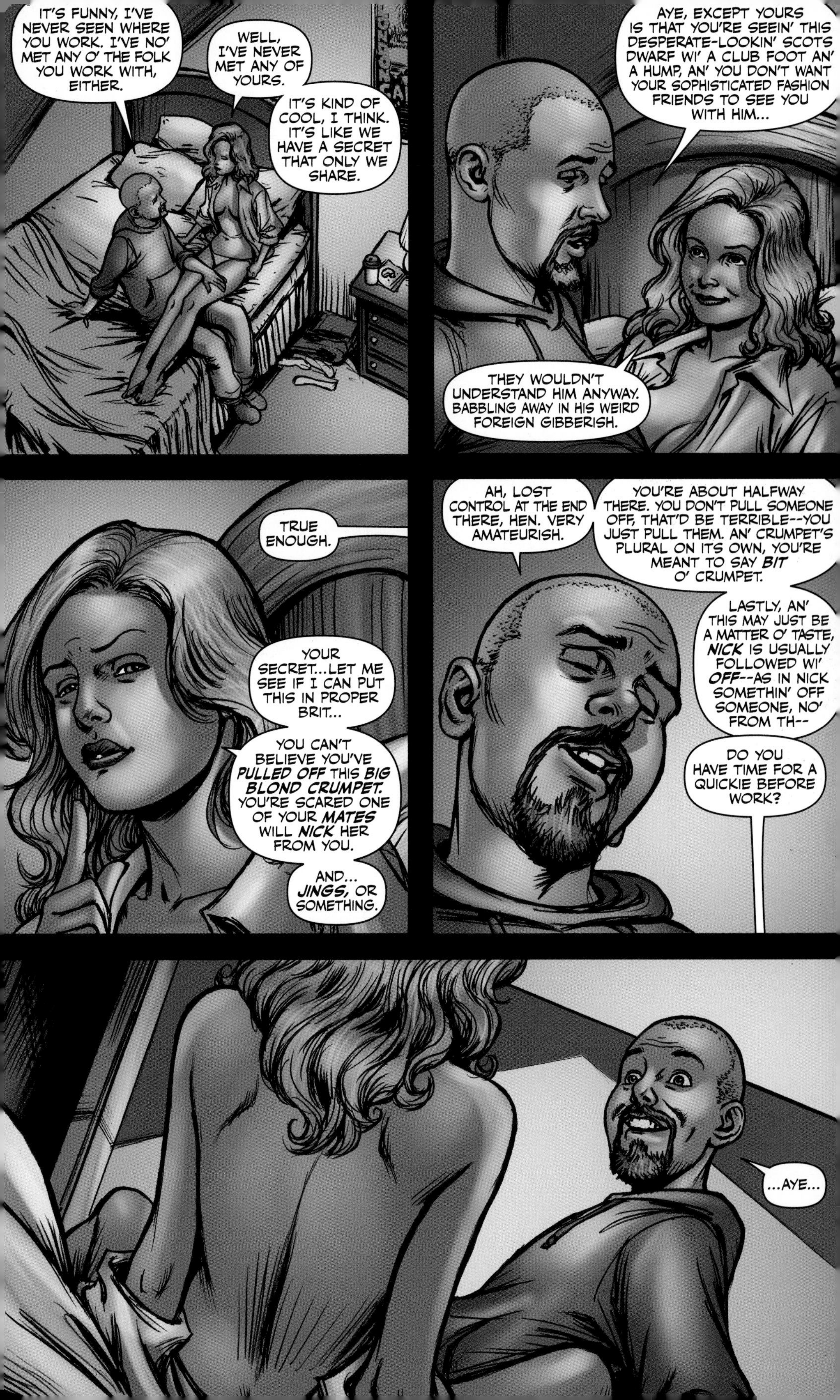

IT'S FUNNY, I'VE NEVER SEEN WHERE YOU WORK. I'VE NO' MET ANY O' THE FOLK YOU WORK WITH, EITHER.
WELL, I'VE NEVER MET ANY OF YOURS.
IT'S KIND OF COOL, I THINK. IT'S LIKE WE HAVE A SECRET THAT ONLY WE SHARE.
AYE, EXCEPT YOURS IS THAT YOU'RE SEEIN' THIS DESPERATE-LOOKIN' SCOTS DWARF WI' A CLUB FOOT AN' A HUMP, AN' YOU DON'T WANT YOUR SOPHISTICATED FASHION FRIENDS TO SEE YOU WITH HIM...
THEY WOULDN'T UNDERSTAND HIM ANYWAY. BABBLING AWAY IN HIS WEIRD FOREIGN GIBBERISH.
TRUE ENOUGH.
YOUR SECRET...LET ME SEE IF I CAN PUT THIS IN PROPER BRIT...
YOU CAN'T BELIEVE YOU'VE *PULLED OFF* THIS *BIG BLOND CRUMPET.* YOU'RE SCARED ONE OF YOUR *MATES* WILL *NICK* HER FROM YOU.
AND... *JINGS,* OR SOMETHING.
AH, LOST CONTROL AT THE END THERE, HEN. VERY AMATEURISH.
YOU'RE ABOUT HALFWAY THERE. YOU DON'T PULL SOMEONE OFF, THAT'D BE TERRIBLE--YOU JUST PULL THEM. AN' CRUMPET'S PLURAL ON ITS OWN, YOU'RE MEANT TO SAY *BIT* O' CRUMPET.
LASTLY, AN' THIS MAY JUST BE A MATTER O' TASTE, *NICK* IS USUALLY FOLLOWED WI' *OFF*--AS IN NICK SOMETHIN' OFF SOMEONE, NO' FROM TH--
DO YOU HAVE TIME FOR A QUICKIE BEFORE WORK?
...AYE...

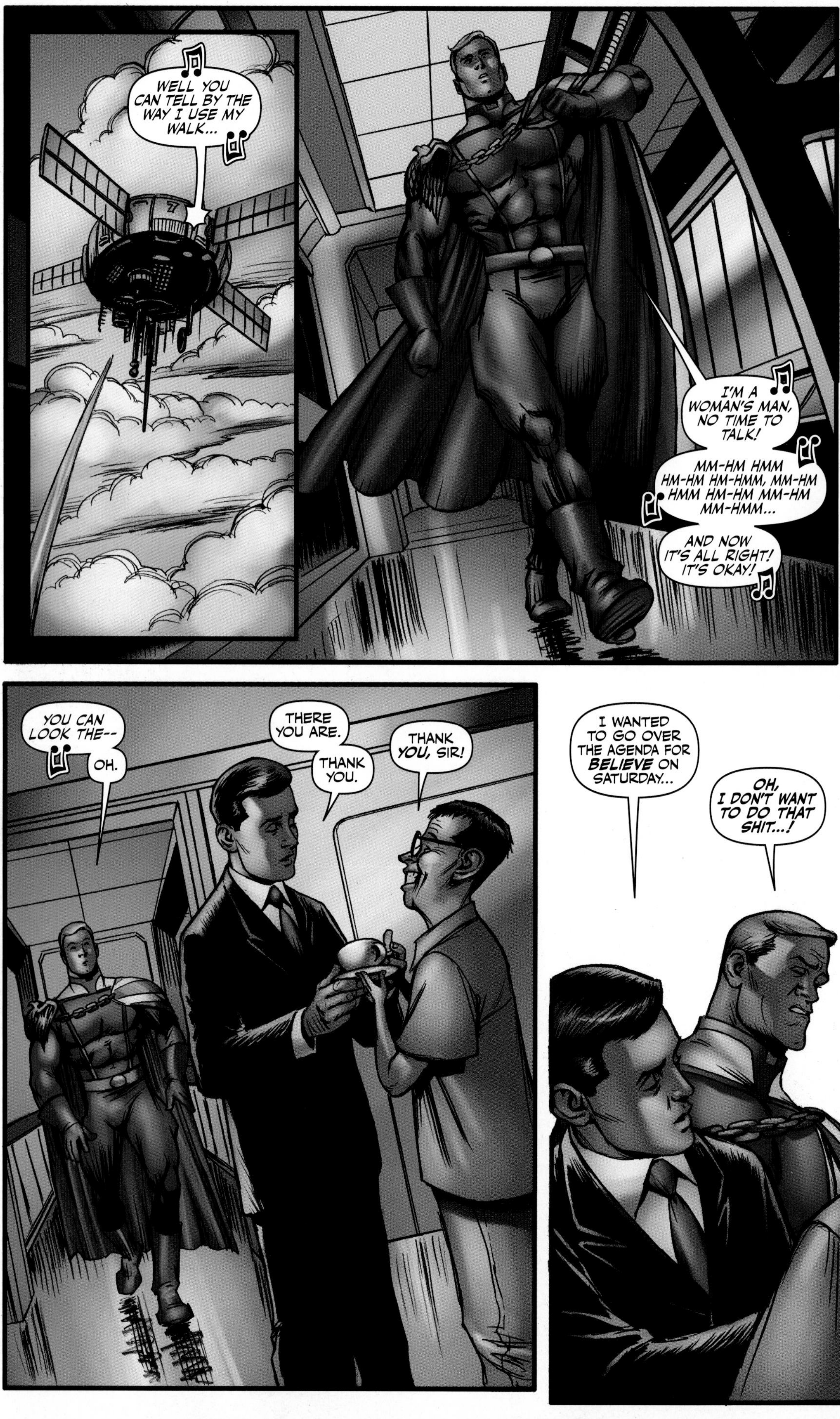
WELL YOU CAN TELL BY THE WAY I USE MY WALK...
I'M A WOMAN'S MAN, NO TIME TO TALK!
MM-HM HMM HM-HM HM-HMM, MM-HM HMM HM-HM MM-HM MM-HMM...
AND NOW IT'S ALL RIGHT! IT'S OKAY!
YOU CAN LOOK THE--
OH.
THERE YOU ARE.
THANK YOU.
THANK YOU, SIR!
I WANTED TO GO OVER THE AGENDA FOR BELIEVE ON SATURDAY...
OH, I DON'T WANT TO DO THAT SHIT...!

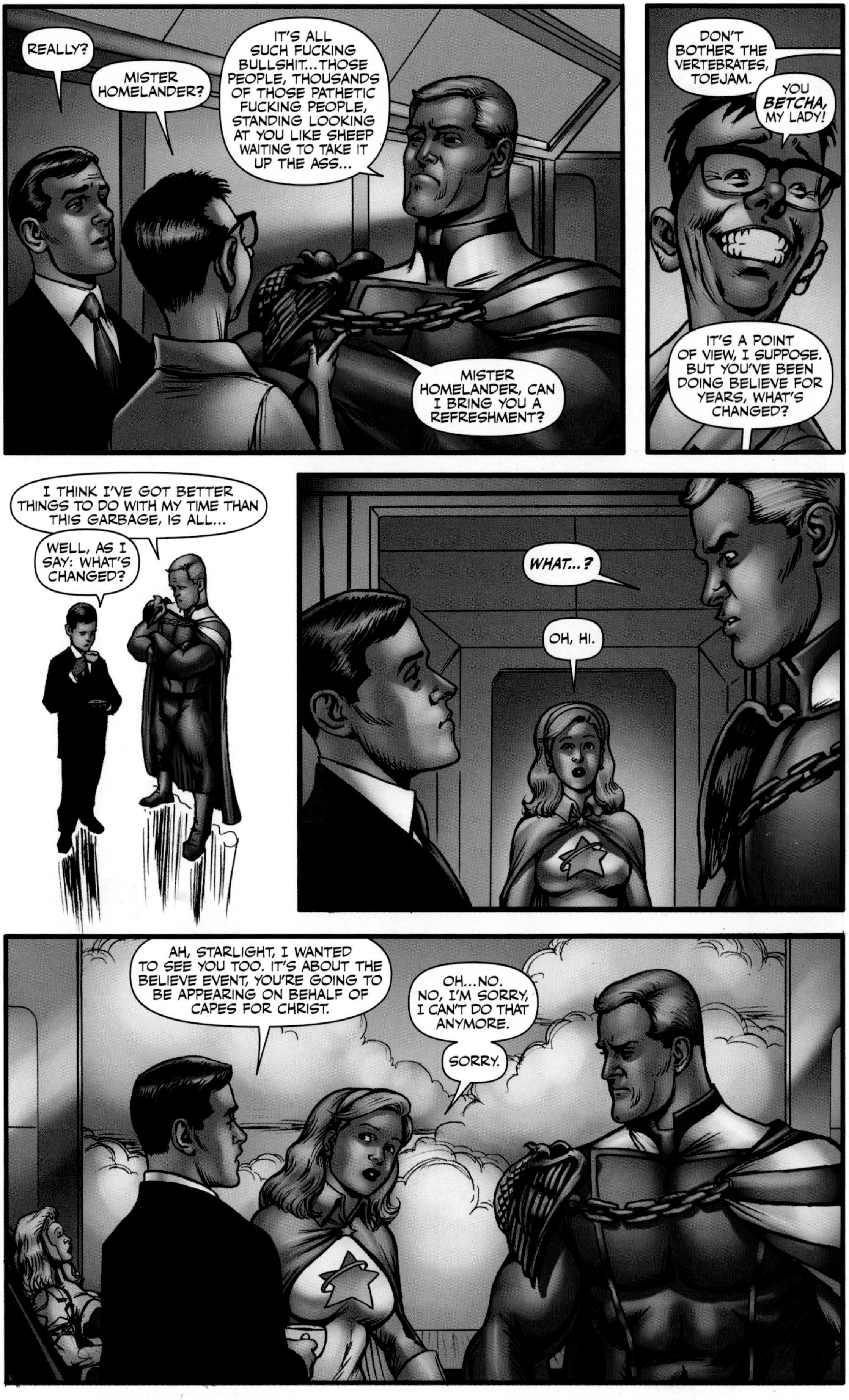
REALLY?
MISTER HOMELANDER?
IT'S ALL SUCH FUCKING BULLSHIT...THOSE PEOPLE, THOUSANDS OF THOSE PATHETIC FUCKING PEOPLE, STANDING LOOKING AT YOU LIKE SHEEP WAITING TO TAKE IT UP THE ASS...
MISTER HOMELANDER, CAN I BRING YOU A REFRESHMENT?
DON'T BOTHER THE VERTEBRATES, TOEJAM.
YOU BETCHA, MY LADY!
IT'S A POINT OF VIEW, I SUPPOSE. BUT YOU'VE BEEN DOING BELIEVE FOR YEARS, WHAT'S CHANGED?
I THINK I'VE GOT BETTER THINGS TO DO WITH MY TIME THAN THIS GARBAGE, IS ALL...
WELL, AS I SAY: WHAT'S CHANGED?
WHAT...?
OH, HI.
AH, STARLIGHT, I WANTED TO SEE YOU TOO. IT'S ABOUT THE BELIEVE EVENT, YOU'RE GOING TO BE APPEARING ON BEHALF OF CAPES FOR CHRIST.
OH...NO. NO, I'M SORRY, I CAN'T DO THAT ANYMORE.
SORRY.

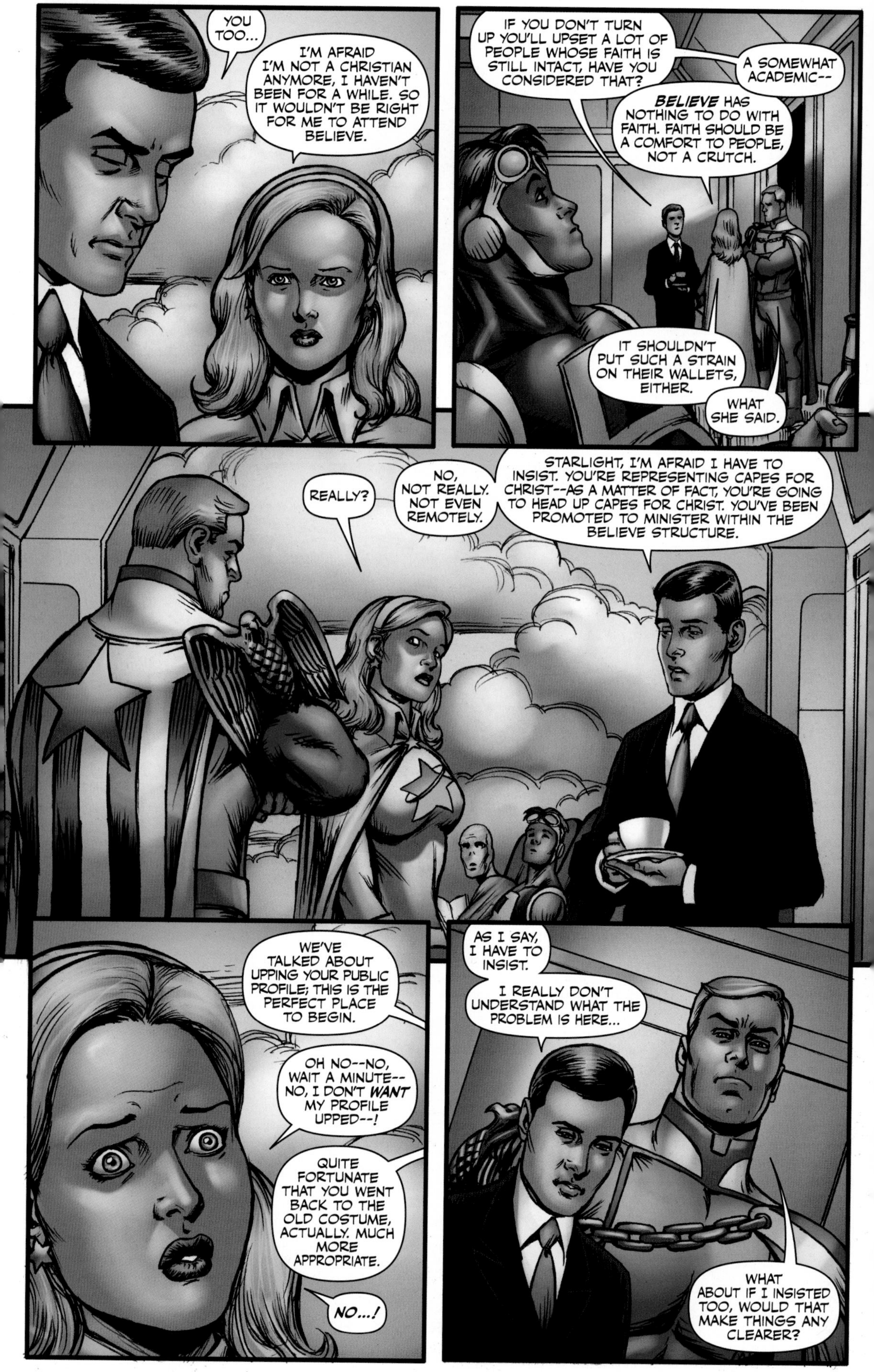

YOU TOO...
I'M AFRAID I'M NOT A CHRISTIAN ANYMORE, I HAVEN'T BEEN FOR A WHILE. SO IT WOULDN'T BE RIGHT FOR ME TO ATTEND BELIEVE.
IF YOU DON'T TURN UP YOU'LL UPSET A LOT OF PEOPLE WHOSE FAITH IS STILL INTACT, HAVE YOU CONSIDERED THAT?
A SOMEWHAT ACADEMIC--
BELIEVE HAS NOTHING TO DO WITH FAITH. FAITH SHOULD BE A COMFORT TO PEOPLE, NOT A CRUTCH.
IT SHOULDN'T PUT SUCH A STRAIN ON THEIR WALLETS, EITHER.
WHAT SHE SAID.
REALLY?
NO, NOT REALLY. NOT EVEN REMOTELY.
STARLIGHT, I'M AFRAID I HAVE TO INSIST. YOU'RE REPRESENTING CAPES FOR CHRIST--AS A MATTER OF FACT, YOU'RE GOING TO HEAD UP CAPES FOR CHRIST. YOU'VE BEEN PROMOTED TO MINISTER WITHIN THE BELIEVE STRUCTURE.
WE'VE TALKED ABOUT UPPING YOUR PUBLIC PROFILE; THIS IS THE PERFECT PLACE TO BEGIN.
OH NO--NO, WAIT A MINUTE--NO, I DON'T *WANT* MY PROFILE UPPED--!
QUITE FORTUNATE THAT YOU WENT BACK TO THE OLD COSTUME, ACTUALLY. MUCH MORE APPROPRIATE.
NO...!
AS I SAY, I HAVE TO INSIST.
I REALLY DON'T UNDERSTAND WHAT THE PROBLEM IS HERE...
WHAT ABOUT IF I INSISTED TOO, WOULD THAT MAKE THINGS ANY CLEARER?

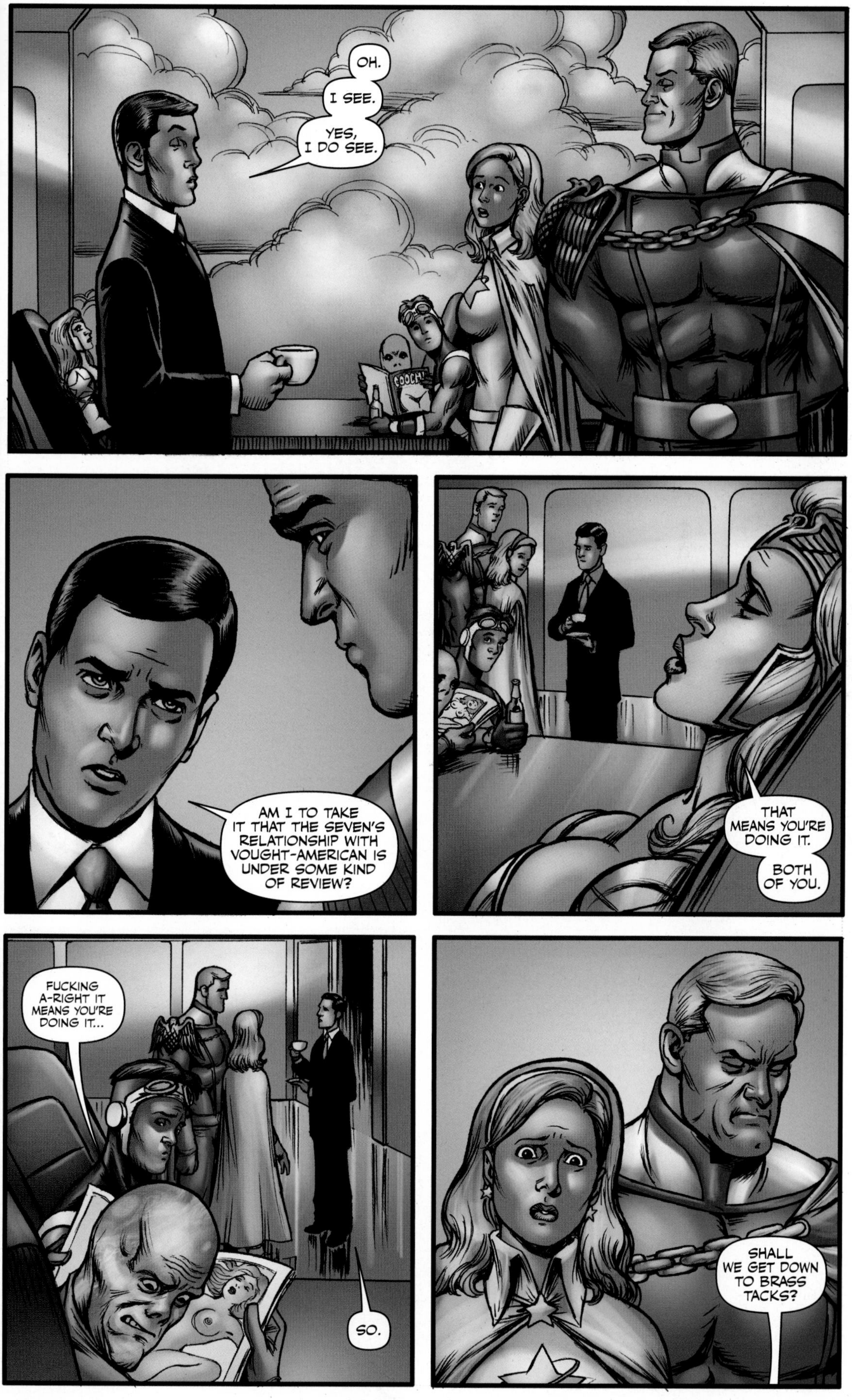
OH.
I SEE.
YES, I DO SEE.
COOCH!
AM I TO TAKE IT THAT THE SEVEN'S RELATIONSHIP WITH VOUGHT-AMERICAN IS UNDER SOME KIND OF REVIEW?
THAT MEANS YOU'RE DOING IT.
BOTH OF YOU.
FUCKING A-RIGHT IT MEANS YOU'RE DOING IT...
SO.
SHALL WE GET DOWN TO BRASS TACKS?

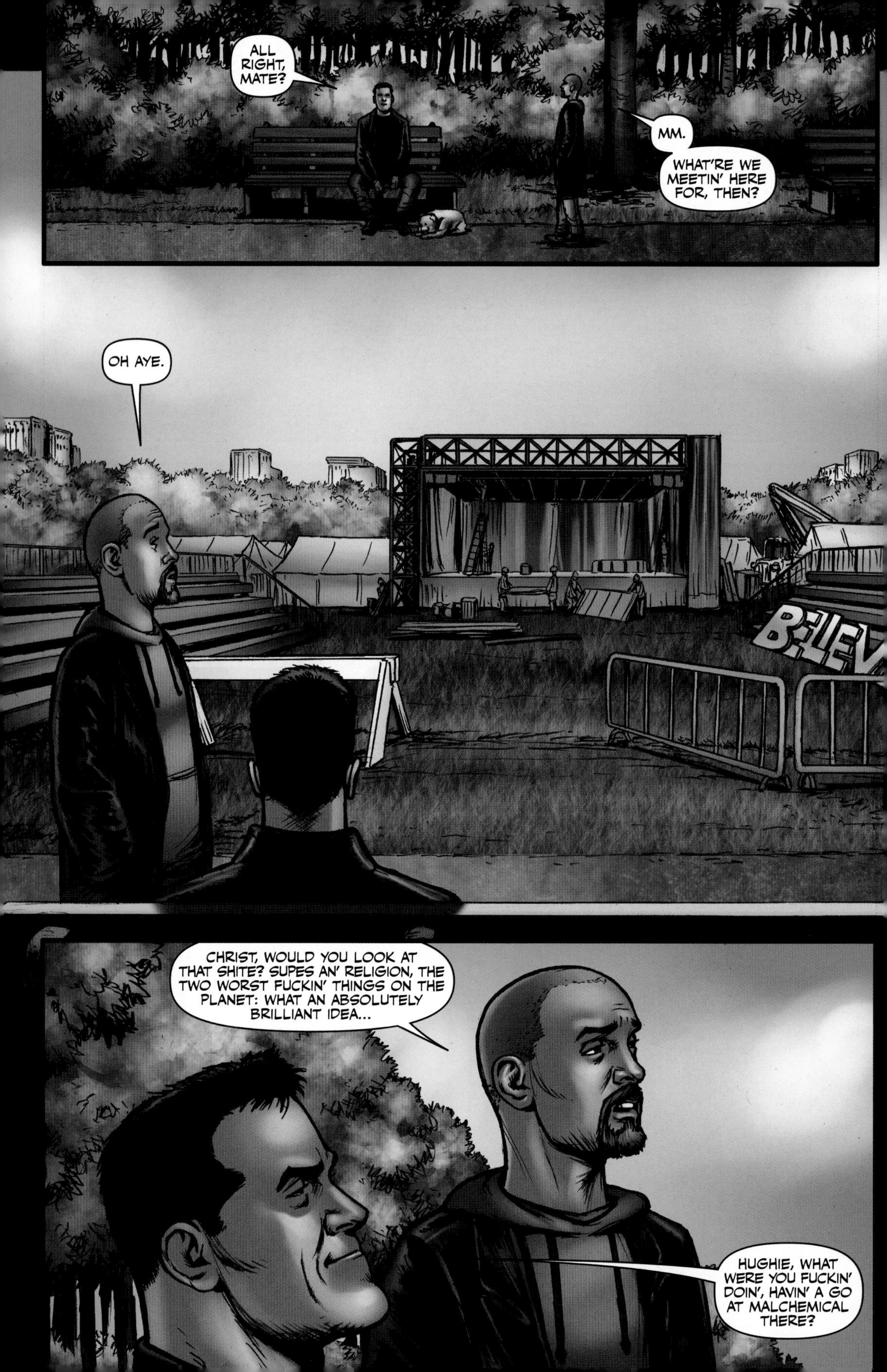
ALL RIGHT, MATE?
MM.
WHAT'RE WE MEETIN' HERE FOR, THEN?
OH AYE.
BELIEV
CHRIST, WOULD YOU LOOK AT THAT SHITE? SUPES AN' RELIGION, THE TWO WORST FUCKIN' THINGS ON THE PLANET: WHAT AN ABSOLUTELY BRILLIANT IDEA...
HUGHIE, WHAT WERE YOU FUCKIN' DOIN', HAVIN' A GO AT MALCHEMICAL THERE?

I...

I WASN'T GONNA GIVE YOU A BOLLOCKIN' WHILE YOU WAS IN HOSPITAL. BUT NOW IT'S TIME TO GO BACK TO WORK.

WANNA SIT DOWN?

I JUST--LOOK, FOR CHRIST'S SAKE, HE WAS GONNA RAPE THEM. MALCHEMICAL, HE WAS GONNA MAKE THOSE TWO WEE LASSIES SUCK HIM OFF, THE FUCKIN' DISGUSTIN' PRICK...

DONE A FUCKSIGHT WORSE'N THAT IN HIS TIME. YOU READ THE FILE.

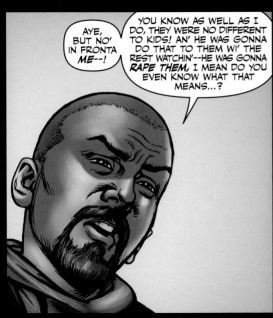

AYE, BUT NO' IN FRONTA *ME*--!

YOU KNOW AS WELL AS I DO, THEY WERE NO DIFFERENT TO KIDS! AN' HE WAS GONNA DO THAT TO THEM WI' THE REST WATCHIN'--HE WAS GONNA *RAPE THEM*, I MEAN DO YOU EVEN KNOW WHAT THAT MEANS...?

YEAH, I THINK I MIGHT HAVE AN INKLIN'.

AW FUCK.

SORRY.

SIT DOWN, WILL YOU? YOU'RE GIVIN' ME A FUCKIN' CRICK IN ME NECK.

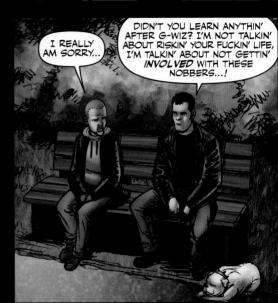

I REALLY AM SORRY...

DIDN'T YOU LEARN ANYTHIN' AFTER G-WIZ? I'M NOT TALKIN' ABOUT RISKIN' YOUR FUCKIN' LIFE, I'M TALKIN' ABOUT NOT GETTIN' *INVOLVED* WITH THESE NOBBERS...!

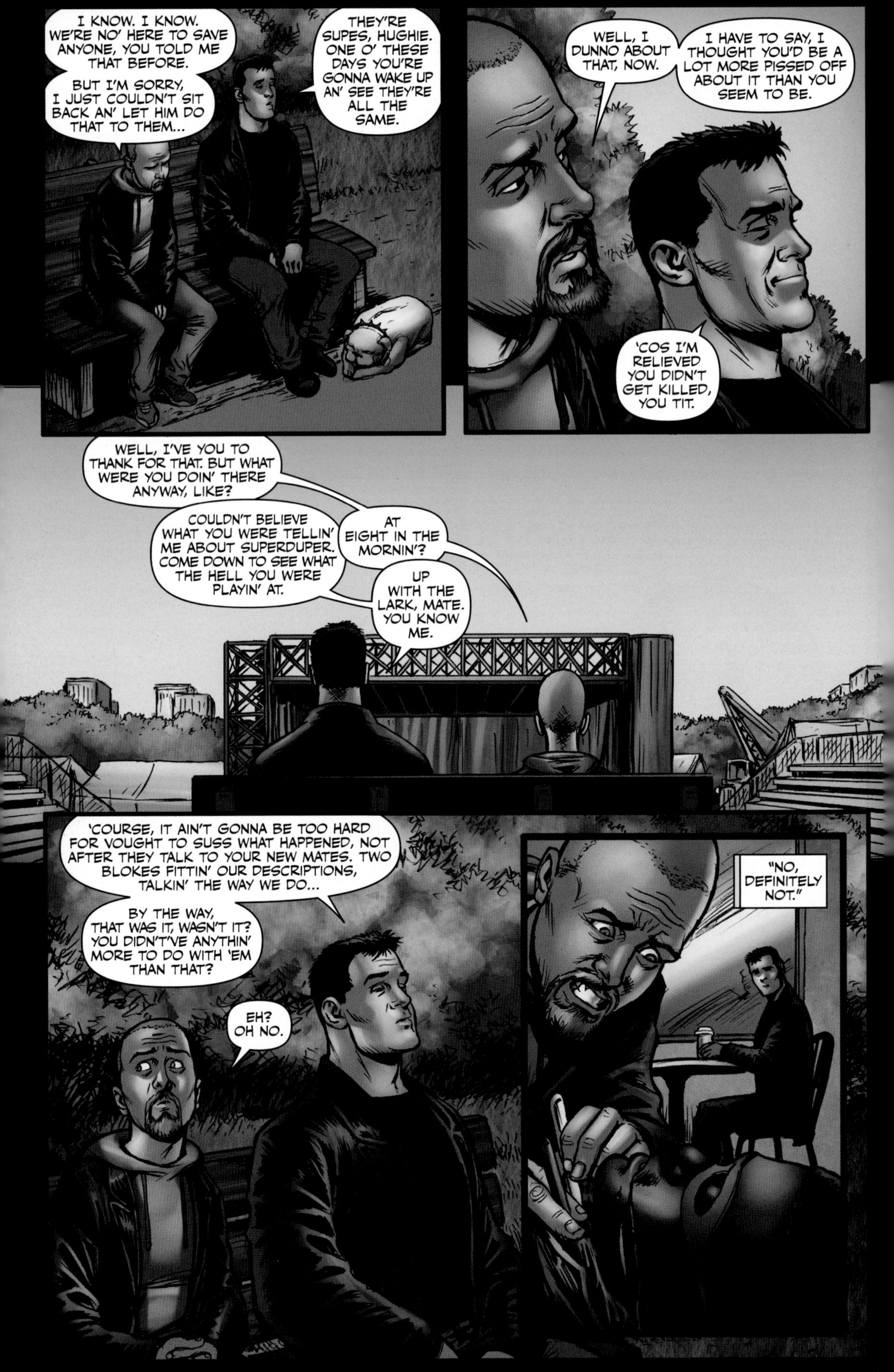
I KNOW. I KNOW. WE'RE NO' HERE TO SAVE ANYONE, YOU TOLD ME THAT BEFORE.
BUT I'M SORRY, I JUST COULDN'T SIT BACK AN' LET HIM DO THAT TO THEM...
THEY'RE SUPES, HUGHIE. ONE O' THESE DAYS YOU'RE GONNA WAKE UP AN' SEE THEY'RE ALL THE SAME.
WELL, I DUNNO ABOUT THAT, NOW.
I HAVE TO SAY, I THOUGHT YOU'D BE A LOT MORE PISSED OFF ABOUT IT THAN YOU SEEM TO BE.
'COS I'M RELIEVED YOU DIDN'T GET KILLED, YOU TIT.
WELL, I'VE YOU TO THANK FOR THAT. BUT WHAT WERE YOU DOIN' THERE ANYWAY, LIKE?
COULDN'T BELIEVE WHAT YOU WERE TELLIN' ME ABOUT SUPERDUPER. COME DOWN TO SEE WHAT THE HELL YOU WERE PLAYIN' AT.
AT EIGHT IN THE MORNIN'?
UP WITH THE LARK, MATE. YOU KNOW ME.
'COURSE, IT AIN'T GONNA BE TOO HARD FOR VOUGHT TO SUSS WHAT HAPPENED, NOT AFTER THEY TALK TO YOUR NEW MATES. TWO BLOKES FITTIN' OUR DESCRIPTIONS, TALKIN' THE WAY WE DO...
BY THE WAY, THAT WAS IT, WASN'T IT? YOU DIDN'T'VE ANYTHIN' MORE TO DO WITH 'EM THAN THAT?
EH? OH NO.
"NO, DEFINITELY NOT."

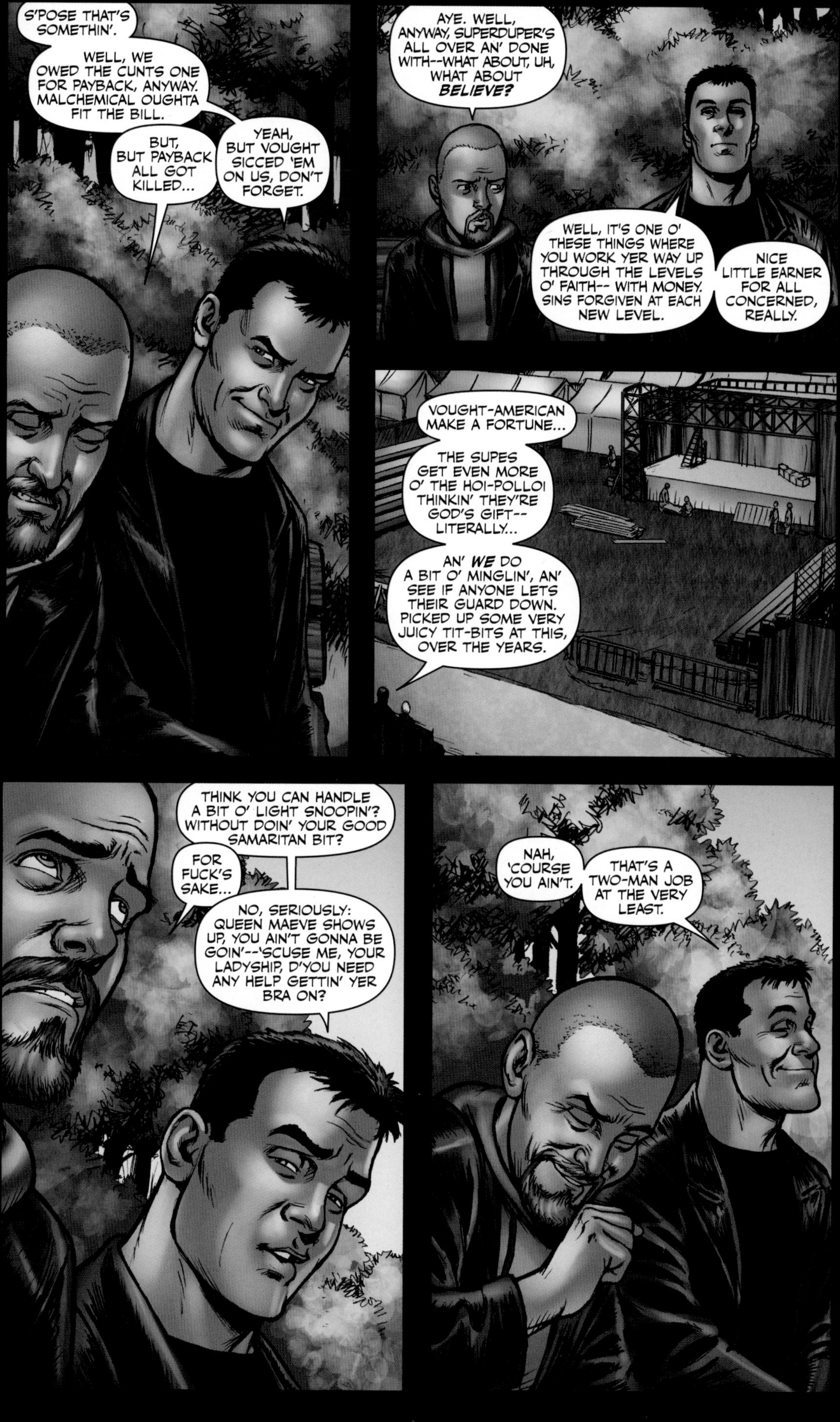
S'POSE THAT'S SOMETHIN'.
WELL, WE OWED THE CUNTS ONE FOR PAYBACK, ANYWAY. MALCHEMICAL OUGHTA FIT THE BILL.
BUT, BUT PAYBACK ALL GOT KILLED...
YEAH, BUT VOUGHT SICCED 'EM ON US, DON'T FORGET.
AYE. WELL, ANYWAY, SUPERDUPER'S ALL OVER AN' DONE WITH--WHAT ABOUT, UH, WHAT ABOUT ***BELIEVE?***
WELL, IT'S ONE O' THESE THINGS WHERE YOU WORK YER WAY UP THROUGH THE LEVELS O' FAITH-- WITH MONEY. SINS FORGIVEN AT EACH NEW LEVEL.
NICE LITTLE EARNER FOR ALL CONCERNED, REALLY.
VOUGHT-AMERICAN MAKE A FORTUNE...
THE SUPES GET EVEN MORE O' THE HOI-POLLOI THINKIN' THEY'RE GOD'S GIFT-- LITERALLY...
AN' ***WE*** DO A BIT O' MINGLIN', AN' SEE IF ANYONE LETS THEIR GUARD DOWN. PICKED UP SOME VERY JUICY TIT-BITS AT THIS, OVER THE YEARS.
THINK YOU CAN HANDLE A BIT O' LIGHT SNOOPIN'? WITHOUT DOIN' YOUR GOOD SAMARITAN BIT?
FOR FUCK'S SAKE...
NO, SERIOUSLY: QUEEN MAEVE SHOWS UP, YOU AIN'T GONNA BE GOIN'--'SCUSE ME, YOUR LADYSHIP, D'YOU NEED ANY HELP GETTIN' YER BRA ON?
NAH, 'COURSE YOU AIN'T.
THAT'S A TWO-MAN JOB AT THE VERY LEAST.

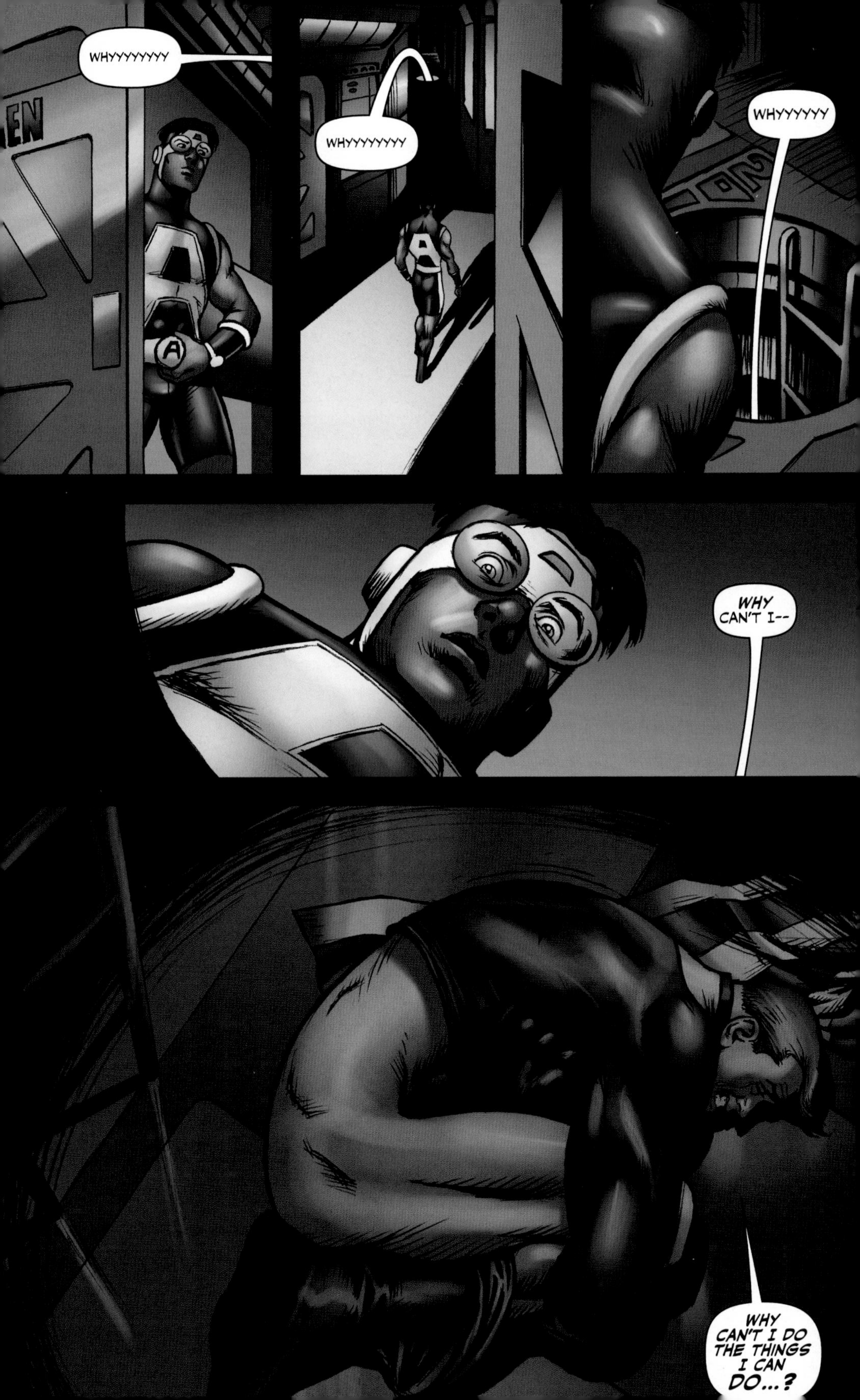

WHYYYYYYYY
WHYYYYYYYY
WHYYYYYY
WHY CAN'T I--
WHY CAN'T I DO THE THINGS I CAN DO...?

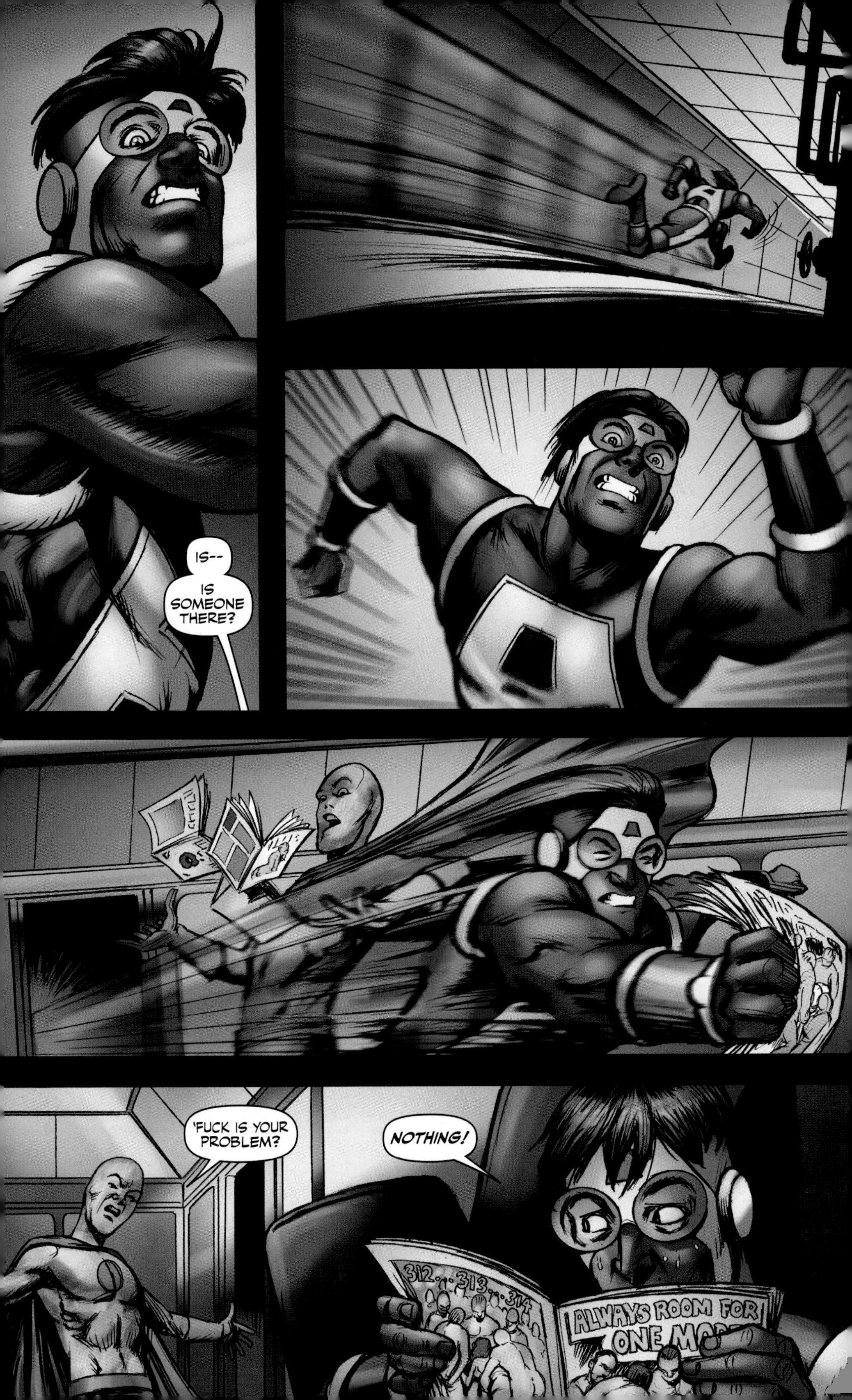
IS--
IS SOMEONE THERE?
'FUCK IS YOUR PROBLEM?
NOTHING!
312...313...314
ALWAYS ROOM FOR ONE MO

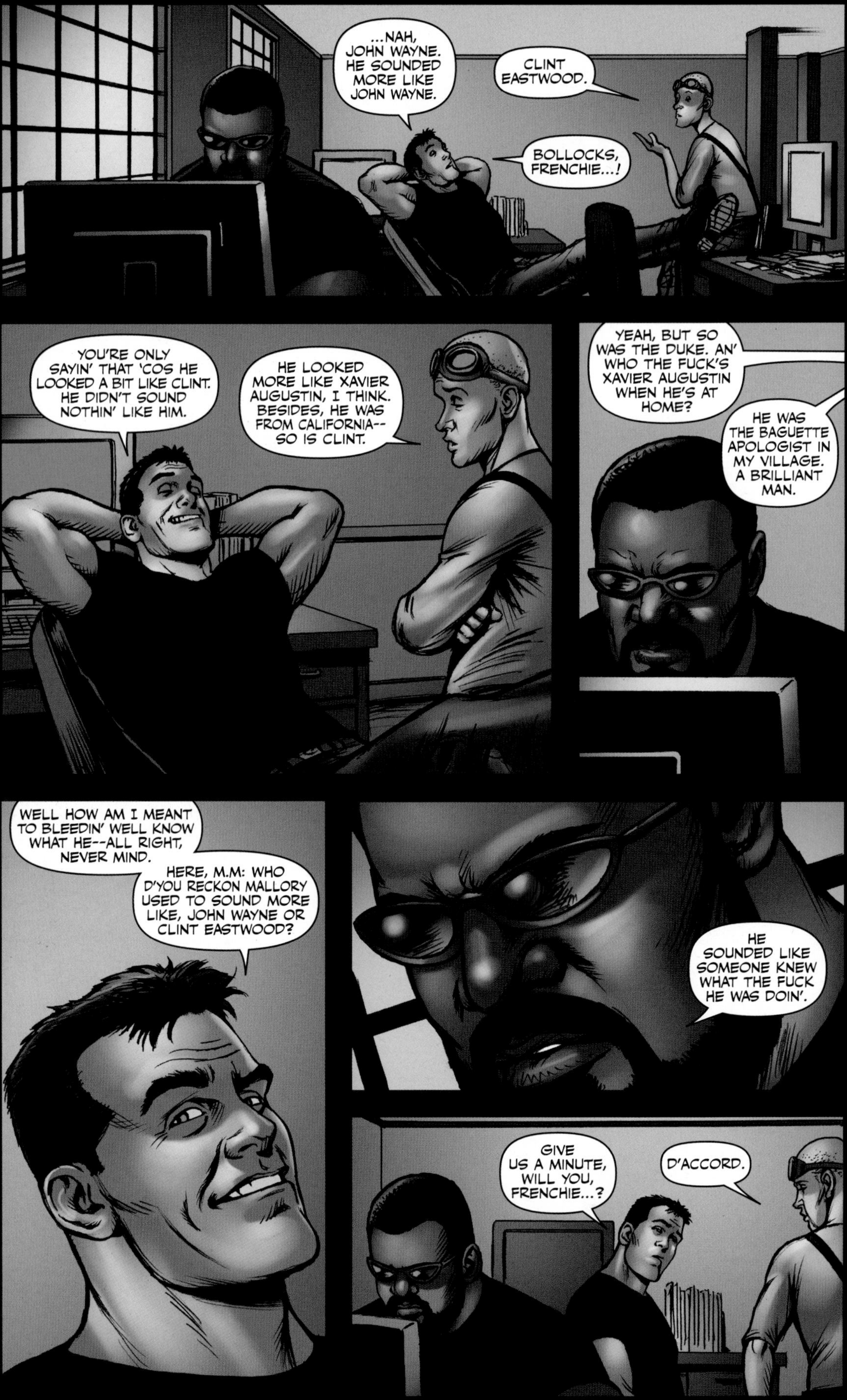
...NAH, JOHN WAYNE. HE SOUNDED MORE LIKE JOHN WAYNE.
CLINT EASTWOOD.
BOLLOCKS, FRENCHIE...!
YOU'RE ONLY SAYIN' THAT 'COS HE LOOKED A BIT LIKE CLINT. HE DIDN'T SOUND NOTHIN' LIKE HIM.
HE LOOKED MORE LIKE XAVIER AUGUSTIN, I THINK. BESIDES, HE WAS FROM CALIFORNIA-- SO IS CLINT.
YEAH, BUT SO WAS THE DUKE. AN' WHO THE FUCK'S XAVIER AUGUSTIN WHEN HE'S AT HOME?
HE WAS THE BAGUETTE APOLOGIST IN MY VILLAGE. A BRILLIANT MAN.
WELL HOW AM I MEANT TO BLEEDIN' WELL KNOW WHAT HE--ALL RIGHT, NEVER MIND.
HERE, M.M: WHO D'YOU RECKON MALLORY USED TO SOUND MORE LIKE, JOHN WAYNE OR CLINT EASTWOOD?
HE SOUNDED LIKE SOMEONE KNEW WHAT THE FUCK HE WAS DOIN'.
GIVE US A MINUTE, WILL YOU, FRENCHIE...?
D'ACCORD.

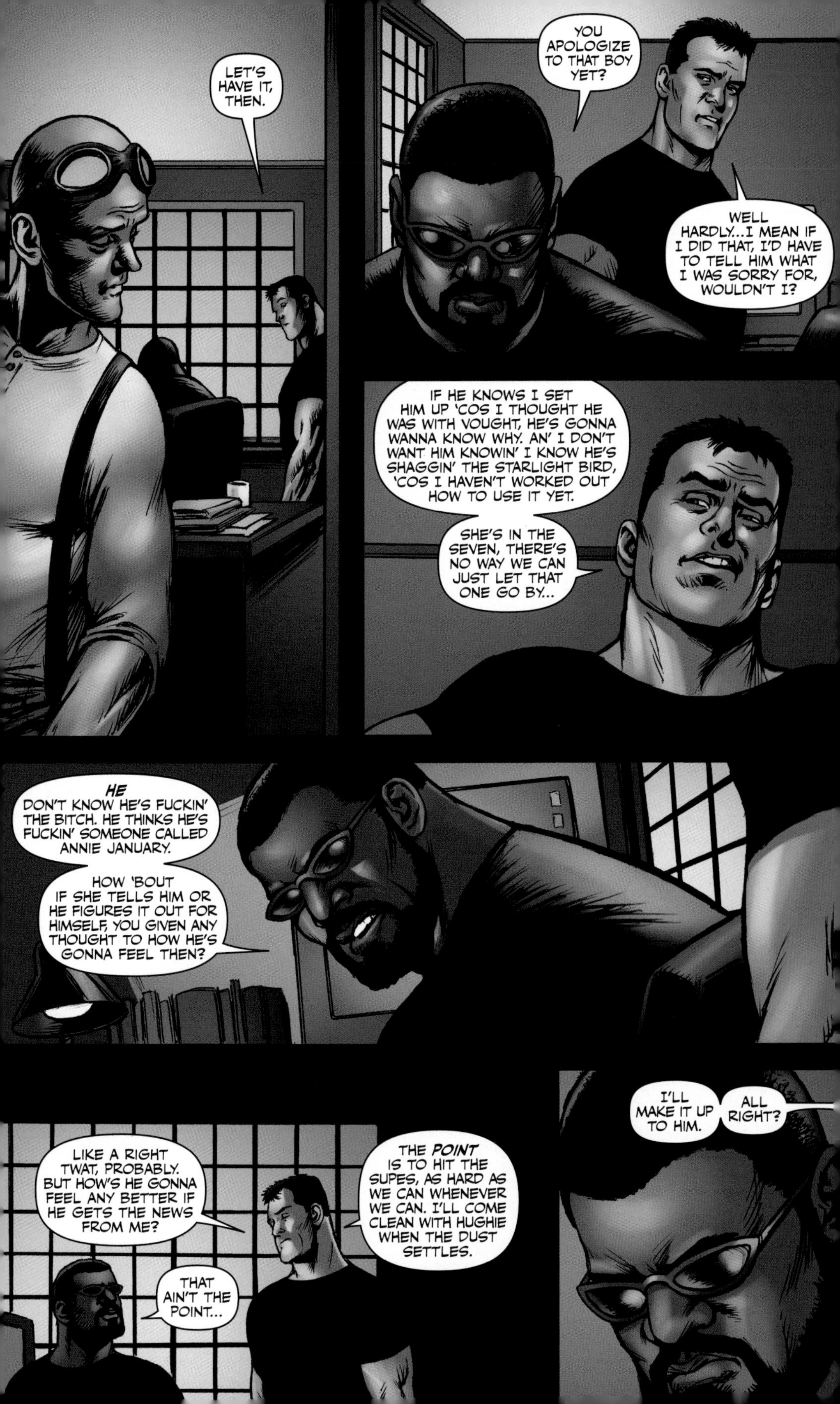
LET'S HAVE IT, THEN.
YOU APOLOGIZE TO THAT BOY YET?
WELL HARDLY...I MEAN IF I DID THAT, I'D HAVE TO TELL HIM WHAT I WAS SORRY FOR, WOULDN'T I?
IF HE KNOWS I SET HIM UP 'COS I THOUGHT HE WAS WITH VOUGHT, HE'S GONNA WANNA KNOW WHY. AN' I DON'T WANT HIM KNOWIN' I KNOW HE'S SHAGGIN' THE STARLIGHT BIRD, 'COS I HAVEN'T WORKED OUT HOW TO USE IT YET.
SHE'S IN THE SEVEN, THERE'S NO WAY WE CAN JUST LET THAT ONE GO BY...
HE DON'T KNOW HE'S FUCKIN' THE BITCH. HE THINKS HE'S FUCKIN' SOMEONE CALLED ANNIE JANUARY.
HOW 'BOUT IF SHE TELLS HIM OR HE FIGURES IT OUT FOR HIMSELF, YOU GIVEN ANY THOUGHT TO HOW HE'S GONNA FEEL THEN?
LIKE A RIGHT TWAT, PROBABLY. BUT HOW'S HE GONNA FEEL ANY BETTER IF HE GETS THE NEWS FROM ME?
THAT AIN'T THE POINT...
THE *POINT* IS TO HIT THE SUPES, AS HARD AS WE CAN WHENEVER WE CAN. I'LL COME CLEAN WITH HUGHIE WHEN THE DUST SETTLES.
I'LL MAKE IT UP TO HIM.
ALL RIGHT?

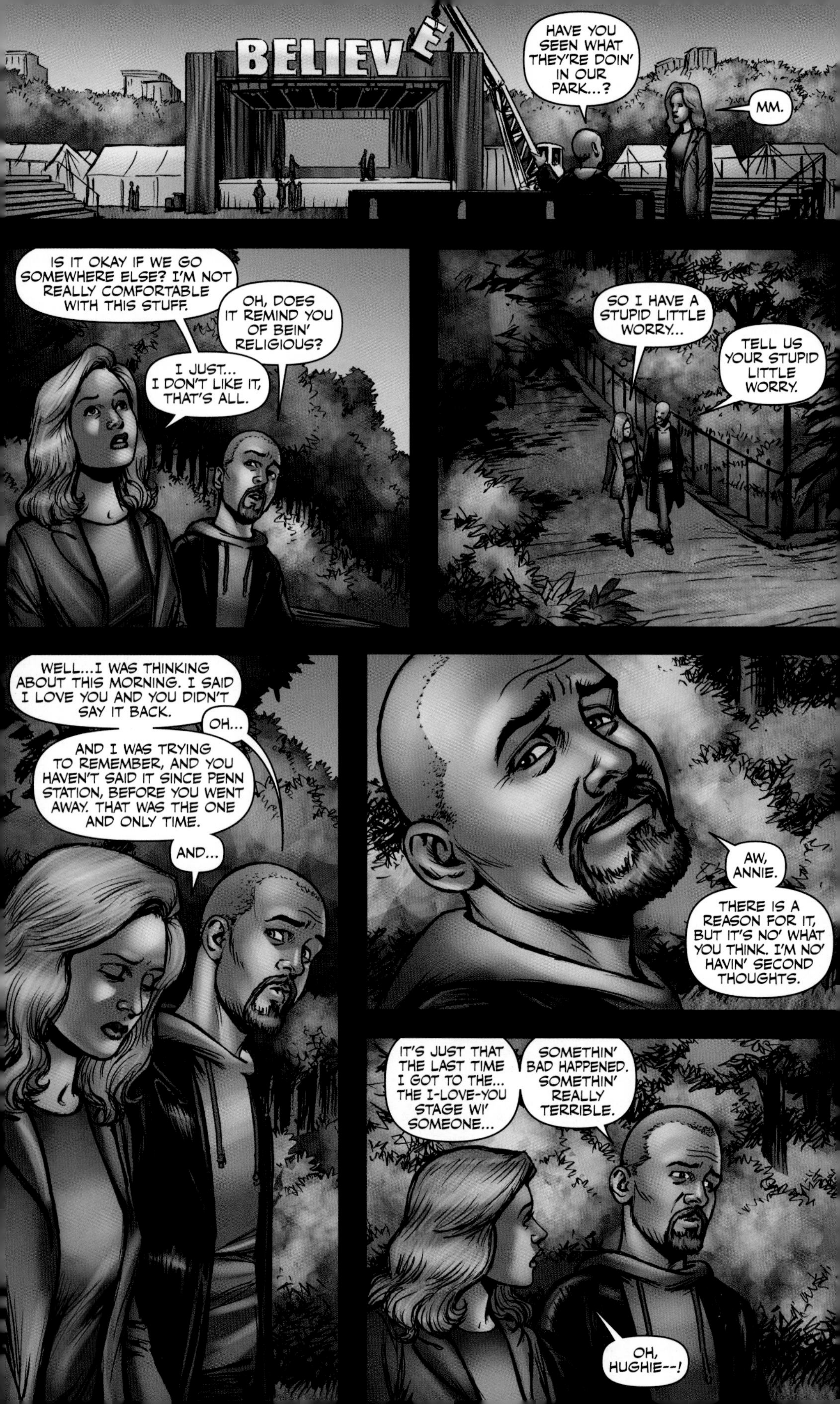
BELIEVE
HAVE YOU SEEN WHAT THEY'RE DOIN' IN OUR PARK...?
MM.
IS IT OKAY IF WE GO SOMEWHERE ELSE? I'M NOT REALLY COMFORTABLE WITH THIS STUFF.
OH, DOES IT REMIND YOU OF BEIN' RELIGIOUS?
I JUST... I DON'T LIKE IT, THAT'S ALL.
SO I HAVE A STUPID LITTLE WORRY...
TELL US YOUR STUPID LITTLE WORRY.
WELL...I WAS THINKING ABOUT THIS MORNING. I SAID I LOVE YOU AND YOU DIDN'T SAY IT BACK.
OH...
AND I WAS TRYING TO REMEMBER, AND YOU HAVEN'T SAID IT SINCE PENN STATION, BEFORE YOU WENT AWAY. THAT WAS THE ONE AND ONLY TIME.
AND...
AW, ANNIE.
THERE IS A REASON FOR IT, BUT IT'S NO' WHAT YOU THINK. I'M NO' HAVIN' SECOND THOUGHTS.
IT'S JUST THAT THE LAST TIME I GOT TO THE... THE I-LOVE-YOU STAGE WI' SOMEONE...
SOMETHIN' BAD HAPPENED. SOMETHIN' REALLY TERRIBLE.
OH, HUGHIE--!

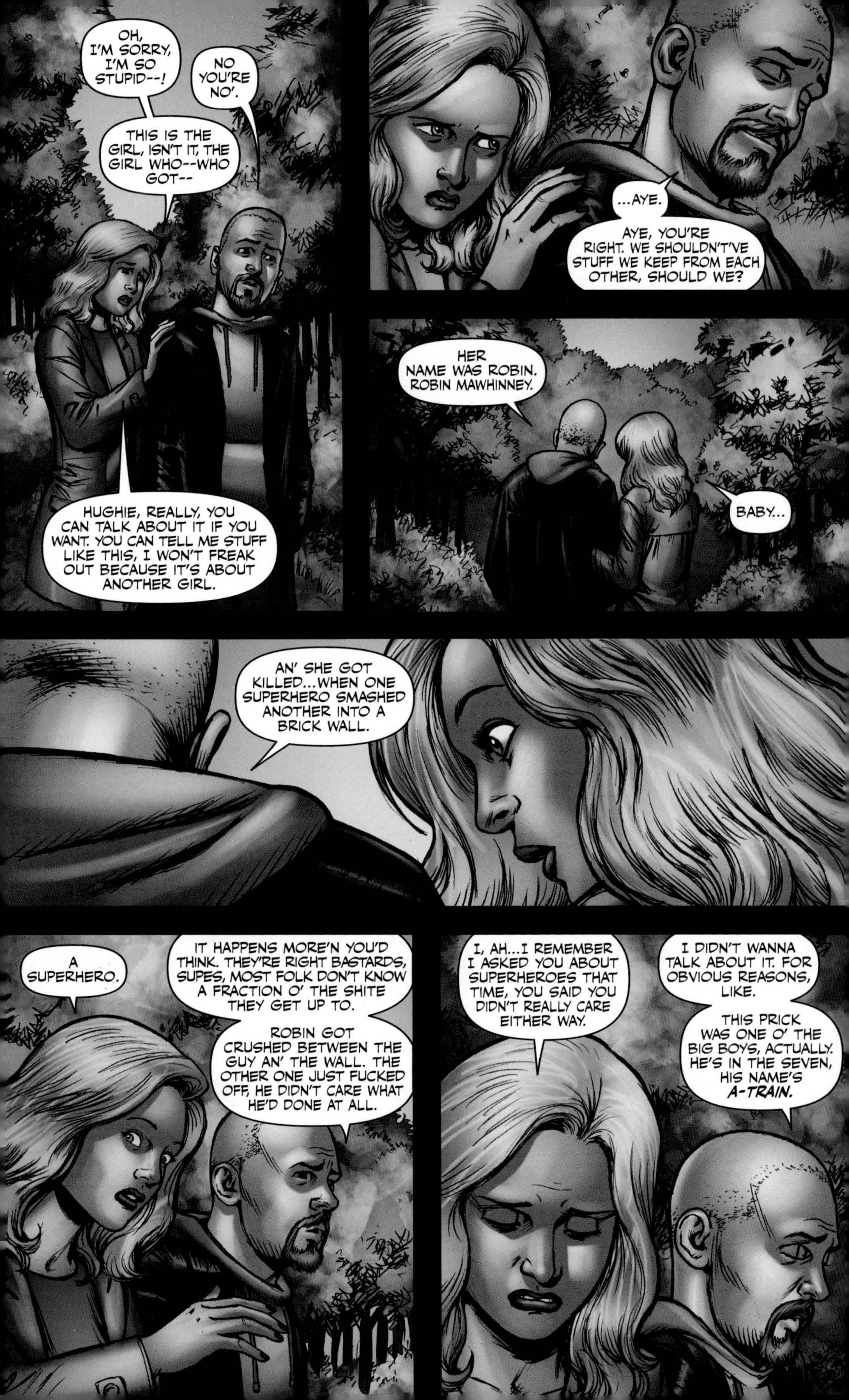
OH, I'M SORRY, I'M SO STUPID--!
NO YOU'RE NO'.
THIS IS THE GIRL, ISN'T IT, THE GIRL WHO--WHO GOT--
HUGHIE, REALLY, YOU CAN TALK ABOUT IT IF YOU WANT. YOU CAN TELL ME STUFF LIKE THIS, I WON'T FREAK OUT BECAUSE IT'S ABOUT ANOTHER GIRL.
...AYE.
AYE, YOU'RE RIGHT. WE SHOULDN'T'VE STUFF WE KEEP FROM EACH OTHER, SHOULD WE?
HER NAME WAS ROBIN. ROBIN MAWHINNEY.
BABY...
AN' SHE GOT KILLED...WHEN ONE SUPERHERO SMASHED ANOTHER INTO A BRICK WALL.
A SUPERHERO.
IT HAPPENS MORE'N YOU'D THINK. THEY'RE RIGHT BASTARDS, SUPES, MOST FOLK DON'T KNOW A FRACTION O' THE SHITE THEY GET UP TO.
ROBIN GOT CRUSHED BETWEEN THE GUY AN' THE WALL. THE OTHER ONE JUST FUCKED OFF, HE DIDN'T CARE WHAT HE'D DONE AT ALL.
I, AH...I REMEMBER I ASKED YOU ABOUT SUPERHEROES THAT TIME, YOU SAID YOU DIDN'T REALLY CARE EITHER WAY.
I DIDN'T WANNA TALK ABOUT IT. FOR OBVIOUS REASONS, LIKE.
THIS PRICK WAS ONE O' THE BIG BOYS, ACTUALLY. HE'S IN THE SEVEN, HIS NAME'S *A-TRAIN.*

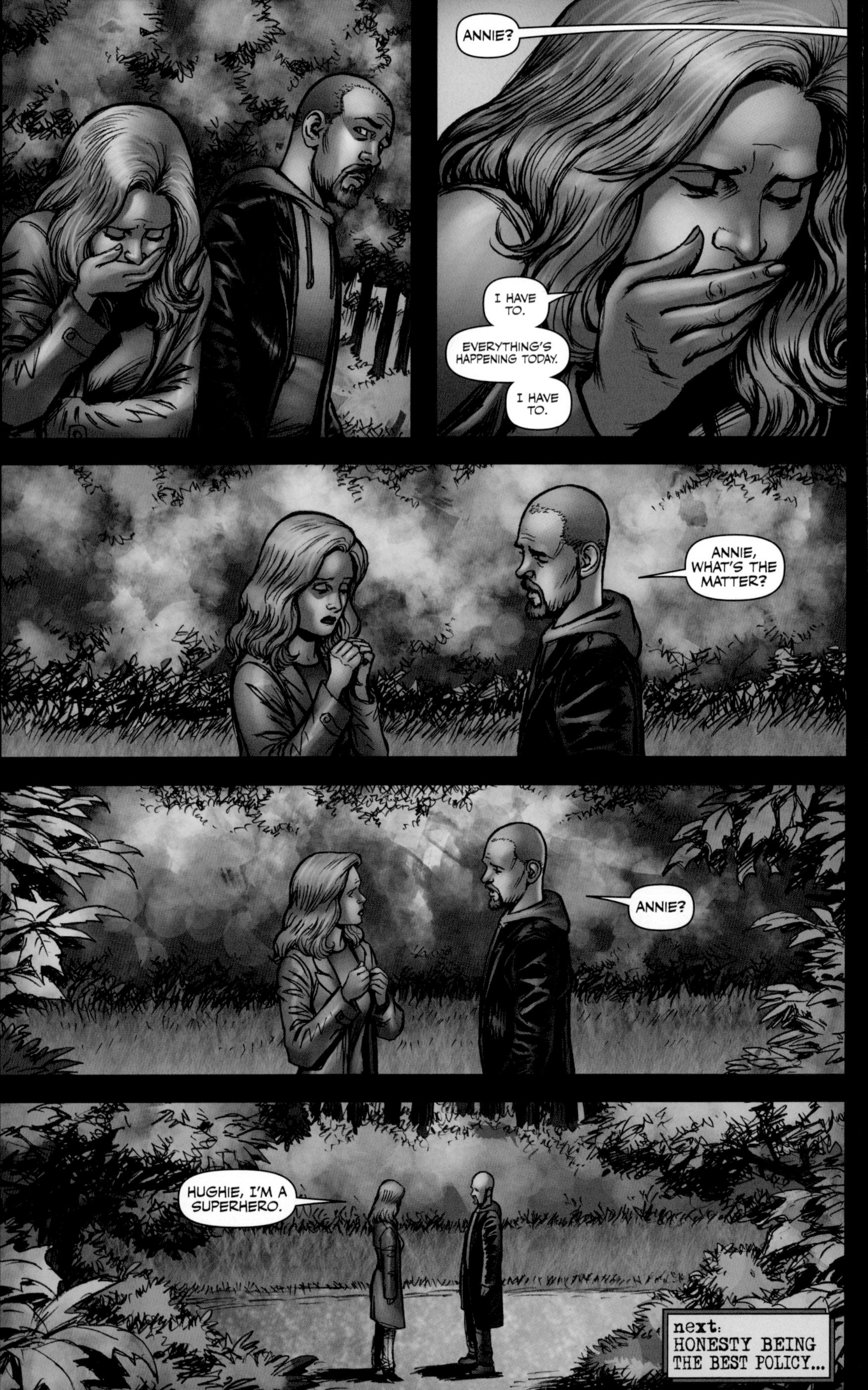
ANNIE?
I HAVE TO.
EVERYTHING'S HAPPENING TODAY.
I HAVE TO.
ANNIE, WHAT'S THE MATTER?
ANNIE?
HUGHIE, I'M A SUPERHERO.
next: HONESTY BEING THE BEST POLICY...

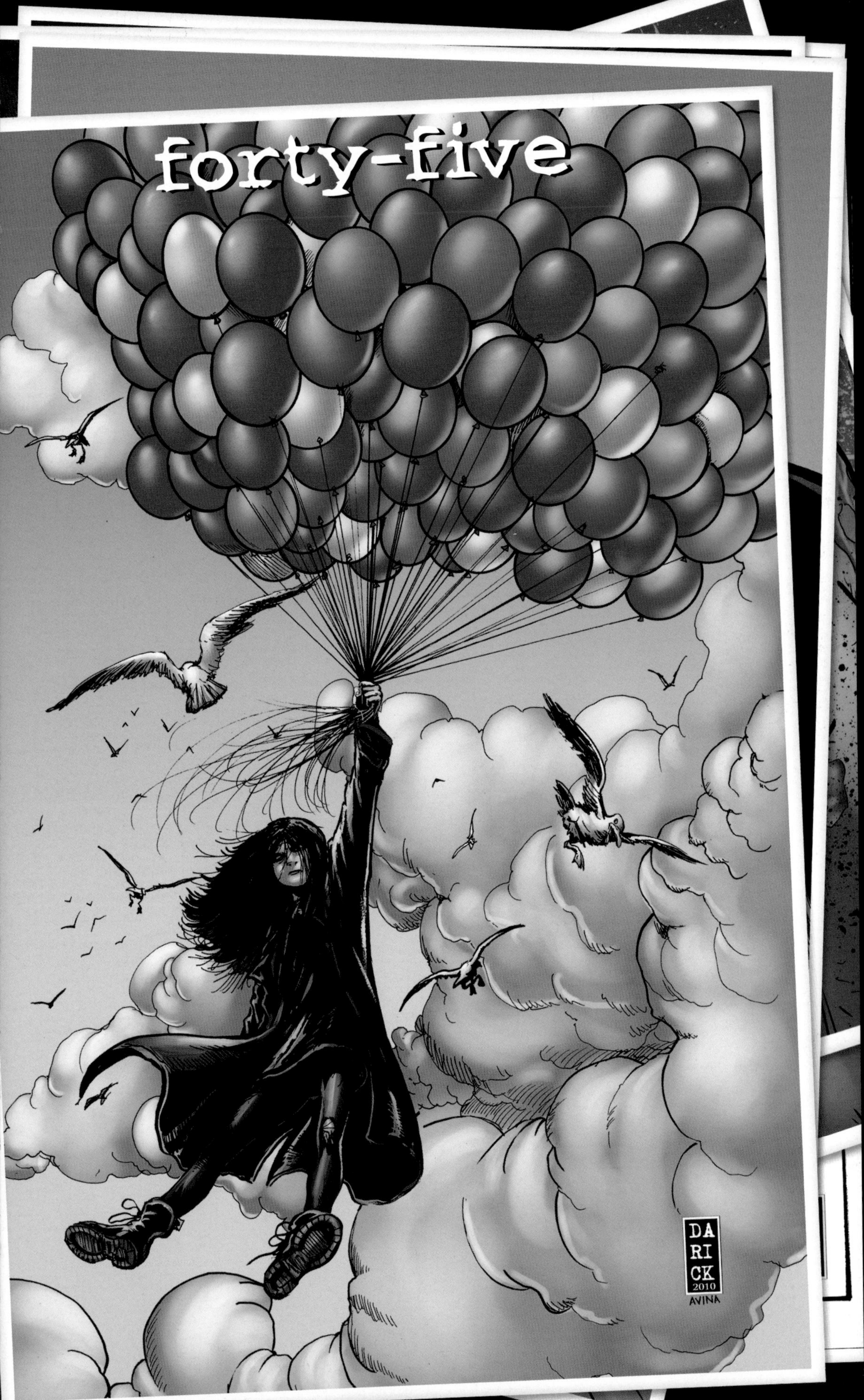
forty-five
DA
RI
CK
2010
AVINA

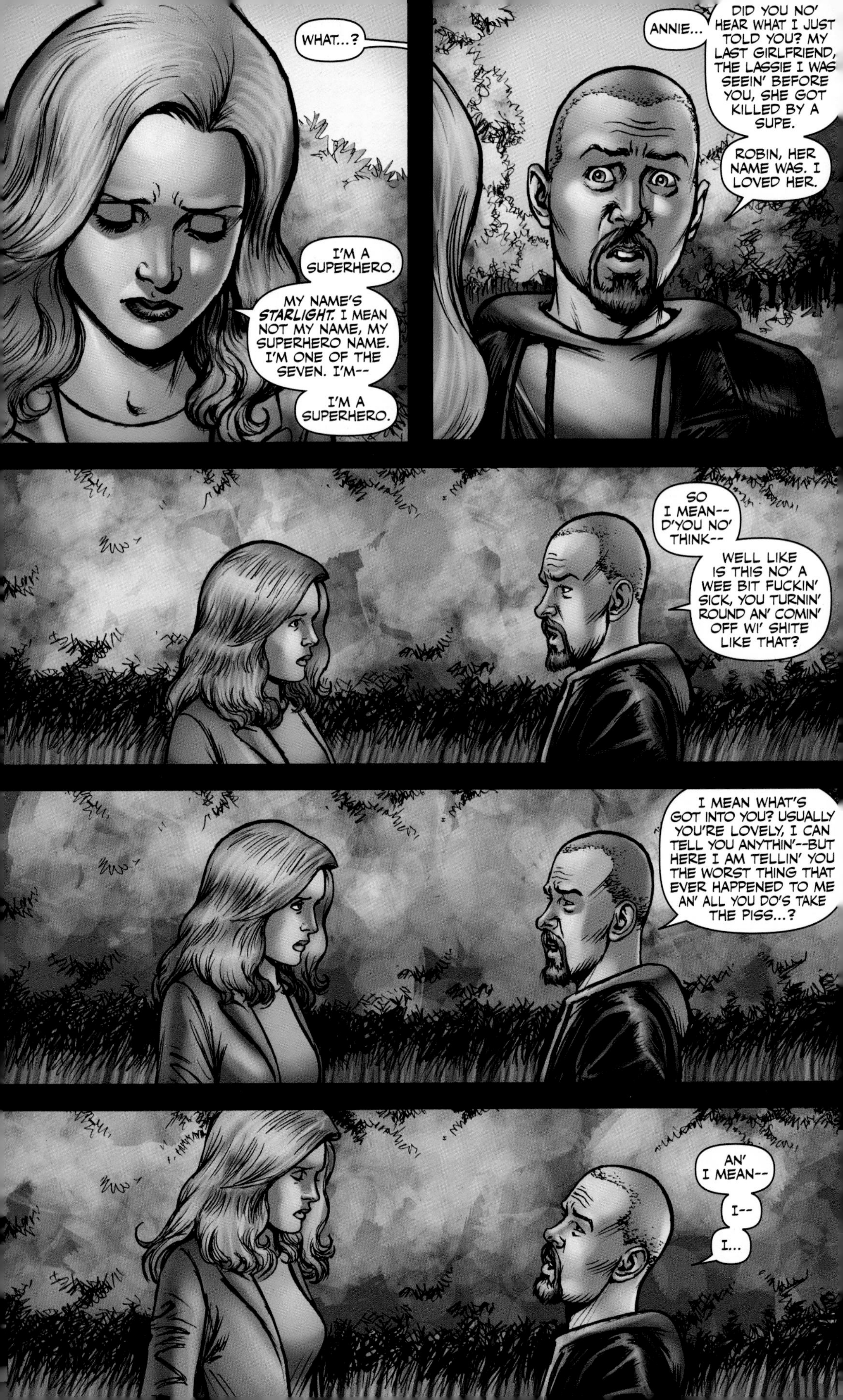
WHAT...?
I'M A SUPERHERO.
MY NAME'S *STARLIGHT.* I MEAN NOT MY NAME, MY SUPERHERO NAME. I'M ONE OF THE SEVEN. I'M--
I'M A SUPERHERO.
ANNIE...
DID YOU NO' HEAR WHAT I JUST TOLD YOU? MY LAST GIRLFRIEND, THE LASSIE I WAS SEEIN' BEFORE YOU, SHE GOT KILLED BY A SUPE.
ROBIN, HER NAME WAS. I LOVED HER.
SO I MEAN-- D'YOU NO' THINK--
WELL LIKE IS THIS NO' A WEE BIT FUCKIN' SICK, YOU TURNIN' ROUND AN' COMIN' OFF WI' SHITE LIKE THAT?
I MEAN WHAT'S GOT INTO YOU? USUALLY YOU'RE LOVELY, I CAN TELL YOU ANYTHIN'--BUT HERE I AM TELLIN' YOU THE WORST THING THAT EVER HAPPENED TO ME AN' ALL YOU DO'S TAKE THE PISS...?
AN' I MEAN--
I--
I...

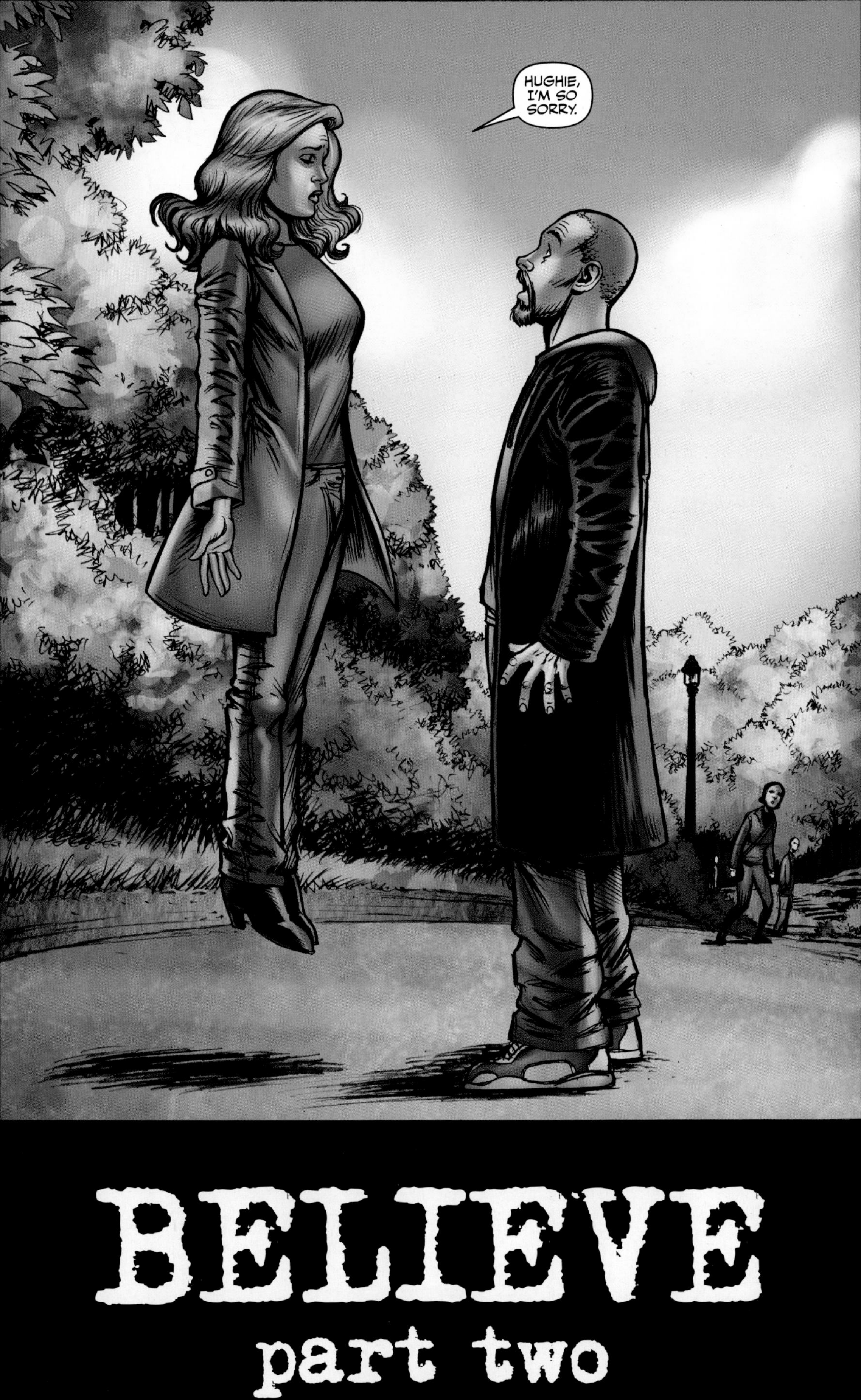
HUGHIE, I'M SO SORRY.

BELIEVE
part two

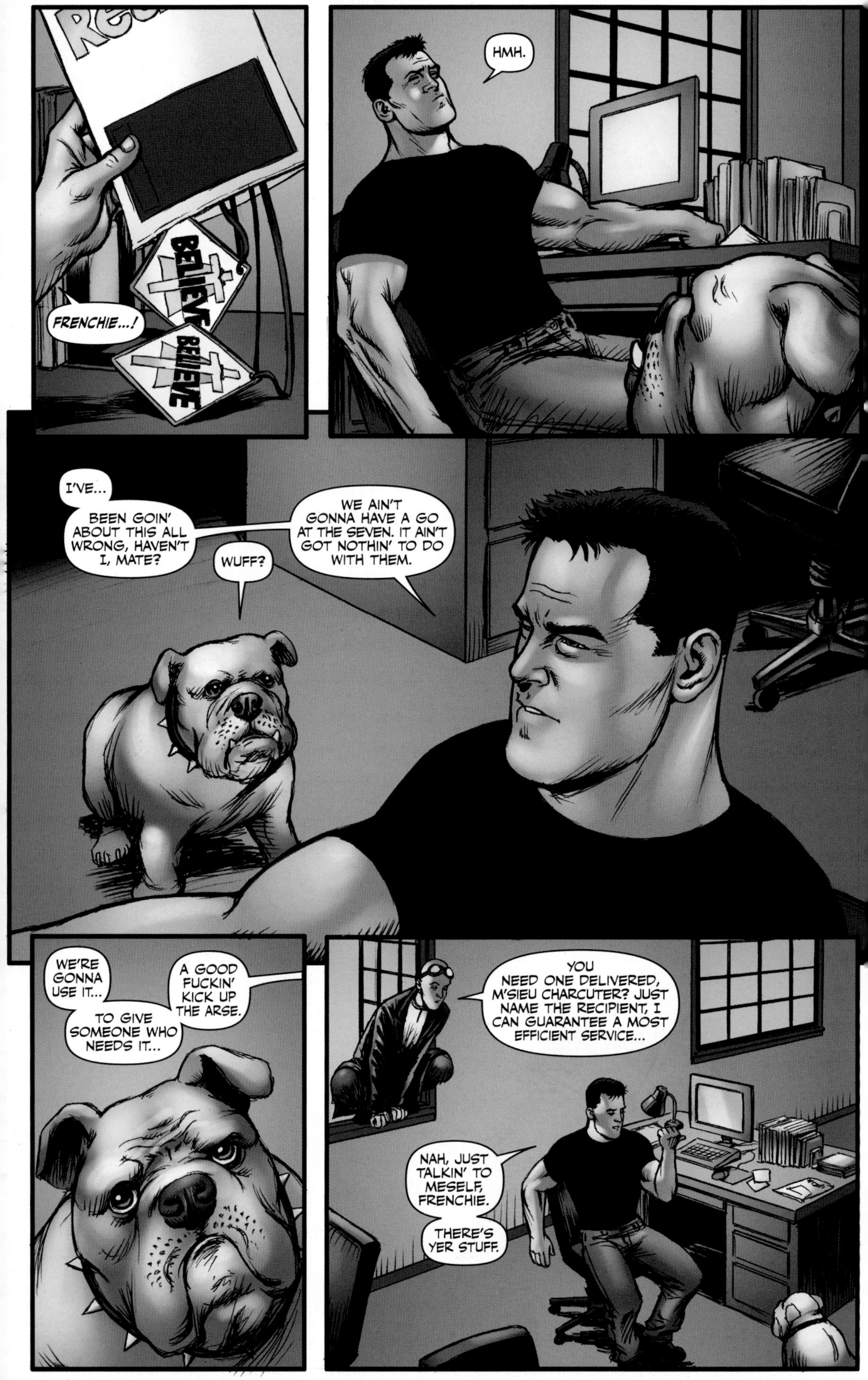
FRENCHIE...!
BELIEVE
BELIEVE
HMH.
I'VE...
BEEN GOIN' ABOUT THIS ALL WRONG, HAVEN'T I, MATE?
WUFF?
WE AIN'T GONNA HAVE A GO AT THE SEVEN. IT AIN'T GOT NOTHIN' TO DO WITH THEM.
WE'RE GONNA USE IT...
TO GIVE SOMEONE WHO NEEDS IT...
A GOOD FUCKIN' KICK UP THE ARSE.
YOU NEED ONE DELIVERED, M'SIEU CHARCUTER? JUST NAME THE RECIPIENT, I CAN GUARANTEE A MOST EFFICIENT SERVICE...
NAH, JUST TALKIN' TO MESELF, FRENCHIE.
THERE'S YER STUFF.

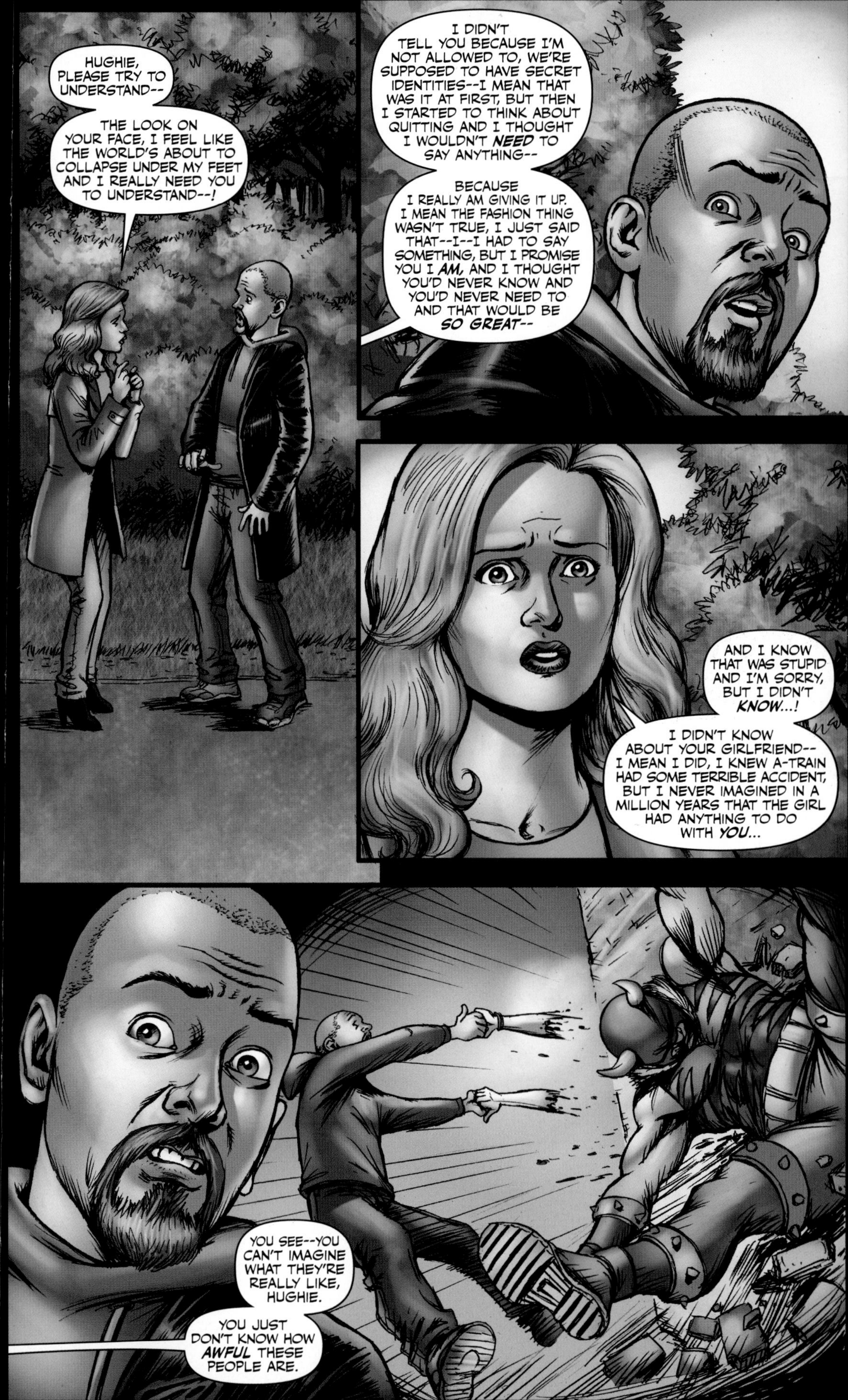
HUGHIE, PLEASE TRY TO UNDERSTAND--
THE LOOK ON YOUR FACE, I FEEL LIKE THE WORLD'S ABOUT TO COLLAPSE UNDER MY FEET AND I REALLY NEED YOU TO UNDERSTAND--!
I DIDN'T TELL YOU BECAUSE I'M NOT ALLOWED TO, WE'RE SUPPOSED TO HAVE SECRET IDENTITIES--I MEAN THAT WAS IT AT FIRST, BUT THEN I STARTED TO THINK ABOUT QUITTING AND I THOUGHT I WOULDN'T *NEED* TO SAY ANYTHING--
BECAUSE I REALLY AM GIVING IT UP. I MEAN THE FASHION THING WASN'T TRUE, I JUST SAID THAT--I--I HAD TO SAY SOMETHING, BUT I PROMISE YOU I *AM,* AND I THOUGHT YOU'D NEVER KNOW AND YOU'D NEVER NEED TO AND THAT WOULD BE *SO GREAT*--
AND I KNOW THAT WAS STUPID AND I'M SORRY, BUT I DIDN'T *KNOW*...!
I DIDN'T KNOW ABOUT YOUR GIRLFRIEND--I MEAN I DID, I KNEW A-TRAIN HAD SOME TERRIBLE ACCIDENT, BUT I NEVER IMAGINED IN A MILLION YEARS THAT THE GIRL HAD ANYTHING TO DO WITH *YOU*...
YOU SEE--YOU CAN'T IMAGINE WHAT THEY'RE REALLY LIKE, HUGHIE.
YOU JUST DON'T KNOW HOW *AWFUL* THESE PEOPLE ARE.

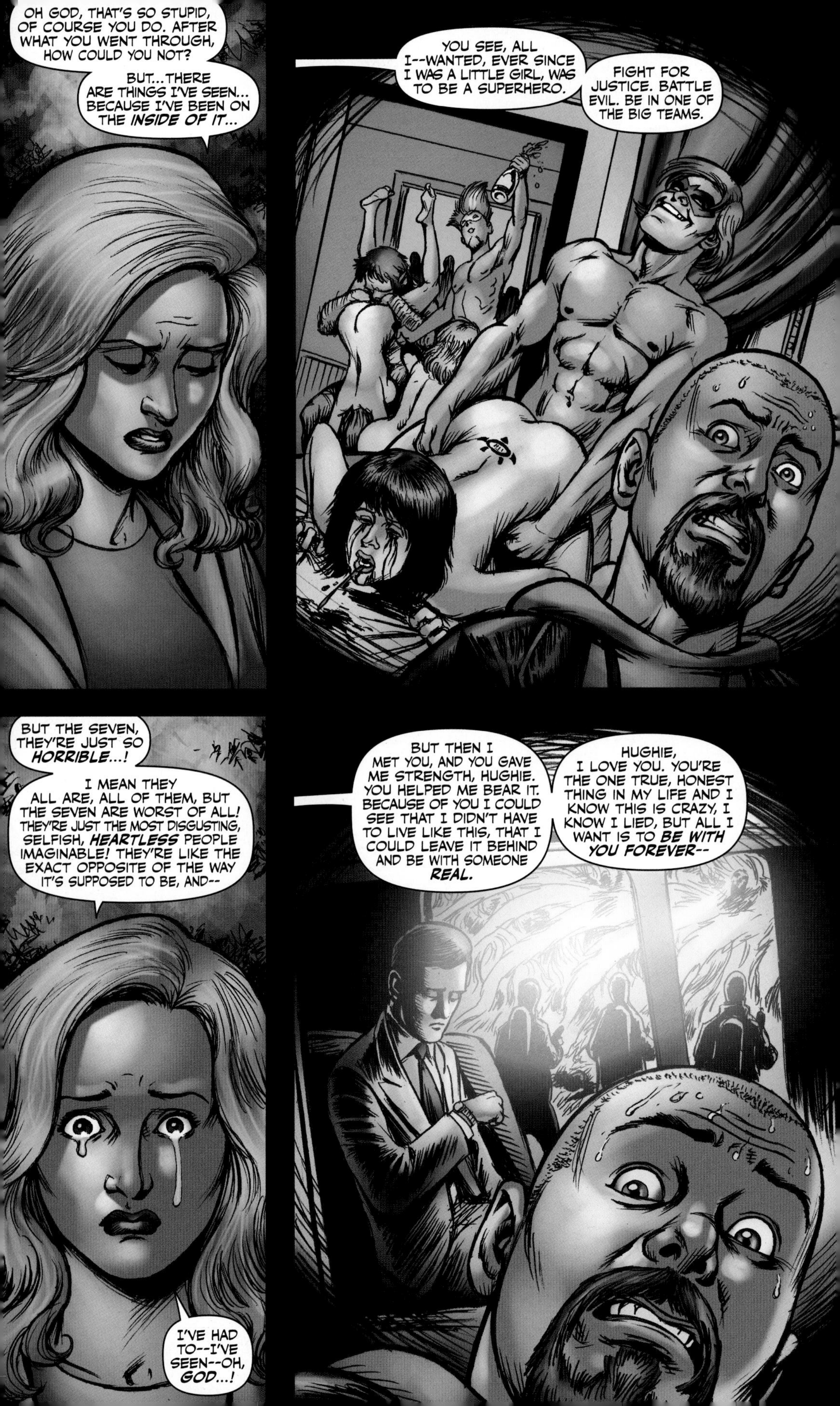

OH GOD, THAT'S SO STUPID, OF COURSE YOU DO. AFTER WHAT YOU WENT THROUGH, HOW COULD YOU NOT?
BUT...THERE ARE THINGS I'VE SEEN... BECAUSE I'VE BEEN ON THE *INSIDE OF IT*...
YOU SEE, ALL I--WANTED, EVER SINCE I WAS A LITTLE GIRL, WAS TO BE A SUPERHERO.
FIGHT FOR JUSTICE. BATTLE EVIL. BE IN ONE OF THE BIG TEAMS.
BUT THE SEVEN, THEY'RE JUST SO *HORRIBLE*...!
I MEAN THEY ALL ARE, ALL OF THEM, BUT THE SEVEN ARE WORST OF ALL! THEY'RE JUST THE MOST DISGUSTING, SELFISH, *HEARTLESS* PEOPLE IMAGINABLE! THEY'RE LIKE THE EXACT OPPOSITE OF THE WAY IT'S SUPPOSED TO BE, AND--
I'VE HAD TO--I'VE SEEN--OH, *GOD*...!
BUT THEN I MET YOU, AND YOU GAVE ME STRENGTH, HUGHIE. YOU HELPED ME BEAR IT. BECAUSE OF YOU I COULD SEE THAT I DIDN'T HAVE TO LIVE LIKE THIS, THAT I COULD LEAVE IT BEHIND AND BE WITH SOMEONE *REAL.*
HUGHIE, I LOVE YOU. YOU'RE THE ONE TRUE, HONEST THING IN MY LIFE AND I KNOW THIS IS CRAZY, I KNOW I LIED, BUT ALL I WANT IS TO *BE WITH YOU FOREVER*--

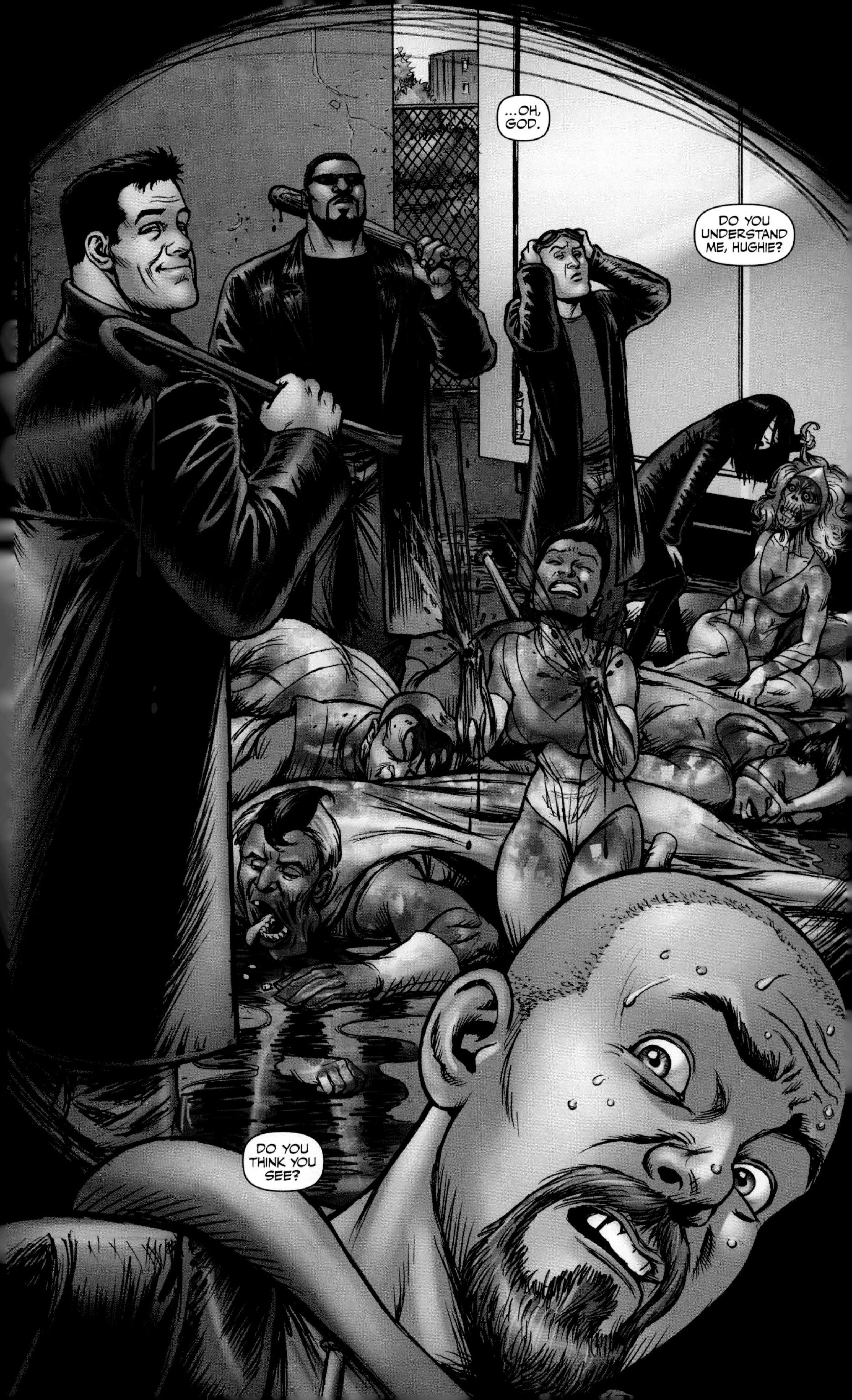
...OH, GOD.
DO YOU UNDERSTAND ME, HUGHIE?
DO YOU THINK YOU SEE?

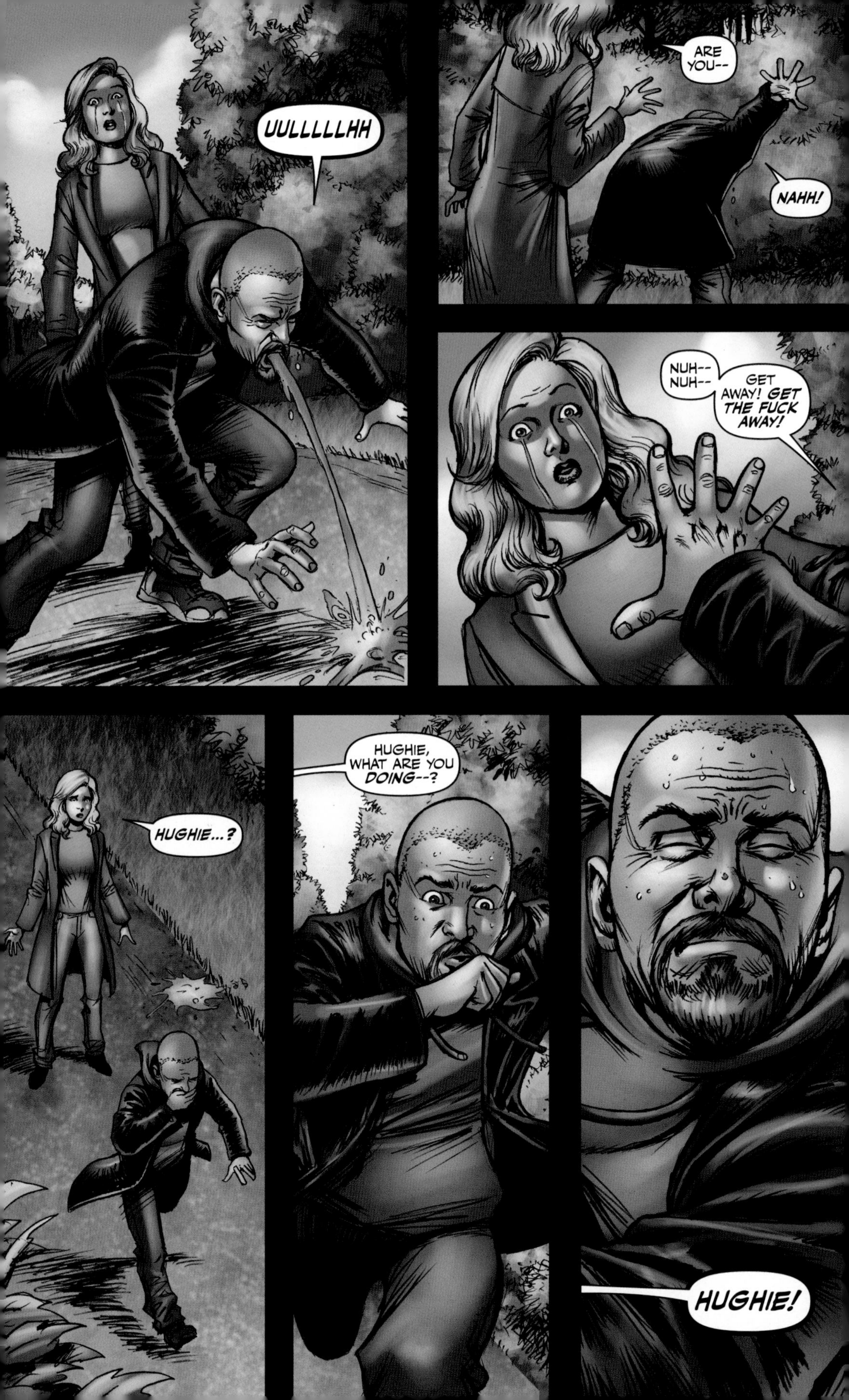
UULLLLLLHH
ARE YOU--
NAHH!
NUH-- NUH--
GET AWAY! GET THE FUCK AWAY!
HUGHIE...?
HUGHIE, WHAT ARE YOU DOING--?
HUGHIE!

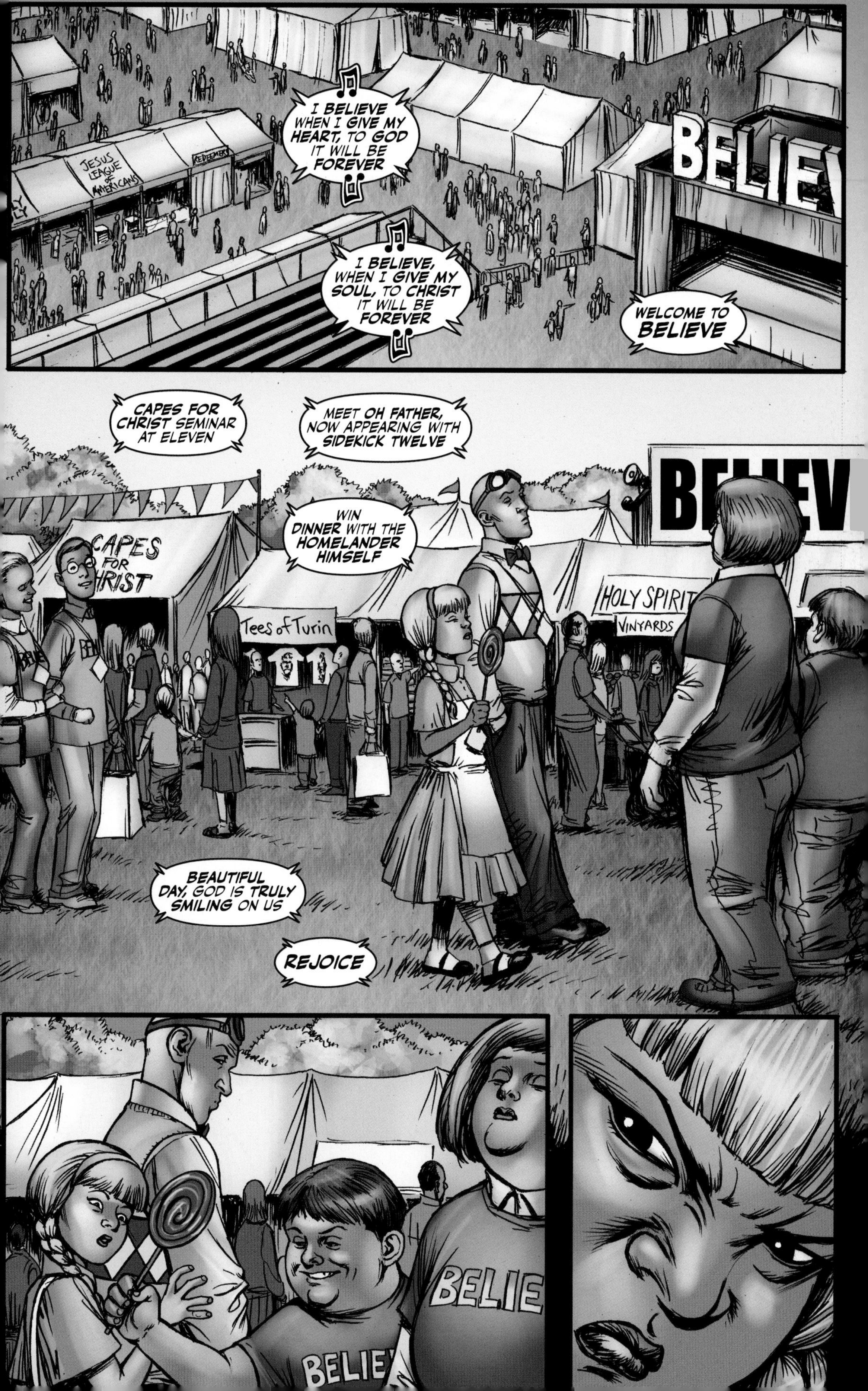

JESUS LEAGUE OF AMERICANS
REDEEMERS
BELIEVE
I BELIEVE WHEN I GIVE MY HEART, TO GOD IT WILL BE FOREVER
I BELIEVE, WHEN I GIVE MY SOUL, TO CHRIST IT WILL BE FOREVER
WELCOME TO BELIEVE
CAPES FOR CHRIST SEMINAR AT ELEVEN
MEET OH FATHER, NOW APPEARING WITH SIDEKICK TWELVE
WIN DINNER WITH THE HOMELANDER HIMSELF
CAPES FOR CHRIST
Tees of Turin
HOLY SPIRIT VINYARDS
BELIEV
BEAUTIFUL DAY, GOD IS TRULY SMILING ON US
REJOICE
BELIE
BELIE

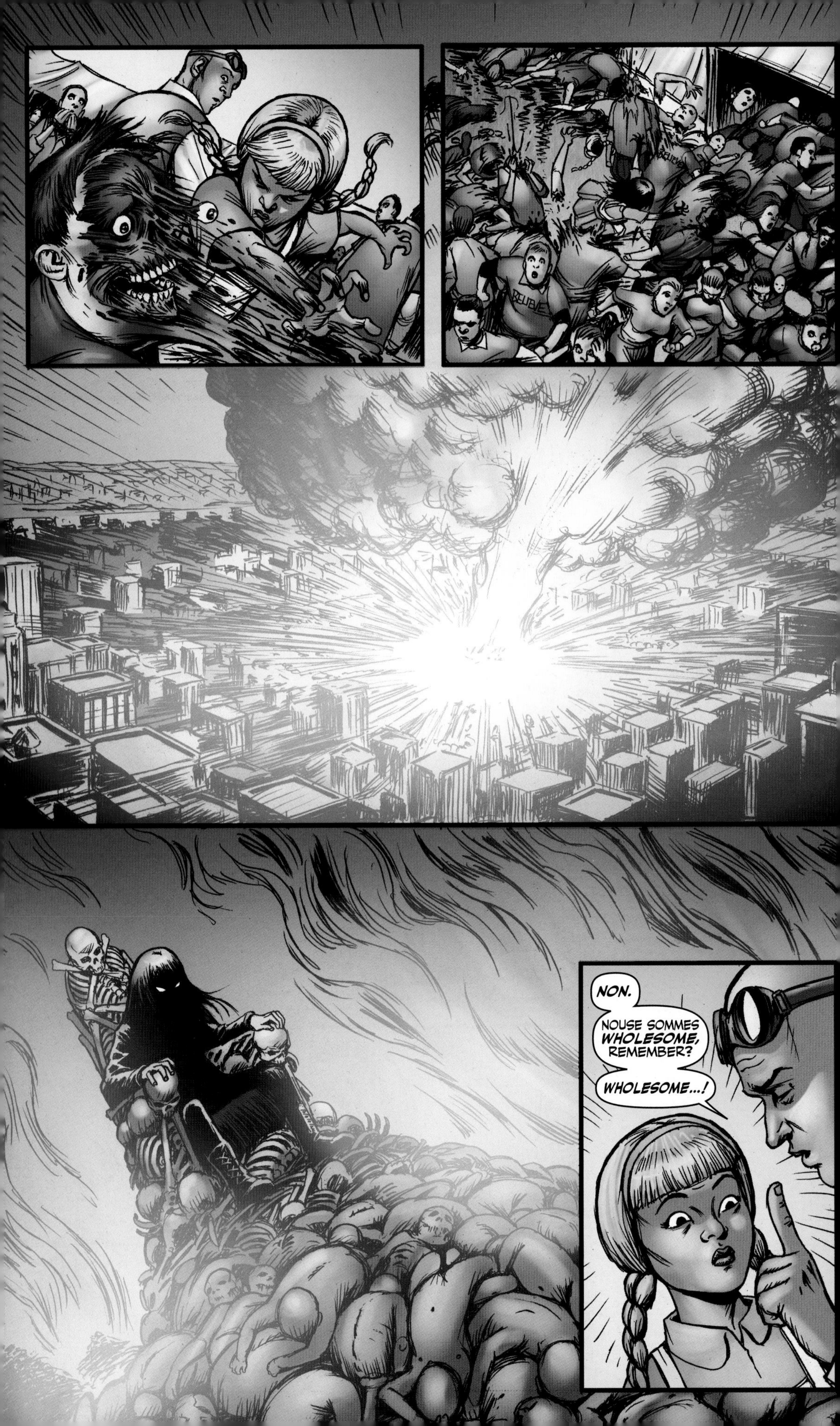

NON.
NOUSE SOMMES WHOLESOME, REMEMBER?
WHOLESOME...!

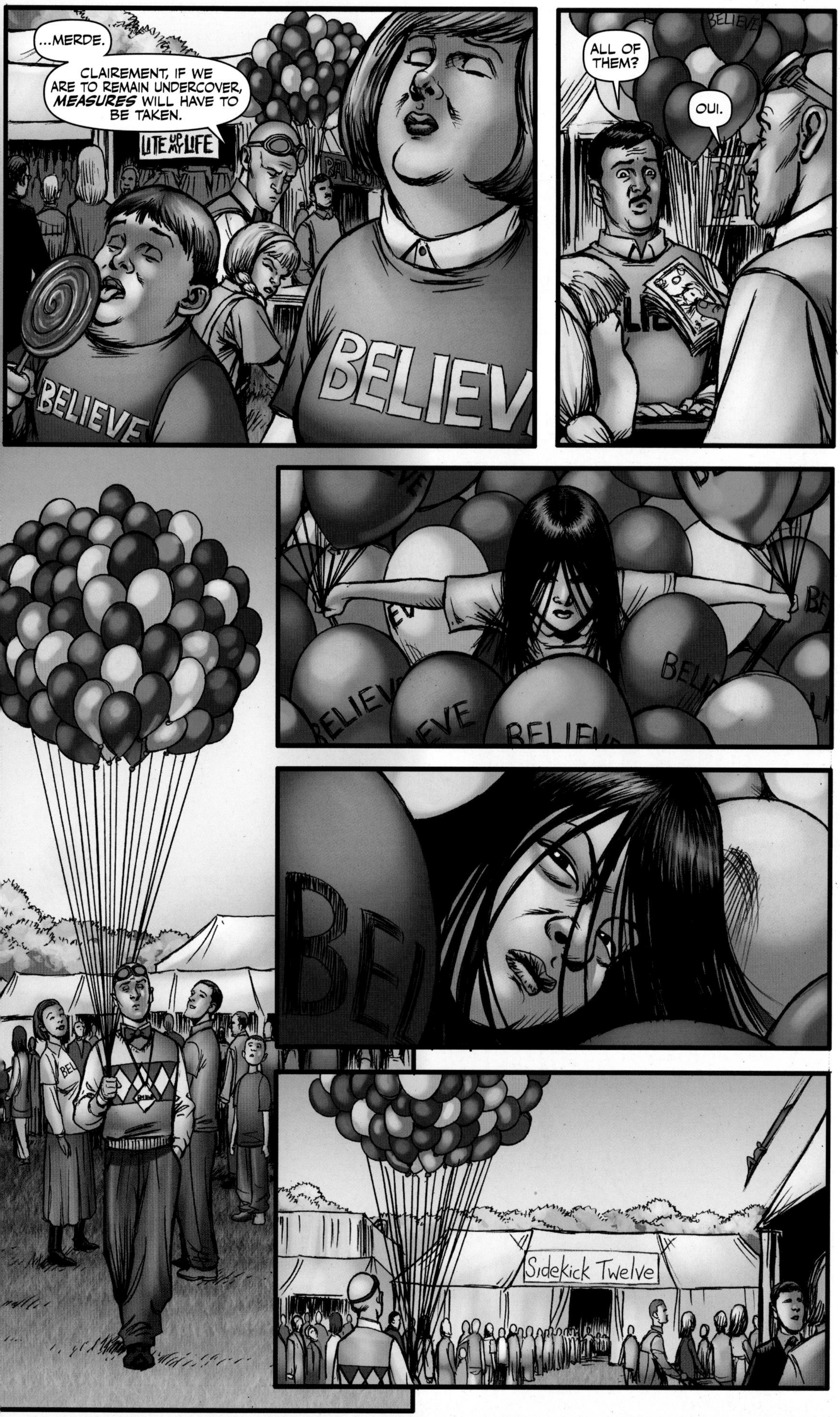
...MERDE.
CLAIREMENT, IF WE ARE TO REMAIN UNDERCOVER, MEASURES WILL HAVE TO BE TAKEN.
LITE UP MY LIFE
BELIEVE
BELIEVE
ALL OF THEM?
OUI.
BELIEVE
BELIEVE
Sidekick Twelve

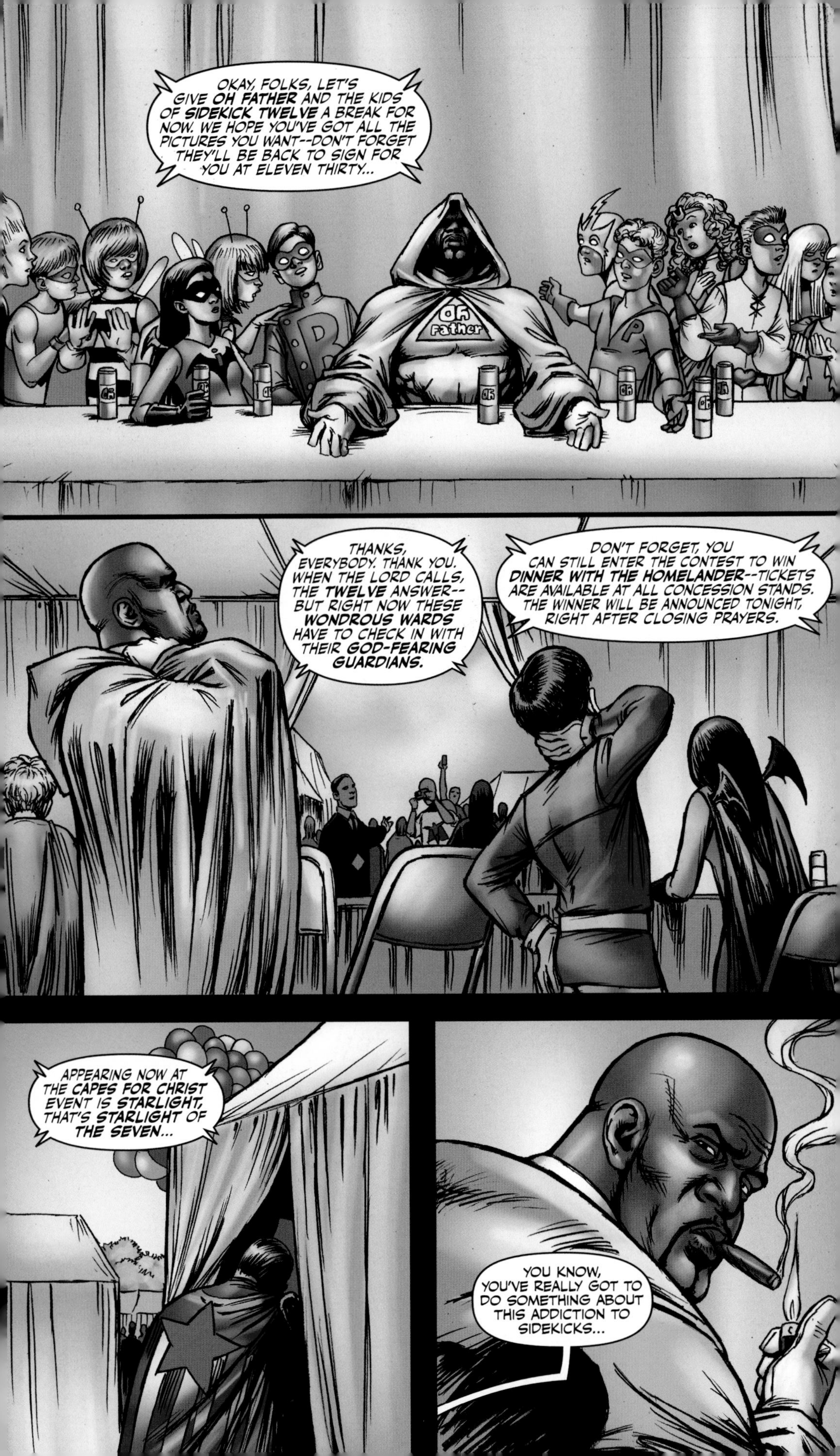
OKAY, FOLKS, LET'S GIVE OH FATHER AND THE KIDS OF SIDEKICK TWELVE A BREAK FOR NOW. WE HOPE YOU'VE GOT ALL THE PICTURES YOU WANT--DON'T FORGET THEY'LL BE BACK TO SIGN FOR YOU AT ELEVEN THIRTY...
THANKS, EVERYBODY. THANK YOU. WHEN THE LORD CALLS, THE TWELVE ANSWER--BUT RIGHT NOW THESE WONDROUS WARDS HAVE TO CHECK IN WITH THEIR GOD-FEARING GUARDIANS.
DON'T FORGET, YOU CAN STILL ENTER THE CONTEST TO WIN DINNER WITH THE HOMELANDER--TICKETS ARE AVAILABLE AT ALL CONCESSION STANDS. THE WINNER WILL BE ANNOUNCED TONIGHT, RIGHT AFTER CLOSING PRAYERS.
APPEARING NOW AT THE CAPES FOR CHRIST EVENT IS STARLIGHT, THAT'S STARLIGHT OF THE SEVEN...
YOU KNOW, YOU'VE REALLY GOT TO DO SOMETHING ABOUT THIS ADDICTION TO SIDEKICKS...

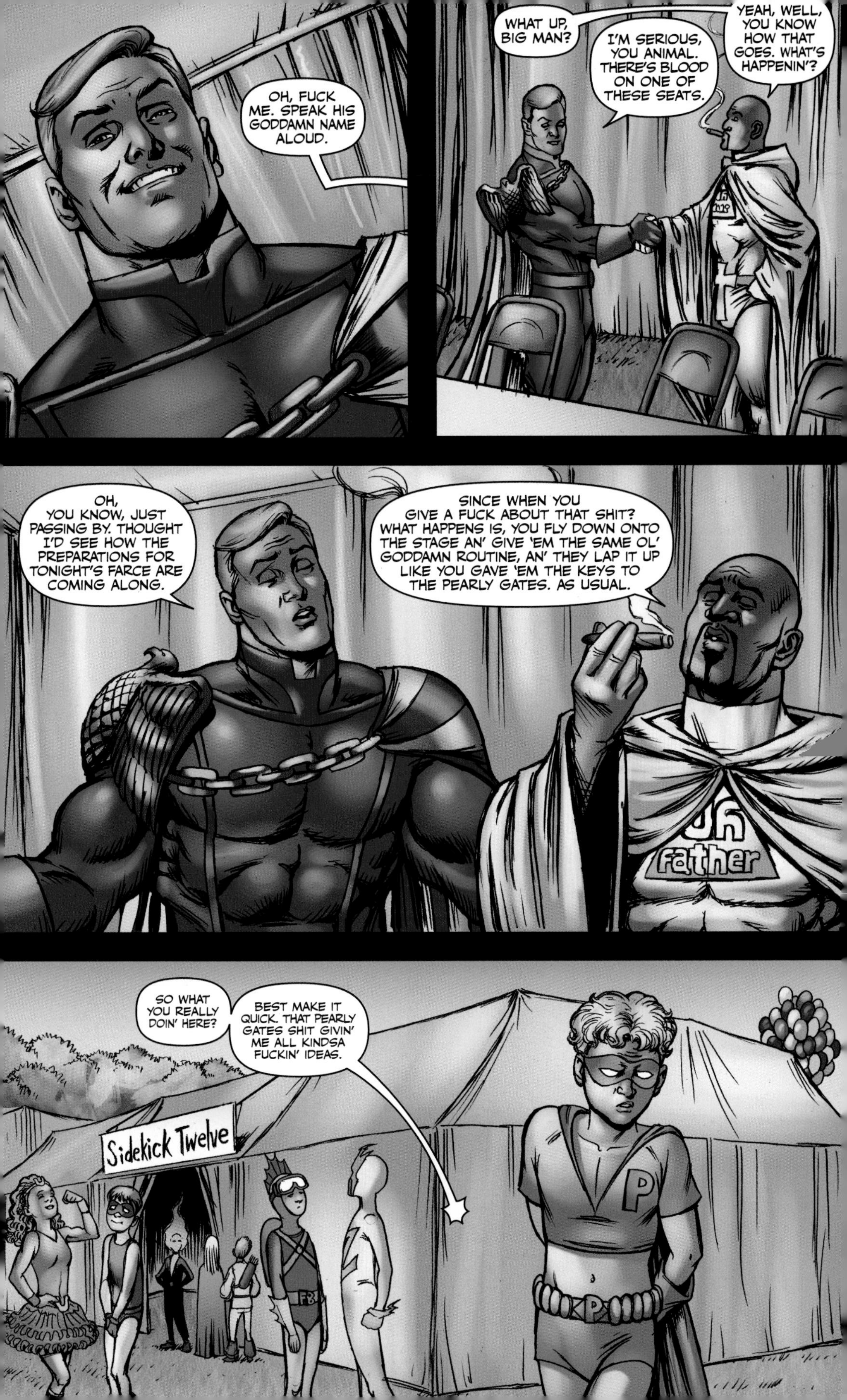
OH, FUCK ME. SPEAK HIS GODDAMN NAME ALOUD.
WHAT UP, BIG MAN?
YEAH, WELL, YOU KNOW HOW THAT GOES. WHAT'S HAPPENIN'?
I'M SERIOUS, YOU ANIMAL. THERE'S BLOOD ON ONE OF THESE SEATS.
OH, YOU KNOW, JUST PASSING BY. THOUGHT I'D SEE HOW THE PREPARATIONS FOR TONIGHT'S FARCE ARE COMING ALONG.
SINCE WHEN YOU GIVE A FUCK ABOUT THAT SHIT? WHAT HAPPENS IS, YOU FLY DOWN ONTO THE STAGE AN' GIVE 'EM THE SAME OL' GODDAMN ROUTINE, AN' THEY LAP IT UP LIKE YOU GAVE 'EM THE KEYS TO THE PEARLY GATES. AS USUAL.
Father
SO WHAT YOU REALLY DOIN' HERE?
BEST MAKE IT QUICK. THAT PEARLY GATES SHIT GIVIN' ME ALL KINDSA FUCKIN' IDEAS.
Sidekick Twelve

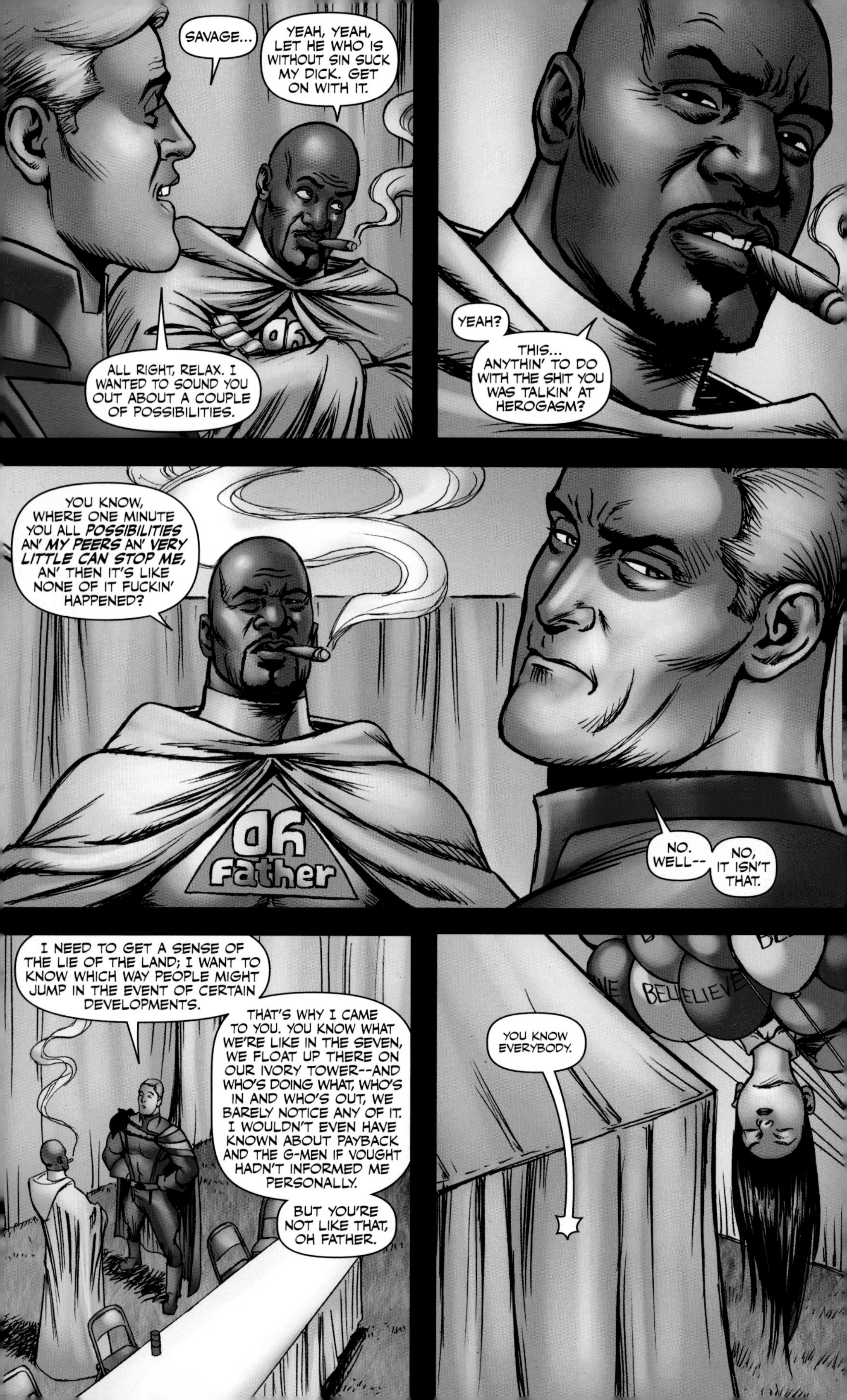
SAVAGE...
YEAH, YEAH, LET HE WHO IS WITHOUT SIN SUCK MY DICK. GET ON WITH IT.
ALL RIGHT, RELAX. I WANTED TO SOUND YOU OUT ABOUT A COUPLE OF POSSIBILITIES.
YEAH?
THIS... ANYTHIN' TO DO WITH THE SHIT YOU WAS TALKIN' AT HEROGASM?
YOU KNOW, WHERE ONE MINUTE YOU ALL *POSSIBILITIES* AN' *MY PEERS* AN' *VERY LITTLE CAN STOP ME,* AN' THEN IT'S LIKE NONE OF IT FUCKIN' HAPPENED?
OH Father
NO. WELL--
NO, IT ISN'T THAT.
I NEED TO GET A SENSE OF THE LIE OF THE LAND; I WANT TO KNOW WHICH WAY PEOPLE MIGHT JUMP IN THE EVENT OF CERTAIN DEVELOPMENTS.
THAT'S WHY I CAME TO YOU. YOU KNOW WHAT WE'RE LIKE IN THE SEVEN, WE FLOAT UP THERE ON OUR IVORY TOWER--AND WHO'S DOING WHAT, WHO'S IN AND WHO'S OUT, WE BARELY NOTICE ANY OF IT. I WOULDN'T EVEN HAVE KNOWN ABOUT PAYBACK AND THE G-MEN IF VOUGHT HADN'T INFORMED ME PERSONALLY.
BUT YOU'RE NOT LIKE THAT, OH FATHER.
YOU KNOW EVERYBODY.
BELIEVE

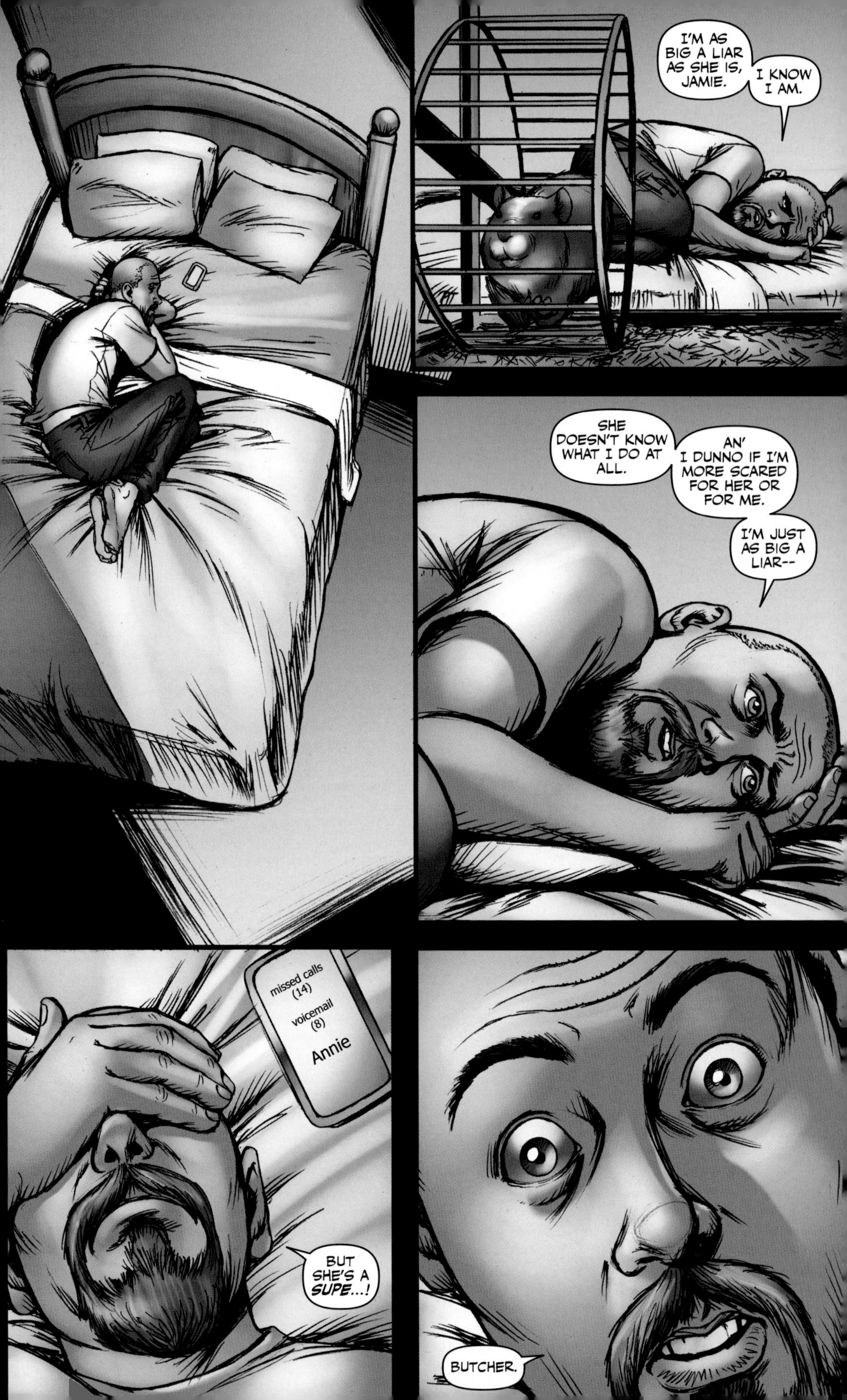
I'M AS BIG A LIAR AS SHE IS, JAMIE.
I KNOW I AM.
SHE DOESN'T KNOW WHAT I DO AT ALL.
AN' I DUNNO IF I'M MORE SCARED FOR HER OR FOR ME.
I'M JUST AS BIG A LIAR--
missed calls (14)
voicemail (8)
Annie
BUT SHE'S A *SUPE*...!
BUTCHER.

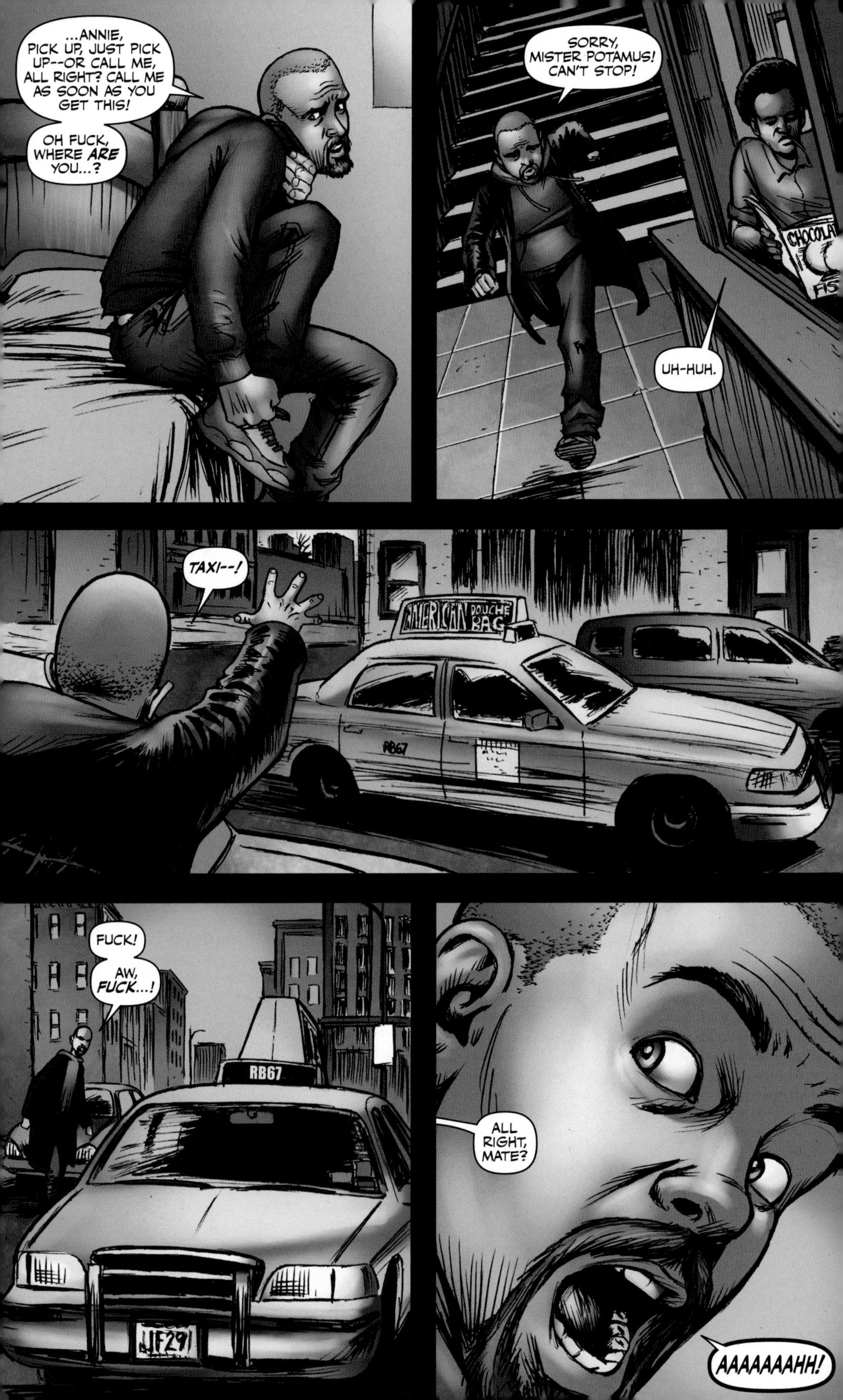
...ANNIE, PICK UP, JUST PICK UP--OR CALL ME, ALL RIGHT? CALL ME AS SOON AS YOU GET THIS!
OH FUCK, WHERE *ARE* YOU...?
SORRY, MISTER POTAMUS! CAN'T STOP!
CHOCOLA
FIS
UH-HUH.
TAXI--!
AMERICAN DOUCHE BAG
RB67
FUCK!
AW, *FUCK*...!
RB67
JJF291
ALL RIGHT, MATE?
AAAAAAAHH!

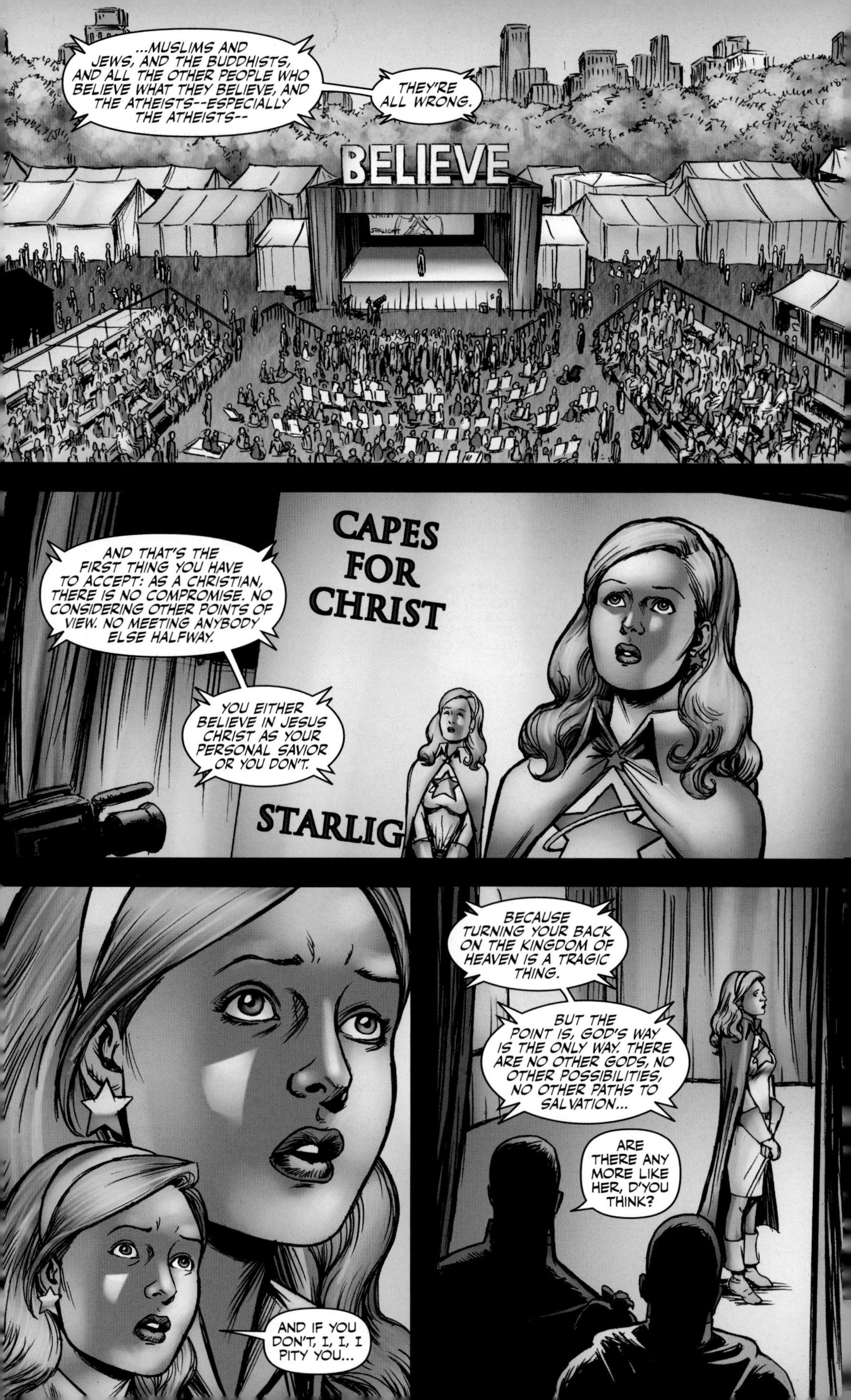
...MUSLIMS AND JEWS, AND THE BUDDHISTS, AND ALL THE OTHER PEOPLE WHO BELIEVE WHAT THEY BELIEVE, AND THE ATHEISTS--ESPECIALLY THE ATHEISTS--
THEY'RE ALL WRONG.
BELIEVE
CAPES FOR CHRIST
AND THAT'S THE FIRST THING YOU HAVE TO ACCEPT: AS A CHRISTIAN, THERE IS NO COMPROMISE. NO CONSIDERING OTHER POINTS OF VIEW. NO MEETING ANYBODY ELSE HALFWAY.
YOU EITHER BELIEVE IN JESUS CHRIST AS YOUR PERSONAL SAVIOR OR YOU DON'T.
STARLIG
AND IF YOU DON'T, I, I, I PITY YOU...
BECAUSE TURNING YOUR BACK ON THE KINGDOM OF HEAVEN IS A TRAGIC THING.
BUT THE POINT IS, GOD'S WAY IS THE ONLY WAY. THERE ARE NO OTHER GODS, NO OTHER POSSIBILITIES, NO OTHER PATHS TO SALVATION...
ARE THERE ANY MORE LIKE HER, D'YOU THINK?

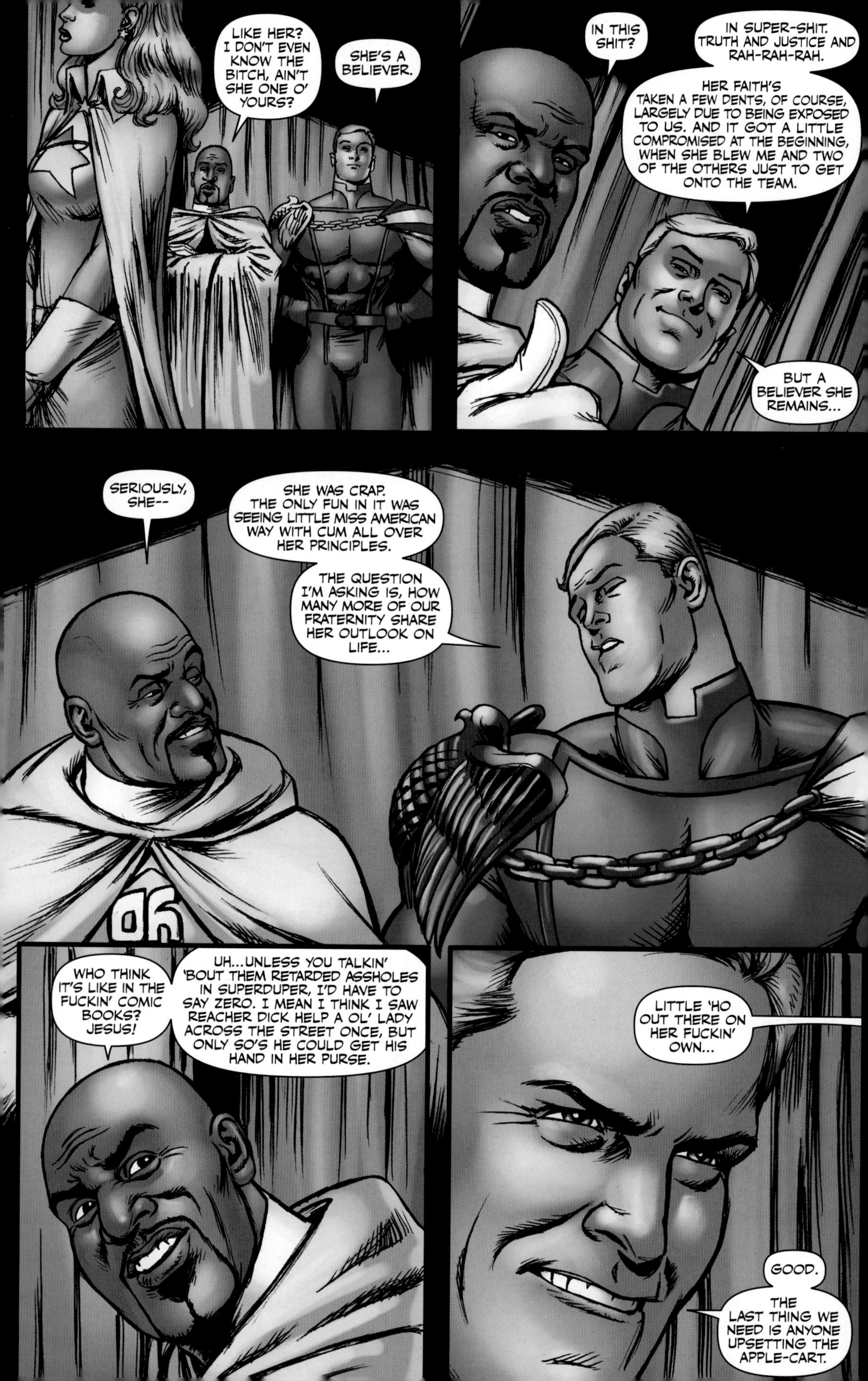
LIKE HER? I DON'T EVEN KNOW THE BITCH, AIN'T SHE ONE O' YOURS?
SHE'S A BELIEVER.
IN THIS SHIT?
IN SUPER-SHIT. TRUTH AND JUSTICE AND RAH-RAH-RAH.
HER FAITH'S TAKEN A FEW DENTS, OF COURSE, LARGELY DUE TO BEING EXPOSED TO US. AND IT GOT A LITTLE COMPROMISED AT THE BEGINNING, WHEN SHE BLEW ME AND TWO OF THE OTHERS JUST TO GET ONTO THE TEAM.
BUT A BELIEVER SHE REMAINS...
SERIOUSLY, SHE--
SHE WAS CRAP. THE ONLY FUN IN IT WAS SEEING LITTLE MISS AMERICAN WAY WITH CUM ALL OVER HER PRINCIPLES.
THE QUESTION I'M ASKING IS, HOW MANY MORE OF OUR FRATERNITY SHARE HER OUTLOOK ON LIFE...
WHO THINK IT'S LIKE IN THE FUCKIN' COMIC BOOKS? JESUS!
UH...UNLESS YOU TALKIN' 'BOUT THEM RETARDED ASSHOLES IN SUPERDUPER, I'D HAVE TO SAY ZERO. I MEAN I THINK I SAW REACHER DICK HELP A OL' LADY ACROSS THE STREET ONCE, BUT ONLY SO'S HE COULD GET HIS HAND IN HER PURSE.
LITTLE 'HO OUT THERE ON HER FUCKIN' OWN...
GOOD.
THE LAST THING WE NEED IS ANYONE UPSETTING THE APPLE-CART.

YOU KNOW HOW VOUGHT ARE PUSHING THIS AGENDA OF THEIRS, THIS SUPERPOWER FOR NATIONAL DEFENSE THING?

OH FUCK, AIN'T THEY GIVEN UP ON THAT YET? SHIT AIN'T NEVER GONNA WORK, A GODDAMN BLIND MAN CAN SEE IT...

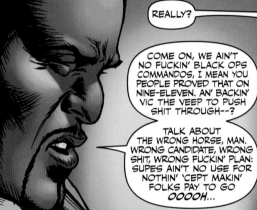

REALLY?

COME ON, WE AIN'T NO FUCKIN' BLACK OPS COMMANDOS, I MEAN YOU PEOPLE PROVED THAT ON NINE-ELEVEN. AN' BACKIN' VIC THE VEEP TO PUSH SHIT THROUGH--?

TALK ABOUT THE WRONG HORSE, MAN. WRONG CANDIDATE, WRONG SHIT, WRONG FUCKIN' PLAN: SUPES AIN'T NO USE FOR NOTHIN' 'CEPT MAKIN' FOLKS PAY TO GO *OOOOH...*

SUPPOSING THAT CHANGED. SUPPOSING THE PLAN WAS SUDDENLY VIABLE.

HOW FAR DO YOU THINK OUR PEOPLE WOULD GO TO ENSURE IT WAS A SUCCESS?

YOU MEAN HOW THEY GONNA FEEL ABOUT GETTIN' FUCKIN' DRAFTED?

NO: ABOUT GETTING THE PLAN ITSELF IMPLEMENTED.

IF VOUGHT WANTED THEIR HELP IN FORCING THE ISSUE.

YOU TALKIN' 'BOUT... WHAT I THINK YOU TALKIN' 'BOUT...?

GIVING VIC WHATEVER SUPPORT HE NEEDS IN WHATEVER CIRCUMSTANCES ARISE.

IF IT REALLY COMES TO IT.

OH, SHIT...

HOW MANY WOULD GO ALONG WITH THAT? IN YOUR OPINION?

UH...HOW THE FUCK YOU GONNA SELL IT, JUST TO START WITH?

LOOK HOW WELL WE DO OUT OF VOUGHT RIGHT NOW. IMAGINE HOW GRATEFUL THEY'D BE IF WE BACKED THEM ON SOMETHING LIKE THIS.

HUH. WELL. I SEE WHY YOU ASKIN' IF WE GOT ANY TRUE BELIEVERS OUT THERE.

'KAY...I DON'T THINK SECURITY GONNA BE A PROBLEM, ALL YOU GOTTA SAY IS *VOUGHT* AN' EVERYONE GONNA SHUT THE FUCK UP. BUT HOW MANY GONNA GO ALONG WITH IT...?

SIXTY, MAYBE SIXTY-FIVE PERCENT. TOPS.

OKAY.

CAN YOU ARRANGE A GET-TOGETHER FOR LATER ON? WITH WHOEVER YOU THINK'LL COME ON BOARD FOR THIS?

SOUND THEM OUT, KEEP IT VAGUE, AND I'LL TELL YOU WHERE AND WHEN.

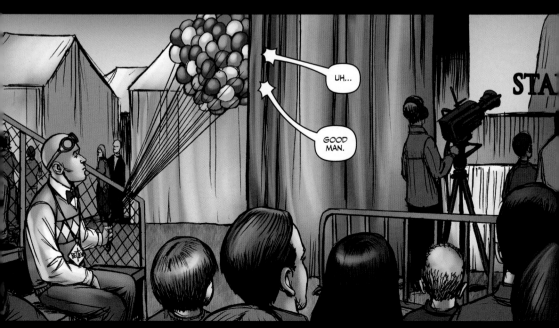

UH...

GOOD MAN.

STA

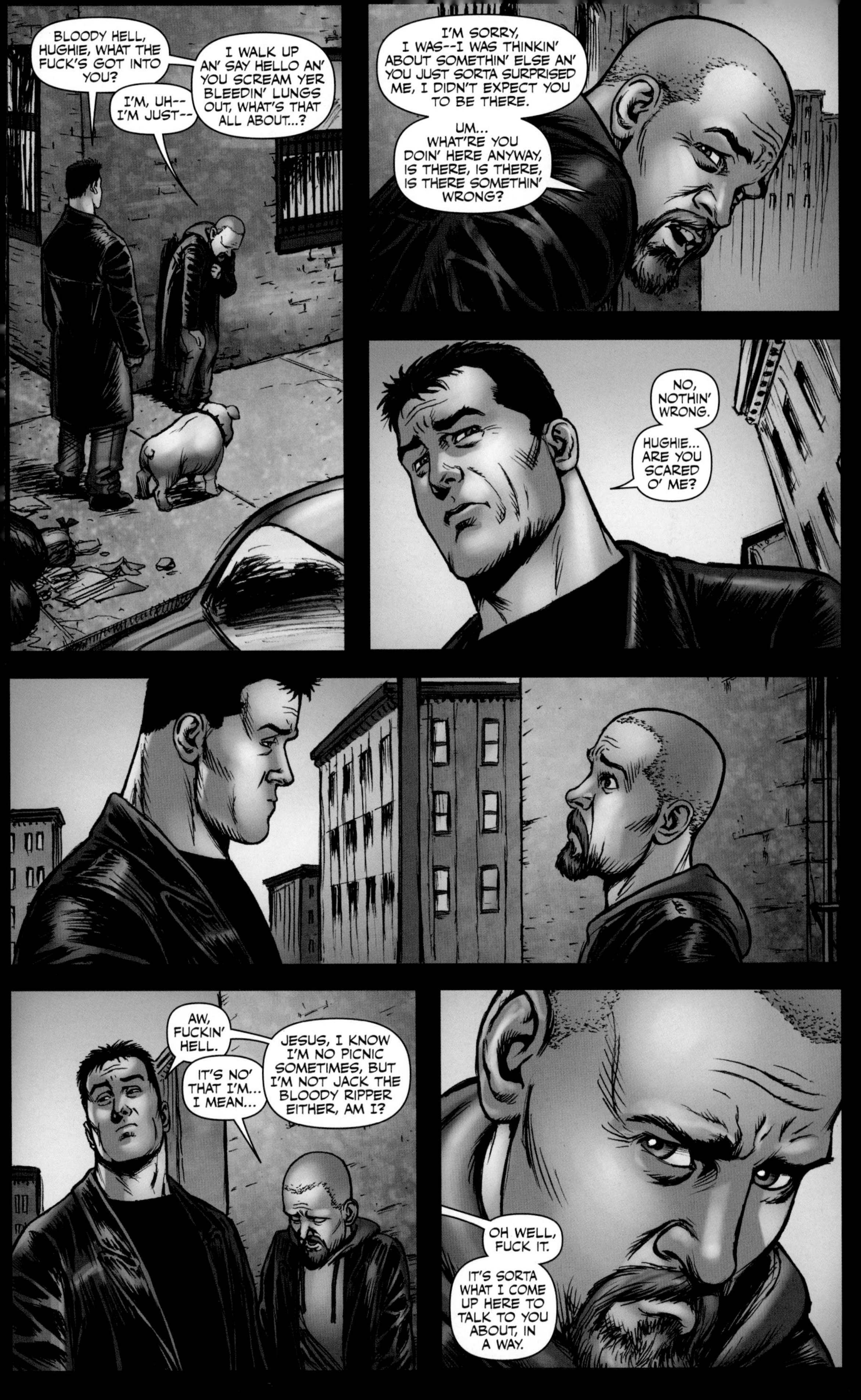
BLOODY HELL, HUGHIE, WHAT THE FUCK'S GOT INTO YOU?
I WALK UP AN' SAY HELLO AN' YOU SCREAM YER BLEEDIN' LUNGS OUT, WHAT'S THAT ALL ABOUT...?
I'M, UH-- I'M JUST--
I'M SORRY, I WAS--I WAS THINKIN' ABOUT SOMETHIN' ELSE AN' YOU JUST SORTA SURPRISED ME, I DIDN'T EXPECT YOU TO BE THERE.
UM... WHAT'RE YOU DOIN' HERE ANYWAY, IS THERE, IS THERE, IS THERE SOMETHIN' WRONG?
NO, NOTHIN' WRONG.
HUGHIE... ARE YOU SCARED O' ME?
AW, FUCKIN' HELL.
JESUS, I KNOW I'M NO PICNIC SOMETIMES, BUT I'M NOT JACK THE BLOODY RIPPER EITHER, AM I?
IT'S NO' THAT I'M... I MEAN...
OH WELL, FUCK IT.
IT'S SORTA WHAT I COME UP HERE TO TALK TO YOU ABOUT, IN A WAY.

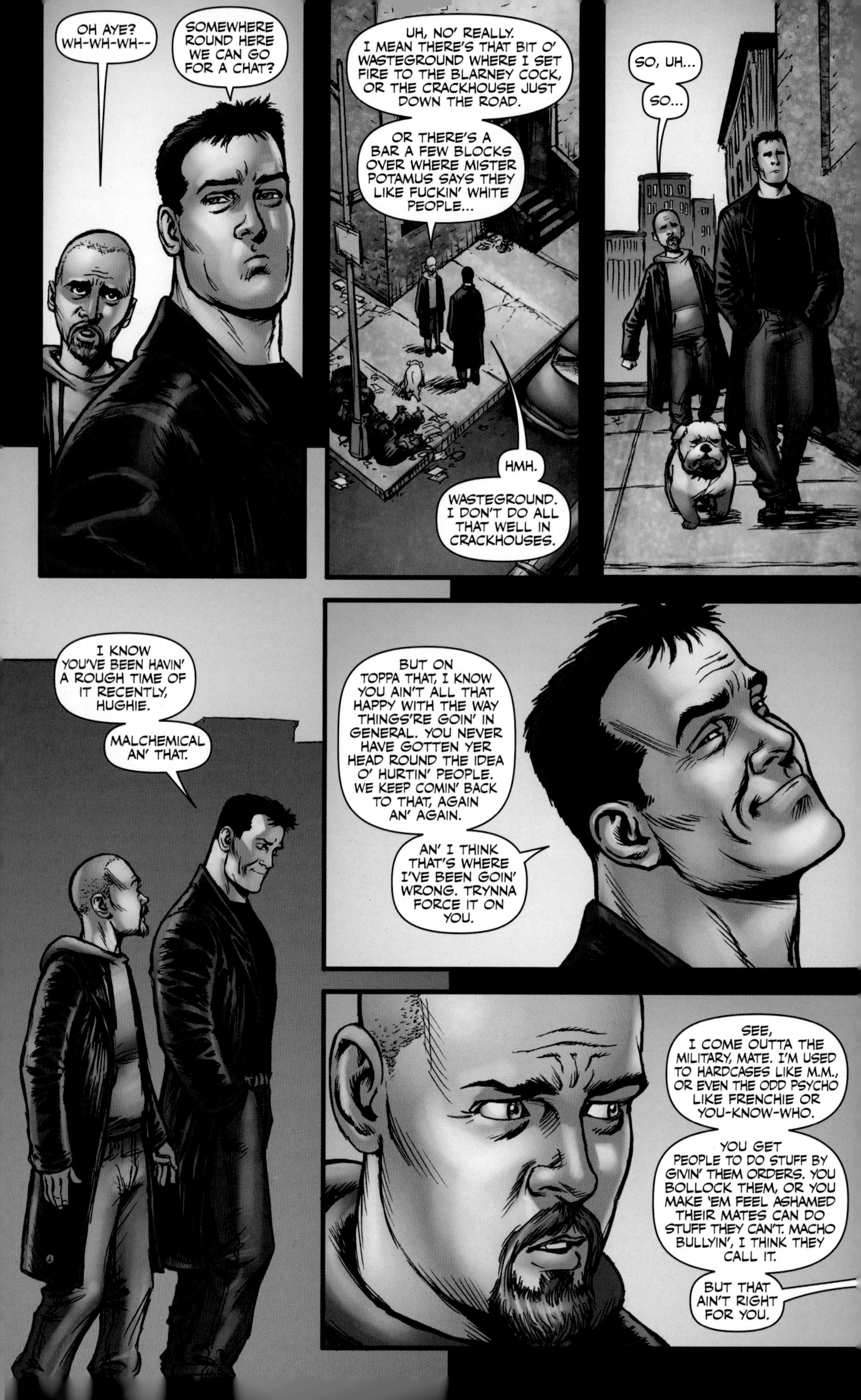
OH AYE? WH-WH-WH--
SOMEWHERE ROUND HERE WE CAN GO FOR A CHAT?
UH, NO' REALLY. I MEAN THERE'S THAT BIT O' WASTEGROUND WHERE I SET FIRE TO THE BLARNEY COCK, OR THE CRACKHOUSE JUST DOWN THE ROAD.
OR THERE'S A BAR A FEW BLOCKS OVER WHERE MISTER POTAMUS SAYS THEY LIKE FUCKIN' WHITE PEOPLE...
HMH.
WASTEGROUND. I DON'T DO ALL THAT WELL IN CRACKHOUSES.
SO, UH...
SO...
I KNOW YOU'VE BEEN HAVIN' A ROUGH TIME OF IT RECENTLY, HUGHIE.
MALCHEMICAL AN' THAT.
BUT ON TOPPA THAT, I KNOW YOU AIN'T ALL THAT HAPPY WITH THE WAY THINGS'RE GOIN' IN GENERAL. YOU NEVER HAVE GOTTEN YER HEAD ROUND THE IDEA O' HURTIN' PEOPLE. WE KEEP COMIN' BACK TO THAT, AGAIN AN' AGAIN.
AN' I THINK THAT'S WHERE I'VE BEEN GOIN' WRONG. TRYNNA FORCE IT ON YOU.
SEE, I COME OUTTA THE MILITARY, MATE. I'M USED TO HARDCASES LIKE M.M., OR EVEN THE ODD PSYCHO LIKE FRENCHIE OR YOU-KNOW-WHO.
YOU GET PEOPLE TO DO STUFF BY GIVIN' THEM ORDERS. YOU BOLLOCK THEM, OR YOU MAKE 'EM FEEL ASHAMED THEIR MATES CAN DO STUFF THEY CAN'T. MACHO BULLYIN', I THINK THEY CALL IT.
BUT THAT AIN'T RIGHT FOR YOU.

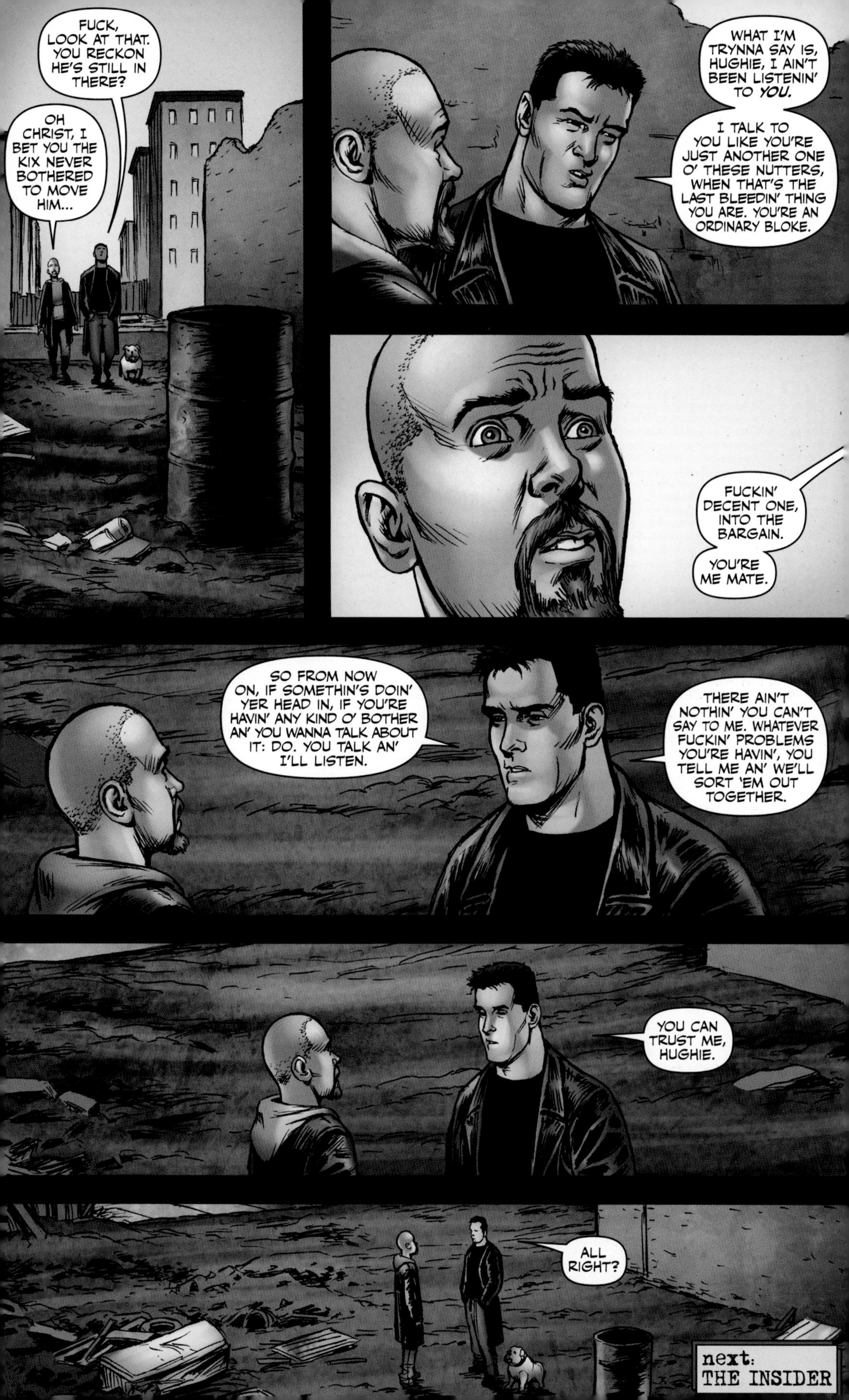
FUCK, LOOK AT THAT. YOU RECKON HE'S STILL IN THERE?
OH CHRIST, I BET YOU THE KIX NEVER BOTHERED TO MOVE HIM...
WHAT I'M TRYNNA SAY IS, HUGHIE, I AIN'T BEEN LISTENIN' TO YOU.
I TALK TO YOU LIKE YOU'RE JUST ANOTHER ONE O' THESE NUTTERS, WHEN THAT'S THE LAST BLEEDIN' THING YOU ARE. YOU'RE AN ORDINARY BLOKE.
FUCKIN' DECENT ONE, INTO THE BARGAIN.
YOU'RE ME MATE.
SO FROM NOW ON, IF SOMETHIN'S DOIN' YER HEAD IN, IF YOU'RE HAVIN' ANY KIND O' BOTHER AN' YOU WANNA TALK ABOUT IT: DO. YOU TALK AN' I'LL LISTEN.
THERE AIN'T NOTHIN' YOU CAN'T SAY TO ME. WHATEVER FUCKIN' PROBLEMS YOU'RE HAVIN', YOU TELL ME AN' WE'LL SORT 'EM OUT TOGETHER.
YOU CAN TRUST ME, HUGHIE.
ALL RIGHT?
next: THE INSIDER

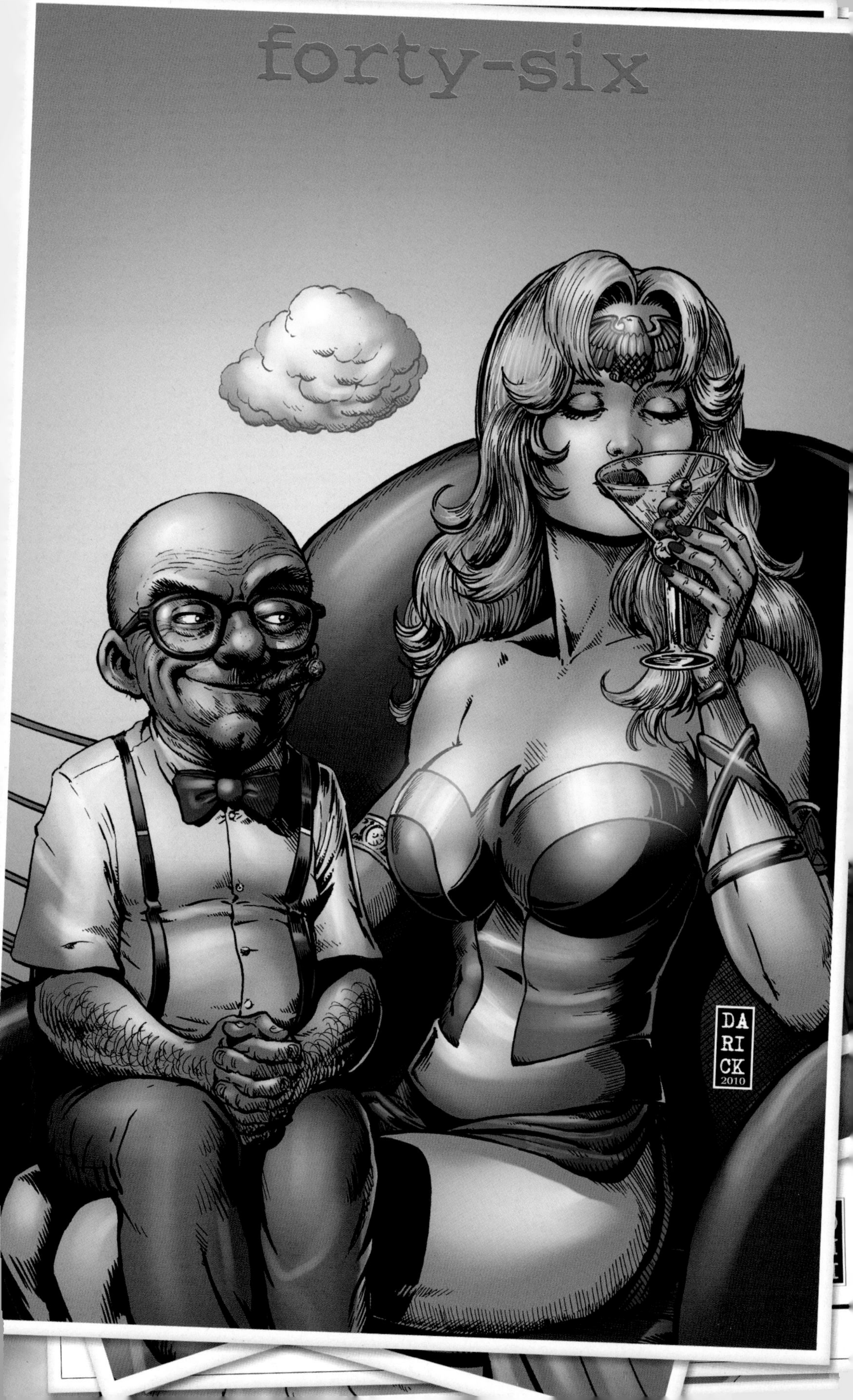
forty-six
DA
RI
CK
2010

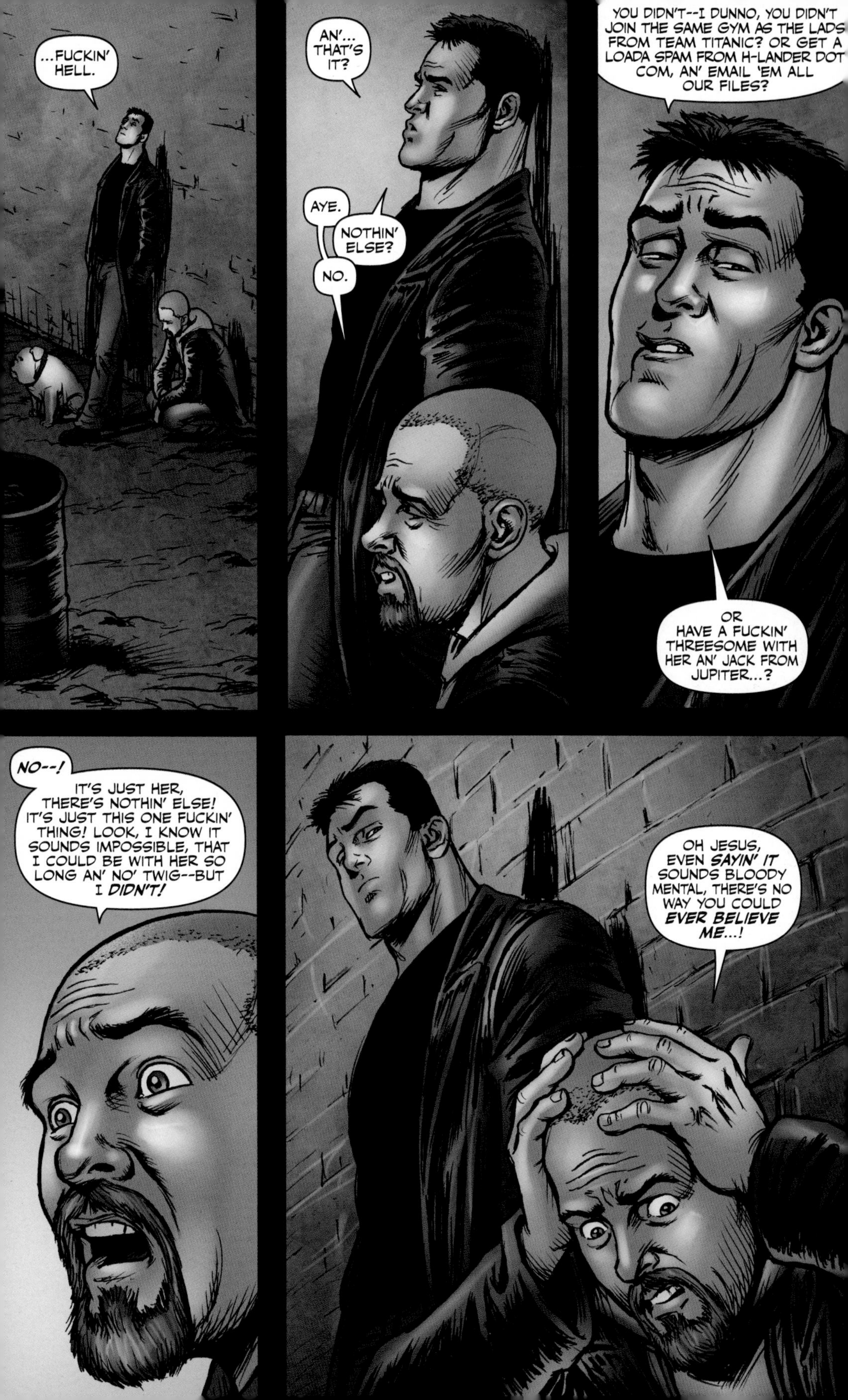
...FUCKIN' HELL.
AN'... THAT'S IT?
AYE.
NOTHIN' ELSE?
NO.
YOU DIDN'T--I DUNNO, YOU DIDN'T JOIN THE SAME GYM AS THE LADS FROM TEAM TITANIC? OR GET A LOADA SPAM FROM H-LANDER DOT COM, AN' EMAIL 'EM ALL OUR FILES?
OR HAVE A FUCKIN' THREESOME WITH HER AN' JACK FROM JUPITER...?
NO--!
IT'S JUST HER, THERE'S NOTHIN' ELSE! IT'S JUST THIS ONE FUCKIN' THING! LOOK, I KNOW IT SOUNDS IMPOSSIBLE, THAT I COULD BE WITH HER SO LONG AN' NO' TWIG--BUT I DIDN'T!
OH JESUS, EVEN SAYIN' IT SOUNDS BLOODY MENTAL, THERE'S NO WAY YOU COULD EVER BELIEVE ME...!

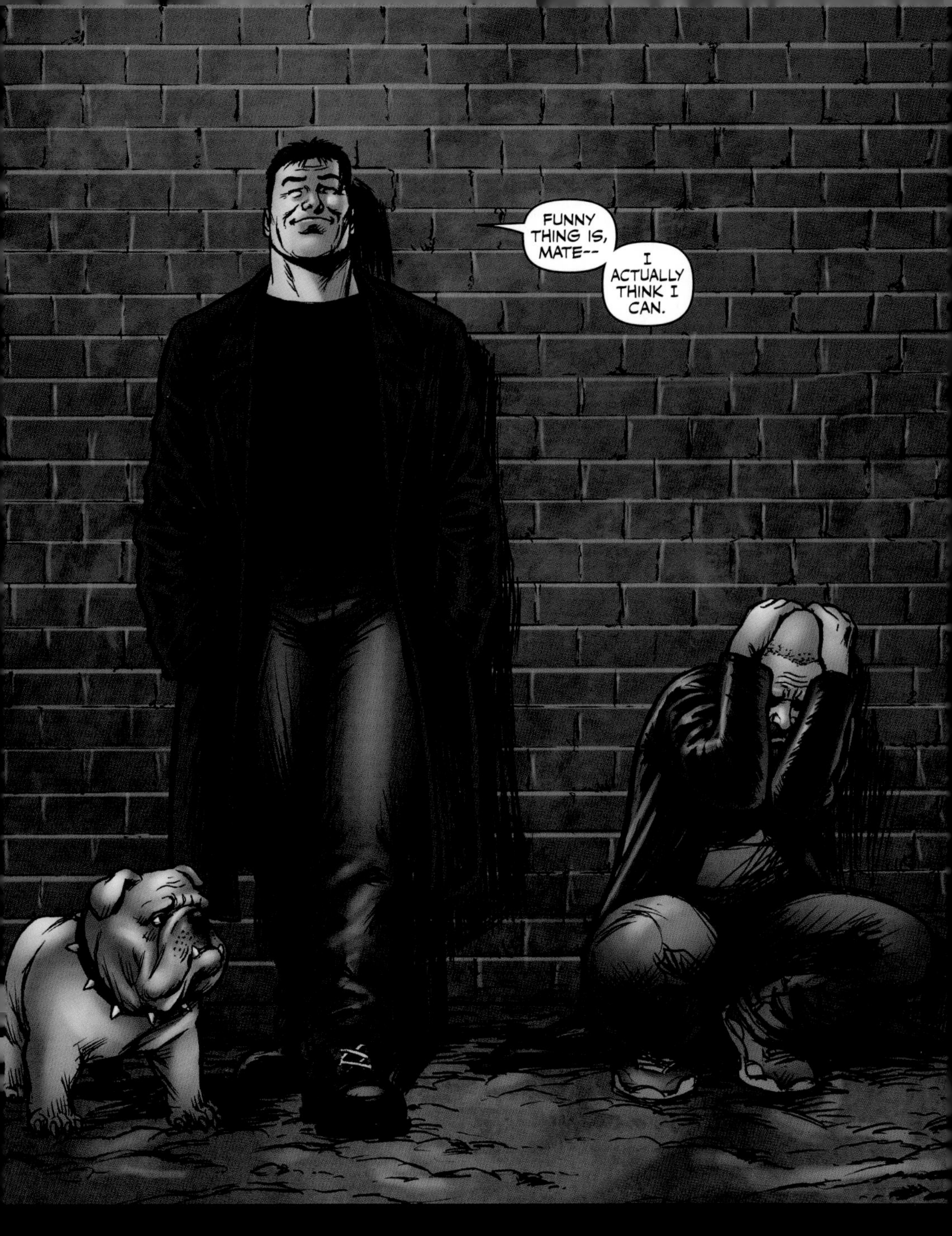
FUNNY THING IS, MATE--
I ACTUALLY THINK I CAN.

BELIEVE
part three

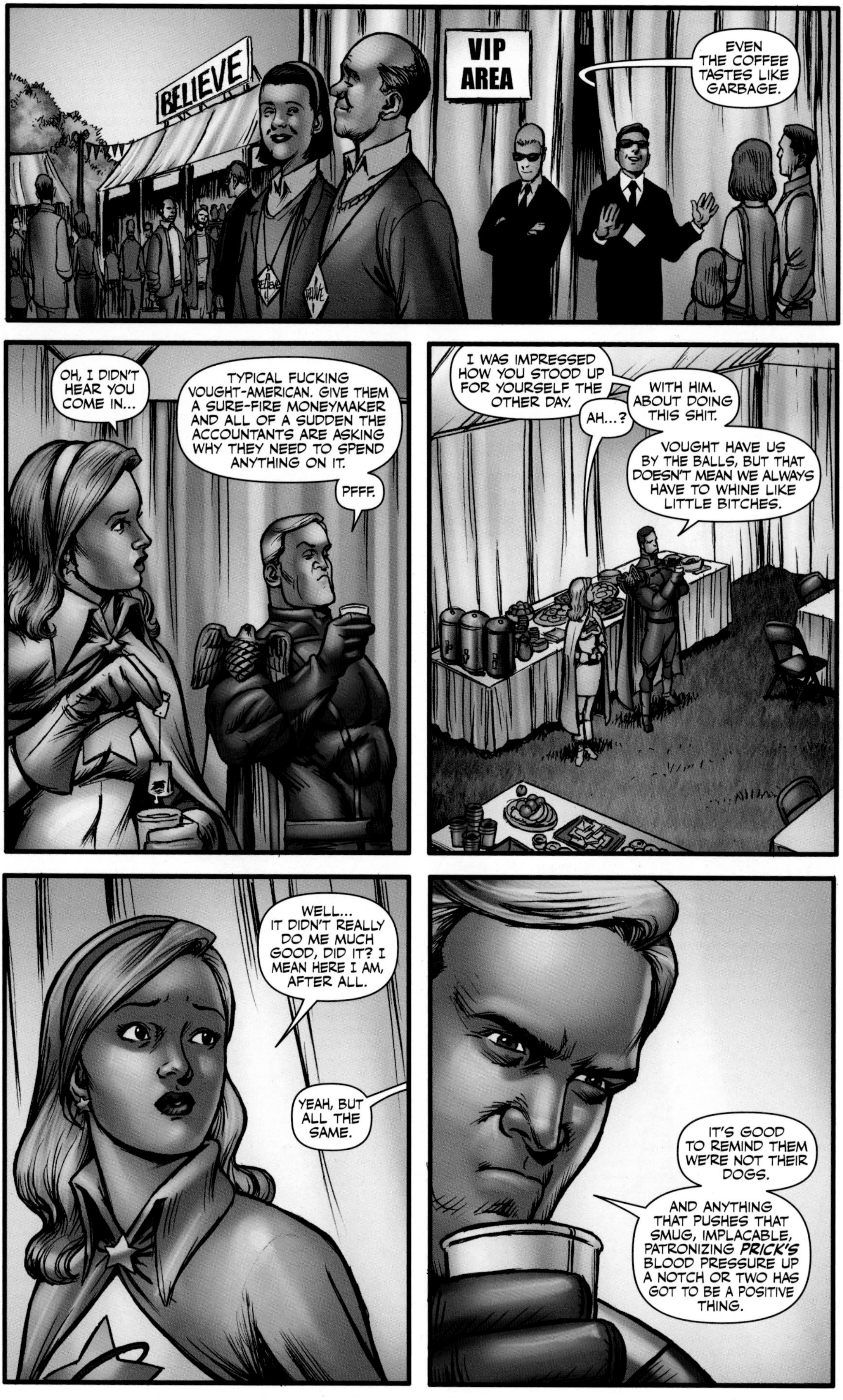
BELIEVE
VIP AREA
EVEN THE COFFEE TASTES LIKE GARBAGE.
OH, I DIDN'T HEAR YOU COME IN...
TYPICAL FUCKING VOUGHT-AMERICAN. GIVE THEM A SURE-FIRE MONEYMAKER AND ALL OF A SUDDEN THE ACCOUNTANTS ARE ASKING WHY THEY NEED TO SPEND ANYTHING ON IT.
PFFF.
I WAS IMPRESSED HOW YOU STOOD UP FOR YOURSELF THE OTHER DAY.
AH...?
WITH HIM. ABOUT DOING THIS SHIT.
VOUGHT HAVE US BY THE BALLS, BUT THAT DOESN'T MEAN WE ALWAYS HAVE TO WHINE LIKE LITTLE BITCHES.
WELL... IT DIDN'T REALLY DO ME MUCH GOOD, DID IT? I MEAN HERE I AM, AFTER ALL.
YEAH, BUT ALL THE SAME.
IT'S GOOD TO REMIND THEM WE'RE NOT THEIR DOGS.
AND ANYTHING THAT PUSHES THAT SMUG, IMPLACABLE, PATRONIZING *PRICK'S* BLOOD PRESSURE UP A NOTCH OR TWO HAS GOT TO BE A POSITIVE THING.

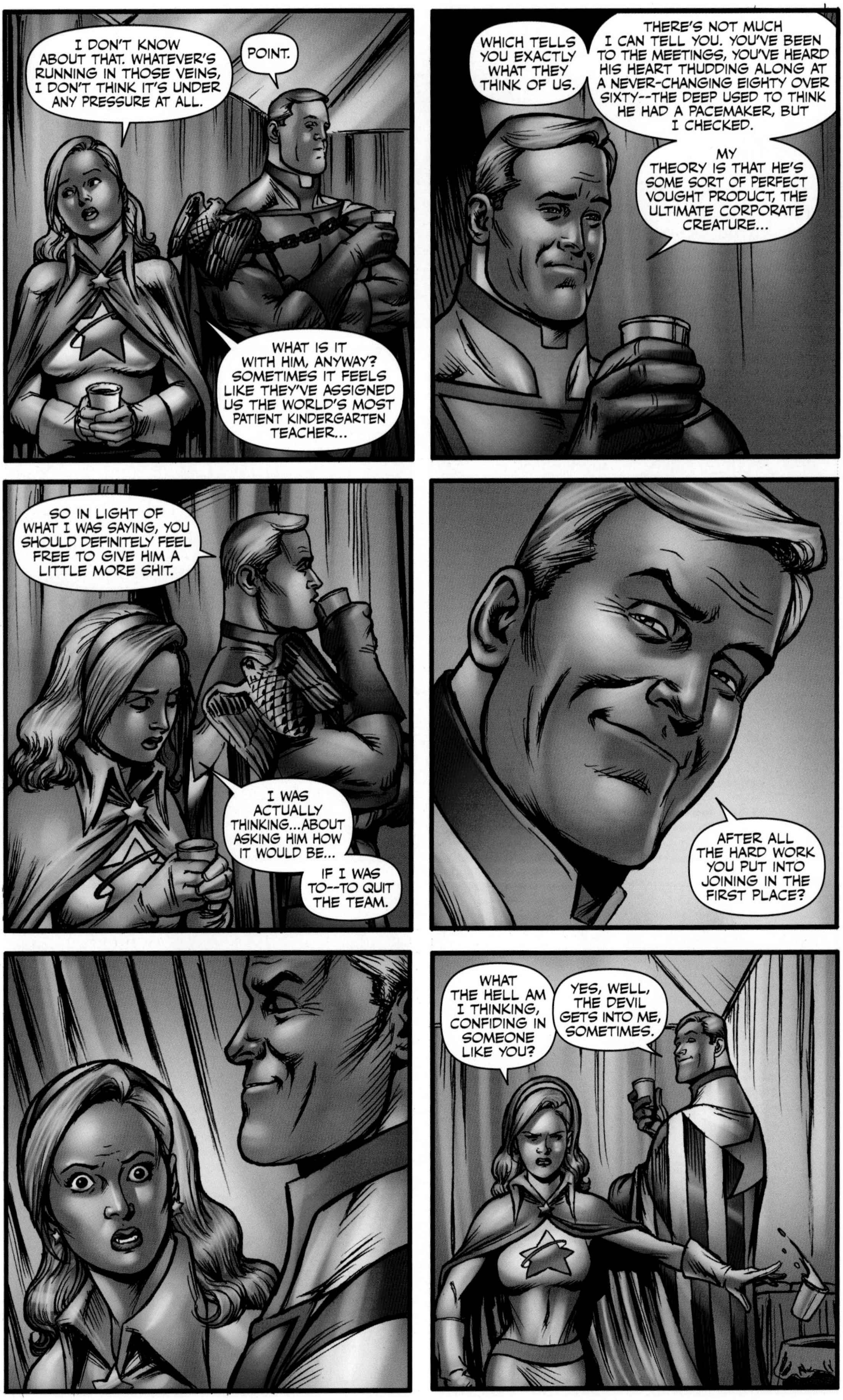
I DON'T KNOW ABOUT THAT. WHATEVER'S RUNNING IN THOSE VEINS, I DON'T THINK IT'S UNDER ANY PRESSURE AT ALL.
POINT.
WHAT IS IT WITH HIM, ANYWAY? SOMETIMES IT FEELS LIKE THEY'VE ASSIGNED US THE WORLD'S MOST PATIENT KINDERGARTEN TEACHER...
WHICH TELLS YOU EXACTLY WHAT THEY THINK OF US.
THERE'S NOT MUCH I CAN TELL YOU. YOU'VE BEEN TO THE MEETINGS, YOU'VE HEARD HIS HEART THUDDING ALONG AT A NEVER-CHANGING EIGHTY OVER SIXTY--THE DEEP USED TO THINK HE HAD A PACEMAKER, BUT I CHECKED.
MY THEORY IS THAT HE'S SOME SORT OF PERFECT VOUGHT PRODUCT, THE ULTIMATE CORPORATE CREATURE...
SO IN LIGHT OF WHAT I WAS SAYING, YOU SHOULD DEFINITELY FEEL FREE TO GIVE HIM A LITTLE MORE SHIT.
I WAS ACTUALLY THINKING...ABOUT ASKING HIM HOW IT WOULD BE...
IF I WAS TO--TO QUIT THE TEAM.
AFTER ALL THE HARD WORK YOU PUT INTO JOINING IN THE FIRST PLACE?
WHAT THE HELL AM I THINKING, CONFIDING IN SOMEONE LIKE YOU?
YES, WELL, THE DEVIL GETS INTO ME, SOMETIMES.

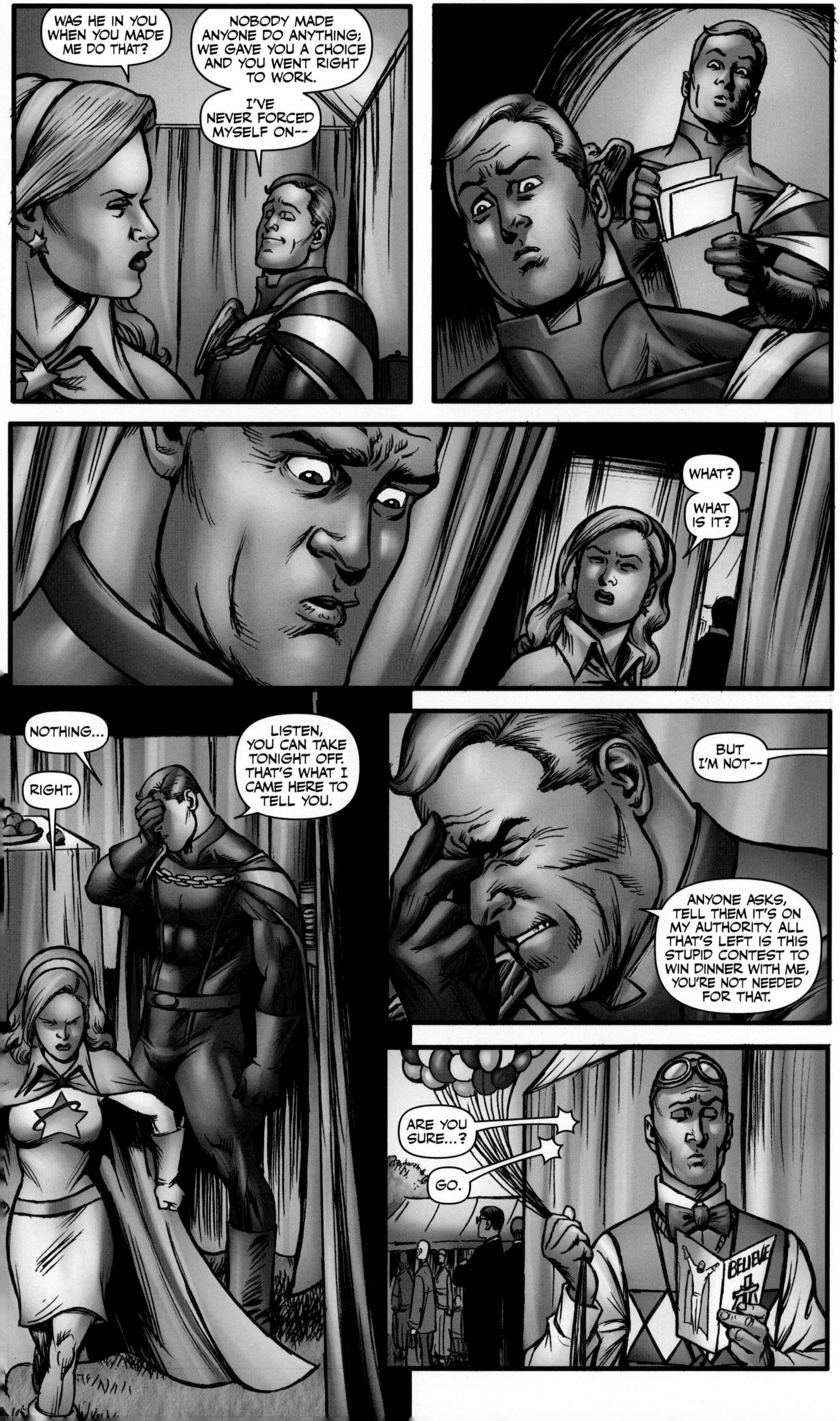
WAS HE IN YOU WHEN YOU MADE ME DO THAT?
NOBODY MADE ANYONE DO ANYTHING; WE GAVE YOU A CHOICE AND YOU WENT RIGHT TO WORK.
I'VE NEVER FORCED MYSELF ON--
WHAT?
WHAT IS IT?
NOTHING...
RIGHT.
LISTEN, YOU CAN TAKE TONIGHT OFF. THAT'S WHAT I CAME HERE TO TELL YOU.
BUT I'M NOT--
ANYONE ASKS, TELL THEM IT'S ON MY AUTHORITY. ALL THAT'S LEFT IS THIS STUPID CONTEST TO WIN DINNER WITH ME, YOU'RE NOT NEEDED FOR THAT.
ARE YOU SURE...?
GO.
BELIEVE

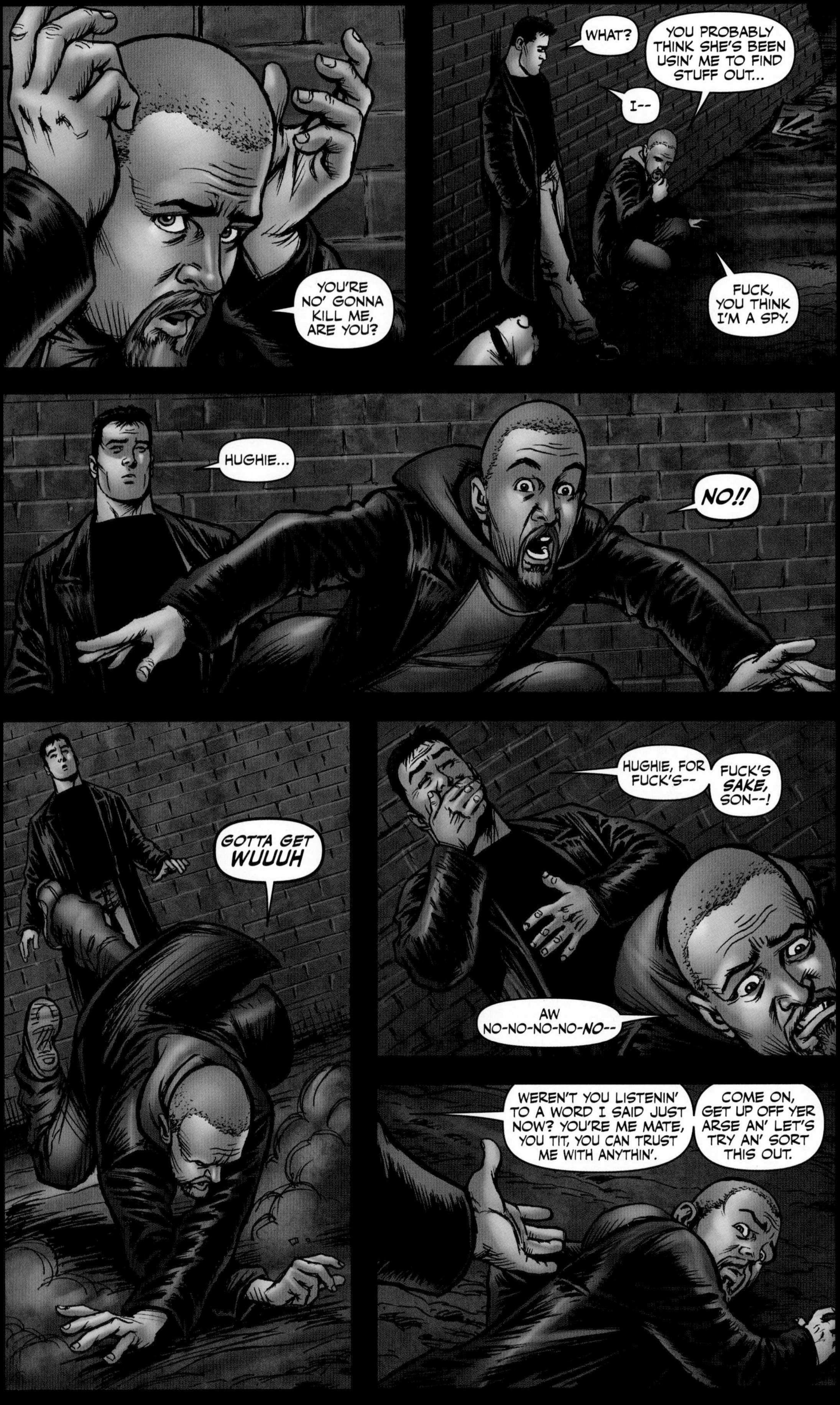
YOU'RE NO' GONNA KILL ME, ARE YOU?
WHAT?
YOU PROBABLY THINK SHE'S BEEN USIN' ME TO FIND STUFF OUT...
I--
FUCK, YOU THINK I'M A SPY.
HUGHIE...
NO!!
GOTTA GET WUUUH
HUGHIE, FOR FUCK'S--
FUCK'S SAKE, SON--!
AW NO-NO-NO-NO-NO--
WEREN'T YOU LISTENIN' TO A WORD I SAID JUST NOW? YOU'RE ME MATE, YOU TIT, YOU CAN TRUST ME WITH ANYTHIN'.
COME ON, GET UP OFF YER ARSE AN' LET'S TRY AN' SORT THIS OUT.

I THOUGHT YOU'D BE REALLY FUCKED OFF...!

HHHH. C'MON, THEN.

'COURSE I AM. BUT WHAT I AM MORE'N THAT IS FUCKIN' GOBSMACKED.

I MEAN ONLY YOU, HUGHIE...

START AT THE BEGINNIN'. WHERE AN' WHEN?

UH...

NO' THAT LONG AFTER I STARTED WI' YOU, ACTUALLY. IT--

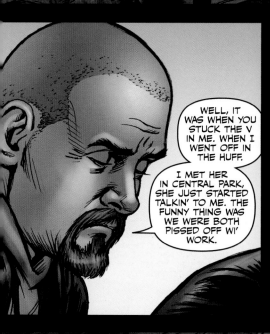

WELL, IT WAS WHEN YOU STUCK THE V IN ME. WHEN I WENT OFF IN THE HUFF.

I MET HER IN CENTRAL PARK, SHE JUST STARTED TALKIN' TO ME. THE FUNNY THING WAS WE WERE BOTH PISSED OFF WI' WORK.

SHE SAID... SHE SAID SHE'D HAD TO DO SOMETHIN' SHE DIDN'T LIKE, TO GET SOMETHIN' SHE WANTED--LATER ON SHE SAID SHE MEANT THE JOB.

THAT'S WHAT WAS GETTIN' HER DOWN, LIKE.

OH YEAH?

NOW UP 'TIL YESTERDAY I THOUGHT SHE WORKED IN FASHION OR WHATEVER, BUT OBVIOUSLY SHE WAS TALKIN' ABOUT THE SEVEN. RIGHT ENOUGH, SHE SAID THEY WERE FUCKIN' HORRIBLE.

WHAT'D YOU TELL HER YOU DONE?

INSURANCE.

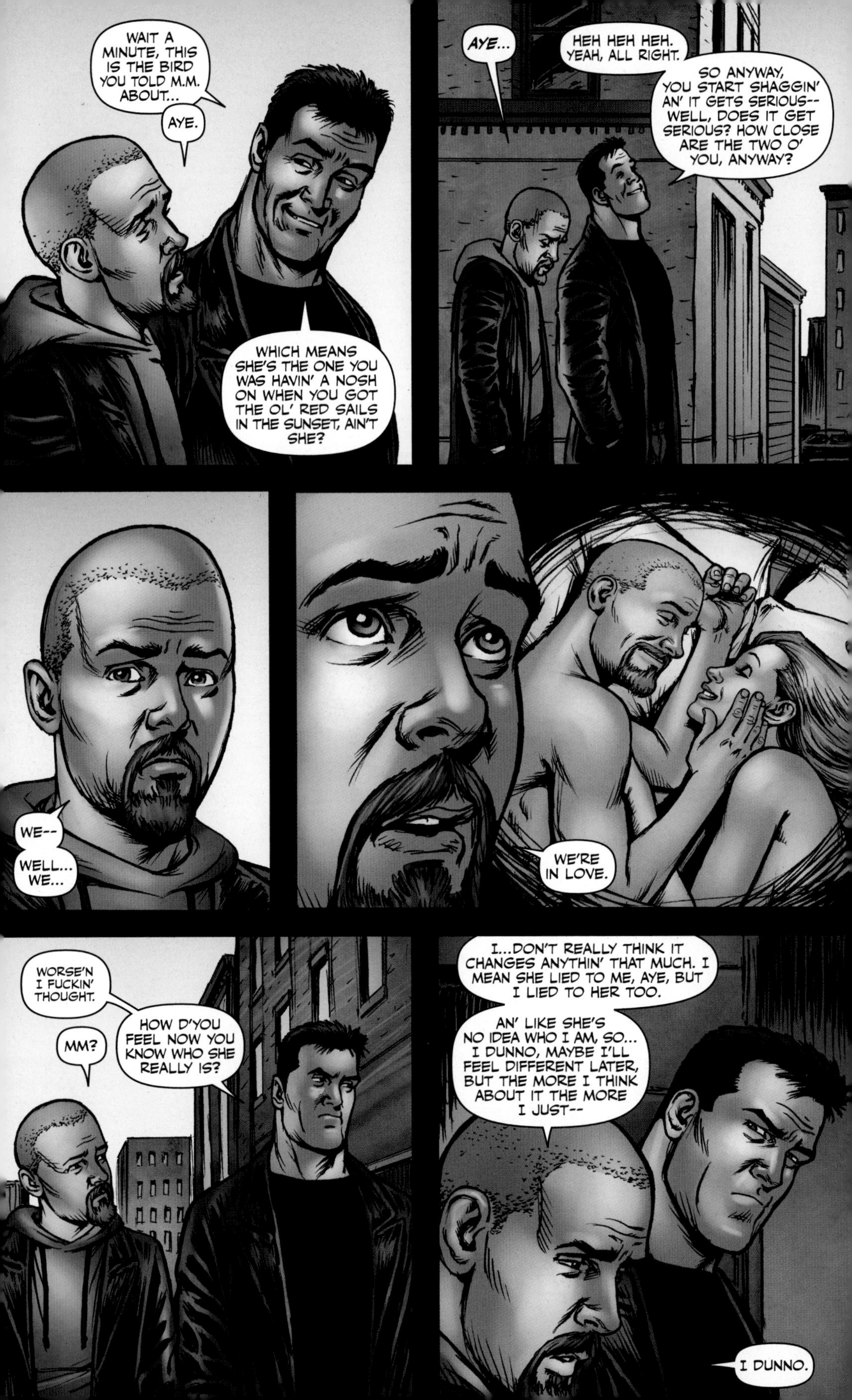
WAIT A MINUTE, THIS IS THE BIRD YOU TOLD M.M. ABOUT...
AYE.
WHICH MEANS SHE'S THE ONE YOU WAS HAVIN' A NOSH ON WHEN YOU GOT THE OL' RED SAILS IN THE SUNSET, AIN'T SHE?
AYE...
HEH HEH HEH. YEAH, ALL RIGHT.
SO ANYWAY, YOU START SHAGGIN' AN' IT GETS SERIOUS-- WELL, DOES IT GET SERIOUS? HOW CLOSE ARE THE TWO O' YOU, ANYWAY?
WE--
WELL... WE...
WE'RE IN LOVE.
WORSE'N I FUCKIN' THOUGHT.
MM?
HOW D'YOU FEEL NOW YOU KNOW WHO SHE REALLY IS?
I...DON'T REALLY THINK IT CHANGES ANYTHIN' THAT MUCH. I MEAN SHE LIED TO ME, AYE, BUT I LIED TO HER TOO.
AN' LIKE SHE'S NO IDEA WHO I AM, SO... I DUNNO, MAYBE I'LL FEEL DIFFERENT LATER, BUT THE MORE I THINK ABOUT IT THE MORE I JUST--
I DUNNO.

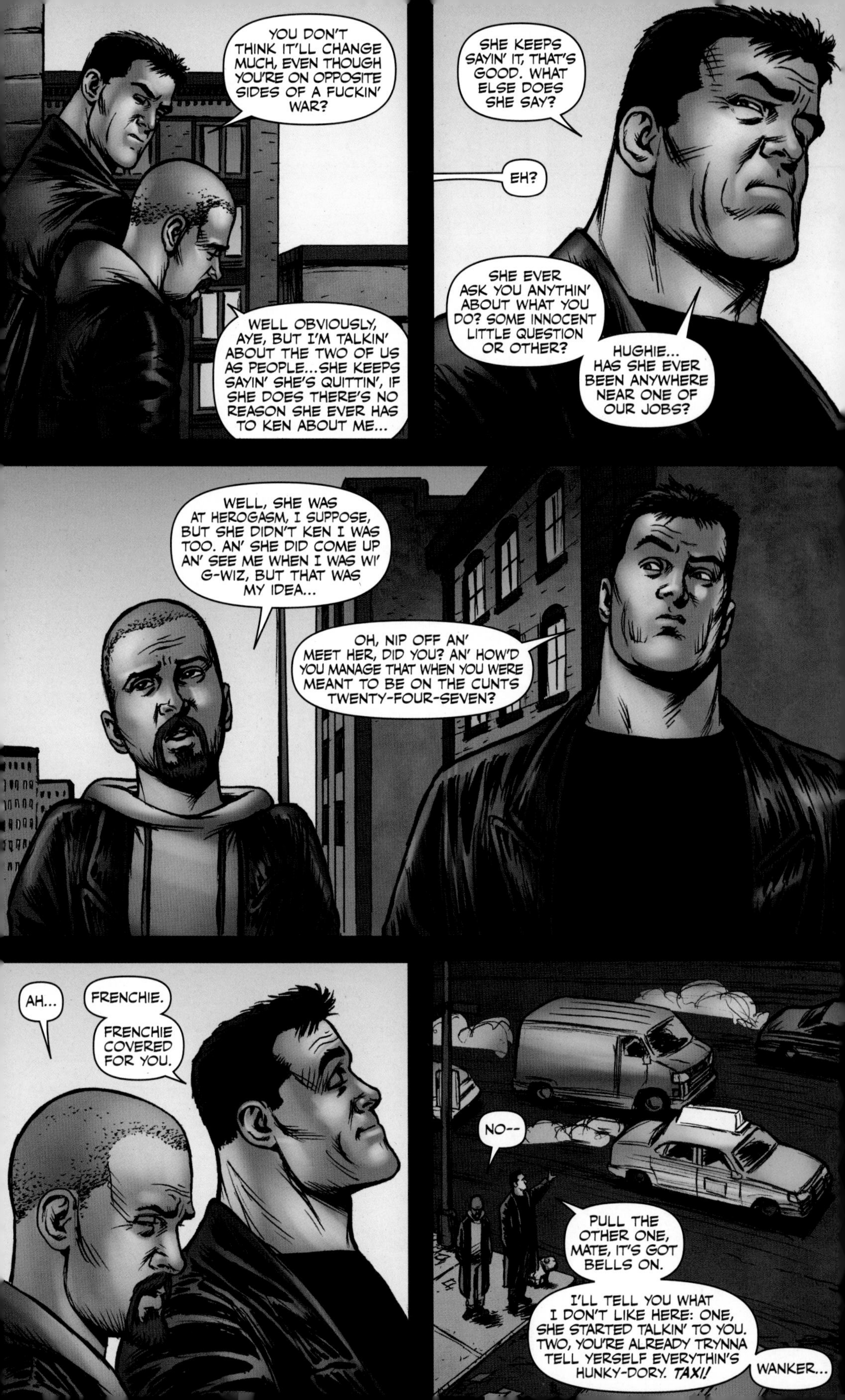
YOU DON'T THINK IT'LL CHANGE MUCH, EVEN THOUGH YOU'RE ON OPPOSITE SIDES OF A FUCKIN' WAR?
WELL OBVIOUSLY, AYE, BUT I'M TALKIN' ABOUT THE TWO OF US AS PEOPLE...SHE KEEPS SAYIN' SHE'S QUITTIN', IF SHE DOES THERE'S NO REASON SHE EVER HAS TO KEN ABOUT ME...
SHE KEEPS SAYIN' IT, THAT'S GOOD. WHAT ELSE DOES SHE SAY?
EH?
SHE EVER ASK YOU ANYTHIN' ABOUT WHAT YOU DO? SOME INNOCENT LITTLE QUESTION OR OTHER?
HUGHIE... HAS SHE EVER BEEN ANYWHERE NEAR ONE OF OUR JOBS?
WELL, SHE WAS AT HEROGASM, I SUPPOSE, BUT SHE DIDN'T KEN I WAS TOO. AN' SHE DID COME UP AN' SEE ME WHEN I WAS WI' G-WIZ, BUT THAT WAS MY IDEA...
OH, NIP OFF AN' MEET HER, DID YOU? AN' HOW'D YOU MANAGE THAT WHEN YOU WERE MEANT TO BE ON THE CUNTS TWENTY-FOUR-SEVEN?
AH...
FRENCHIE.
FRENCHIE COVERED FOR YOU.
NO--
PULL THE OTHER ONE, MATE, IT'S GOT BELLS ON.
I'LL TELL YOU WHAT I DON'T LIKE HERE: ONE, SHE STARTED TALKIN' TO YOU. TWO, YOU'RE ALREADY TRYNNA TELL YERSELF EVERYTHIN'S HUNKY-DORY. *TAXI!*
WANKER...

FRENCHIE! WE WAS JUST TALKIN' ABOUT YOU, MY SON!

OUI...?

NOTHING IS AMISS, M'SIEU CHARCUTER?

'COURSE NOT! WHAT MAKES YOU SAY THAT, MATE?

AH...I THOUGHT I DETECTED SOMETHING MILDLY... CARNIVOROUS, IN YOUR TONE...

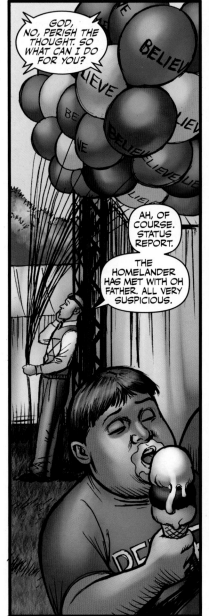

GOD, NO, PERISH THE THOUGHT. SO WHAT CAN I DO FOR YOU?

AH, OF COURSE. STATUS REPORT.

THE HOMELANDER HAS MET WITH OH FATHER. ALL VERY SUSPICIOUS.

OH YEAH? WHAT'S THE CUNT WANT WITH THAT FUCKIN' PEDO, THEN?

SEEMED TO BE...SOUNDING HIM OUT. ABOUT WHICH OF THE SUPES WOULD BACK VOUGHT-AMERICAN AND VIC THE VEEP IN, AH, EXTREME CIRCUMSTANCES.

NOW THAT IS INTERESTIN'...

THE QUESTION WAS ONE OF FORCING THROUGH A CERTAIN PLAN. OH FATHER BELIEVES THAT A MAJORITY WOULD GO ALONG WITH IT.

A MEETING WAS CALLED FOR LATER ON.

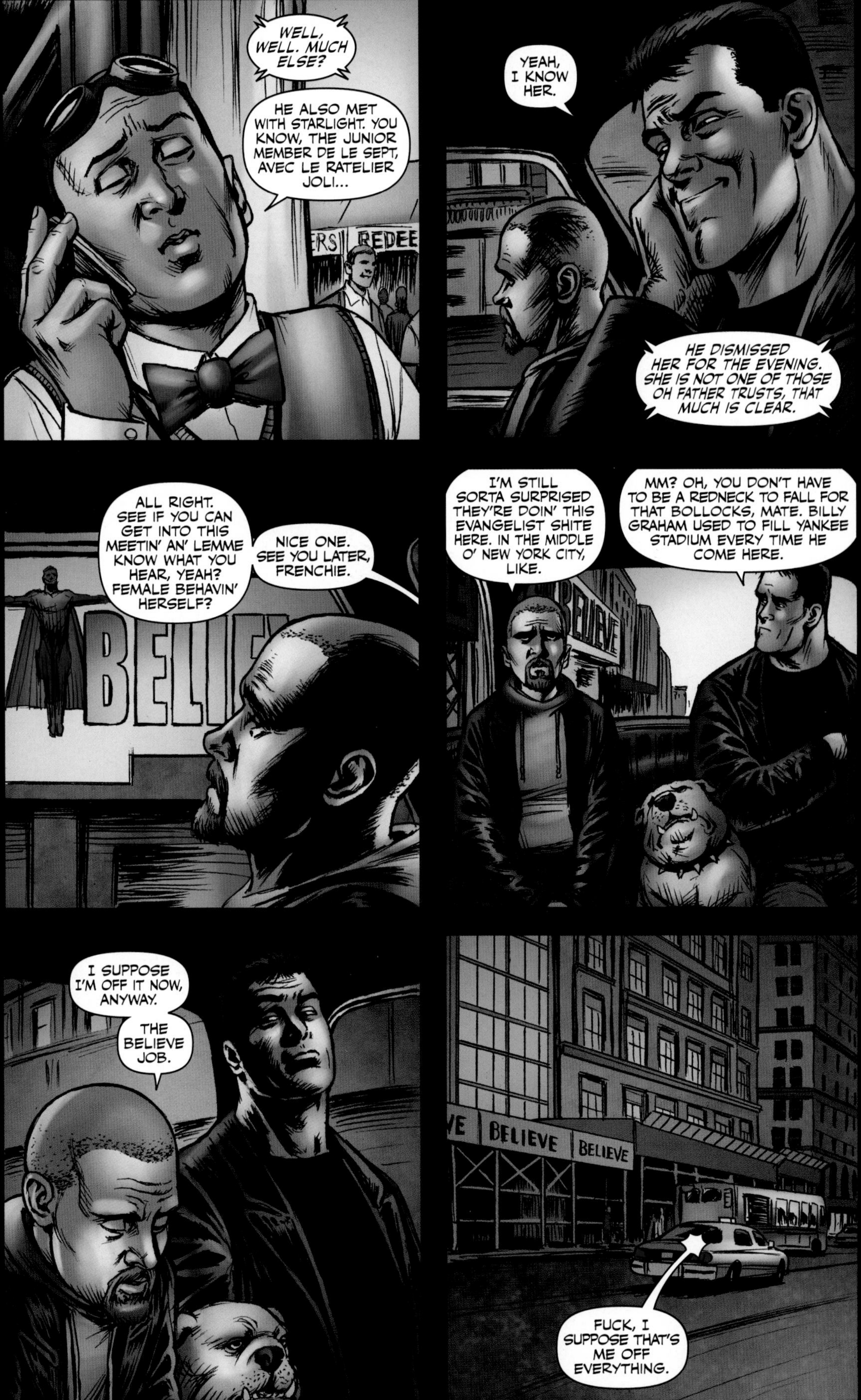
WELL, WELL. MUCH ELSE?
HE ALSO MET WITH STARLIGHT. YOU KNOW, THE JUNIOR MEMBER DE LE SEPT, AVEC LE RATELIER JOLI...
YEAH, I KNOW HER.
HE DISMISSED HER FOR THE EVENING. SHE IS NOT ONE OF THOSE OH FATHER TRUSTS, THAT MUCH IS CLEAR.
ALL RIGHT. SEE IF YOU CAN GET INTO THIS MEETIN' AN' LEMME KNOW WHAT YOU HEAR, YEAH? FEMALE BEHAVIN' HERSELF?
NICE ONE. SEE YOU LATER, FRENCHIE.
BELIE
I'M STILL SORTA SURPRISED THEY'RE DOIN' THIS EVANGELIST SHITE HERE. IN THE MIDDLE O' NEW YORK CITY, LIKE.
MM? OH, YOU DON'T HAVE TO BE A REDNECK TO FALL FOR THAT BOLLOCKS, MATE. BILLY GRAHAM USED TO FILL YANKEE STADIUM EVERY TIME HE COME HERE.
BELIEVE
I SUPPOSE I'M OFF IT NOW, ANYWAY.
THE BELIEVE JOB.
BELIEVE
BELIEVE
FUCK, I SUPPOSE THAT'S ME OFF EVERYTHING.

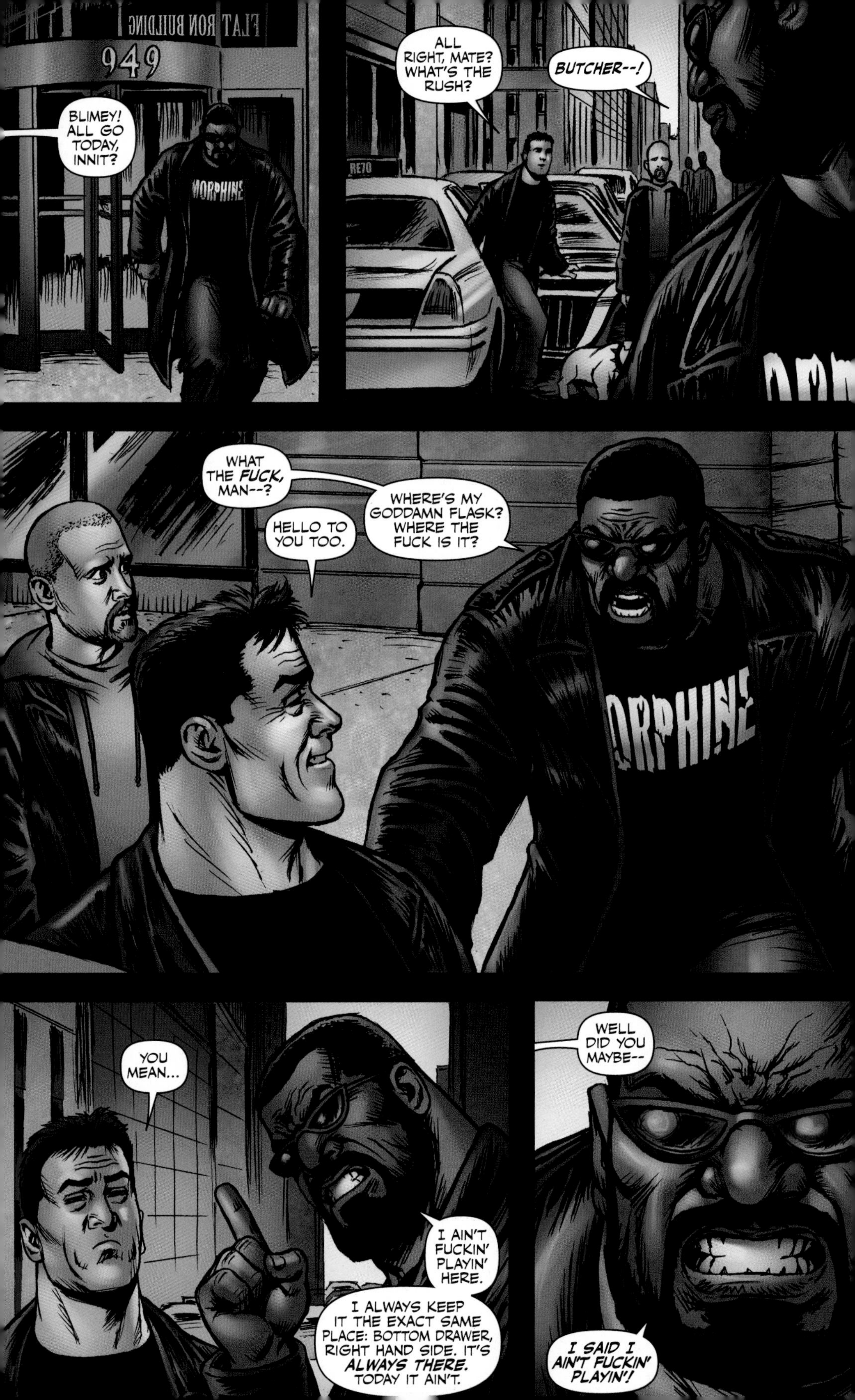
949
MORPHINE
BLIMEY! ALL GO TODAY, INNIT?
ALL RIGHT, MATE? WHAT'S THE RUSH?
BUTCHER--!
WHAT THE FUCK, MAN--?
HELLO TO YOU TOO.
WHERE'S MY GODDAMN FLASK? WHERE THE FUCK IS IT?
MORPHINE
YOU MEAN...
I AIN'T FUCKIN' PLAYIN' HERE.
I ALWAYS KEEP IT THE EXACT SAME PLACE: BOTTOM DRAWER, RIGHT HAND SIDE. IT'S ALWAYS THERE. TODAY IT AIN'T.
WELL DID YOU MAYBE--
I SAID I AIN'T FUCKIN' PLAYIN'!

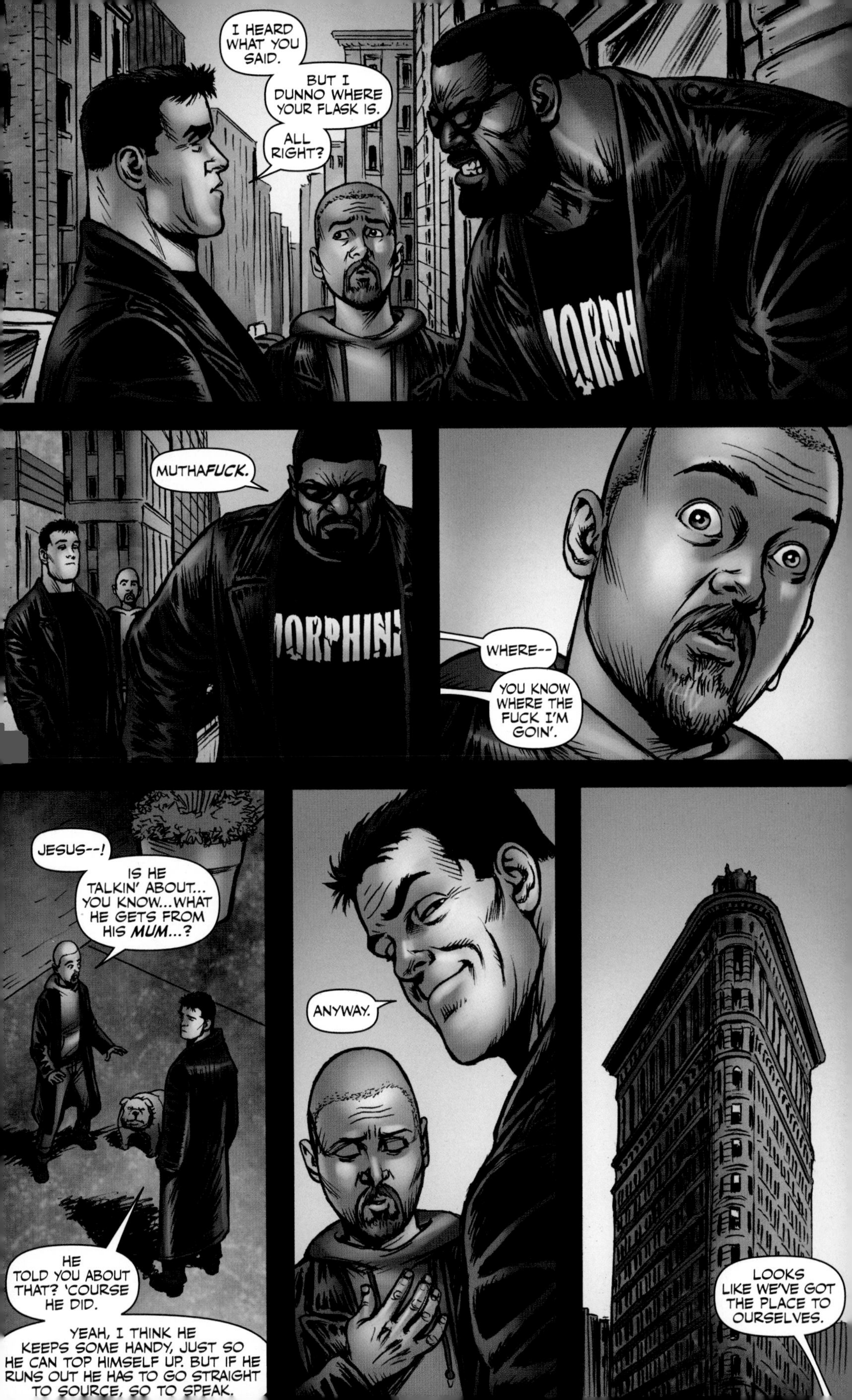
I HEARD WHAT YOU SAID.
BUT I DUNNO WHERE YOUR FLASK IS.
ALL RIGHT?
MORPH
MUTHAFUCK.
MORPHINE
WHERE--
YOU KNOW WHERE THE FUCK I'M GOIN'.
JESUS--!
IS HE TALKIN' ABOUT... YOU KNOW...WHAT HE GETS FROM HIS MUM...?
HE TOLD YOU ABOUT THAT? 'COURSE HE DID.
YEAH, I THINK HE KEEPS SOME HANDY, JUST SO HE CAN TOP HIMSELF UP. BUT IF HE RUNS OUT HE HAS TO GO STRAIGHT TO SOURCE, SO TO SPEAK.
ANYWAY.
LOOKS LIKE WE'VE GOT THE PLACE TO OURSELVES.

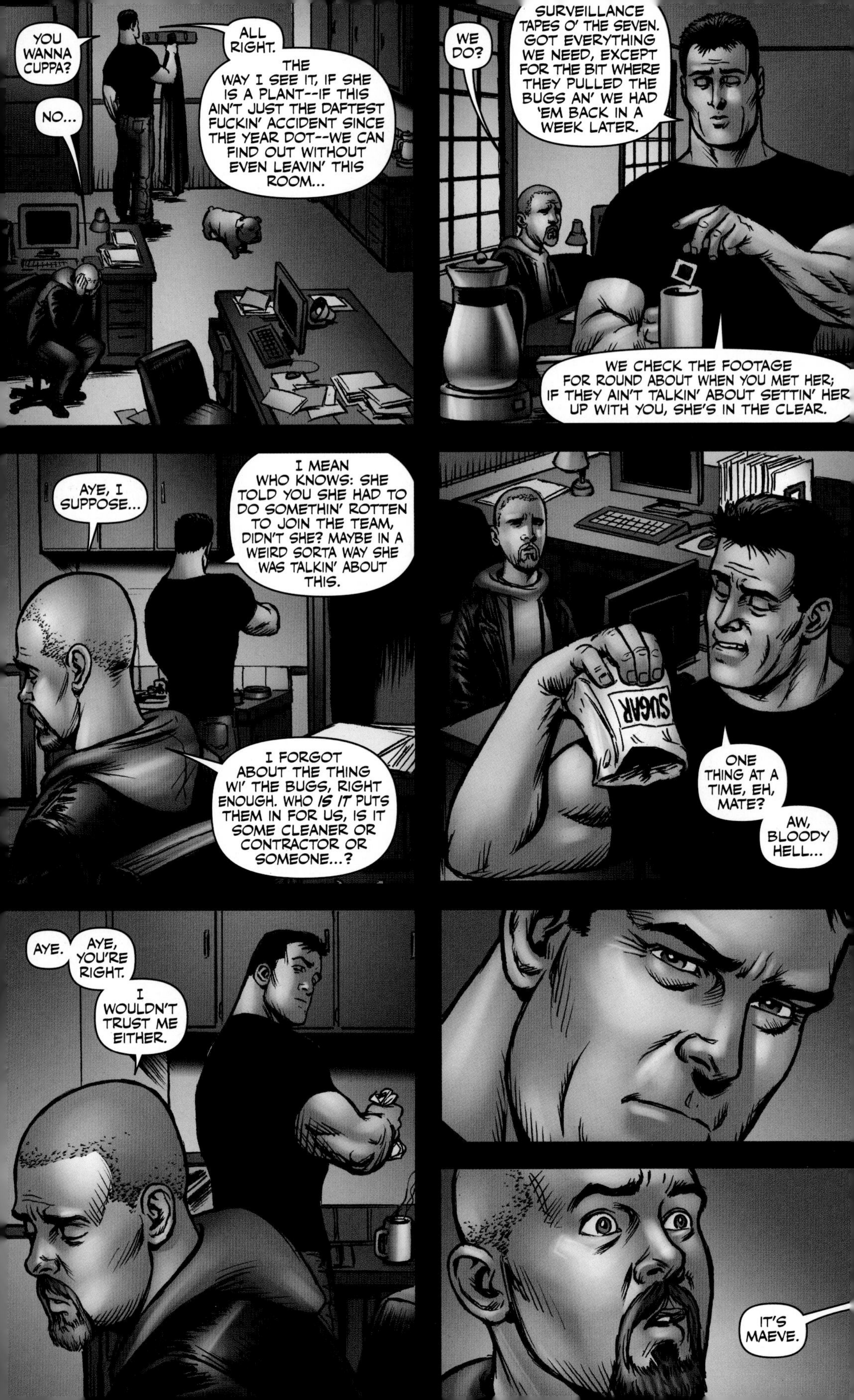
YOU WANNA CUPPA?
ALL RIGHT.
NO...
THE WAY I SEE IT, IF SHE IS A PLANT--IF THIS AIN'T JUST THE DAFTEST FUCKIN' ACCIDENT SINCE THE YEAR DOT--WE CAN FIND OUT WITHOUT EVEN LEAVIN' THIS ROOM...
WE DO?
SURVEILLANCE TAPES O' THE SEVEN. GOT EVERYTHING WE NEED, EXCEPT FOR THE BIT WHERE THEY PULLED THE BUGS AN' WE HAD 'EM BACK IN A WEEK LATER.
WE CHECK THE FOOTAGE FOR ROUND ABOUT WHEN YOU MET HER; IF THEY AIN'T TALKIN' ABOUT SETTIN' HER UP WITH YOU, SHE'S IN THE CLEAR.
AYE, I SUPPOSE...
I MEAN WHO KNOWS: SHE TOLD YOU SHE HAD TO DO SOMETHIN' ROTTEN TO JOIN THE TEAM, DIDN'T SHE? MAYBE IN A WEIRD SORTA WAY SHE WAS TALKIN' ABOUT THIS.
I FORGOT ABOUT THE THING WI' THE BUGS, RIGHT ENOUGH. WHO *IS IT* PUTS THEM IN FOR US, IS IT SOME CLEANER OR CONTRACTOR OR SOMEONE...?
SUGAR
ONE THING AT A TIME, EH, MATE?
AW, BLOODY HELL...
AYE.
AYE, YOU'RE RIGHT.
I WOULDN'T TRUST ME EITHER.
IT'S MAEVE.

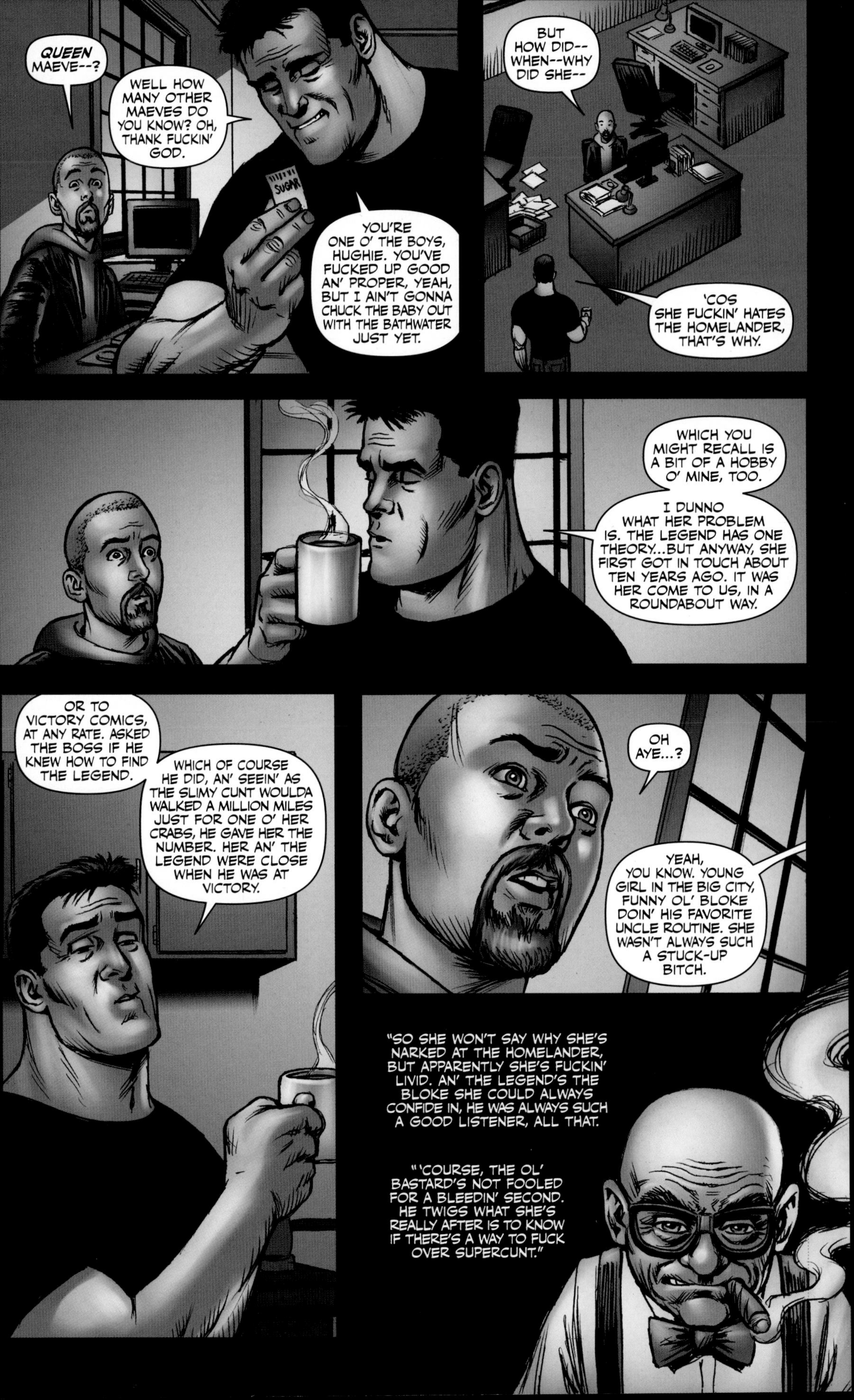
QUEEN MAEVE--?
WELL HOW MANY OTHER MAEVES DO YOU KNOW? OH, THANK FUCKIN' GOD.
SUGAR
YOU'RE ONE O' THE BOYS, HUGHIE. YOU'VE FUCKED UP GOOD AN' PROPER, YEAH, BUT I AIN'T GONNA CHUCK THE BABY OUT WITH THE BATHWATER JUST YET.
BUT HOW DID-- WHEN--WHY DID SHE--
'COS SHE FUCKIN' HATES THE HOMELANDER, THAT'S WHY.
WHICH YOU MIGHT RECALL IS A BIT OF A HOBBY O' MINE, TOO.
I DUNNO WHAT HER PROBLEM IS. THE LEGEND HAS ONE THEORY...BUT ANYWAY, SHE FIRST GOT IN TOUCH ABOUT TEN YEARS AGO. IT WAS HER COME TO US, IN A ROUNDABOUT WAY.
OR TO VICTORY COMICS, AT ANY RATE. ASKED THE BOSS IF HE KNEW HOW TO FIND THE LEGEND.
WHICH OF COURSE HE DID, AN' SEEIN' AS THE SLIMY CUNT WOULDA WALKED A MILLION MILES JUST FOR ONE O' HER CRABS, HE GAVE HER THE NUMBER. HER AN' THE LEGEND WERE CLOSE WHEN HE WAS AT VICTORY.
OH AYE...?
YEAH, YOU KNOW. YOUNG GIRL IN THE BIG CITY, FUNNY OL' BLOKE DOIN' HIS FAVORITE UNCLE ROUTINE. SHE WASN'T ALWAYS SUCH A STUCK-UP BITCH.
"SO SHE WON'T SAY WHY SHE'S NARKED AT THE HOMELANDER, BUT APPARENTLY SHE'S FUCKIN' LIVID. AN' THE LEGEND'S THE BLOKE SHE COULD ALWAYS CONFIDE IN, HE WAS ALWAYS SUCH A GOOD LISTENER, ALL THAT.
"'COURSE, THE OL' BASTARD'S NOT FOOLED FOR A BLEEDIN' SECOND. HE TWIGS WHAT SHE'S REALLY AFTER IS TO KNOW IF THERE'S A WAY TO FUCK OVER SUPERCUNT."

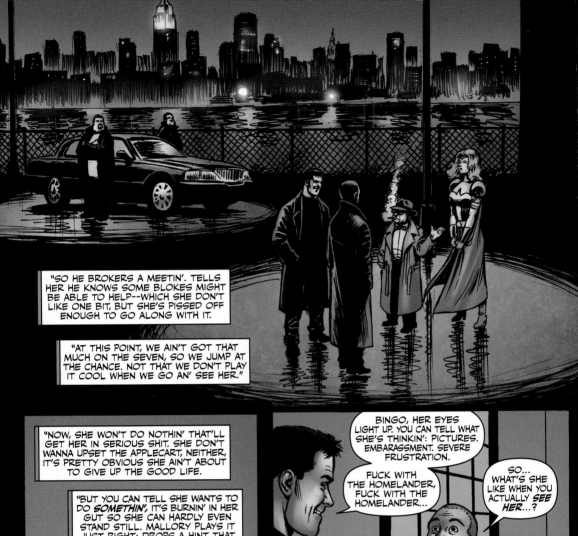

"SO HE BROKERS A MEETIN'. TELLS HER HE KNOWS SOME BLOKES MIGHT BE ABLE TO HELP--WHICH SHE DON'T LIKE ONE BIT, BUT SHE'S PISSED OFF ENOUGH TO GO ALONG WITH IT.

"AT THIS POINT, WE AIN'T GOT THAT MUCH ON THE SEVEN, SO WE JUMP AT THE CHANCE. NOT THAT WE DON'T PLAY IT COOL WHEN WE GO AN' SEE HER."

"NOW, SHE WON'T DO NOTHIN' THAT'LL GET HER IN SERIOUS SHIT. SHE DON'T WANNA UPSET THE APPLECART, NEITHER, IT'S PRETTY OBVIOUS SHE AIN'T ABOUT TO GIVE UP THE GOOD LIFE.

"BUT YOU CAN TELL SHE WANTS TO DO *SOMETHIN'*, IT'S BURNIN' IN HER GUT SO SHE CAN HARDLY EVEN STAND STILL. MALLORY PLAYS IT JUST RIGHT: DROPS A HINT THAT WE'RE FEDERAL, SAYS WE DON'T WANNA FINISH THE SEVEN EITHER, FAR FROM IT--

BINGO, HER EYES LIGHT UP. YOU CAN TELL WHAT SHE'S THINKIN': PICTURES. EMBARASSMENT. SEVERE FRUSTRATION.

FUCK WITH THE HOMELANDER, FUCK WITH THE HOMELANDER...

SO... WHAT'S SHE ACTUALLY *SEE* HER...?

"BUT HOW ABOUT STICKIN' IN A COUPLA CAMERAS FOR US?"

"TYPICAL OLDER BIRD WITH MONEY. QUITE TASTY, 'TIL YOU GET CLOSE ENOUGH TO SEE THE CRACKS...

"OH, BLOODY HELL, HUGHIE, YOU'RE NOT TRYNNA TELL ME YOU FUCKIN' FANCY *MAEVE*...!"

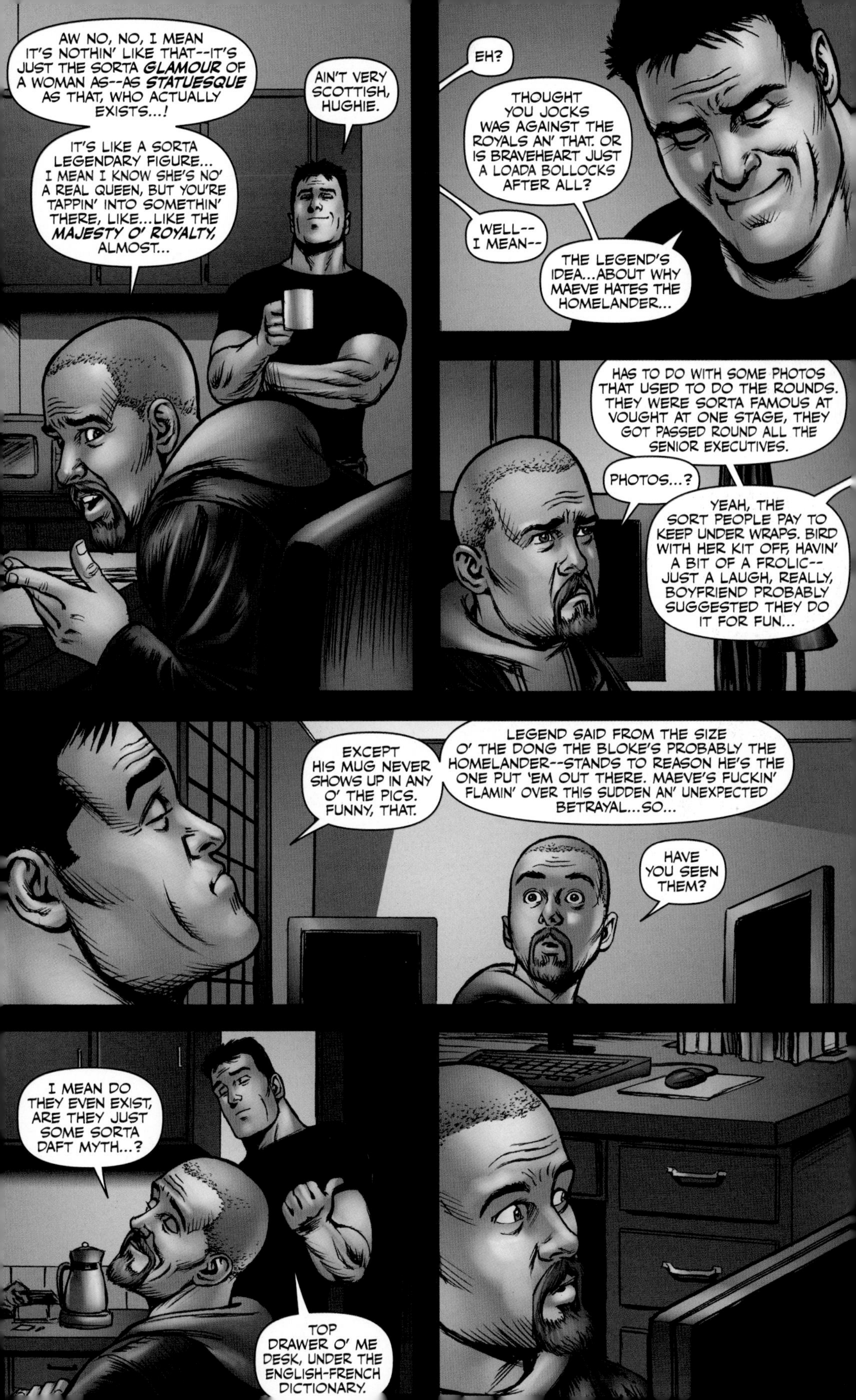
AW NO, NO, I MEAN IT'S NOTHIN' LIKE THAT--IT'S JUST THE SORTA GLAMOUR OF A WOMAN AS--AS STATUESQUE AS THAT, WHO ACTUALLY EXISTS...!
IT'S LIKE A SORTA LEGENDARY FIGURE... I MEAN I KNOW SHE'S NO' A REAL QUEEN, BUT YOU'RE TAPPIN' INTO SOMETHIN' THERE, LIKE...LIKE THE MAJESTY O' ROYALTY, ALMOST...
AIN'T VERY SCOTTISH, HUGHIE.
EH?
THOUGHT YOU JOCKS WAS AGAINST THE ROYALS AN' THAT. OR IS BRAVEHEART JUST A LOADA BOLLOCKS AFTER ALL?
WELL-- I MEAN--
THE LEGEND'S IDEA...ABOUT WHY MAEVE HATES THE HOMELANDER...
HAS TO DO WITH SOME PHOTOS THAT USED TO DO THE ROUNDS. THEY WERE SORTA FAMOUS AT VOUGHT AT ONE STAGE, THEY GOT PASSED ROUND ALL THE SENIOR EXECUTIVES.
PHOTOS...?
YEAH, THE SORT PEOPLE PAY TO KEEP UNDER WRAPS. BIRD WITH HER KIT OFF, HAVIN' A BIT OF A FROLIC-- JUST A LAUGH, REALLY, BOYFRIEND PROBABLY SUGGESTED THEY DO IT FOR FUN...
LEGEND SAID FROM THE SIZE O' THE DONG THE BLOKE'S PROBABLY THE HOMELANDER--STANDS TO REASON HE'S THE ONE PUT 'EM OUT THERE. MAEVE'S FUCKIN' FLAMIN' OVER THIS SUDDEN AN' UNEXPECTED BETRAYAL...SO...
EXCEPT HIS MUG NEVER SHOWS UP IN ANY O' THE PICS. FUNNY, THAT.
HAVE YOU SEEN THEM?
I MEAN DO THEY EVEN EXIST, ARE THEY JUST SOME SORTA DAFT MYTH...?
TOP DRAWER O' ME DESK, UNDER THE ENGLISH-FRENCH DICTIONARY.

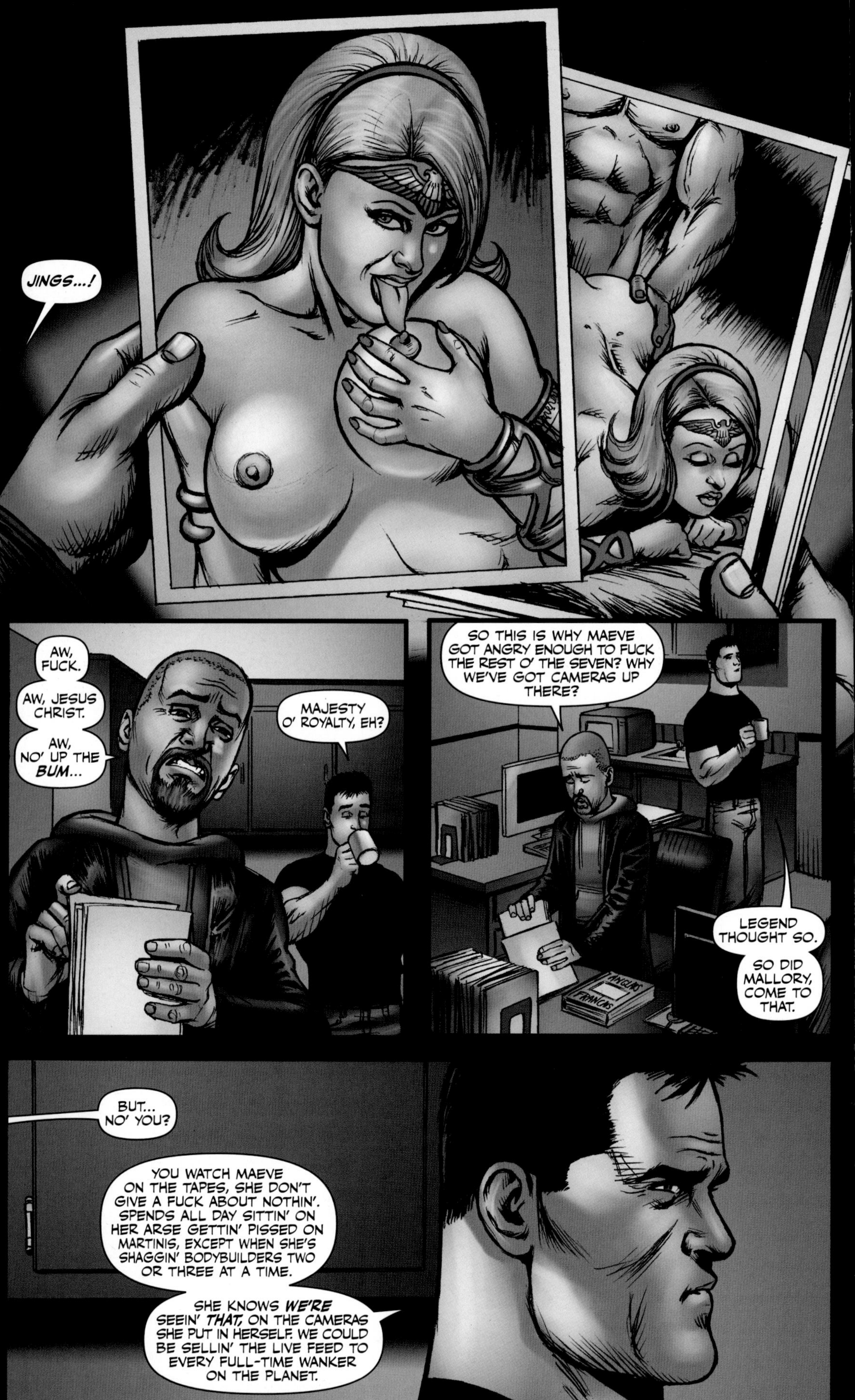
JINGS...!
AW, FUCK.
AW, JESUS CHRIST.
AW, NO' UP THE *BUM*...
MAJESTY O' ROYALTY, EH?
SO THIS IS WHY MAEVE GOT ANGRY ENOUGH TO FUCK THE REST O' THE SEVEN? WHY WE'VE GOT CAMERAS UP THERE?
LEGEND THOUGHT SO.
SO DID MALLORY, COME TO THAT.
BUT... NO' YOU?
YOU WATCH MAEVE ON THE TAPES, SHE DON'T GIVE A FUCK ABOUT NOTHIN'. SPENDS ALL DAY SITTIN' ON HER ARSE GETTIN' PISSED ON MARTINIS, EXCEPT WHEN SHE'S SHAGGIN' BODYBUILDERS TWO OR THREE AT A TIME.
SHE KNOWS *WE'RE* SEEIN' *THAT*, ON THE CAMERAS SHE PUT IN HERSELF. WE COULD BE SELLIN' THE LIVE FEED TO EVERY FULL-TIME WANKER ON THE PLANET.

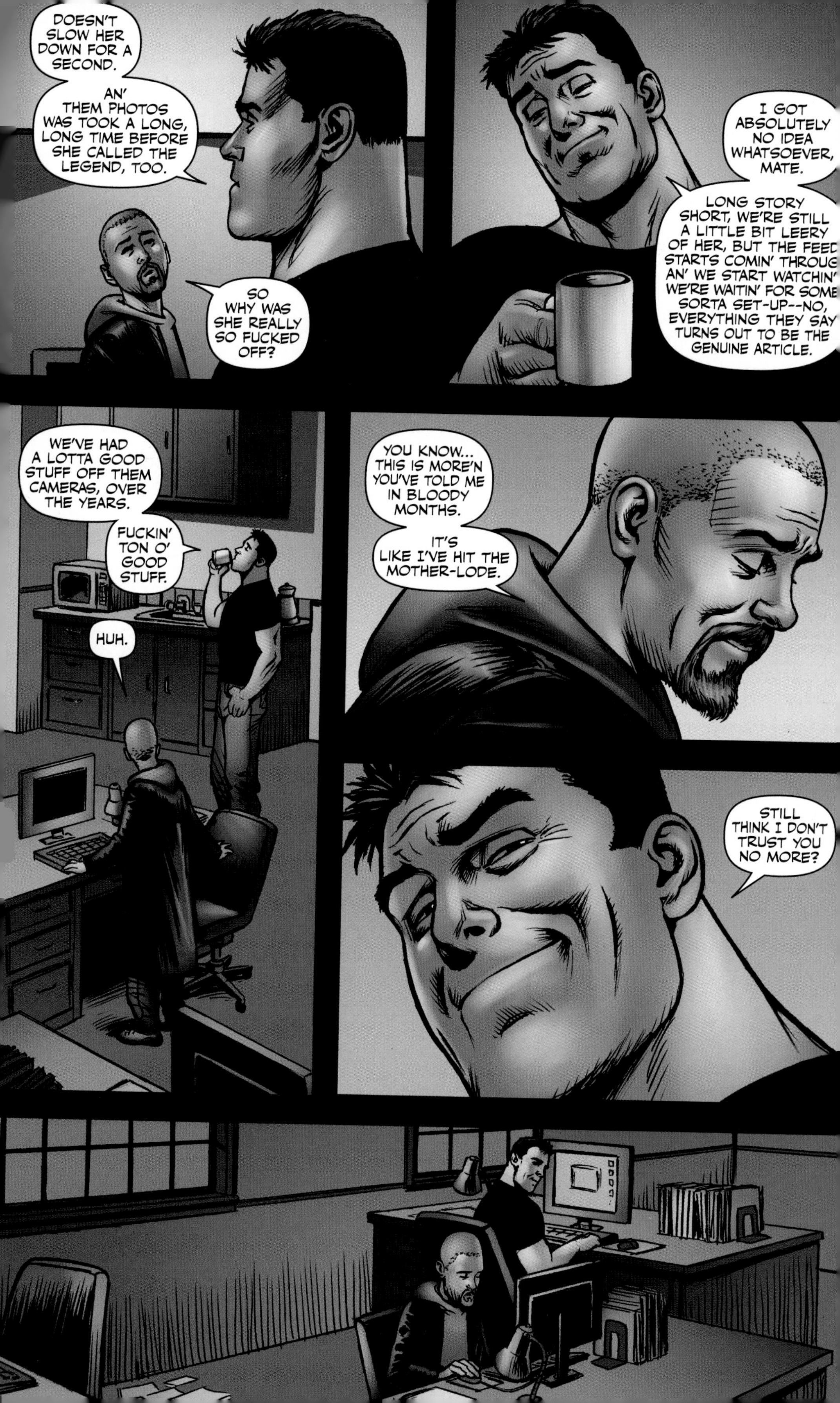
DOESN'T SLOW HER DOWN FOR A SECOND.
AN' THEM PHOTOS WAS TOOK A LONG, LONG TIME BEFORE SHE CALLED THE LEGEND, TOO.
SO WHY WAS SHE REALLY SO FUCKED OFF?
I GOT ABSOLUTELY NO IDEA WHATSOEVER, MATE.
LONG STORY SHORT, WE'RE STILL A LITTLE BIT LEERY OF HER, BUT THE FEED STARTS COMIN' THROUG AN' WE START WATCHIN' WE'RE WAITIN' FOR SOME SORTA SET-UP--NO, EVERYTHING THEY SAY TURNS OUT TO BE THE GENUINE ARTICLE.
WE'VE HAD A LOTTA GOOD STUFF OFF THEM CAMERAS, OVER THE YEARS.
FUCKIN' TON O' GOOD STUFF.
HUH.
YOU KNOW... THIS IS MORE'N YOU'VE TOLD ME IN BLOODY MONTHS.
IT'S LIKE I'VE HIT THE MOTHER-LODE.
STILL THINK I DON'T TRUST YOU NO MORE?

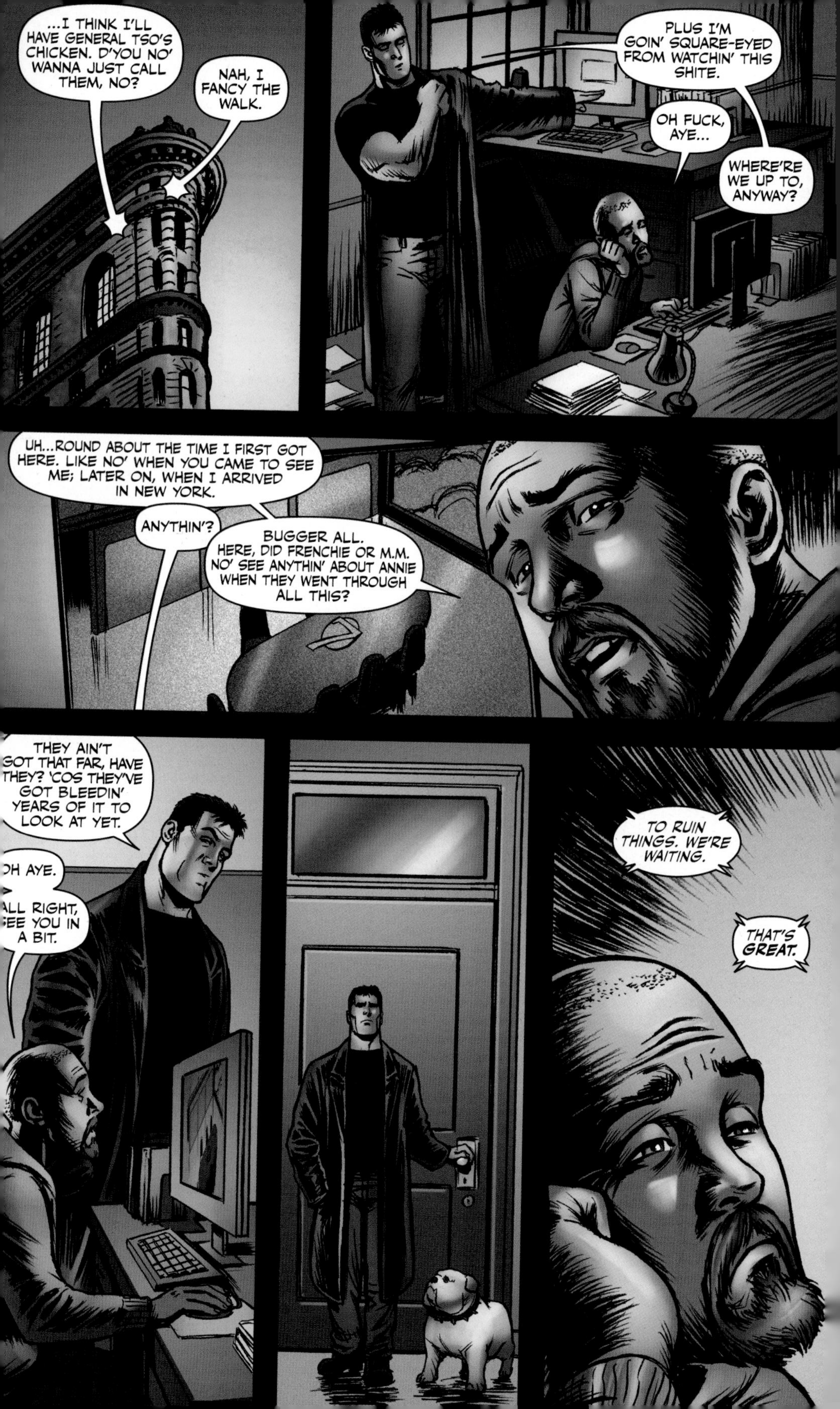
...I THINK I'LL HAVE GENERAL TSO'S CHICKEN. D'YOU NO' WANNA JUST CALL THEM, NO?
NAH, I FANCY THE WALK.
PLUS I'M GOIN' SQUARE-EYED FROM WATCHIN' THIS SHITE.
OH FUCK, AYE...
WHERE'RE WE UP TO, ANYWAY?
UH...ROUND ABOUT THE TIME I FIRST GOT HERE. LIKE NO' WHEN YOU CAME TO SEE ME; LATER ON, WHEN I ARRIVED IN NEW YORK.
ANYTHIN'?
BUGGER ALL. HERE, DID FRENCHIE OR M.M. NO' SEE ANYTHIN' ABOUT ANNIE WHEN THEY WENT THROUGH ALL THIS?
THEY AIN'T GOT THAT FAR, HAVE THEY? 'COS THEY'VE GOT BLEEDIN' YEARS OF IT TO LOOK AT YET.
OH AYE.
ALL RIGHT, SEE YOU IN A BIT.
TO RUIN THINGS. WE'RE WAITING.
THAT'S GREAT.

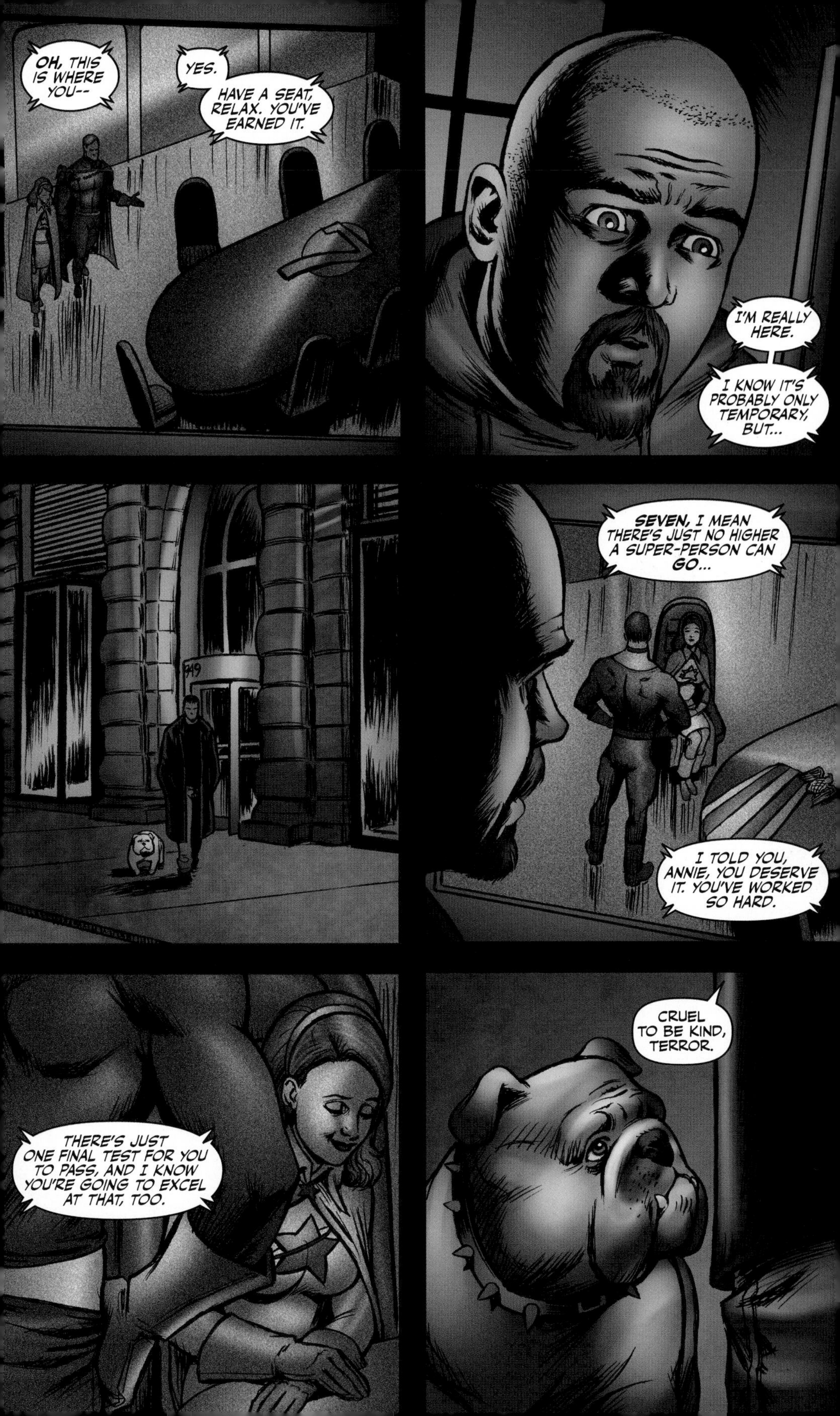
OH, THIS IS WHERE YOU--
YES.
HAVE A SEAT, RELAX. YOU'VE EARNED IT.
I'M REALLY HERE.
I KNOW IT'S PROBABLY ONLY TEMPORARY, BUT...
949
SEVEN, I MEAN THERE'S JUST NO HIGHER A SUPER-PERSON CAN GO...
I TOLD YOU, ANNIE, YOU DESERVE IT. YOU'VE WORKED SO HARD.
THERE'S JUST ONE FINAL TEST FOR YOU TO PASS, AND I KNOW YOU'RE GOING TO EXCEL AT THAT, TOO.
CRUEL TO BE KIND, TERROR.

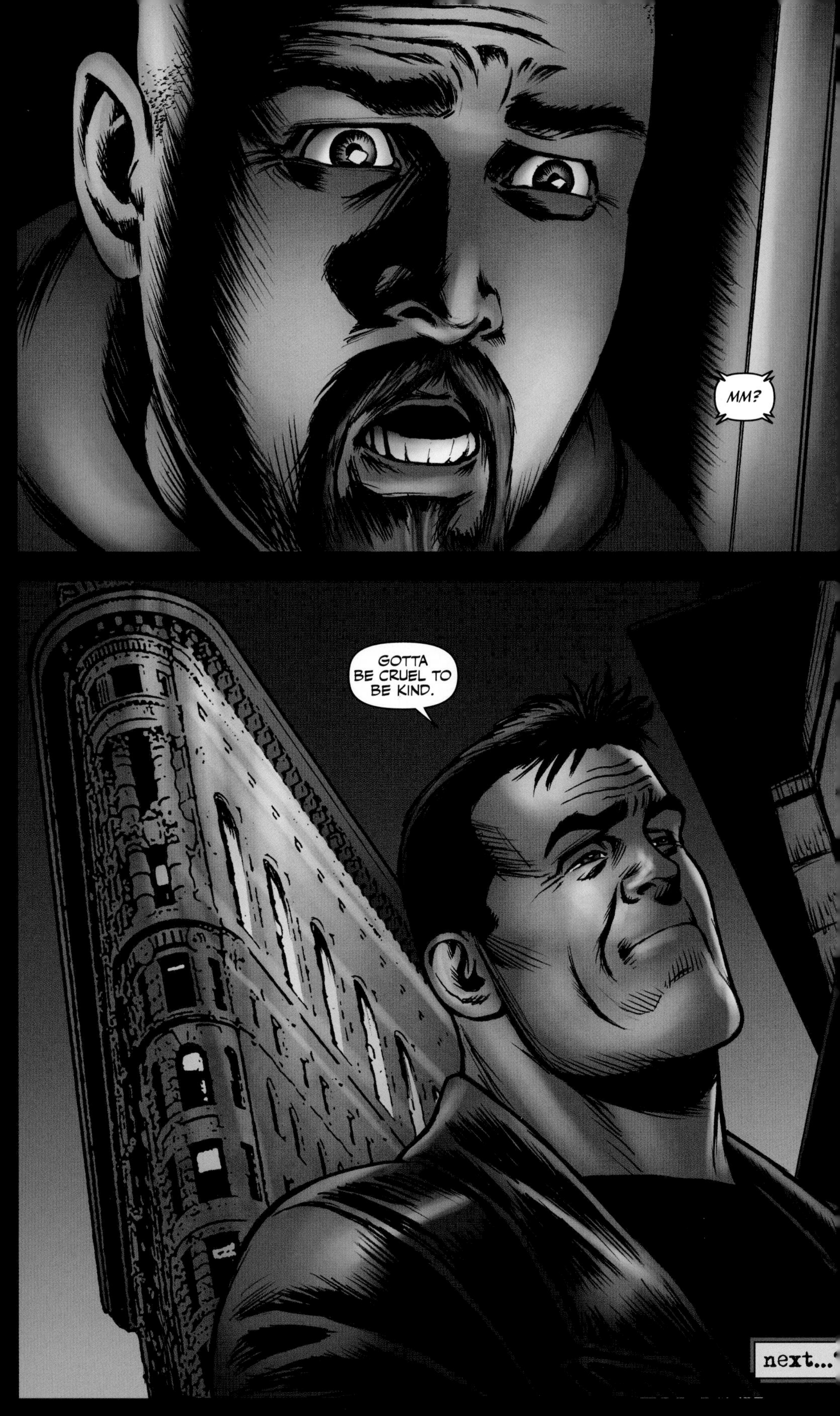
MM?
GOTTA BE CRUEL TO BE KIND.
next...

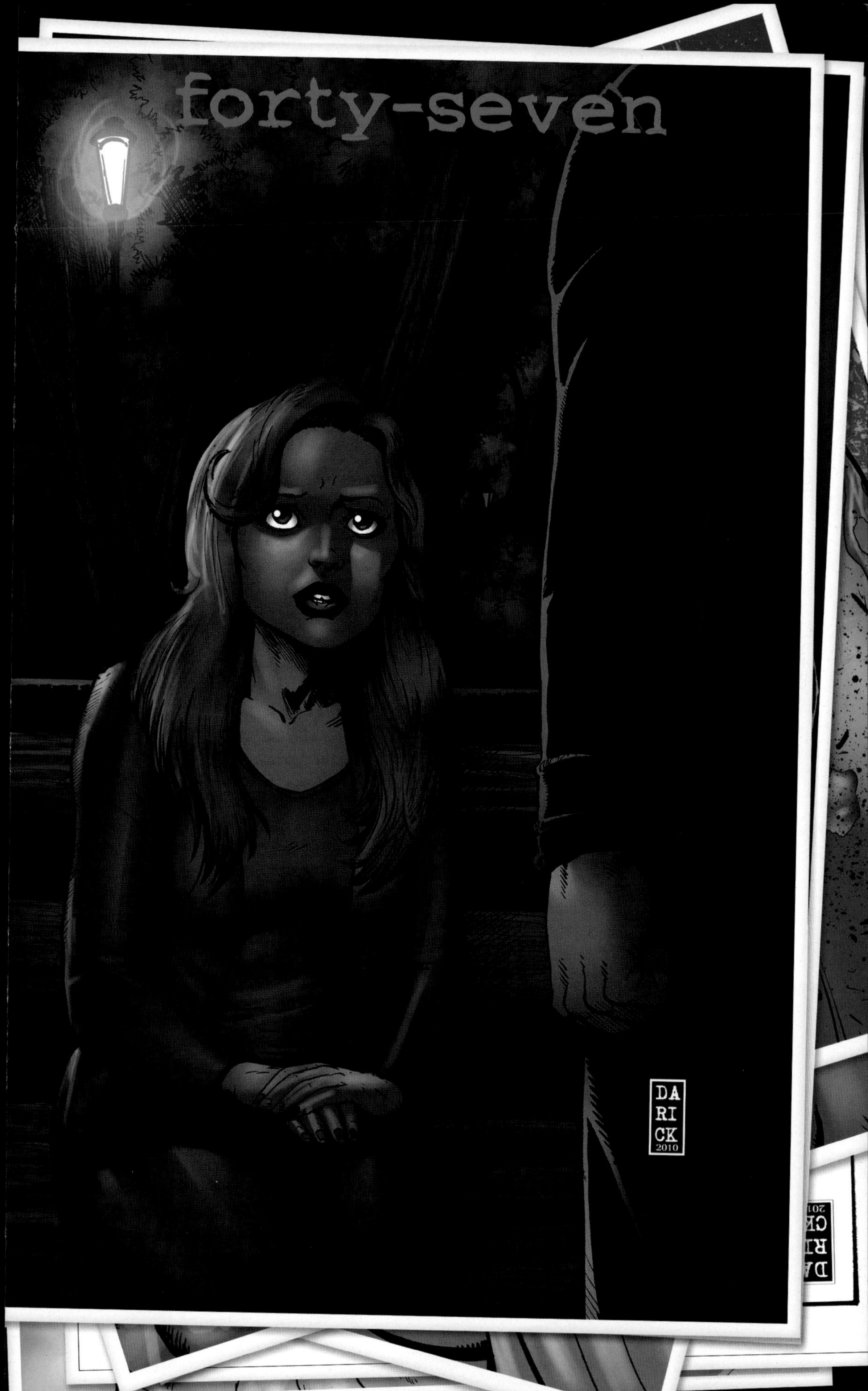
forty-seven
DA
RI
CK
2010

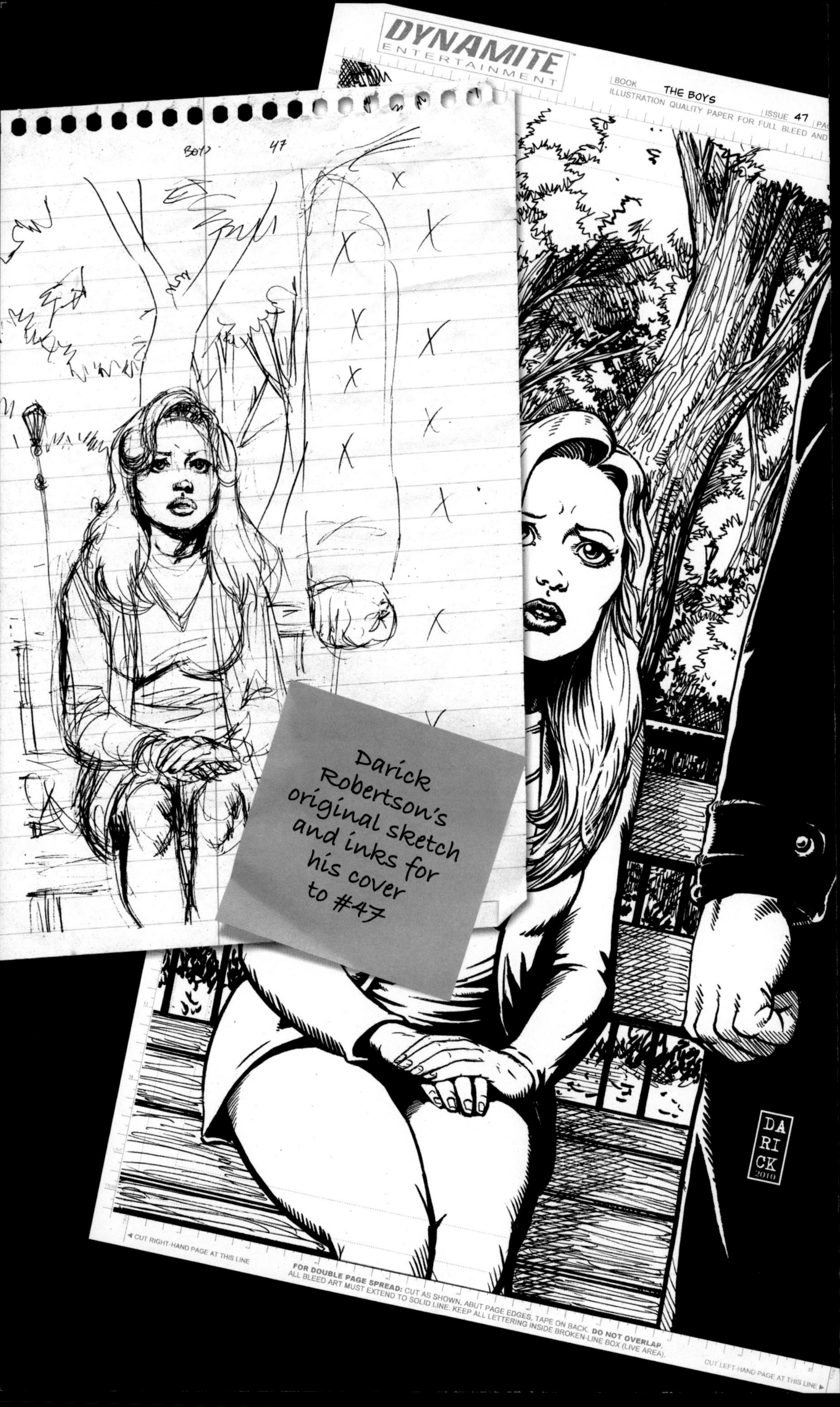
DYNAMITE ENTERTAINMENT
BOOK THE BOYS
ILLUSTRATION QUALITY PAPER FOR FULL BLEED AND
ISSUE 47
BOYS 47
Darick Robertson's original sketch and inks for his cover to #47
DA RI CK 2010
CUT RIGHT-HAND PAGE AT THIS LINE
FOR DOUBLE PAGE SPREAD: CUT AS SHOWN, ABUT PAGE EDGES, TAPE ON BACK. DO NOT OVERLAP.
ALL BLEED ART MUST EXTEND TO SOLID LINE. KEEP ALL LETTERING INSIDE BROKEN-LINE BOX (LIVE AREA).
CUT LEFT-HAND PAGE AT THIS LINE

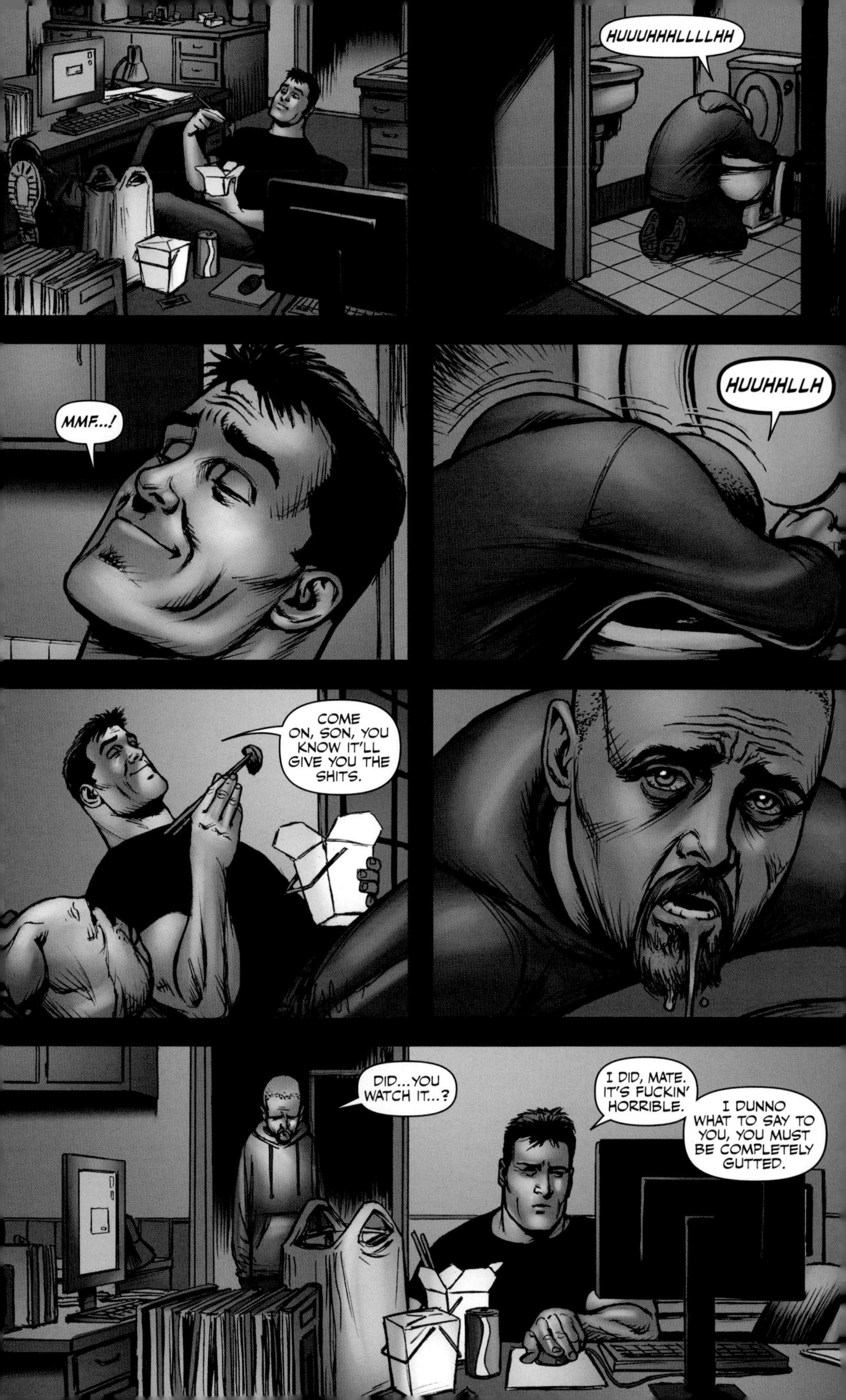
HUUUHHHLLLLHH
MMF...!
HUUHHLLH
COME ON, SON, YOU KNOW IT'LL GIVE YOU THE SHITS.
DID...YOU WATCH IT...?
I DID, MATE. IT'S FUCKIN' HORRIBLE.
I DUNNO WHAT TO SAY TO YOU, YOU MUST BE COMPLETELY GUTTED.

I NEVER THOUGHT...

I JUST DIDN'T...

YEAH, I KNOW.

IN A WAY, IT AIN'T NOTHIN' NEW, HUGHIE. YOUNG GIRL WANTS TO GET AHEAD, SOME DIRTY OL' FUCKER GIVES HER A CHOICE...

BUT WE'RE TALKIN' ABOUT SUPES HERE, AIN'T WE?

AN' THAT MAKES ALL THE DIFFERENCE.

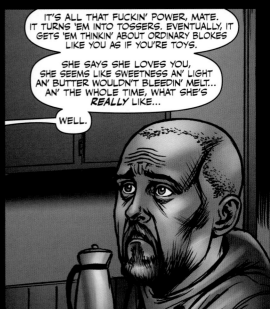

IT'S ALL THAT FUCKIN' POWER, MATE. IT TURNS 'EM INTO TOSSERS. EVENTUALLY, IT GETS 'EM THINKIN' ABOUT ORDINARY BLOKES LIKE YOU AS IF YOU'RE TOYS.

SHE SAYS SHE LOVES YOU, SHE SEEMS LIKE SWEETNESS AN' LIGHT AN' BUTTER WOULDN'T BLEEDIN' MELT... AN' THE WHOLE TIME, WHAT SHE'S *REALLY* LIKE...

WELL.

THAT'S WHAT I WAS TRYNNA TEACH YOU.

ALL THEM TIMES YOU WANTED TO HELP THE BASTARDS.

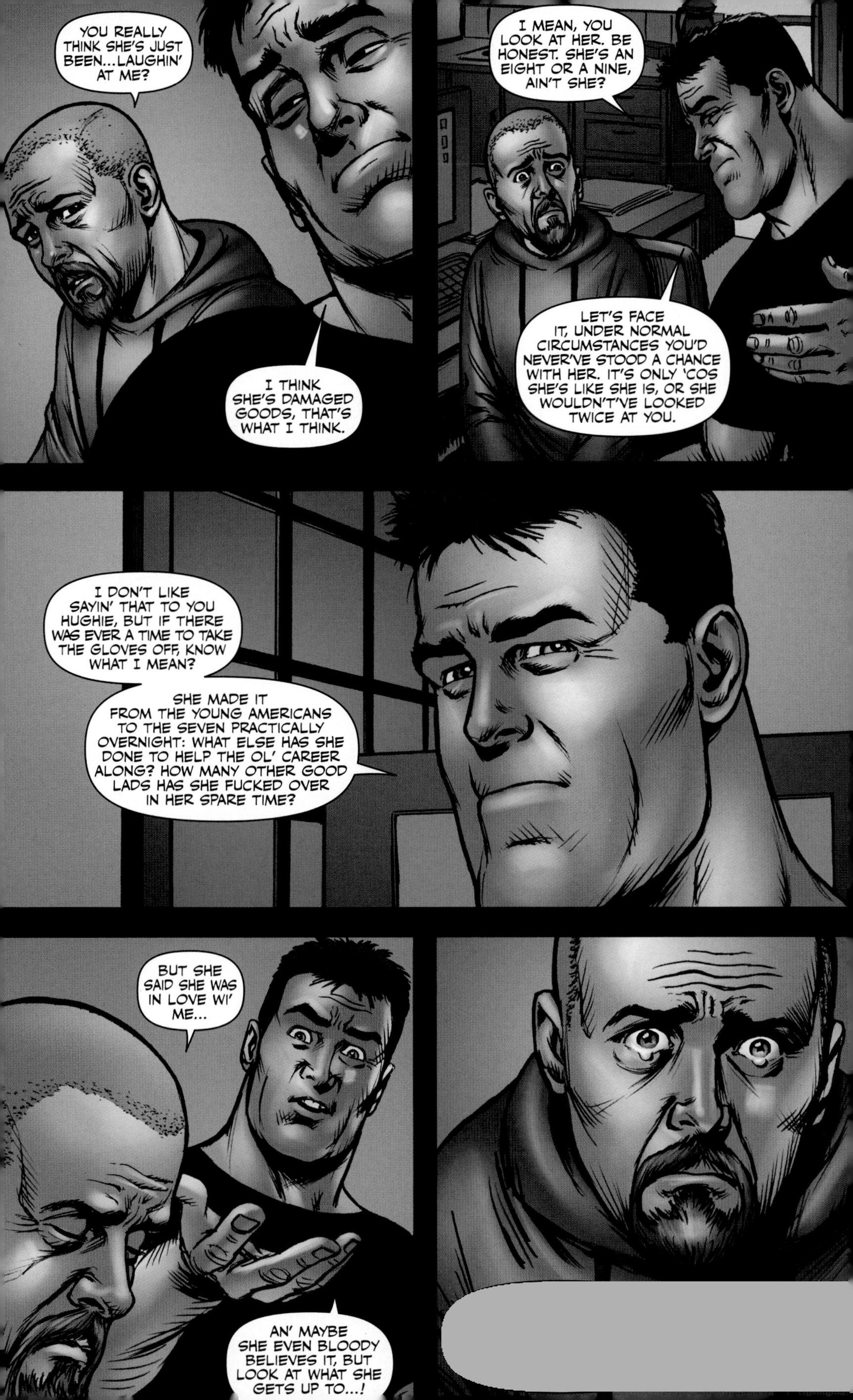
YOU REALLY THINK SHE'S JUST BEEN...LAUGHIN' AT ME?
I THINK SHE'S DAMAGED GOODS, THAT'S WHAT I THINK.
I MEAN, YOU LOOK AT HER. BE HONEST. SHE'S AN EIGHT OR A NINE, AIN'T SHE?
LET'S FACE IT, UNDER NORMAL CIRCUMSTANCES YOU'D NEVER'VE STOOD A CHANCE WITH HER. IT'S ONLY 'COS SHE'S LIKE SHE IS, OR SHE WOULDN'T'VE LOOKED TWICE AT YOU.
I DON'T LIKE SAYIN' THAT TO YOU HUGHIE, BUT IF THERE WAS EVER A TIME TO TAKE THE GLOVES OFF, KNOW WHAT I MEAN?
SHE MADE IT FROM THE YOUNG AMERICANS TO THE SEVEN PRACTICALLY OVERNIGHT: WHAT ELSE HAS SHE DONE TO HELP THE OL' CAREER ALONG? HOW MANY OTHER GOOD LADS HAS SHE FUCKED OVER IN HER SPARE TIME?
BUT SHE SAID SHE WAS IN LOVE WI' ME...
AN' MAYBE SHE EVEN BLOODY BELIEVES IT, BUT LOOK AT WHAT SHE GETS UP TO...!

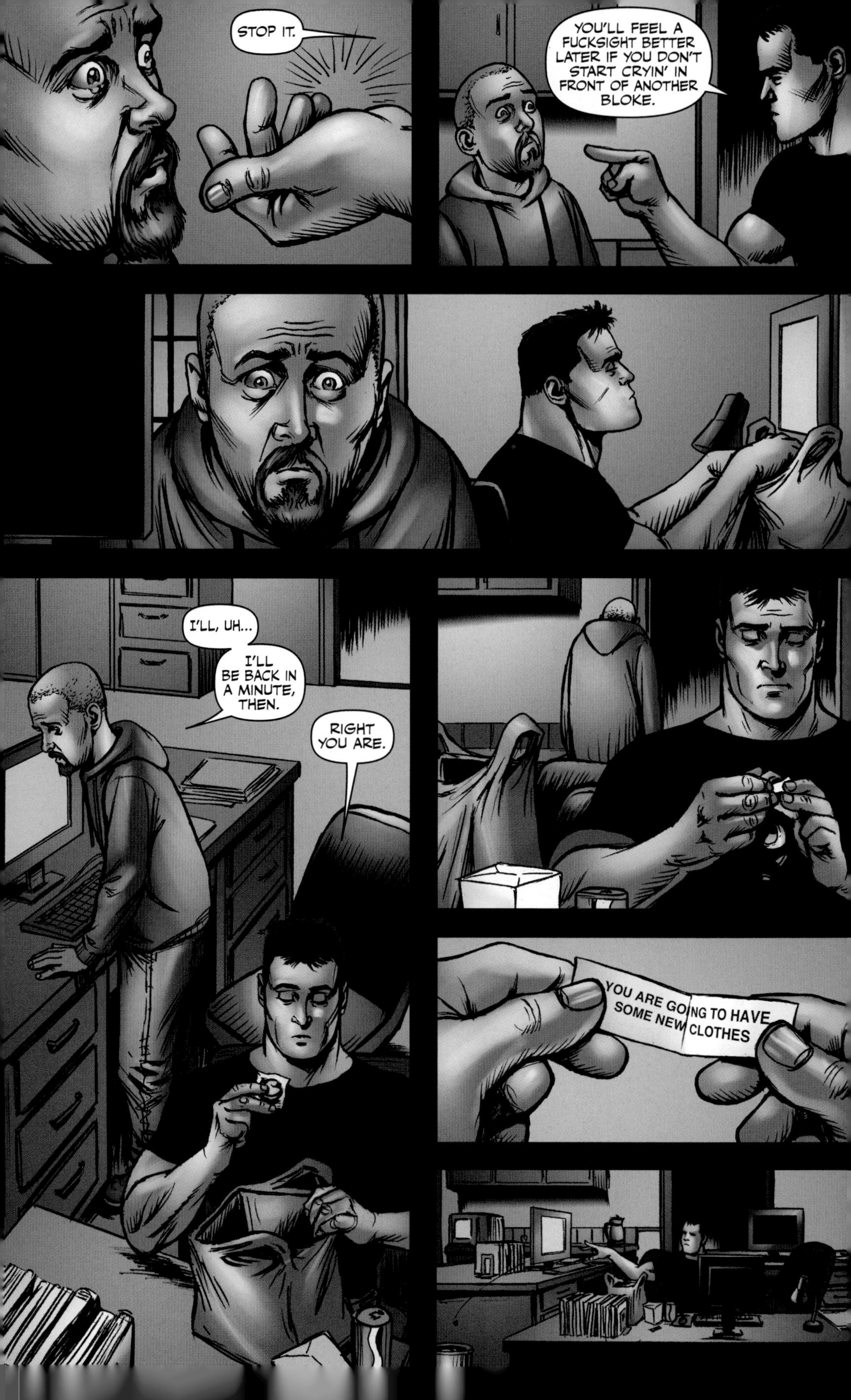
STOP IT.
YOU'LL FEEL A FUCKSIGHT BETTER LATER IF YOU DON'T START CRYIN' IN FRONT OF ANOTHER BLOKE.
I'LL, UH...
I'LL BE BACK IN A MINUTE, THEN.
RIGHT YOU ARE.
YOU ARE GOING TO HAVE SOME NEW CLOTHES

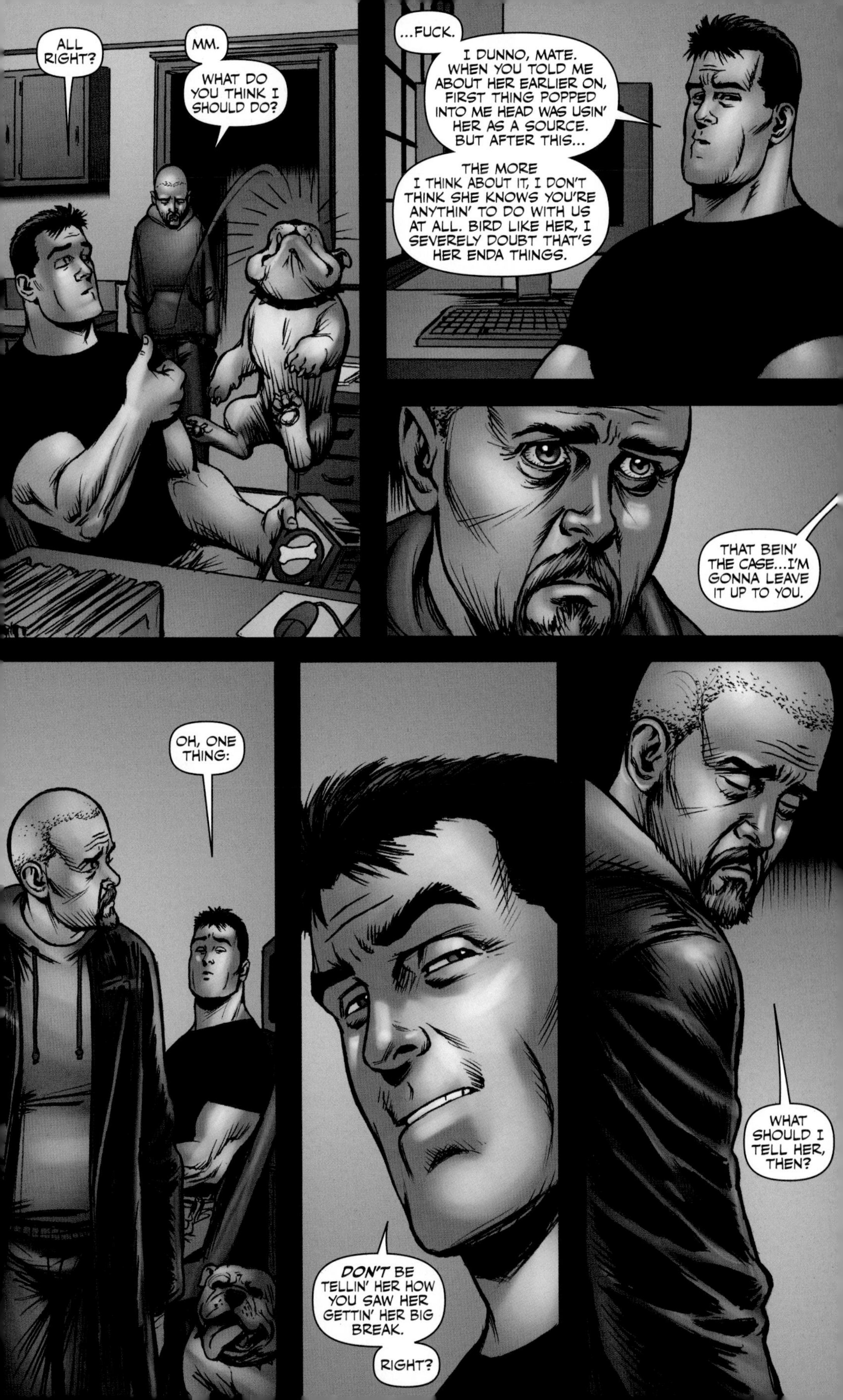
ALL RIGHT?
MM.
WHAT DO YOU THINK I SHOULD DO?
...FUCK.
I DUNNO, MATE. WHEN YOU TOLD ME ABOUT HER EARLIER ON, FIRST THING POPPED INTO ME HEAD WAS USIN' HER AS A SOURCE. BUT AFTER THIS...
THE MORE I THINK ABOUT IT, I DON'T THINK SHE KNOWS YOU'RE ANYTHIN' TO DO WITH US AT ALL. BIRD LIKE HER, I SEVERELY DOUBT THAT'S HER ENDA THINGS.
THAT BEIN' THE CASE...I'M GONNA LEAVE IT UP TO YOU.
OH, ONE THING:
DON'T BE TELLIN' HER HOW YOU SAW HER GETTIN' HER BIG BREAK.
RIGHT?
WHAT SHOULD I TELL HER, THEN?

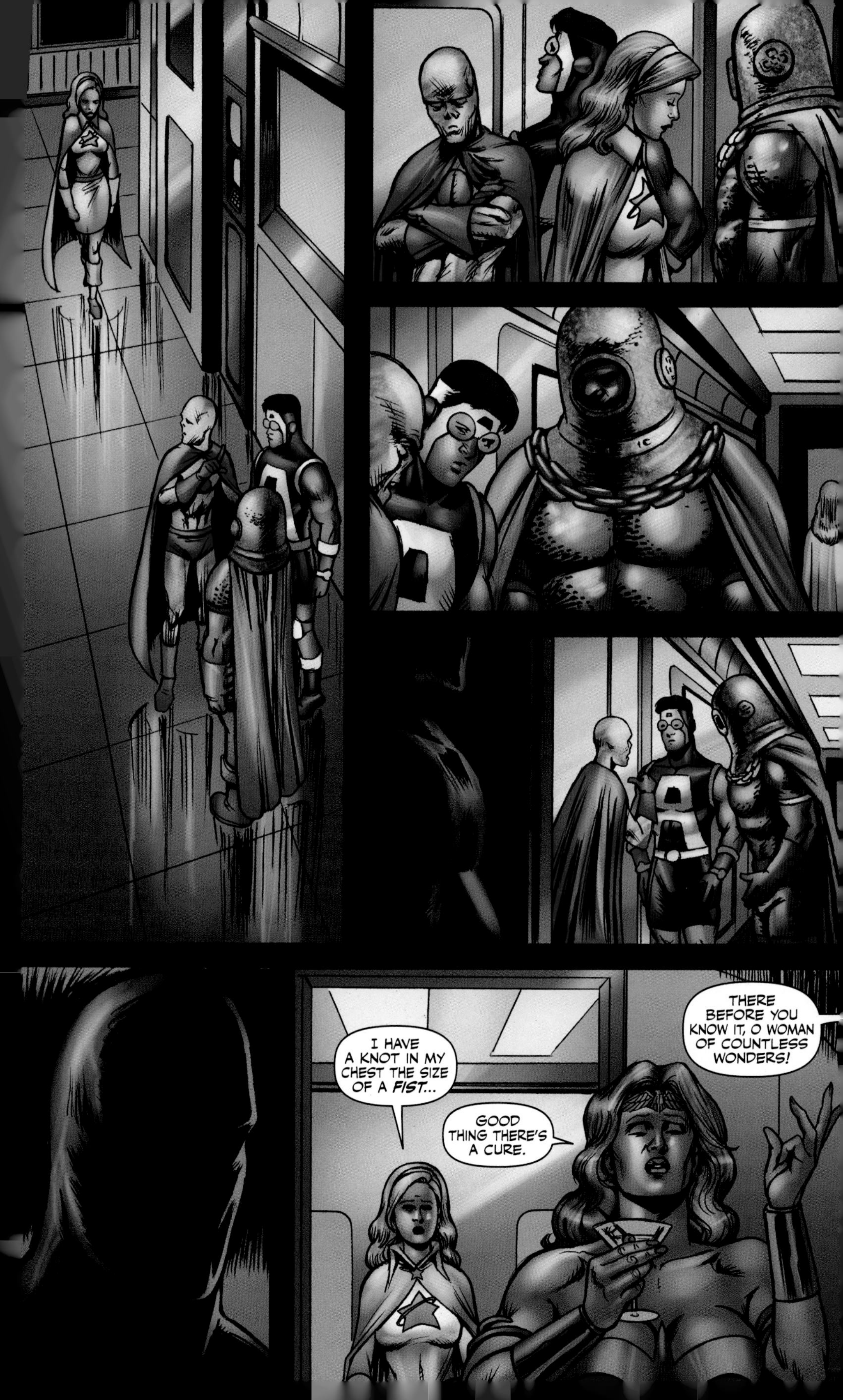
I HAVE A KNOT IN MY CHEST THE SIZE OF A *FIST*...
GOOD THING THERE'S A CURE.
THERE BEFORE YOU KNOW IT, O WOMAN OF COUNTLESS WONDERS!

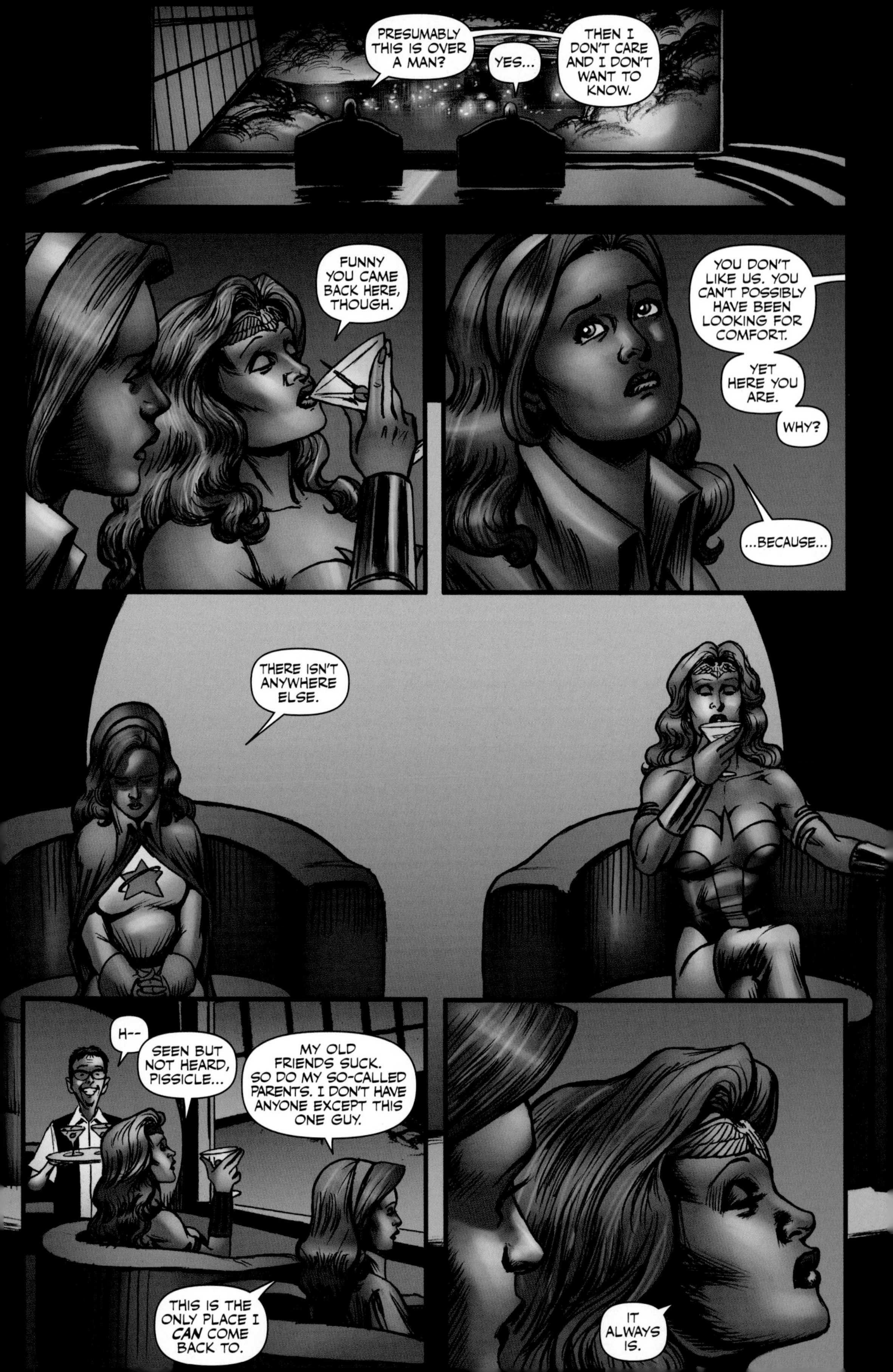
PRESUMABLY THIS IS OVER A MAN?
YES...
THEN I DON'T CARE AND I DON'T WANT TO KNOW.
FUNNY YOU CAME BACK HERE, THOUGH.
YOU DON'T LIKE US. YOU CAN'T POSSIBLY HAVE BEEN LOOKING FOR COMFORT.
YET HERE YOU ARE.
WHY?
...BECAUSE...
THERE ISN'T ANYWHERE ELSE.
H--
SEEN BUT NOT HEARD, PISSICLE...
MY OLD FRIENDS SUCK. SO DO MY SO-CALLED PARENTS. I DON'T HAVE ANYONE EXCEPT THIS ONE GUY.
THIS IS THE ONLY PLACE I *CAN* COME BACK TO.
IT ALWAYS IS.

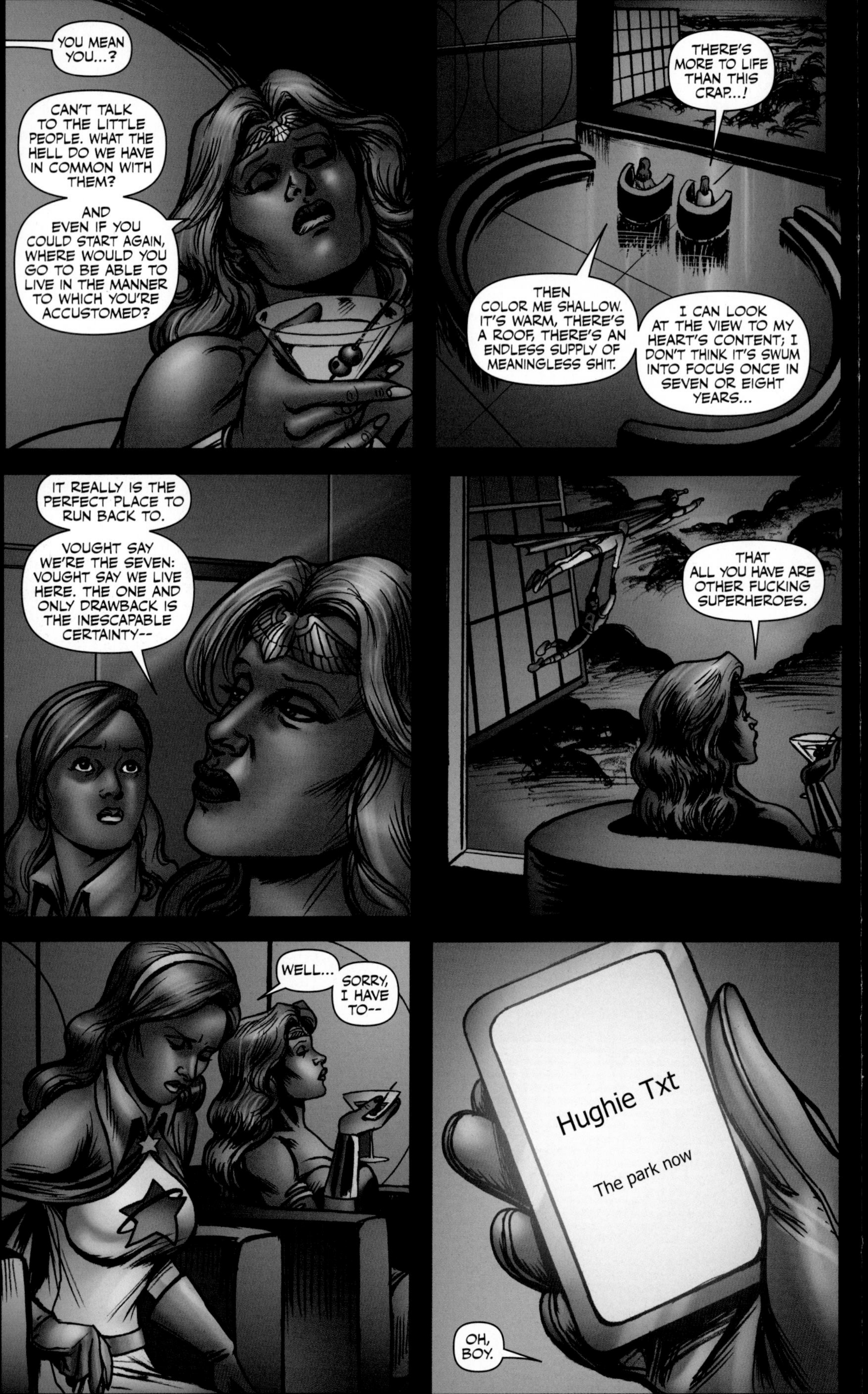
YOU MEAN YOU...?
CAN'T TALK TO THE LITTLE PEOPLE. WHAT THE HELL DO WE HAVE IN COMMON WITH THEM?
AND EVEN IF YOU COULD START AGAIN, WHERE WOULD YOU GO TO BE ABLE TO LIVE IN THE MANNER TO WHICH YOU'RE ACCUSTOMED?
THERE'S MORE TO LIFE THAN THIS CRAP...!
THEN COLOR ME SHALLOW. IT'S WARM, THERE'S A ROOF, THERE'S AN ENDLESS SUPPLY OF MEANINGLESS SHIT.
I CAN LOOK AT THE VIEW TO MY HEART'S CONTENT; I DON'T THINK IT'S SWUM INTO FOCUS ONCE IN SEVEN OR EIGHT YEARS...
IT REALLY IS THE PERFECT PLACE TO RUN BACK TO.
VOUGHT SAY WE'RE THE SEVEN: VOUGHT SAY WE LIVE HERE. THE ONE AND ONLY DRAWBACK IS THE INESCAPABLE CERTAINTY--
THAT ALL YOU HAVE ARE OTHER FUCKING SUPERHEROES.
WELL...
SORRY, I HAVE TO--
Hughie Txt
The park now
OH, BOY.

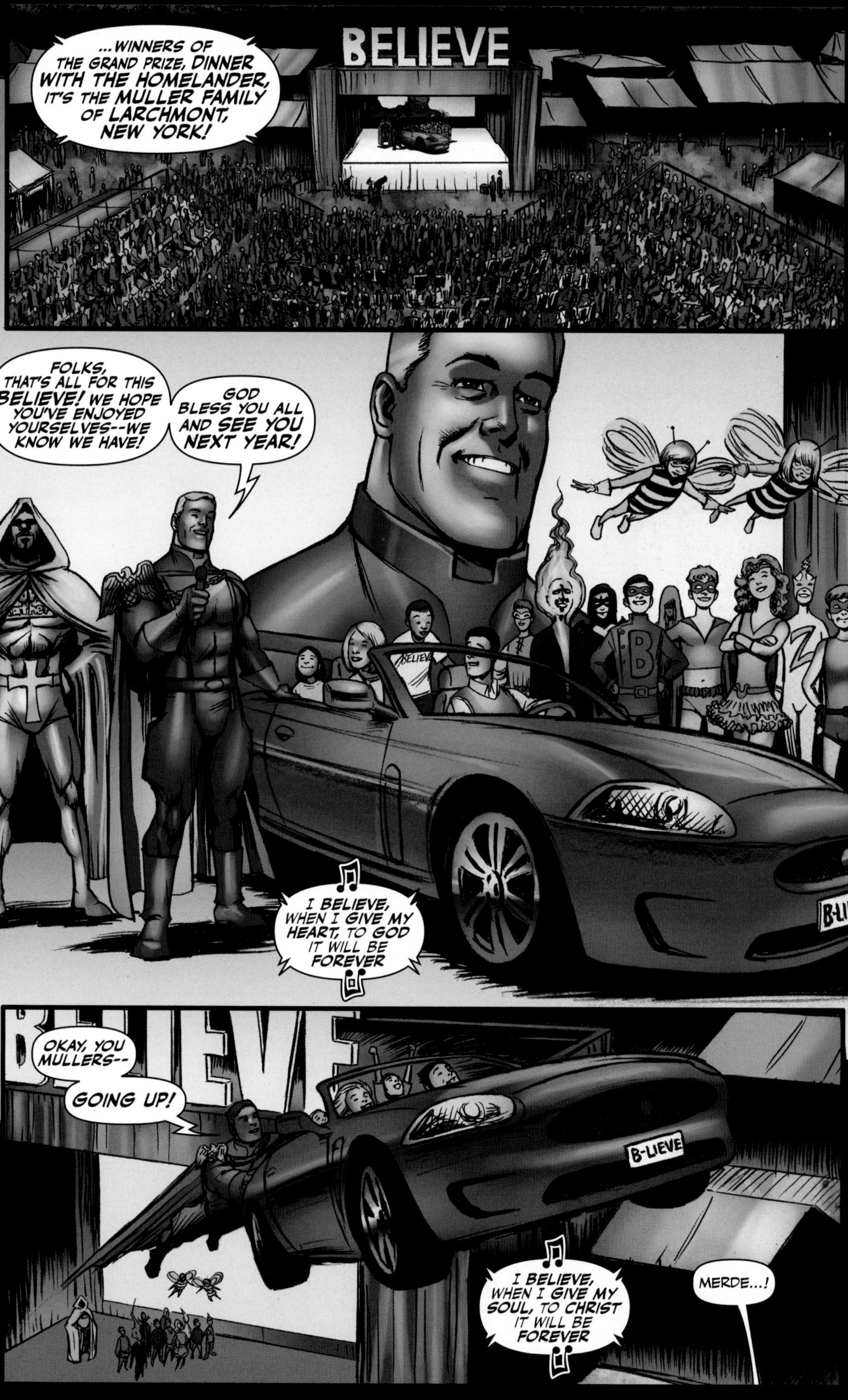
BELIEVE
...WINNERS OF THE GRAND PRIZE, DINNER WITH THE HOMELANDER, IT'S THE MULLER FAMILY OF LARCHMONT, NEW YORK!
FOLKS, THAT'S ALL FOR THIS BELIEVE! WE HOPE YOU'VE ENJOYED YOURSELVES--WE KNOW WE HAVE!
GOD BLESS YOU ALL AND SEE YOU NEXT YEAR!
BELIEVE
B-LIEVE
I BELIEVE, WHEN I GIVE MY HEART, TO GOD IT WILL BE FOREVER
OKAY, YOU MULLERS--
GOING UP!
B-LIEVE
I BELIEVE, WHEN I GIVE MY SOUL, TO CHRIST IT WILL BE FOREVER
MERDE...!

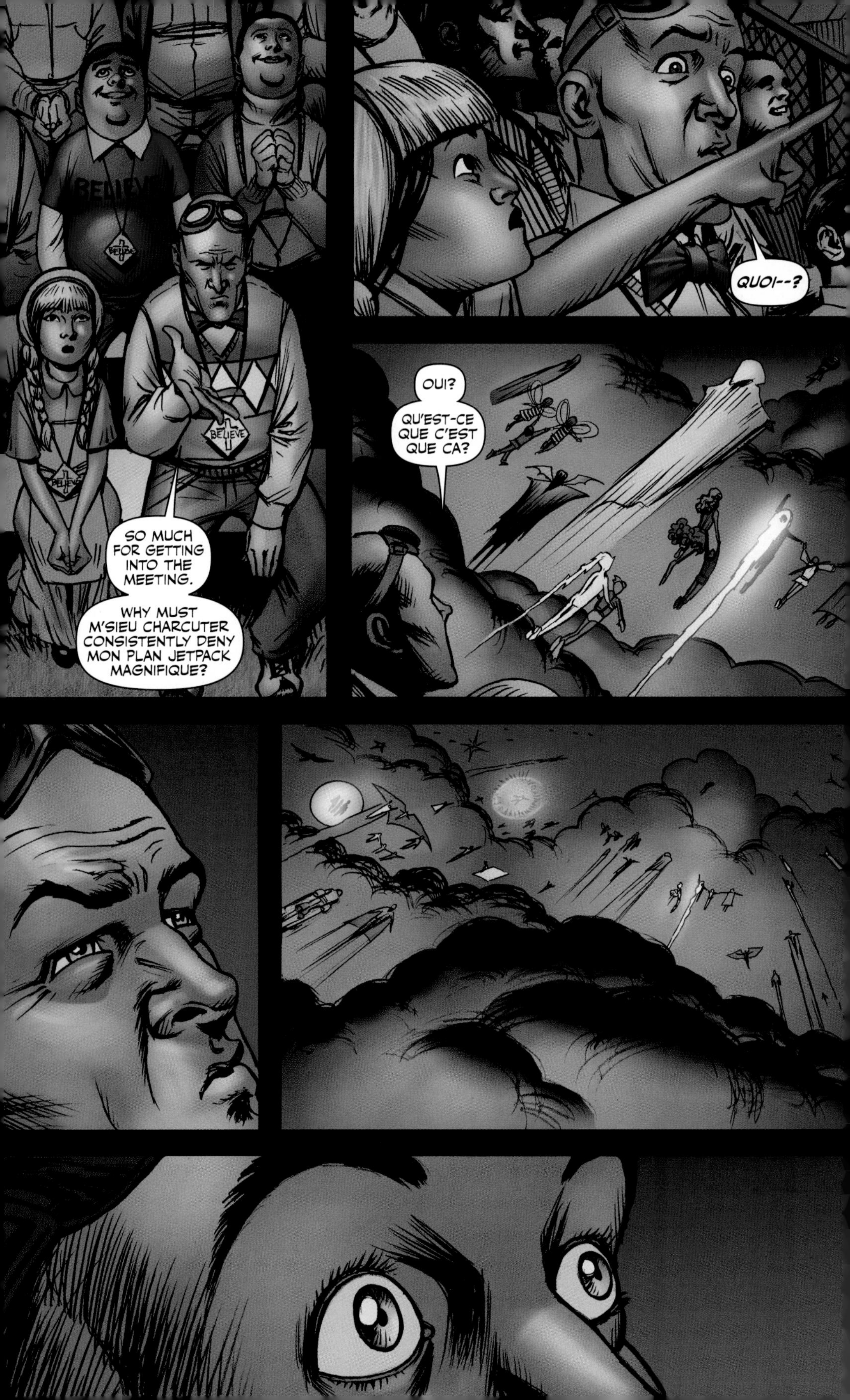
SO MUCH FOR GETTING INTO THE MEETING.
WHY MUST M'SIEU CHARCUTER CONSISTENTLY DENY MON PLAN JETPACK MAGNIFIQUE?
QUOI--?
OUI?
QU'EST-CE QUE C'EST QUE CA?

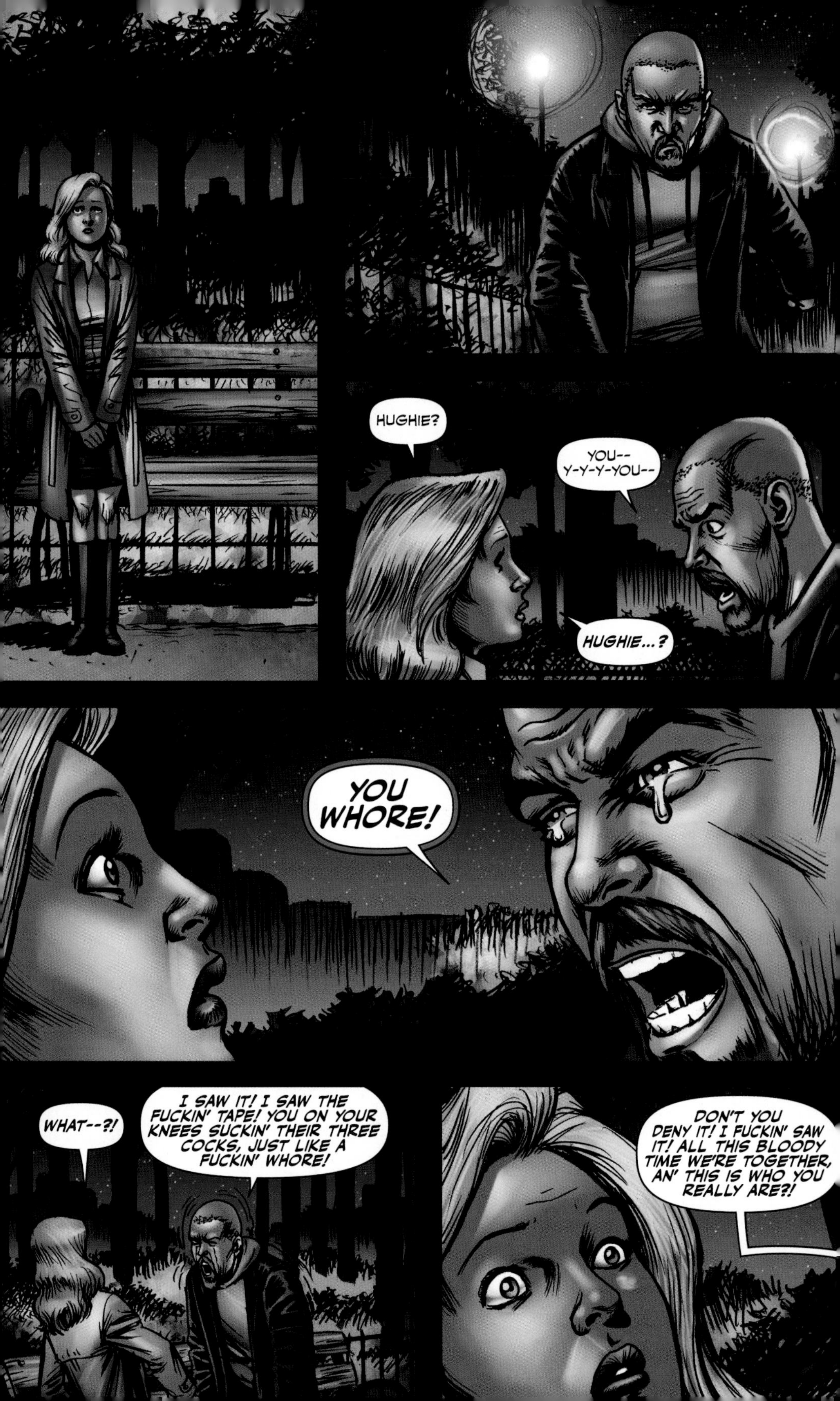
HUGHIE?
YOU--
Y-Y-Y-YOU--
HUGHIE...?
YOU WHORE!
WHAT--?!
I SAW IT! I SAW THE FUCKIN' TAPE! YOU ON YOUR KNEES SUCKIN' THEIR THREE COCKS, JUST LIKE A FUCKIN' WHORE!
DON'T YOU DENY IT! I FUCKIN' SAW IT! ALL THIS BLOODY TIME WE'RE TOGETHER, AN' THIS IS WHO YOU REALLY ARE?!

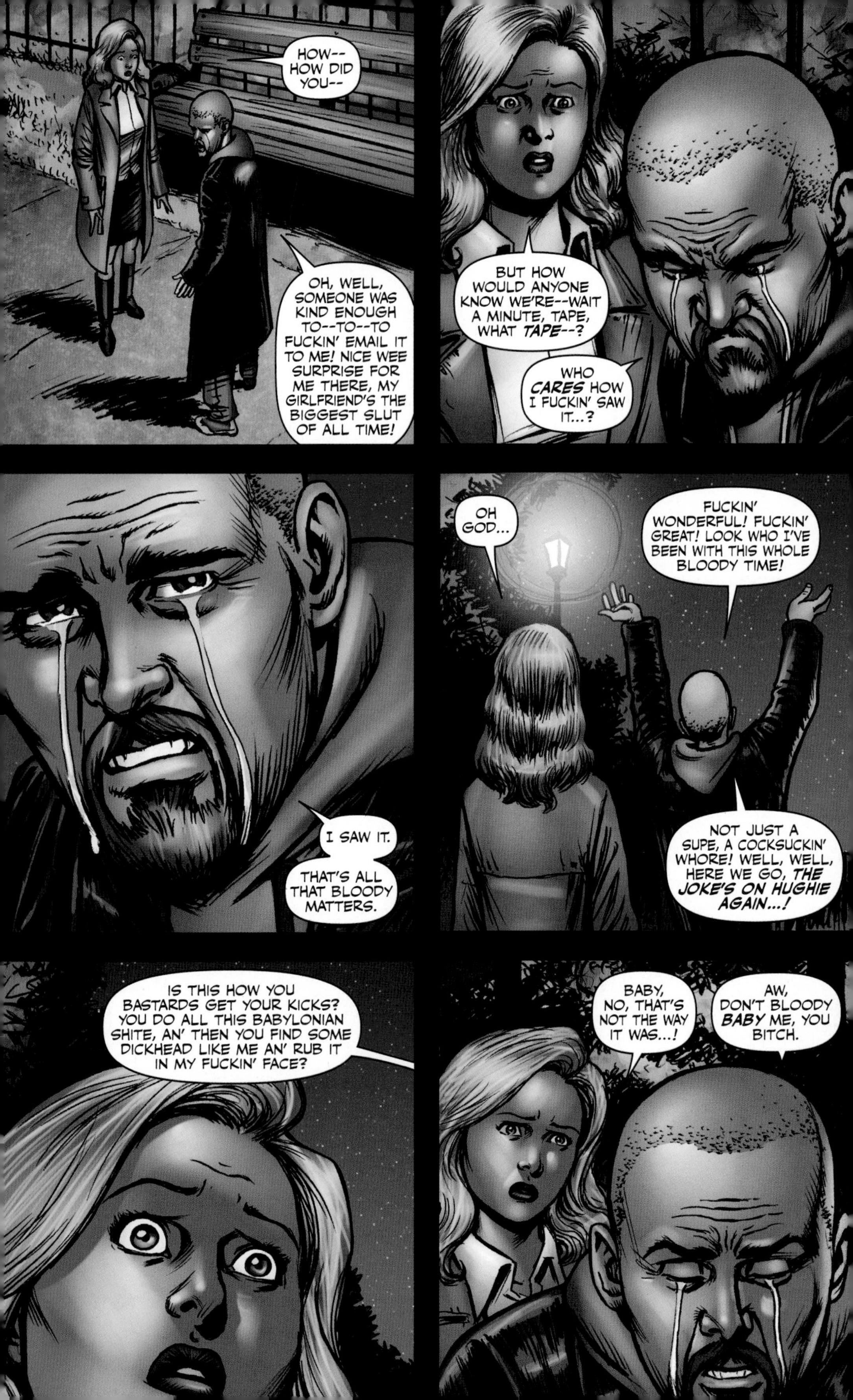
HOW-- HOW DID YOU--
OH, WELL, SOMEONE WAS KIND ENOUGH TO--TO--TO FUCKIN' EMAIL IT TO ME! NICE WEE SURPRISE FOR ME THERE, MY GIRLFRIEND'S THE BIGGEST SLUT OF ALL TIME!
BUT HOW WOULD ANYONE KNOW WE'RE--WAIT A MINUTE, TAPE, WHAT *TAPE*--?
WHO *CARES* HOW I FUCKIN' SAW IT...?
I SAW IT.
THAT'S ALL THAT BLOODY MATTERS.
OH GOD...
FUCKIN' WONDERFUL! FUCKIN' GREAT! LOOK WHO I'VE BEEN WITH THIS WHOLE BLOODY TIME!
NOT JUST A SUPE, A COCKSUCKIN' WHORE! WELL, WELL, HERE WE GO, ***THE JOKE'S ON HUGHIE AGAIN...!***
IS THIS HOW YOU BASTARDS GET YOUR KICKS? YOU DO ALL THIS BABYLONIAN SHITE, AN' THEN YOU FIND SOME DICKHEAD LIKE ME AN' RUB IT IN MY FUCKIN' FACE?
BABY, NO, THAT'S NOT THE WAY IT WAS...!
AW, DON'T BLOODY *BABY* ME, YOU BITCH.

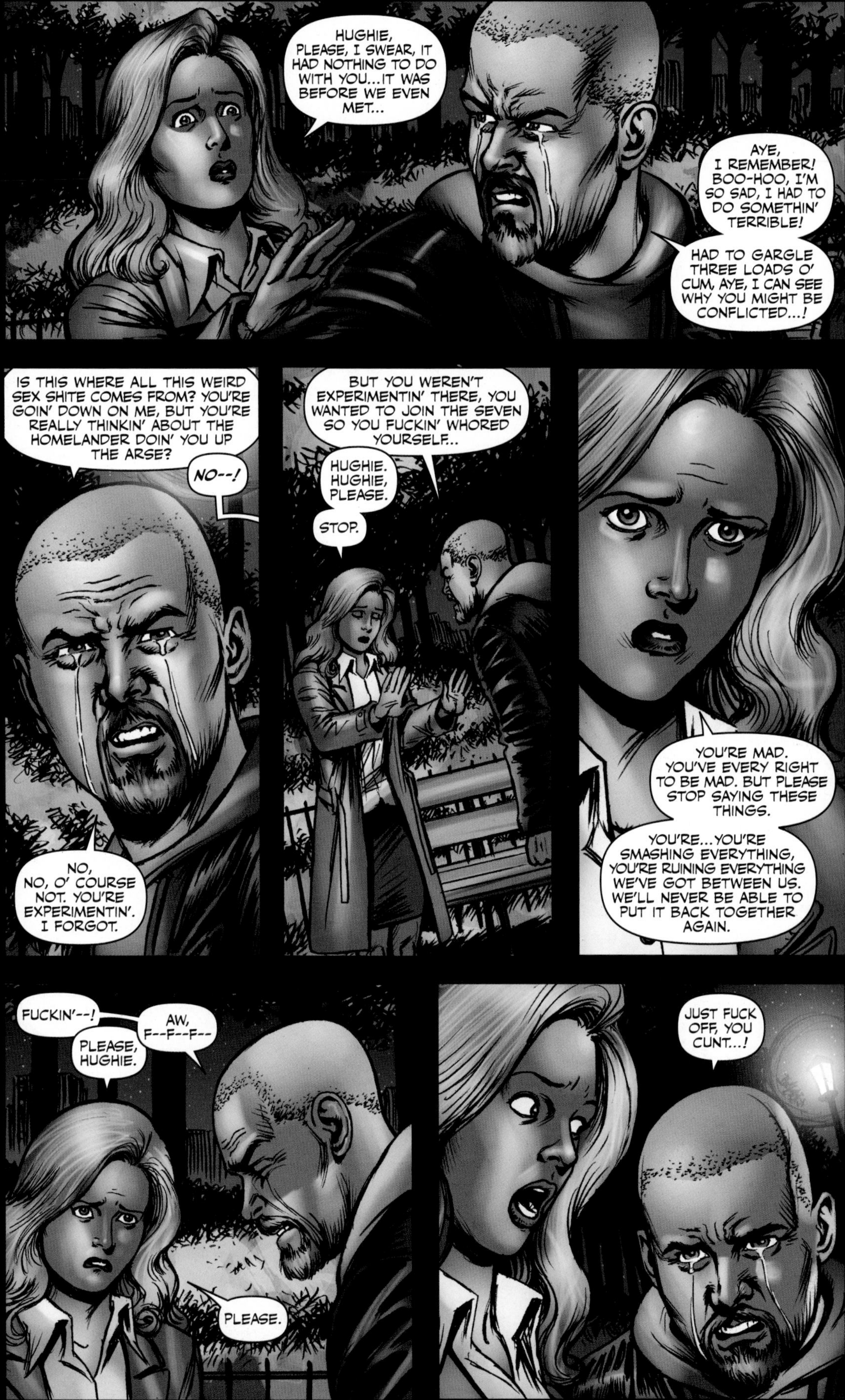
HUGHIE, PLEASE, I SWEAR, IT HAD NOTHING TO DO WITH YOU...IT WAS BEFORE WE EVEN MET...
AYE, I REMEMBER! BOO-HOO, I'M SO SAD, I HAD TO DO SOMETHIN' TERRIBLE!
HAD TO GARGLE THREE LOADS O' CUM, AYE, I CAN SEE WHY YOU MIGHT BE CONFLICTED...!
IS THIS WHERE ALL THIS WEIRD SEX SHITE COMES FROM? YOU'RE GOIN' DOWN ON ME, BUT YOU'RE REALLY THINKIN' ABOUT THE HOMELANDER DOIN' YOU UP THE ARSE?
NO--!
NO, NO, O' COURSE NOT. YOU'RE EXPERIMENTIN'. I FORGOT.
BUT YOU WEREN'T EXPERIMENTIN' THERE, YOU WANTED TO JOIN THE SEVEN SO YOU FUCKIN' WHORED YOURSELF...
HUGHIE. HUGHIE, PLEASE.
STOP.
YOU'RE MAD. YOU'VE EVERY RIGHT TO BE MAD. BUT PLEASE STOP SAYING THESE THINGS.
YOU'RE...YOU'RE SMASHING EVERYTHING, YOU'RE RUINING EVERYTHING WE'VE GOT BETWEEN US. WE'LL NEVER BE ABLE TO PUT IT BACK TOGETHER AGAIN.
FUCKIN'--!
AW, F--F--F--
PLEASE, HUGHIE.
PLEASE.
JUST FUCK OFF, YOU CUNT...!

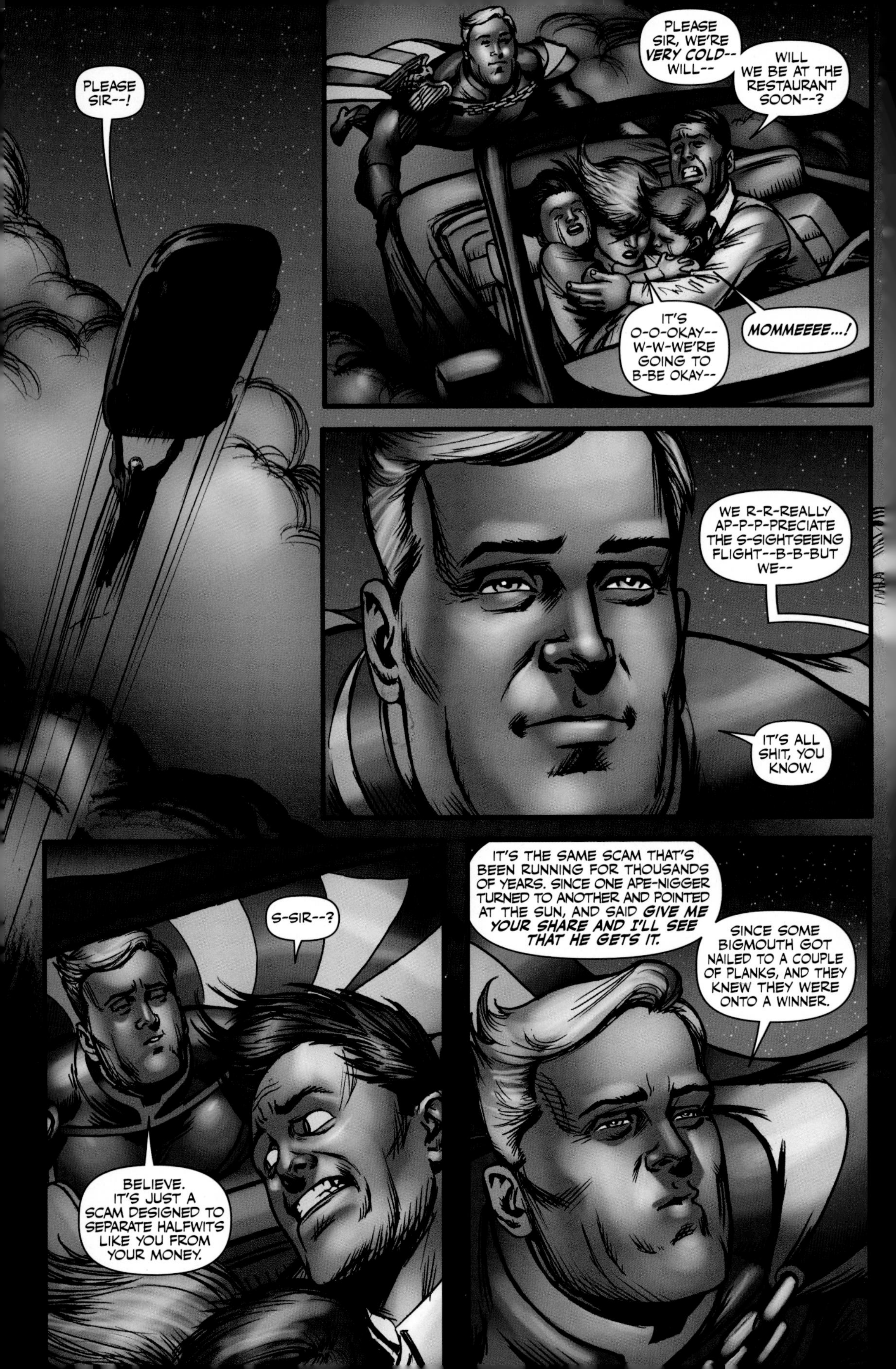
PLEASE SIR--!
PLEASE SIR, WE'RE *VERY COLD*-- WILL--
WILL WE BE AT THE RESTAURANT SOON--?
IT'S O-O-OKAY-- W-W-WE'RE GOING TO B-BE OKAY--
MOMMEEEE...!
WE R-R-REALLY AP-P-P-PRECIATE THE S-SIGHTSEEING FLIGHT--B-B-BUT WE--
IT'S ALL SHIT, YOU KNOW.
S-SIR--?
BELIEVE. IT'S JUST A SCAM DESIGNED TO SEPARATE HALFWITS LIKE YOU FROM YOUR MONEY.
IT'S THE SAME SCAM THAT'S BEEN RUNNING FOR THOUSANDS OF YEARS. SINCE ONE APE-NIGGER TURNED TO ANOTHER AND POINTED AT THE SUN, AND SAID ***GIVE ME YOUR SHARE AND I'LL SEE THAT HE GETS IT.***
SINCE SOME BIGMOUTH GOT NAILED TO A COUPLE OF PLANKS, AND THEY KNEW THEY WERE ONTO A WINNER.

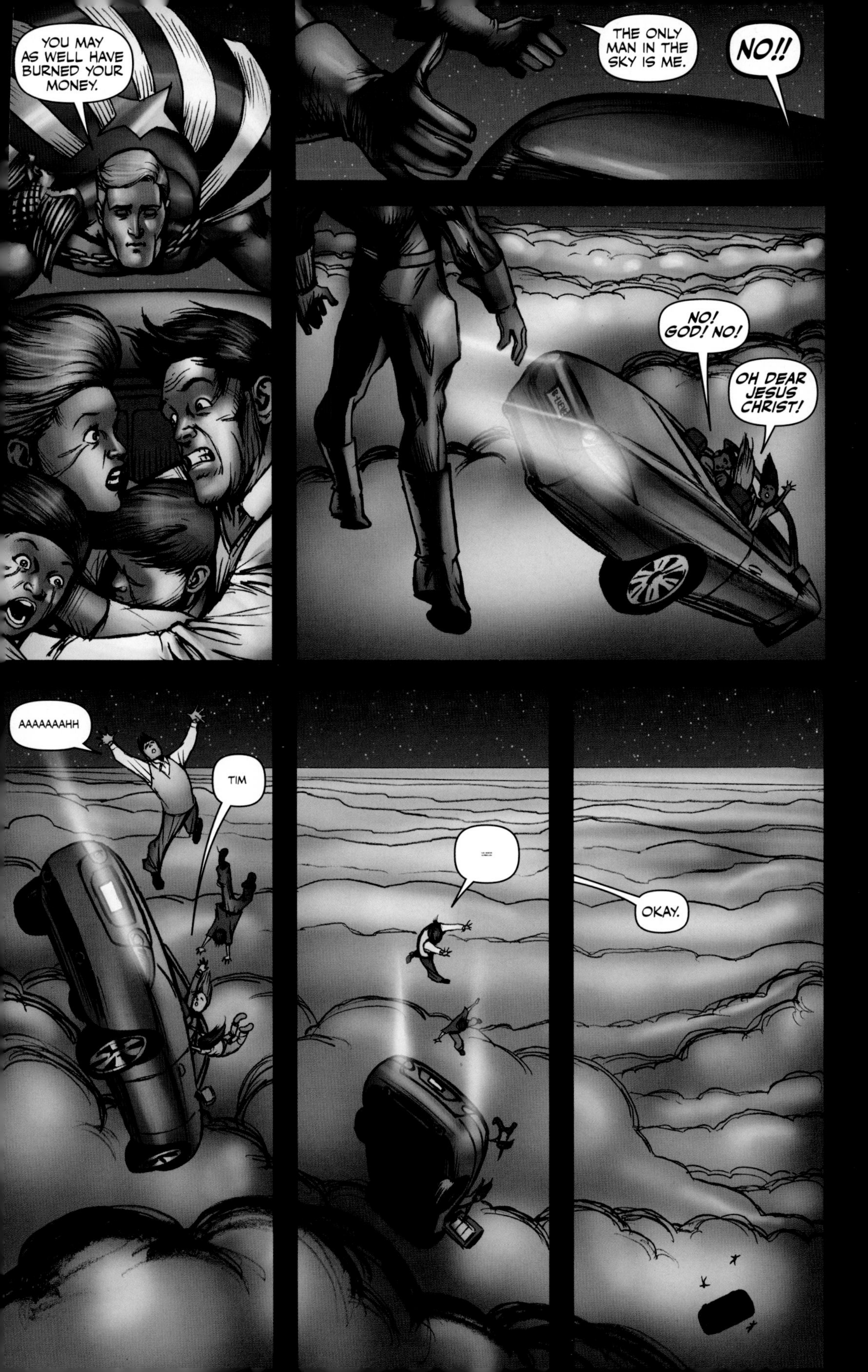
YOU MAY AS WELL HAVE BURNED YOUR MONEY.
THE ONLY MAN IN THE SKY IS ME.
NO!!
NO! GOD! NO!
OH DEAR JESUS CHRIST!
AAAAAAAHH
TIM
OKAY.

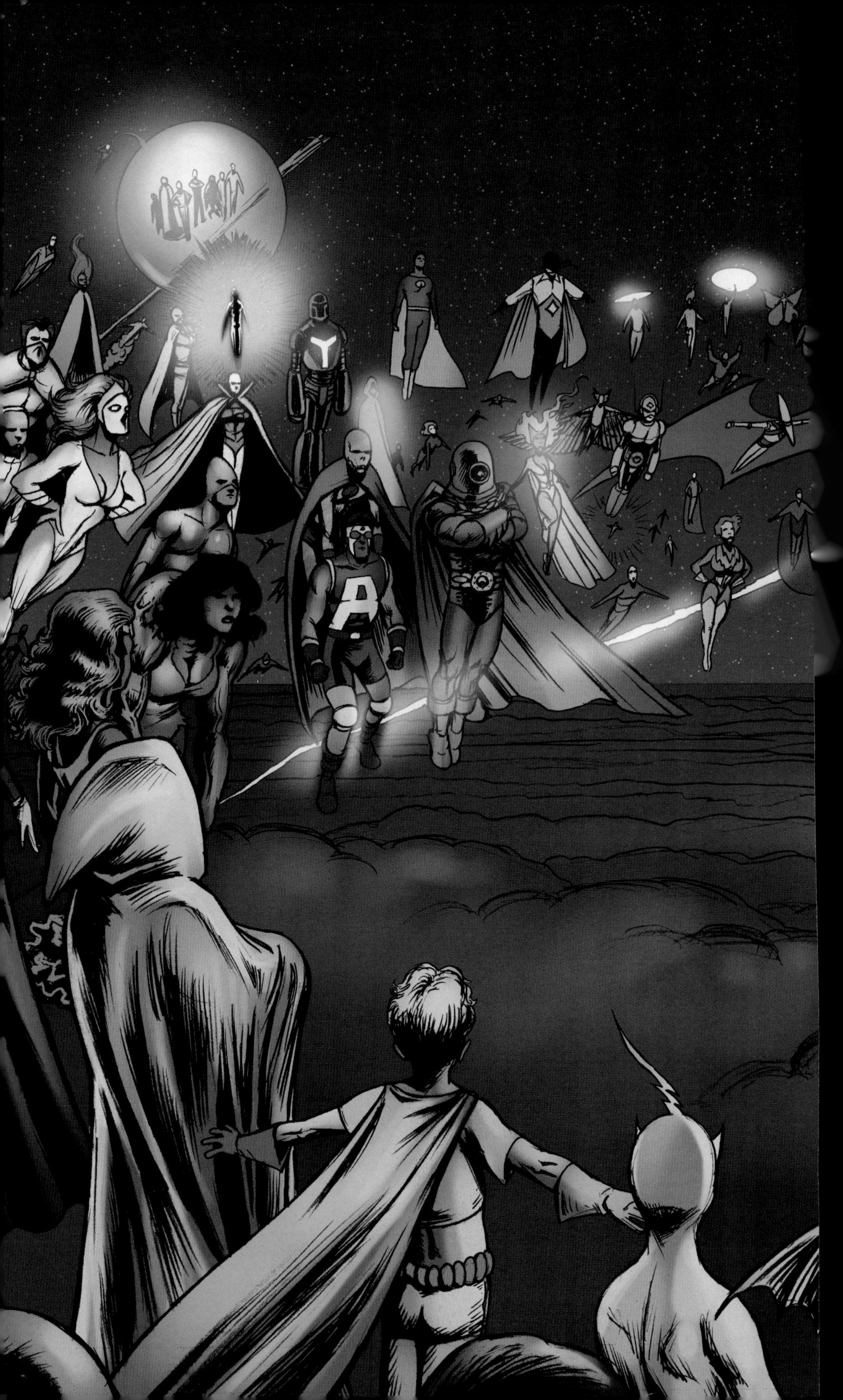

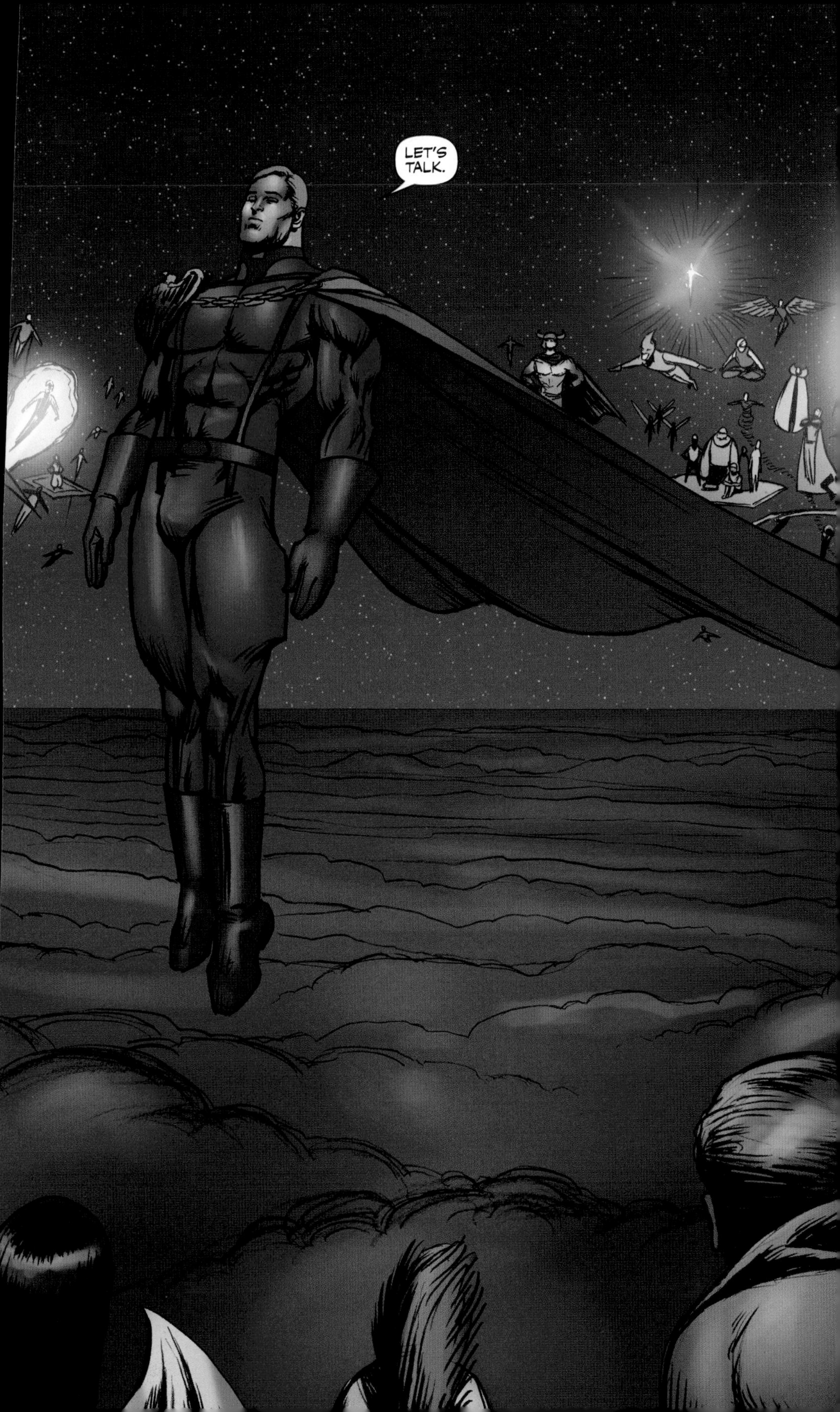
LET'S TALK.

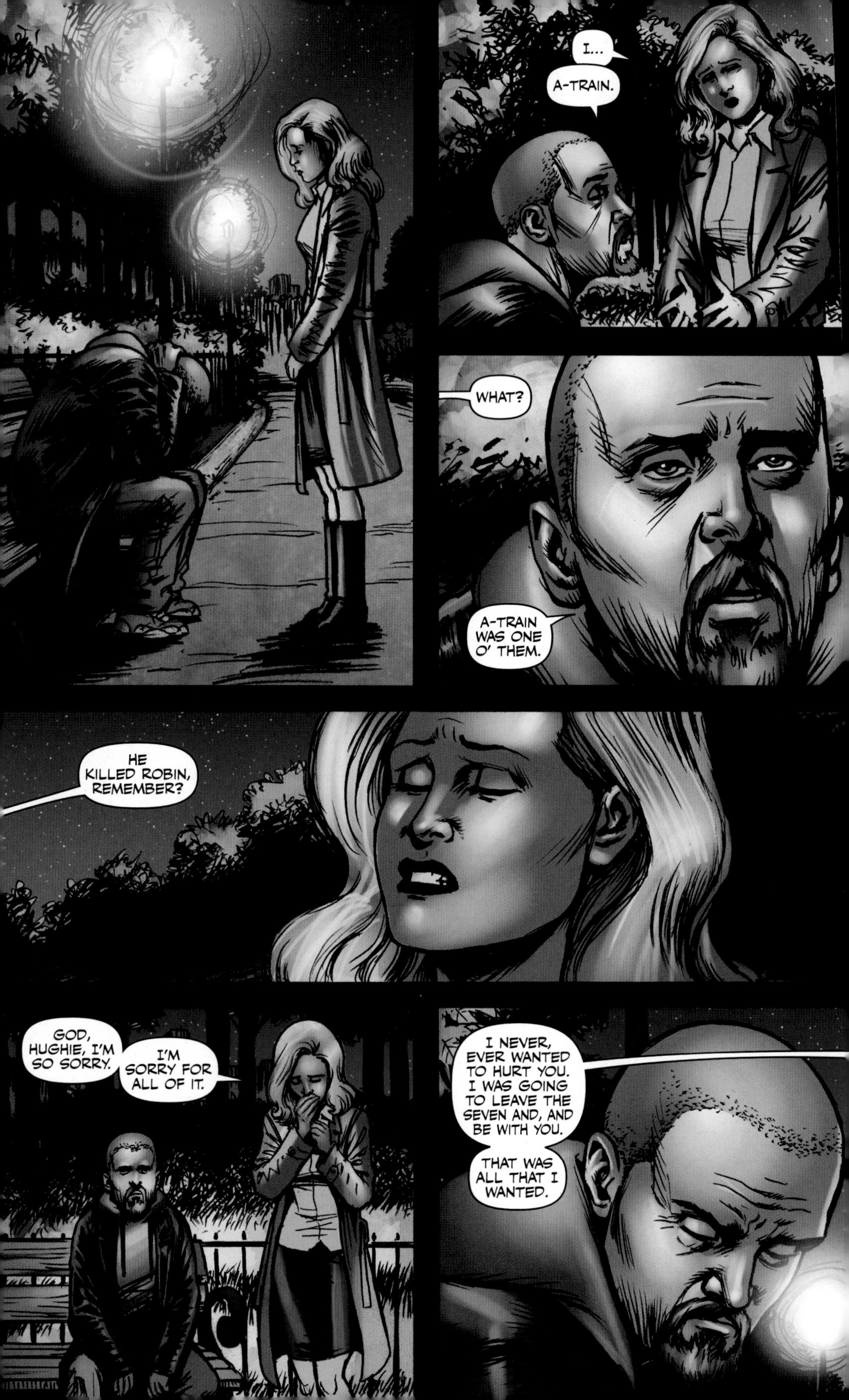

I...
A-TRAIN.
WHAT?
A-TRAIN WAS ONE O' THEM.
HE KILLED ROBIN, REMEMBER?
GOD, HUGHIE, I'M SO SORRY.
I'M SORRY FOR ALL OF IT.
I NEVER, EVER WANTED TO HURT YOU. I WAS GOING TO LEAVE THE SEVEN AND, AND BE WITH YOU.
THAT WAS ALL THAT I WANTED.

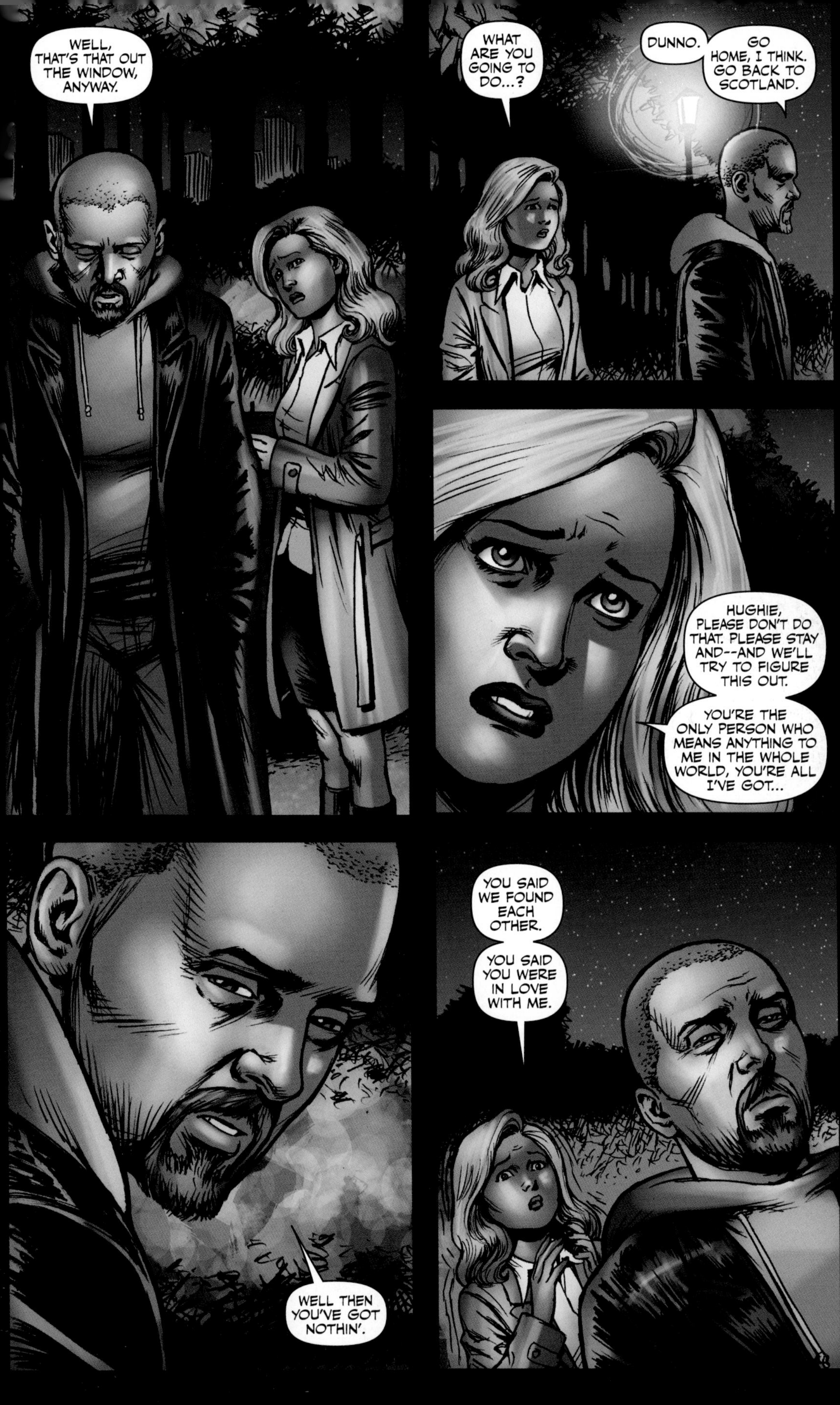
WELL, THAT'S THAT OUT THE WINDOW, ANYWAY.
WHAT ARE YOU GOING TO DO...?
DUNNO.
GO HOME, I THINK. GO BACK TO SCOTLAND.
HUGHIE, PLEASE DON'T DO THAT. PLEASE STAY AND--AND WE'LL TRY TO FIGURE THIS OUT.
YOU'RE THE ONLY PERSON WHO MEANS ANYTHING TO ME IN THE WHOLE WORLD, YOU'RE ALL I'VE GOT...
WELL THEN YOU'VE GOT NOTHIN'.
YOU SAID WE FOUND EACH OTHER.
YOU SAID YOU WERE IN LOVE WITH ME.

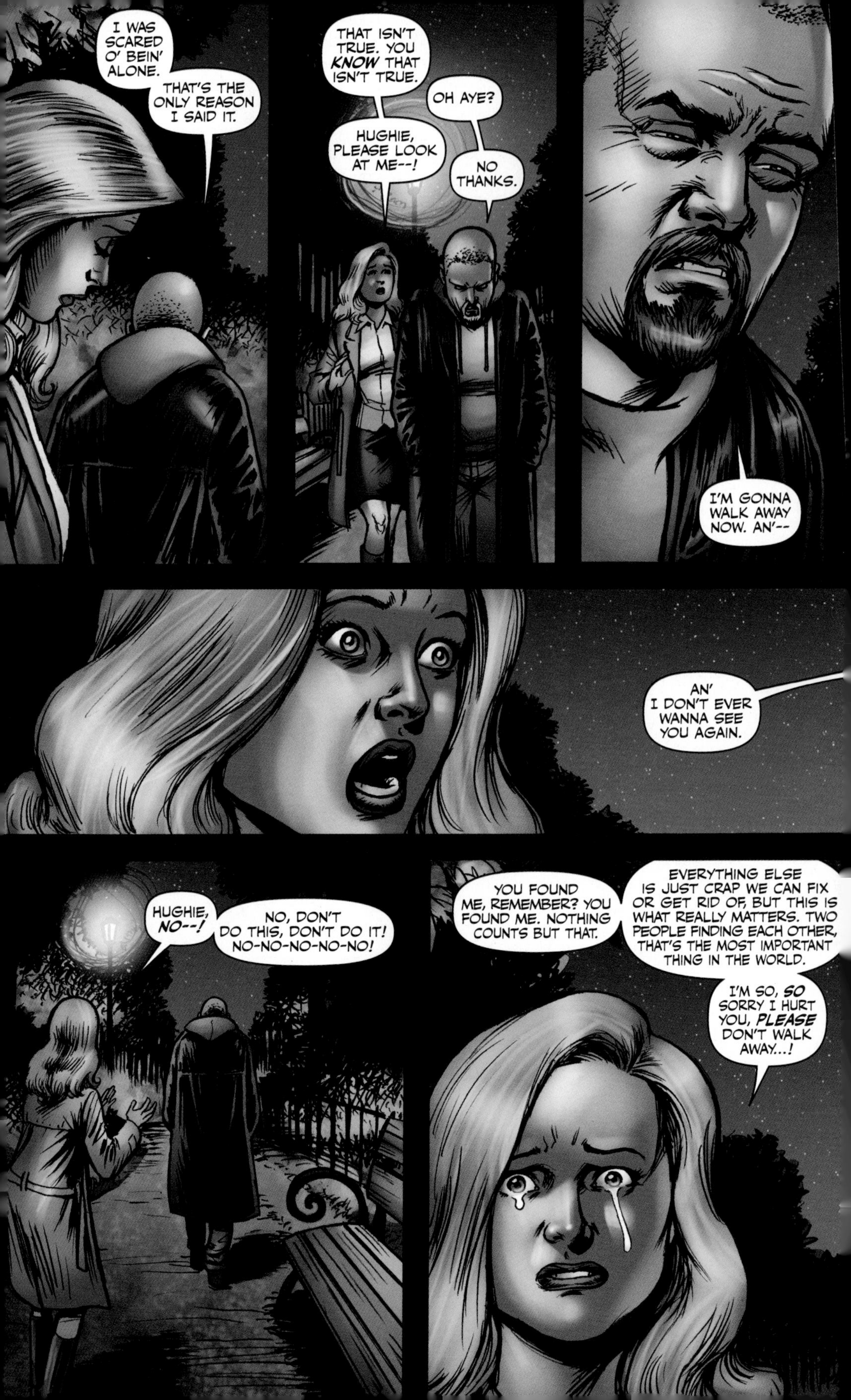
I WAS SCARED O' BEIN' ALONE.
THAT'S THE ONLY REASON I SAID IT.
THAT ISN'T TRUE. YOU KNOW THAT ISN'T TRUE.
OH AYE?
HUGHIE, PLEASE LOOK AT ME--!
NO THANKS.
I'M GONNA WALK AWAY NOW. AN'--
AN' I DON'T EVER WANNA SEE YOU AGAIN.
HUGHIE, NO--!
NO, DON'T DO THIS, DON'T DO IT! NO-NO-NO-NO-NO!
YOU FOUND ME, REMEMBER? YOU FOUND ME. NOTHING COUNTS BUT THAT.
EVERYTHING ELSE IS JUST CRAP WE CAN FIX OR GET RID OF, BUT THIS IS WHAT REALLY MATTERS. TWO PEOPLE FINDING EACH OTHER, THAT'S THE MOST IMPORTANT THING IN THE WORLD.
I'M SO, SO SORRY I HURT YOU, PLEASE DON'T WALK AWAY...!

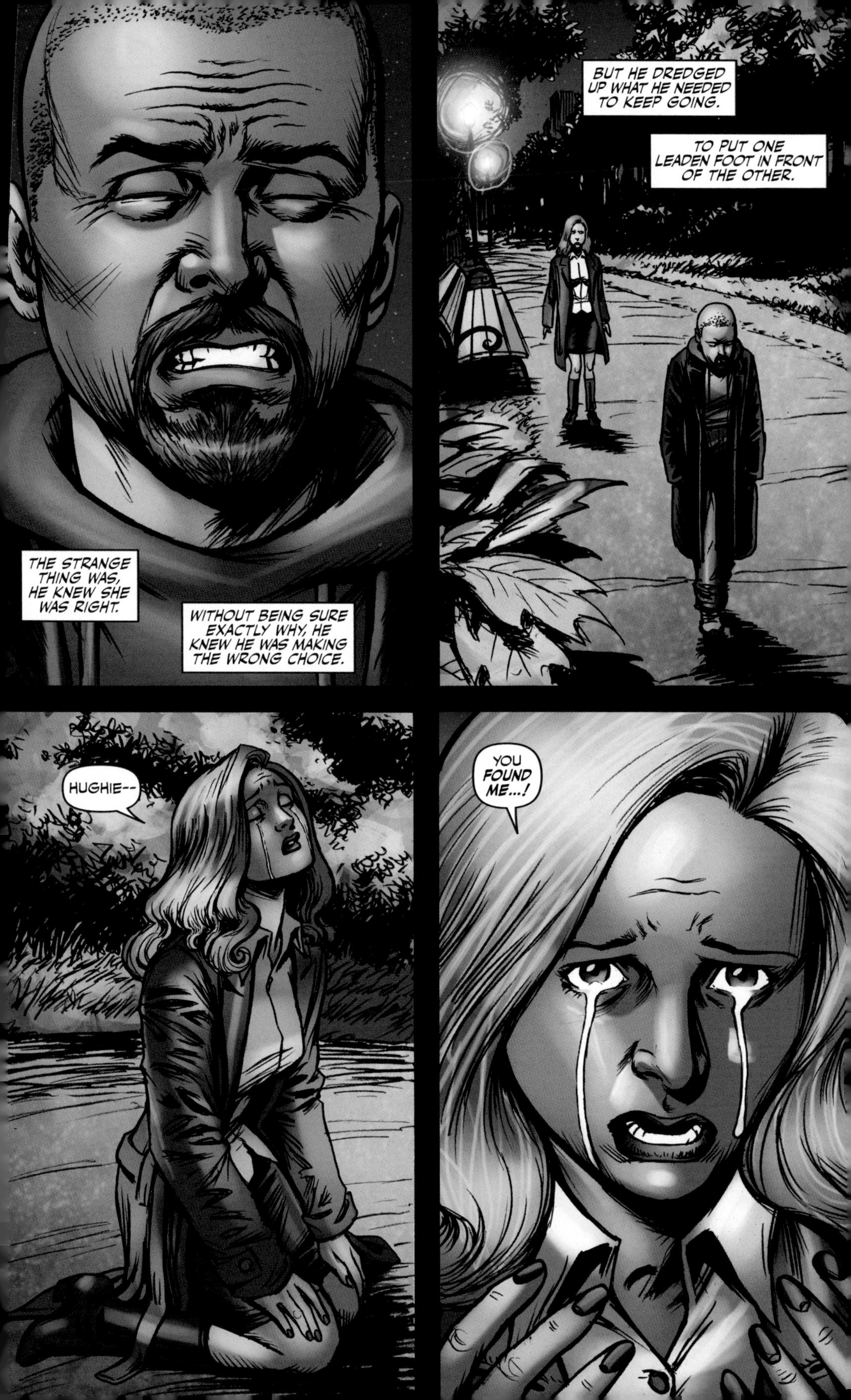
THE STRANGE THING WAS, HE KNEW SHE WAS RIGHT.
WITHOUT BEING SURE EXACTLY WHY, HE KNEW HE WAS MAKING THE WRONG CHOICE.
BUT HE DREDGED UP WHAT HE NEEDED TO KEEP GOING.
TO PUT ONE LEADEN FOOT IN FRONT OF THE OTHER.
HUGHIE--
YOU FOUND ME...!

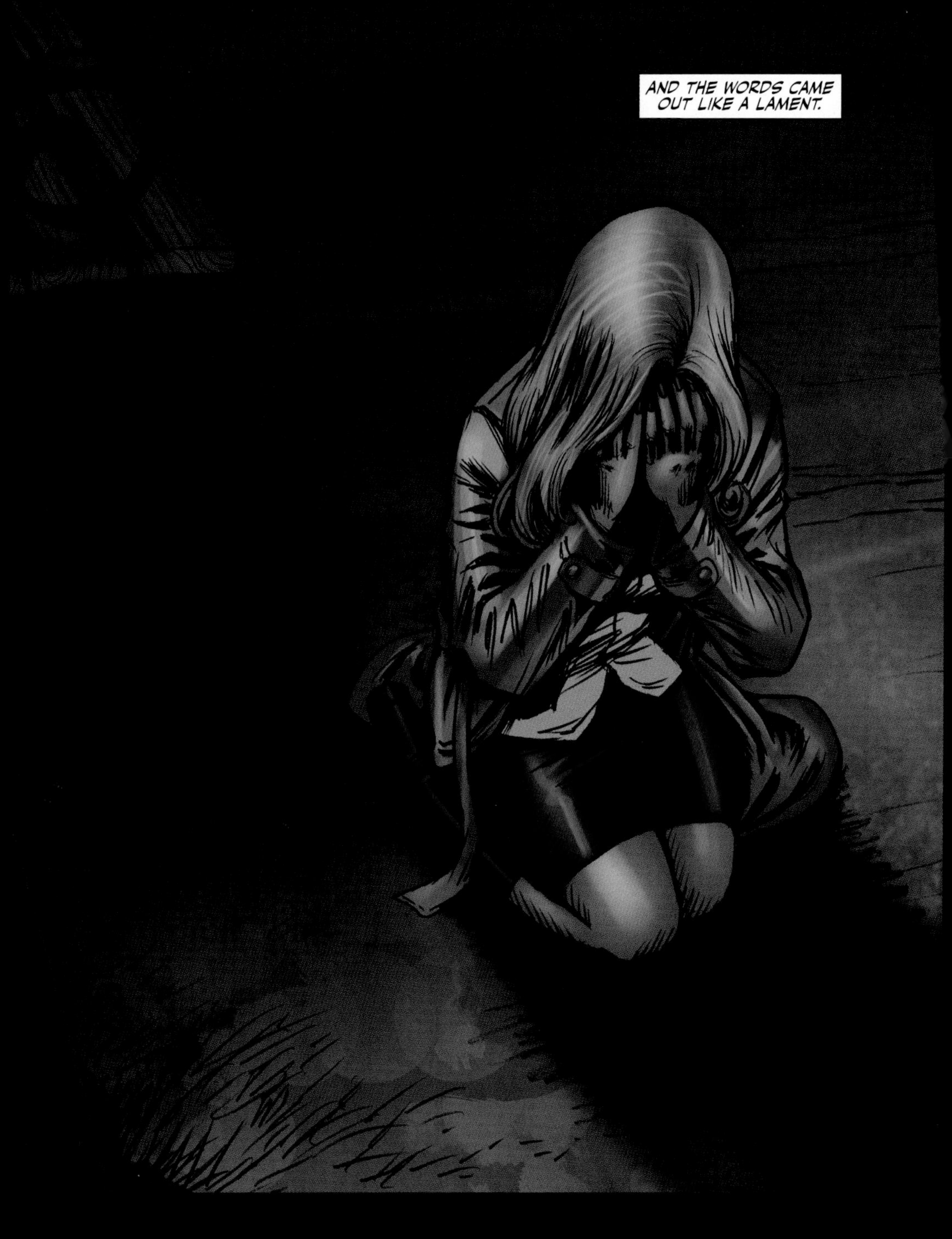
AND THE WORDS CAME OUT LIKE A LAMENT.

BELIEVE
conclusion

From *New York Times* Best-Selling Writer

GARTH ENNIS (Preacher, The Boys)

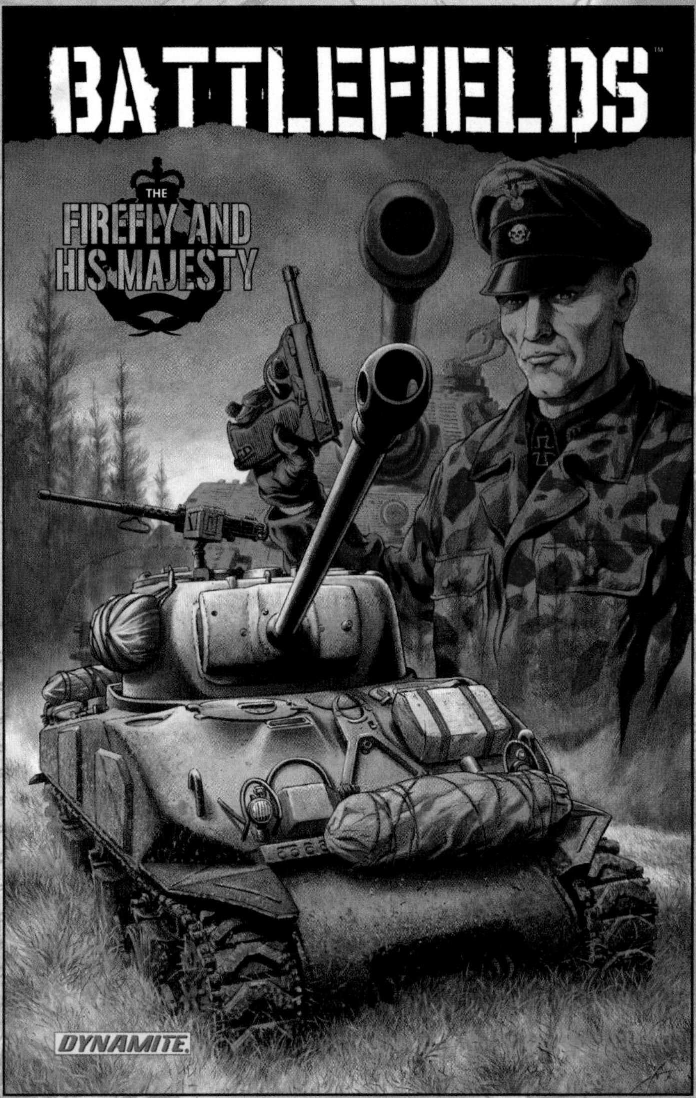
BATTLEFIELDS™
THE
FIREFLY AND
HIS MAJESTY
DYNAMITE

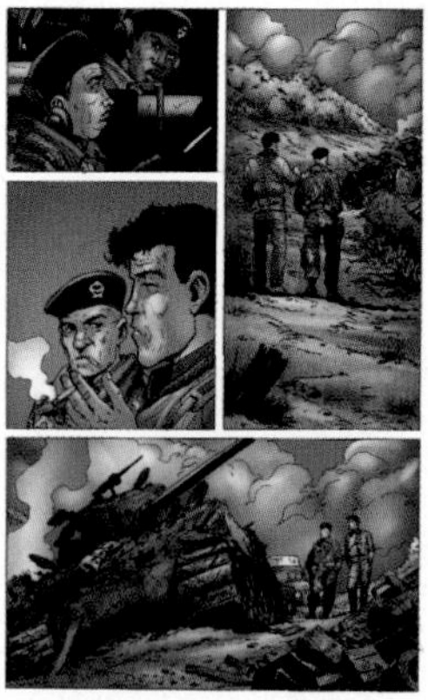

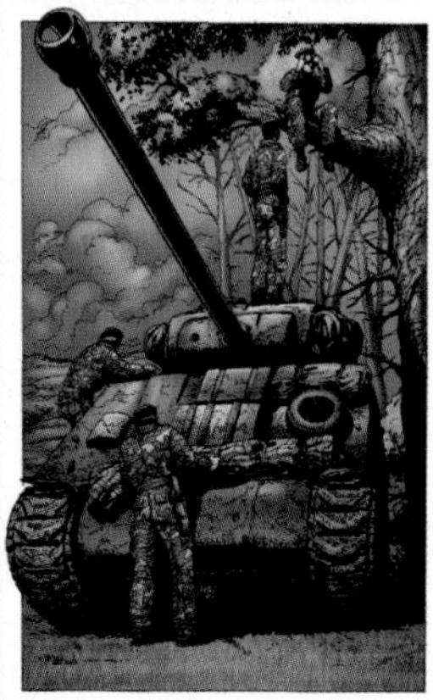

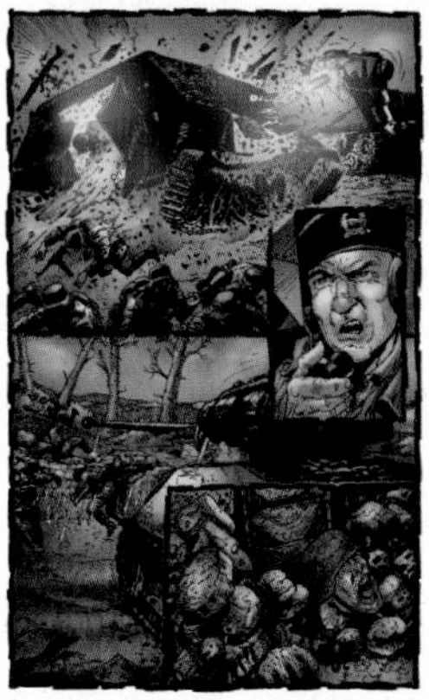

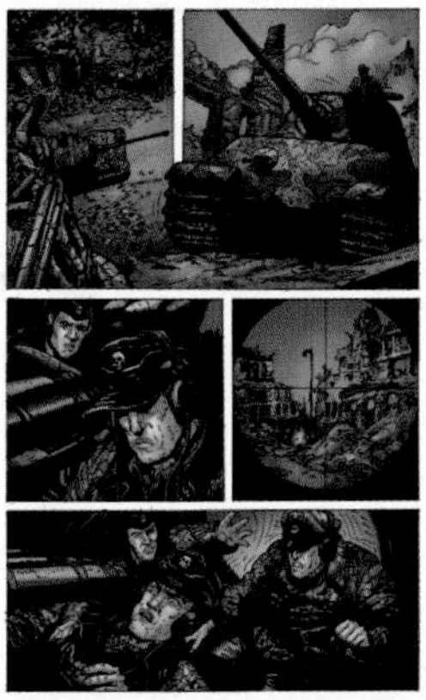

BATTLEFIELDS VOL. 5: THE FIREFLY AND HIS MAJESTY TRADE PAPERBACK

written by **GARTH ENNIS**
art by **CARLOS EZQUERRA** cover by **GARRY LEACH**

The Tankies' Sergeant Stiles returns, recently promoted and angrier than ever! He's got a new crew and a new tank — a Sherman Firefly with a high-velocity gun capable of taking out even the fearsome German Tiger. Too bad the enemy have a new tank of their own — the mighty King Tiger, with twice the armor and firepower of the original. As Stiles and his men join the Allied advance into the Nazi homeland, they soon realize that every inch of ground will be bitterly contested by the foe... and that there are worse horrors than Tigers lurking in the gloom of the last German winter. Reprinting issues #4-6 (parts 1-3), with a complete cover gallery.

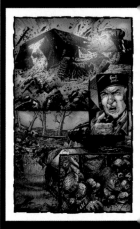

COMING SOON FROM DYNAMITE

WWW.DYNAMITEENTERTAINMENT.COM

DON'T MISS THESE GREAT COLLECTIONS FROM *NEW YORK TIMES* BEST-SELLING AUTHO

GARTH ENNIS & DYNAMIT

THE NEW YORK TIMES BEST-SELLING SERIES CONTINUES!
Garth Ennis Darick Robertson Carlos Ezquerra
The BOYS
volume six: THE SELF-PRESERVATION SOCIETY
WANTED
DEAD
For Crimes Against SUPERHUMANITY
DYNAMITE

THE COMPLETE
BATTLEFIELDS
VOLUME ONE
DYNAMITE

JUST A
PILGRIM
GARTH ENNIS • CARLOS EZQUERRA

GARTH ENNIS GARY ERS
DYNAMITE

HARDCOVERS

THE BOYS DEFINITIVE EDITION VOL. 1 HARDCOVER...........(SOLD OUT!).............193330580
- Collecting issues 1-14 of the hit series by Ennis and Robertson

THE BOYS DEFINITIVE EDITION VOL. 2 HARDCOVER..160690073
- Collecting issues 15-30 of the hit series by Ennis and Robertson

THE COMPLETE BATTLEFIELDS VOL. 1 HARDCOVER...160690079
- Collecting the first 3 Battlefields mini-series by Ennis, Braun, Snejbjerg and Ezquerra

THE COMPLETE JUST A PILGRIM HARDCOVER...160690003
- Both mini-series by Ennis and Ezquerra collected together for the first time

DAN DARE OMNIBUS HARDCOVER..160690027
- Collecting issues 1-7 by Ennis and Erskine

TRADE PAPERBACKS

THE BOYS VOL. 1: THE NAME OF THE GAME...19333057
- Collects issues 1-6 by Ennis & Robertson

THE BOYS VOL. 2: GET SOME...1933305
- Collects issues 7-14 by Ennis, Robertson and Snejbjerg

THE BOYS VOL. 3: GOOD FOR THE SOUL..19333059
- Collects issues 15-22 by Ennis & Robertson

THE BOYS VOL. 4: WE GOTTA GO NOW...160690035
- Collects issues 23-30 by Ennis, Robertson and Higgins

THE BOYS VOL. 5: HEROGASM..160690082X
- Collects issues 1-6 of the hit mini-series by Ennis and McCrea

THE BOYS VOL. 6: THE SELF-PRESERVATION SOCIETY...1606901257
- Collects issues 31-38 by Ennis, Robertson and Ezquerra

BATTLEFIELDS VOL. 1: THE NIGHT WITCHES..1606900285
- Collects issues 1-3 by Ennis and Braun

BATTLEFIELDS VOL. 2: DEAR BILLY...1606900579
- Collects issues 1-3 by Ennis and Snejbjerg

BATTLEFIELDS VOL. 3: THE TANKIES..1606900757
- Collects issues 1-3 by Ennis and Ezquerra

BATTLEFIELDS VOL. 4: HAPPY VALLEY..1606901281
- Collects issues 1-3 by Ennis and Holden

BATTLEFIELDS VOL. 5: THE FIREFLY AND HIS MAJESTY.......................................1606901451
- Collects issues 4-6 by Ennis and Ezquerra

THE COMPLETE JUST A PILGRIM 1606900072
- Both mini-series by Ennis and Ezquerra collected together for the first time

DAN DARE OMNIBUS...1606900404
- Collecting issues 1-7 by Ennis and Erskine

DYNAMITE ENTERTAINMENT WWW.DYNAMITEENTERTAINMENT.COM Newsletters • Contests • Downloads • Forums • More

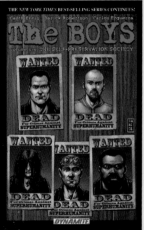

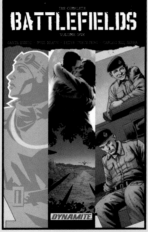

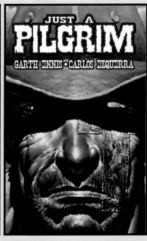

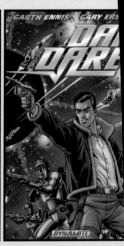

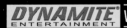